FAILURES IN FAMILY THERAPY

THE GUILFORD FAMILY THERAPY SERIES
Alan S. Gurman, Editor

FAILURES IN FAMILY THERAPY

Edited by

SANDRA B. COLEMAN

*Family Guidance Center of Bucks County
and Hahnemann University*

Foreword by Peggy Papp

THE GUILFORD PRESS
New York   London

© 1985 The Guilford Press
A Division of Guilford Publications, Inc.
200 Park Avenue South, New York, N.Y. 10003

Printed in the United States of America

LIBRARY OF CONGRESS CATALOGING IN PUBLICATION DATA
Main entry under title:

Failures in family therapy.

(The Guilford family therapy series)
Includes index.
1. Family psychotherapy.   2. Psychiatric errors.
I. Coleman, Sandra B.   II. Series.
RC488.5.F27   1985   616.89′156   84-19325
ISBN 0-89862-048-1

This book is dedicated, first, to the families whose very personal traumas and treatment disappointments are described herein. Because of their trust in us, their therapists, and their hope for relief from the troubles that brought them into treatment, they have made an unusual contribution. One can only wish that the product of their pain and our failure to relieve it will be a guidepost for the families and therapists who follow. And, second, this book is dedicated to my own families—my family of origin, who for me surely did not fail, and my family of procreation, whom I trust I have not failed.

S.B.C.

Contributors

Margaret S. Baggett, PhD, Private practice, Atlanta, Georgia

W. Robert Beavers, MD, Department of Psychiatry, University of Texas Health Science Center, Dallas, Texas; Southwest Family Institute, Dallas, Texas

Robert A. Berley, Department of Psychology, University of Washington, Seattle, Washington

Sandra B. Coleman, PhD, Family Guidance Center of Bucks County, Yardley, Pennsylvania; Department of Mental Health Sciences, Hahnemann University, Philadelphia, Pennsylvania

Paul F.Dell, PhD, Eastern Virginia Family Therapy Institute, Department of Psychiatry and Behavioral Sciences, Eastern Virginia Medical School, Virginia Beach, Virginia

Richard Elwood, Department of Psychology, University of Washington, Seattle, Washington

Ilda V. Ficher, PhD, Van Hammett Psychiatric Clinic, Human Sexuality Section, Department of Mental Health Sciences, Hahnemann University, Philadelphia, Pennsylvania

Robert Jay Green, Department of Psychiatry, University of Rochester School of Medicine and Dentistry, Rochester, New York

Alan S. Gurman, PhD, Department of Psychiatry, University of Wisconsin Medical School, Madison, Wisconsin

Neil S. Jacobson, PhD, Department of Psychology, University of Washington, Seattle, Washington

J. Doreene Kaplan, ACSW, Family Guidance Center of Bucks County, Yardley, Pennsylvania

Florence W. Kaslow, PhD, Private practice, West Palm Beach, Florida; Florida Couples and Family Institute, West Palm Beach, Florida; Department of Psychiatry, Duke University Medical School, Durham, North Carolina

David V. Keith, MD, Family Therapy Institute, Inc., St. Paul, Minnesota

Luciano L'Abate, MD, Department of Psychology, Georgia State University, Atlanta, Georgia

Howard A. Liddle, EdD, Division of Family and Community Medicine, University of California School of Medicine, San Francisco, California; Mental Research Institute, Palo Alto, California; Family Institute of San Francisco, San Francisco, California

Kathy Newport Melman, Department of Psychology, University of Washington, Seattle, Washington

Israela Meyerstein, ACSW, Strategic Family Training Program of the Lehigh Valley, Allentown, Pennsylvania

Carolyn Phelps, Department of Psychology, University of Washington, Seattle, Washington

Lynn Segal, LCSW, Brief Therapy Center, Mental Research Institute, Palo Alto, California

Karl Tomm, MD, Department of Psychiatry, University of Calgary Medical Clinic, Calgary, Alberta, Canada

Paul Watzlawick, PhD, Brief Therapy Center, Mental Research Institute, Palo Alto, California

Carl A. Whitaker, MD, Department of Psychiatry, University of Wisconsin Medical School, Clinical Sciences Center, Madison, Wisconsin

Lyman C. Wynne, MD, PhD, Department of Psychiatry, University of Rochester School of Medicine and Dentistry, Rochester, New York

Acknowledgments

Special appreciation is expressed to several people who helped me create a book as complex as this one. I wish to thank Alan Gurman for being inspired by my inspiration to write a book on failures and for listening to all my laments about whether my philosophical ramblings sounded like they came from another planet; Carl Whitaker for being the first of the first-generation family therapists to support my efforts; all the contributors for having the courage to dig into their files and their souls to write about their failures; Doreene Kaplan for sharing in all the phases of my enthusiasm and discouragement and for helping me with so much of the editing; and Cathi Rulis for her incredible patience in having to type and retype everything before we ever got our IBM.

S.B.C.

Foreword

This book comes to unsettle and refresh a field that is surfeited with oversimplified answers to complex problems. The first of its kind, it rips the mask off success and reveals some of the confusion and frustration accompanying the daily practice of therapy.

With the exception of parenting, no other human endeavor involves one so personally in the lives of others as does therapy. This engenders a feeling of awesome responsibility whether one consciously wishes to accept it or not. The consequences of failure so poignantly involve the well-being of others that no theoretical construct can ever completely release the therapist from this sense of accountability. As Gregory Bateson states, ". . . the results of error are likely to be ugliness." Failure is inevitably followed by haunting reflections, lingering regrets, and a wish to petition the gods for more wisdom.

It takes great candor and humility on the part of both the editor and contributors to this book to exhume and re-examine cases that most therapists would keep hidden in a back file. In so doing, contributors are not just exposing their professional work, their therapeutic mistakes, but something extremely personal about themselves. An examination of failure requires that one engage in the kind of soul-searching that can be avoided in describing successes. One must examine not only one's theory but one's values and beliefs; one's illusions, prejudices, and ideological commitment. Questions regarding personal ethics and integrity are raised, doubts about one's professional competence emerge, and a re-evaluation of the ultimate goal of therapy takes place.

An abiding consolation is that there is something to be learned from this critical review of one's work. Fritz Perls contends one never learns from one's successes but only from one's failures. That would seem to be borne out by the accounts in this book, which provide a valuable learning experience not only for the clinicians but for the readers as well. As the clinicians retrace their steps analyzing the different components of their work, readers are given a rare glimpse of the actual way their theory is translated into practice. New perspectives emerge as the authors are compelled to cope with the unexpected, re-examine their concepts, take a different path. In many cases the description of this process proves to be more enlightening than descriptions of their successes in previous publications. Karl Tomm speaks of the extraordinary impact his struggle with a suicidal family had on the future direction of his work. "It prepared me for a major shift in my thinking about mental process and in my method of conducting therapy." Israela Meyerstein and Paul Dell ask at the end of therapy, "How is success defined if therapist and family (and different family members) have different definitions of success?" They conclude that their major therapeutic error was imposing their definition of healthy functioning on the family and pursuing a variety of ends that the family did not want. "Instead of questioning our premises or strategically disengaging . . . we succumbed to battling the 'resistant' family; we continued to advocate our definition of the problem and continued to press for our goals. Today, it is clear to us who was *really* 'resistant.'"

David Keith and Carl Whitaker ask the intriguing question, "Could it be that failure and success are linear ideas that don't apply to a family system?" and urge family therapists to take note of Kipling's famous line for children: "If you can meet with Triumph and Disaster and treat those two imposters just the same."

In Chapter 14, "An Analysis of Family Therapy Failures," Sandra Coleman with Alan Gurman in collaboration integrates the salient factors in the preceding chapters with an eye toward identifying early warning signs and developing possible tenets of failure associated with family work. Their careful dissection of pretreatment factors, current status, historical framework, referral and assessment, process and content issues, motivation, professional and personal transitions, and ecological collisions, provides a pragmatic check list as a step toward possible future prevention.

The field of family therapy owes Sandra Coleman a debt of gratitude for this masterful investigation into the phenomenon of failure in all its complexities.

PEGGY PAPP

Contents

PART THREE. EMERGING PRINCIPLES OF FAILING

PART ONE

INTRODUCTION

Prologue

SANDRA B. COLEMAN

"Don't they ever fall?" I often wonder as I watch the graceful riders artfully guide their majestic horses through the precise ballet-like movement of the Grand Prix de Dressage. How similar is my current awe of the equestrians to that which I experienced in the late 1960s as I watched the artistry of the great family therapy masters as they stroked their brushes across the canvas called The Hillcrest Series (training films made at Eastern Pennsylvania Psychiatric Institute, Philadelphia, Pennsylvania). I remember how I marveled at Murray Bowen, Carl Whitaker, and the late Don Jackson and Nathan Ackerman; each seeing the same family, applying a very different therapeutic magic, and yet emerging with the same result—success. "Don't they ever fail?" I pondered.

During the 1970s I again watched the mastery of the current gurus—Minuchin, Haley, and the Milan maestros. Like the stellar equestrian riders who travel across the country on the grand prix circuit, so did the family therapy experts go "on the road" with their magnificent skills and wisdom. Again, I sometimes wondered if in the midst of a live consultation they ever made a mistake.

Then, in the late 1970s I had a strange experience. A student of mine made a blunder with a family while I was safely away on vacation. Because he was honest and sincere, he never erased the videotape but carefully shielded it until I returned. That tape became one of my most precious possessions. My students seemed to learn more from that bungled therapy mishap than they ever did from some of my more "brilliant" tapes. I began to think about what they were learning from such a muddled session.

Shortly thereafter at one of the American Family Therapy Association (AFTA) meetings, I thought aloud at dinner one night with Howard A. Liddle, telling him about this marvelous failure tape that I had been showing. Laughingly, I said that I would like to see a whole book filled with family therapy failures, that maybe (and here I became more serious and thoughtful) we were finally ready to expose ourselves on both sides. After all, "to err is human."

Sandra B. Coleman. Family Guidance Center of Bucks County, Yardley, Pennsylvania; Department of Mental Health Sciences, Hahnemann University, Philadelphia, Pennsylvania.

Several weeks later I jotted down some ideas and sent them to Alan S. Gurman. I told him that I wanted to write a book about failures, and before I knew it this book was launched.

Like most efforts in this or any other profession, one's ideas are only as productive as their fruition, and this has been a very difficult book to produce. The credibility of a book on failures rests solely on the validity of those who failed, and as I told one earnest author, "In order to earn the right to publicly fail you must first succeed—and do so famously."

In the following pages, those who have gained sufficient respect for the quality of their work open themselves to an in-depth exploration of a case that went awry. In each chapter the author presents his or her theoretical orientation, the case background, the process of therapy, and an analysis of the failure followed by a hypothetical reconstruction toward success (hindsight or an opportunity for redemption). In each instance the work is serious and the therapist is earnest; the problems presented, however, are all remarkably difficult. We all know many of these families—yet we know none of them. Some of the families induce a smile while others enrage us. Some grip our very core and make us wonder how we ever got to be in this field—and why we stay. There are also some really tender moments. At times it is hard to believe that some of the things that took place really happen to people, yet we all know that they do.

As editor, the contributors shared their writing struggles with me by phone, by mail, and in person. I never knew when I heard from them if they were going to quit or hang in. Some did quit but fortunately most had the courage to remain. I have selected some especially insightful comments from the authors as a way of paying tribute to the very difficult task they did and because I believe there are some special thoughts that should be emphasized. Thus, on the subject of failures:

Neil S. Jacobson and coauthors (Chapter 4) talk about the "temporal relativity of failure."

Howard A. Liddle (Chapter 6) says, "Our traditional American response to failures is to reject them, to consign them, metaphorically or actually to the refuse heap. . . ."

Luciano L'Abate and Margaret S. Baggett (Chapter 9) believe that "our therapeutic defeats keep us humble. . . ."

Lynn Segal and Paul Watzlawick (Chapter 3) remind us, "It would be so easy to explain away this failure by using the time-honored argument that the severity of the pathology and the resistance of the family made them unfit for treatment. However, as Don Jackson used to say, 'There are no insolvable cases, there are only inept therapists.'"

Israela Meyerstein and Paul F. Dell (Chapter 10) confess that "We were mesmerized by part of the system. . . ."

Lyman C. Wynne and Robert Jay Green (Chapter 5) (on the family's reaction to learning that there would be no more family therapy): ". . . and the 9 year old jumps up and down shouting, 'We won! We won! We don't have to come anymore.'"

The **Anonymous family** (Chapter 11) stated, "After all, they were the experts and we were the failure."

Ilda V. Ficher and J. Doreene Kaplan (Chapter 8) speculate, "Although one always hopes to learn from one's errors, given identical circumstances, one wonders if the therapist might make the same mistake again."

David V. Keith and Carl A. Whitaker (Chapter 1) suggest that "Grandiosity is a hidden danger" and "There is relief in the collapse of a delusion."

Karl Tomm (Chapter 13) confesses, "I had lost my confidence in my own work and was losing hope."

Florence W. Kaslow (Chapter 12) questions, "Is this then failure or the beginning journey and quest of which the final destination and results may remain unknown to the therapist?"

W. Robert Beavers (Chapter 7) reflects, "It seems to me that success and failure intertwine; they are not opposites but close kin."

W. Robert Beavers's notion of success and failure being "close kin" suggests the episode in "Is God a Taoist?" when God reaches the conclusion of his conversation with the mortal and quotes the writings of Seng-Ts'an:

> If you want to get the plain truth,
> Be not concerned with right and wrong.
> The conflict between right and wrong
> Is the sickness of the mind.

In a sense the arbitrary boundary between success and failure is similar to the Zen view of the conflict between right and wrong. Thus, in extricating failure from its circular arc with success, one necessarily makes failure a linear concept which, as Keith and Whitaker (Chapter 1) suggest, "does not fit with ecosystems." In viewing success as failure and failure as success, these authors question the implied dualism between the two, wondering if they are at times inseparable.

This book and the theory underlying the treatment approaches illustrated therein may be challenged philosophically from a Zen perspective, or, as no doubt will be the case, from any perspective. It is, however, as if each presented case, albeit failure, had a beginning, a middle, and an end. Of course, all these points along the continuum are arbitrary: Even the flatness of the continuum is arbitrary unless it bends enough to form a circle. Thus, it has been difficult to write a book like this because the "new epistemology" clearly tells us that the essence of understanding both life and its meaning is within the delineation of the infamous feedback loop.

So, I worried about this book, fully expecting to have to write a complete apology in the Prologue, lest I and all the thoughtful contributors to this volume be hastily gobbled up by the demon who swallows and regurgitates its tail as it circles the path toward all who espouse noncybernetic ideas. I continued to worry a lot until two things happened, both during the time that my German Shepherd, Quinto, and I were on a solo mountain retreat immersed in completing this book.

First, I had a dream one night that I was aimlessly wandering the halls of an institution of higher learning that turned out to be a medical school. I was terribly dejected, having just learned that I had not passed a very essential examination. My classmates milled about the hallway appearing content and self-assured that they had done okay; they were obviously relaxed, at ease, and in no hurry to get their grades. As I continued to sadly stalk the halls, a friend appeared. At this point I had found a desk and was frenetically flipping pages to search for my unknown answers. The identity of this friend is important. He is one of my "closest people" and has been for more than 30 years. Also, he is an outstanding achiever and a major success in his field. He offered me the use of his entire medical library, saying, "Why not borrow my books? I can give you a complete set." I did not want to be ungrateful or insult him, but I doubted that he could really help since he has been out of medical school for 20 years. He knows me well, however, and quickly read my mind, saying, "Don't worry, I have kept them up to date." I began to relax, not because of his offer of books, but because his presence alone was so reassuring. With the warmth of his support, I awakened knowing that the book would somehow be all right.

Second, *The New York Times* Arts and Leisure section (August 21, 1983), which I had brought along for diversionary reading, serendipitously offered me additional hope. In an article by Roger Copeland called, "The 'Linear' Play Still Retains a Powerful Potential," the author notes that the

> so-called "unities" of time, place and action—the belief that a play should take place in one location, that it should depict a single action and that this action should unfold sequentially, in a linear fashion—now seems hopelessly out of date.

Copeland observes that most of the leading, "intellectually stimulating" theater takes place nonlinearly. After citing several examples, he states:

> What this—and much other evidence—suggests is that those of us who live in the second half of the 20th century have all but lost faith in the concept of "linear" orderliness—as a way of thinking, as a manner of behaving, and certainly as a principle that might apply to the origin of serious plays that capture the complexity of our lives.

However, after much support of this new way of revealing life, on stage or off, Copeland moves on to praise the way in which *'Night Mother*, Marsha Norman's Pulitzer Prize drama, handles time in what he calls the "inexorably linear nature of the evening," which unquestionably gives the drama its power, thrusting the play "squarely in our laps." Thus, although Copeland initially comes at us in a cybernetic swoop, he later relents and underscores the "powerful potential of the linear flow."

It is with Copeland's latter notion in mind that I hope this book is read. The following chapters represent a very sincere and careful effort on the part of each contributor to offer the reader an inside, at times almost voycuristic view of a special family and a masterful slice of work—that did not go so well.

1

Failure: Our Bold Companion

DAVID V. KEITH AND CARL A. WHITAKER

Success and failure in family therapy ought to be easy enough to talk about. Unfortunately they are not, at least for us. Conceptually, it is like solving a Rubik's Cube®; we can get one face organized while the rest is in chaos. There are partial successes and partial failures. Sometimes the individuals succeed and the family fails. Sometimes the family succeeds but a family member may fail. The issue is complicated by the fact that failure can be a success and a success can be a failure. Could it be that failure and success are linear ideas that don't apply to a family system? Family therapists should take note of Kipling's famous line for children: "If you can meet with Triumph and Disaster and treat those two imposters just the same . . ." (Kipling, 1940).

There are two places we like to go to get a handle on slippery conceptual problems. One is our dictionary collection and the other our dreams. In answer to the question "What is failure?" our dictionaries give an interesting answer. The root word for failure has to do with committing a fault on purpose, deceiving, or escaping. Success, on the other hand comes from the root word "cede," which has to do with the act of giving over.

In the midst of our confusion about this chapter, one morning somewhere near dawn I (Keith) struggled awake from a dream about medical practice. I was in a cold sweat. A newspaper headline, "Doctor Abandons Suffering Child," appeared in the dream. Underneath was a picture of myself. The dream represented in the extreme my anxiety about failure, disgrace, and being judged incompetent. As a colleague said, "What's tough about this business isn't what the patients think, it's protecting your reputation from what colleagues think."

In the dream I came upon a 9-year-old girl, in great pain, lying in a shopping center mall surrounded by a large group of people. Her injury was a dislocated hip. I comforted her and splinted the injury so that she couldn't move. When the ambulance arrived I left for the hospital in my car. When she did not arrive at the emergency room, I returned to the shopping center and found that she had been moved to a store. She was given a pair of red shoes

David V. Keith. Family Therapy Institute, Inc., St. Paul, Minnesota.

Carl A. Whitaker. Department of Psychiatry, University of Wisconsin Medical School, Clinical Sciences Center, Madison, Wisconsin.

that corrected the dislocation. A group of people were celebrating her cure. As I approached, I was photographed, jeered by the crowd, and accused of being stupid and unprofessional. That is when I fought my way back to wakefulness.

The fear of failure is a constant haunt for family therapists. "Somebody else could do this better." "I'm not thinking clearly." "I need more data." In the dream I did not feel that I had failed personally. Instead, it reflected our failure as members of the medical community and of the community at large. I made an effort to provide proper treatment, but my plan was not implemented. I was not heard, or I was misunderstood, or somebody with more influence had a better idea. It recalls the kind of situation where after the first interview the family complains to the referring doctor, who does not trust psychiatrists either, and helps them find somebody who will not upset them. In the dream I did the right thing for my frame of reference, yet I was willing to accept the load of guilt imposed by the community for not doing the right thing in somebody else's frame of reference. Here we are dealing with the question of integrity, an important interface between the patient and the healer. Perhaps clinicians are successful if we maintain our integrity and fail if we somehow feel we have lost it. However, it is possible to maintain our integrity and still fail the community.

The girl's dislocated hip brought to mind one of our favorite growth metaphors: the Old Testament story of Jacob and Esau, which speaks to the question of failure in family therapy. Jacob steals his older brother's birthright and then goes off to become a wealthy man. Many years later he returns to his brother's homeland. The night before their reunion he cannot sleep. While walking in the night, he meets an angel of the Lord, and they wrestle. Jacob is defeated and his hip is dislocated. He leaves the place walking with a limp, and his name is changed to Israel. Thus, his life is changed through a wrestling struggle that damages him. Through a defeat and personal injury comes profound change.

Models for Family Psychotherapists

We are always seeking metaphors that illuminate the function of psychotherapy. Sometimes we are like garage mechanics. We don't rebuild cars, mostly we tinker with them to keep them going. Sometimes we are like a ship's pilot, and our job is to steer the family through a difficult channel. Success at this time means that the family suffered no undue damage during a time of crisis, although they may come out of therapy very much as they were when they went in. The metaphor for psychotherapy that we like best is the model of the foster parent in relation to children. So we asked ourselves, "How do parents fail?" or "Do they ever fail?" as a way to understand how family therapists fail.

We think that parents cannot win. They can only choose their way of losing—the strict way or the lenient way. How do they lose? The children go away, of course, and leave them alone. Some children leave with parental blessings, some are angry and fed up, and some leave hoping for more loving but despairing of getting any.

Does it then follow that parents win if the children never leave home but in some way hang around to provide the give-and-take triangulation of oedipal romance? Obviously, that is a costly and mutually debilitating success. The parents' best reward comes from the day-to-day pleasure of sharing in the children's growth, moments of intimacy, and the surprise of change.

There is little consolation for "mothballed" parents. They feel the pain of their children's failures as if their own. While the children's successes bring joy, the fun is only fleeting and the impact on the personhood of the parent is much less.

Parents fail personally when they don't care. Lillian Carter, the former president's mother, represents a model for parent failure when she said, "When I look at my children, it makes me think I should have stayed a virgin."

Parents can fail operationally by being too much of anything:

• too disciplining	• too rigid
• too ambivalent	• too understanding
• too decisive	• too encouraging
• too protective	• too crazy
• too rejecting	• too impatient
• too loving	• too lenient

Another form of parental failure occurs when the parents use their children to vindicate themselves.

Mr. and Mrs. Simms had four children. Mr. Simms's old-fashioned, rigid parenting pattern was a camouflage for a massive hunger for loving. Each teenager went through considerable turmoil in adolescence manifested mainly in loud, sometimes physical fights with the father. Each one left the family for a period of time and then returned to sheepishly admit that their father was right all along.

These examples of parent failure are paradigmatic for ways family therapists fail.

Models of Failure and Success for Patients and Therapists

Perhaps one of the complications of understanding failure in family psychotherapy is that failure is not ordinarily a unilateral process. In our framework the therapist is the real patient. As the therapist continues to grow or stay spontaneous, so can his or her patients. This is not to say that the patients are the therapists; it is in fact the process which is therapeutic. In *The Roots of Psychotherapy* (Whitaker & Malone, 1953) success is defined as a simultaneous increase in the richness of inner life (intrapsychic life or fantasy life) and outer life (personal or social life). We like to think of it as an arrival at personhood, or expansion of one's personal presence. Perhaps we can define success in another way as more free access across the corpus callosum, a free communication between the intuitive (or creative) right brain and the analytic (or communicational) left brain. Or success may be defined as the capacity to be crazy joined simultaneously with the capacity to be adaptive. Defining success as the freedom to be crazy lets us include the wisdom to plan when, how, and with whom to be irrational, nonrational, and creative. The freedom to be adaptive would include the wisdom to be adaptive as needed and in a useful manner as well as the freedom to refuse. Success might also be defined as the enjoyment of being surprised at oneself, or, again, less and less need to *accomplish* and more and more freedom to *be*.

Success in family therapy is when the family achieves a sense of wholeness or integrity, absurdity, and the capacity to deal with the community in relation to the family's problems as individuals and as a group. Success is intensifying the family organization and administrative competence. Often a failure may precipitate this end, as shown in the following case example:

The Hammond family entered therapy when the father's affair was exposed. Therapy went on for a year with considerable change in the family dynamics, yet somehow they never quite finished. Divorce was a constant threat. Mrs. Hammond was unable to give up trying to improve her husband. After 16 months the nun-like wife had a brief affair, which for her was akin to a psychotic episode. Mr. Hammond was furious, not only with his wife, but with the therapist, whom she felt had suggested the affair. He decided to push for divorce. In the war that followed, Mrs. Hammond left her intrapsychic convent, the marriage came alive, and family therapy came to a close. This shift into immorality by the wife and the family's flirtation with self-destruction restored the family to life.

Having defined some parameters for successful therapy, we can direct ourselves toward failing, or unsuccessful therapy. We think the two most important ways the therapist fails include (1) not caring or (2) deceiving or backing out, which we would translate into failure to maintain integrity.

For the individual, a retreat into loneliness would be a failure, as would denial of the self or flight into being a social automaton. For the family, failure is a retreat into isolation with the individuals in the family remaining faceless and role dominated. They never surprise themselves. A family that does not change is a failure, thus failure equals the use of repetitive patterns that are not resilient enough for life-cycle changes.

Perhaps the real failure in family therapy is the failure to have any effect. Are we a failure if we always stay neutral and professional? Failure becomes more likely when there is too much caution. A surgeon who is too cautious to make an incision is as dangerous as a surgeon who operates too frequently.

The Danger of Caution: Failure Phobia

Fourteen-year-old Jenny was an A+ student who had a paper route and played on the school basketball team. She developed anorexia nervosa and was admitted to the hospital. Her family was socially adapted, attractive, pseudomutual, and shallow. Father was a physician. Mother was a beautiful nonentity. The parents had experienced a smooth road to social adaptation, sometimes tedious, but never painful. Jenny's older brother was an honor student away at college. Our impression was that the anorexia was precipitated by the brother's depression and fear of failing in college. We asked where the failure haunt came from in the light of the fact that there were no obvious failures in the family. Suddenly father remembered his college days and the threat of not making it into medical school and ending up as a drug detail man or a pharmacist. This was a very strange menu with a limited selection. Beyond failure was nothingness. Then he remembered a frequent dream of being in college unable to study for an exam the next day. In his dream he becomes overwhelmed by his fears of failing, wakes up in a panic, then remembers that he is a physician, he has made it, and does not have to fear anymore. This unconscious danger in the father is thus being lived out in the daughter. The phobia about failure has caused them to be distant and the daughter embodies their nightmare in her grotesque living pattern. But, she is succeeding as an anorexic.

When psychotherapists are haunted by failure, we may choose to stay cautious and ineffective in an effort to avoid it. It is safer to be a nobody. (Incidentally, this reminds us of our plan to require that everyone fail at least one course in high school and college so that it will not be necessary for them to go through life forever phobic about failure.) We sometimes think of ourself as too harsh or too cold in working with family problems, but more often we fail by being too soft or too tentative. Remember the old story of the man who needed to cut his dog's tail off. He loved the dog so much that he could only cut it off one inch at a time.

Failure as Success

In the following example the therapy process was ended, but the scapegoat was temporarily displaced:

A family with six children came in for therapy because the 11-year-old son, Joe, had become too much for his mother to handle with her parent effectiveness methods. All the children were omnipotent and cynical toward the therapist. After three interviews the therapist became fed up and said that all the children were impossible and that

Joe was just the drum major. He said he was glad that they were not his kids. If they were he would probably have to leave his wife to deal with them. The mother's despair suddenly hit rock bottom. Two months later she called to straighten out the bill. She said that after that interview she switched from being an optimist to a pessimist and felt like she was enjoying the children much more now, although she had no idea why it was so.

In the next example we succeeded with the father and the children, but failed with the mother. Again the therapy failed, but the family did not.

An 18-year-old daughter felt she was being destroyed by her mother's nagging and moved to an apartment. The move precipitated the family into therapy where mother's harangue continued. I (Keith) experienced empathetic hurt with both mother and daughter and their painful love–hate relationship. The mother would go on, and on, and on about her daughter. I felt that I was not getting through to the mother and said so in 20 different ways. In the middle of the eighth interview, I said to the cotherapist, "I have the feeling that if I was married to her I'd pray that she would break her jaw just so I could arrange to have it wired shut for 10 weeks. Then I wouldn't have to listen to her complaining."

When I think of that moment, I wish I had not said it, and I don't suggest that anyone else should. The mother said I was "rude" and left therapy. However, a month later my cotherapist, the family pediatrician, reported that the battle between the mother and daughter was depolarized and peaceful.

In this next example there is a failure to meet for one interview, but the nontherapy is successful.

Mrs. Magnuson had had a year of productive individual psychotherapy with a colleague who left town some months after the therapy had been terminated. A few years later she called one of us (Keith) for family therapy, describing malaise and discomfort within the marriage and a series of difficulties with the children. She agreed to our usual demand that she would bring the husband and children to the first interview.

One week later, on the morning of the interview, the husband called to argue against bringing the kids. We didn't get anywhere, and he canceled the appointment. I never saw them as patients. I felt badly about the situation because I had backed him into a corner. By now, I should have forgotten this interchange, which occurred 5 years ago, but for some reason it stuck in my mind. It was one of those high-affect telephone conversations that don't go away easily. It was engaging even though we gave up on one another. I felt like my discussion with him had been a flop because of my overcommitment to theory about family therapy. On the other hand, he did sound terribly arrogant, and I was relieved not to have to see them.

I had an accidental follow-up on this family from a friend who turned out to be a close friend of Mrs. Magnuson. Both husband and wife were

furious with me. However, neither husband nor wife sought further psychotherapy. They are still married. She launched into an art career, both as
teacher and practitioner. He took the family abroad for a year. I would
not want to overplay the significance of these events, but I do think that my
interaction with him induced a theater-of-the-absurd experience. The wife
had had a good therapy experience with my colleague, and I think she was
only seeking a repeat performance, but with much less anxiety.

A final example raises the question of whether we can prevent some
future tragedy by confusing a preliminary failure.

A family with a depressed father who felt like a failure, a distant but frustrated wife,
and an angry, white-knight daughter came in seeking help for dad's depression. The
family handled father with kid gloves lest they depress him even more. At the end of
the interview the therapists said they could see no hope for them to be helpful to the
family. If they remained protective, dad would stay depressed. It did not appear that
things would get much worse, but they would probably stay the same. They were
panicked by our observation that our efforts were doomed to fail. They chose to
come back and increase the pressure for change.

We prefer to fail early rather than trying to clarify and empathize to a
standstill (another form of failure).

Success as Failure

It is very clear that by inhibiting growth, success can be a failure.

A man came in with a problem of sexual impotence. In the second interview it was
revealed that he was organizing his life around winning a Nobel Prize. His impotence
was cured, but the delusion of being a Nobel Prize winner was never touched.

This is an example of successful treatment of a symptom, but the overall
psychotherapy ending in failure.

Failure Inducing Success

Does failure in psychotherapy produce a paradoxical effect in which the
individual suddenly sees himself going downhill, renews his efforts to integrate himself, and becomes successful a year or two later?

We began therapy with a 41-year-old physician's family around the issue of a dead
marriage. After the fourth interview he fell off his roof and seriously fractured his
femur. He had to remain at bedrest in traction for 6 weeks. During this period he
became reacquainted with his children and started reading novels. He felt as though
he had been Rip Van Winkle, asleep for many years. He reduced the size of his

practice and went back to teaching in a medical school so that he could have the possibility of enjoying himself for awhile before his children grew up.

Therapist Failure and Family Success

The Masons' 16-year-old son was admitted to the pediatric unit with abdominal pain of unknown cause. The evaluation of his psychosomatic problem involved a family interview that didn't get anywhere. The family was discouraged and depressed, yet elusive, about a number of issues including the impact of the economy on their farm, a handicapped younger child, and problems with the in-laws. They agreed to a second interview, but did not show up. The interview was rescheduled at the time of the boy's discharge. Mother and father showed up without the children, so I (Keith) began the interview with the parents and their hospitalized son.

"What happened to the kids?" I asked. Dad answered, "I'm not taking the kids out of school for this." "That's what I'm afraid of. You think this problem is going to go away if you ignore it. I think the danger of it staying the same or getting worse is great," I said. He laughed and put his hat back on. "You don't know nothing about what it takes to run a farm. You ain't got all day to run here and run there just because somebody's sick." His voice was loud and firm. So was mine. "Don't laugh me off, Pa. I don't know nothin' about runnin' a farm, but I know plenty about sick kids and families, and you have troubles starin' you straight in the face. Don't turn your back." "Well I'm takin' my boy home. I don't care what you say." Mother and son were with him. They added their vehemence to his, their anger uniting them.

They made me angry with their bullheadedness, but at the same time I had a feeling of admiration for their courage. They left the hospital. I think they needed more family therapy and I worried about them, but at the same time I enjoyed their initiative.

Success with Individuals, Failure of Therapeutic Relationship

I (Keith) saw a single-parent family with one of the residents. After the interview the mother gave the resident her opinion of me: "I thought he was a real jerk, but I enjoyed talking with him." As I recall the interview, I could say the same thing about her.

Psychotherapy Fails, Change Comes Later

Eight-year-old Johnnie had not spoken a word since his whooping cough episode at 2 years of age. He had worked out a very successful sign language with his soccer pals and his family, pointing at Christmas gifts he wanted in the Sears catalog. Psychotherapy was basically a total failure. I (Whitaker) saw him once a week for 15 weeks. He never said a word to me and any words I said to him remained floating in the air. I accepted the failure. Three weeks later the family called back to say that he had started to talk. That kind of failure I enjoyed.

Failure Based upon Situational Stress

Situational stress may disrupt the efforts of both family and therapist, as the following case illustrates.

Mrs. Zilch was brought in because she was depressed. It turned out the depression had to do with her husband objecting to her overspending the $2000 a month she got beyond her expenses. Behind that was the fact that they had just finished a quarter-million dollar home. This country girl, whom her 30-year-old husband had married as a protest against his father's success in international manufacturing, was making life complicated. This young woman with her seven children and a newborn baby had been dragged into an Evangelical church because of her lavish gifts to various church committees. The husband, a spoiled child, was suddenly projected into international status when his father died. People came from all over the world to investigate his manufacturing techniques, and he was invited as consultant to many countries. His religion would not let him divorce, and our power was not sufficient to hold him in the family scene enough to reconstruct it. Within four interviews he called the Menninger Clinic and his wife was quickly hospitalized there for 2 years, with the first year to be free of any visiting from members of the family or the newborn baby.

  The failure still rankles even though we thought we were over our delusion that we could change the world.

Situational stress disruptions often occur in relation to more dramatic symptoms, like psychosis or an acting-out teenager. The family or the therapist cannot stand the ambiguity or the anxiety, so the family treatment is suspended and the scapegoat enters the hospital, is placed on medication, or winds up in individual therapy. Often these maneuvers are covertly designed to protect the family or one of the members from the painful components of a growth process. However, if the family is not for family therapy and is looking for another mode of treatment it is wise to let them go.

Success or Failure of the Patient–Therapist Interface

In discussing the question of failure and success in experiential family therapy, Malone said, "The psychotherapies are not relevant, the therapist is not relevant, and even the patients are not relevant. What is truly relevant are the interfaces amongst them" (Malone, Warkentin, Felder, & Whitaker, 1978). This confusing point of view reflects the complexity of the question of failure in family therapy. The therapist is in part a patient. We find this particularly true in working with schizophrenics, children, and families. Likewise, the family becomes therapeutic. It is this kind of thinking which led Barbara Betz to say, "The dynamics of therapy are in the person of the therapist" (Betz & Whitehorn, 1975). One way of thinking about success in Malone's model is that the interfaces may lose and then regain their integrity. That process can occur in one interview, or it may happen serially, the way a microscope may go out of focus and then resharpen. The following case illustrates distortion and realignment of the interface:

The Evans family was referred for family therapy because of their son's phobia about living away from home. At the second interview, as the family anxiety began to mount, the parents talked about having Joe come in by himself so that we could learn more about his problem. We turned down the offer and scheduled another family appointment. Joe showed up alone anyway. We reviewed what had happened. He said that his mother told him to come alone. Joe didn't particularly want to be there by himself. We felt double-crossed by the family and told him that it seemed his mother was trying to decide how we should practice, and we didn't accept that arrangement at all. He went home to see if the family wanted to make another appointment. The next day the mother called back. She was sorry and went on to explain. She sounded anxious and we felt anxious about the interaction. She went on to say that she knew what we were talking about vis-à-vis the family. There were things she wanted to talk about but didn't know how to; how could we help her?

In the above example the interface between the therapist and the patient dissolved when the mother decided unilaterally on individual therapy for her son. We were confused about what to do when her son arrived. He was old enough to be an individual patient, the family was a powerful one, and we were wary of double-crossing them. The interface was blurred as the mother became the doctor and we her patients. It was restored by sending the son home and by our telephone conversation. The distortion and realignment of the interface is therapeutic. Failure occurs when the interfaces are too rigidly maintained or when they are not restored after being broken down. If the case ended now, we would consider it only a partial failure, because we did make emotional contact with both the son and the mother. What will be the next impasse?

Standard Patterns of Failure: The Therapist's Contribution

Failure to Be Nonrational

Working with families is a sizeable project that usually begins with the external reality of the family. While much can be done in assisting the family in management of their explicit problems, therapists must also be able to guide patients through nonrational regressive experiences. These events, which may have a psychosomatic quality, are often profound growth experiences. It is our sense that if therapists back away from them it may be damaging.

I (Whitaker) treated a psychiatrist and his wife. The husband had been growing more and more compulsive while she had rediscovered herself in the process of having children. I suggested to the father that he should go crazy to get out of the obsessive corner that he had painted around himself. Two weeks later the father went into a crazy episode in the office. He was a big man and started shouting and throwing pillows around. I felt intimidated by him and slowed him down, "Whoa! Who there! Shut up, that's enough! Now sit down!" The man did stop and did sit down. Later, I felt that I had interrupted a growth process in this man. However, 6 months later, a similar event occurred. This time a joint process developed in which we were crazy together, neither intimidated by the other, and the psychiatrist had a therapeutic experience with it.

Failure to Acknowledge the Whole

We always seek to include three generations in our work with families. Obviously, it is not always possible. We may end up with a majority while some distant members are left out, as the following case illustrates.

Eight months of family therapy had been useful in neutralizing an acrimonious marriage which appeared to be headed for divorce. The dead stillness between the parents had lifted, and the children's cynicism lost much of its power, but the family still felt crippled. The father remained an outsider, not very much alive. The oldest daughter of the family lived in San Francisco and had never attended a family meeting. The therapist decided to have her in by way of speaker-phone. Her presence changed the quality of family process. The family lost its dormant quality and the format for growth emerged. They regained possession of themselves as a whole.

Failure of Systems Communication

For one reason or another—busyness, shyness, or lack of a common language—communication in the community of healers breaks down, and a family may fall into the crevasse.

A family from a city 100 miles away was referred by their physician. The doctor noted in his referral that the middle of three children was depressed, and the diagnosis was accurate. Mary, 8 years old, was a school phobic, suffering numerous somatic problems. A review of the family system gave an inkling of a serious but covert problem in this clean-faced family agonizing over which of the three daughters would become Miss America. The difficulty was the high-pressure war between the mother and the paternal grandmother; the father tried vainly to keep the peace. The family left the meeting appearing anxious, with another interview scheduled. They called later to cancel. When I (Keith) didn't hear from them, I called the family doctor 6 weeks later and learned he had performed a tonsillectomy on Mary. In his estimation she was better.

This was a dismal failure in that the family remains locked into their external reality, ignoring the covert power maneuvers. They discount their own inner life (the wife's anger at her mother-in-law and the husband's confusion). The process that precipitated the depression still haunts the family. It is a ghost that they refuse to acknowledge; thus, it will always haunt them. The failure might have been prevented had I made better connection with the referring physician. The surgery, which was probably unnecessary, might have been averted. However, it provided the girl a chance to regress and be cared for, and in that sense may have been therapeutic, since the treatment took the form of a murderous attack, which perhaps temporarily resolved her guilt in the same way that treatment with electroconvulsive therapy (ECT) does for adults. Failure of family change occurred because of my fear of exposing my failure to the referring doctor. It is a failure because I still feel depressed about the outcome.

Failure to Take Responsibility

This kind of failure occurs when the therapist looks over his or her shoulder and assumes that somebody somewhere else could do it better. The metaphorical prototype would be the young parents who feel dominated by their own parents, or a parent who loses decisiveness as a result of being taken over by community agencies. This failure also occurs when the therapist panics and gives up a treatment case. A better solution is to seek consultation. Failure to take responsibility also occurs when there are a number of treatment systems involved and no one is central.

A 22-year-old man was admitted to the hospital after a drug overdose. During his hospitalization he was connected with two residents who were going to do family therapy, a psychiatrist at a mental health center who was going to follow his medication, and a nurse therapist at a local social service agency. Four months after discharge he committed suicide. A meeting was held to review what had happened. It seemed that while he had been carefully diagnosed and much effort had gone into treatment planning, all of the persons involved had had some contact with him but each had assumed that someone else was in charge of the treatment.

Failing Intentionally to Create Success

Together the authors currently see a man who is left over from a family treatment case. He is a successful psychopath, having made a million dollars twice. He comes in to be defeated. It is hard to say what, if anything, he gets from the interviews. When we asked, he wasn't sure either. We never talk straight to him. We constantly one-up him. He ends up confused and says things like, "Whitaker, I can never get a straight answer out of you." It is our impression that every time his seduction succeeds he loses more personhood. He maneuvers to push us away. The natural response of any therapist is to try to pull him back. However, we push him away and thereby force him to maintain the relationship. This confuses the failure–success issue because he wins by losing. Bear in mind, however, that if you have not been one up, you can't go one down.

Failing by Successful Individual Therapy

In our frame of reference, successful individual therapy may disrupt the family (Whitaker & Keith, 1980). This can occur, for example, in a feminist-oriented family, or in a family in which a member attends Alcoholics Anonymous (AA). We think of it as a failure.

The Hayes family was referred about their 13-year-old son, who was a prepuberty version of Humphrey Pennyworth: overfed and overindulged by both parents. Both parents were immature, hostile–dependent people, who had somehow managed to limp along for 15 years of marriage. Psychotherapy went very well. Both parents began to make some very solid individuation steps, then they ended up getting divorced. The boy has done fairly well. He ended up living with his grandmother. He managed to salvage a year in school, which it had appeared that he was going to have to repeat. Two years later the parents are still shell shocked by the divorce, unable to get back together, or to join with anyone else. They had grown up enough to separate from one another but not enough to rejoin.

Failure by Therapist Revealing Secrets

In our consultations to other family therapists, we are frequently asked what therapists should do with secret information they receive about the family. Our assumption is that there are no such things as family secrets; although there is covert agreement in families not to openly acknowledge anxiety-producing information. When the therapist is made privy to such information, he or she should abide by the family's intuitive judgment.

A young psychiatrist was seeing a family with four young children regarding the mother's battle fatigue, manifested by disabling anxiety attacks. He learned in a telephone call that the mother's mother was an alcoholic, and everyone in the family refused to notice the alcoholism. In a family interview including extended family from both sides, the young psychiatrist decided to put the family's cards on the table and announced that he knew of the alcoholism. A second interview was then planned but never occurred because the young mother made a serious suicide attempt 2 days before, following a number of contacts from family members who were pressuring her.

Defeat

Looking back over our history as therapists, we find many cases that are partial failures and partial successes. Failure and success have bilateral components—contributions from therapists and families. We expect to fail and we do fail. There are another group of therapy experiences that collectively make a heavy dark mass and cause us to think that perhaps we should have gone into obstetrics or radiology. When we began this paper on failure, the first case to come to mind from that heavy dark mass was the following:

Mr. and Mrs. Marker were referred to us by another group of psychiatrists, who ran out of ideas after working individually with Mrs. Marker for a year (6 months as an inpatient). She had performed a series of self-abusive attacks over an 8-month period. At the height of the period, a police officer was posted in her room to protect her from herself. Hospitalization and individual therapy were nonproductive. She was referred to the authors for family therapy. We took them on with a combination of challenge and reservation.

We worked boldly and carefully, like mountain climbers crossing a high, dangerous ridge. We finally reached a place of reduced danger, but it was unclear what lay ahead. At that point, they decided to go no further with us. The wife's suicidal behavior was diminished, the overly conscientious physician husband restructured his work habits, and a tentative flexibility seeped into their overly rigid living pattern.

Mrs. Marker constantly sought to "understand" why she was like she was, and was discouraged by our position that it was virtually impossible, in a crisis, to discover the "whys." At that point she had been out of the hospital for 3 months, and while she appeared to have a great deal of intrapsychic pain, her balance was not so precarious as earlier. Her parents were in for a week of interviews. His parents also came in for interviews. We had a wonderful time with their 4-year-old daughter. Mrs. Marker wanted to leave therapy because she thought a woman therapist could "understand her situation better." We understood them to want to run away from home and said that we didn't agree, but it was their life. They left.

Three weeks later we received a Christmas card from Mrs. Marker with a warm note stating that things were going much better with them. They were very pleased with our psychotherapy. We were pleased that the outcome was satisfactory.

Two days after the card arrived, a woman psychiatrist in town called to say that Mrs. Marker had been admitted to an inpatient unit. The admission was precipitated by a severe slashing of her arms and a failed carbon monoxide suicide. She had been in the hospital 10 days, and had injured herself on four occasions with broken glass, razors, and wire. Please note the irony in the Christmas card written and mailed from the hospital. The psychiatrist was concerned that Mrs. Marker was starting a cycle similar to the one that preceded our work with the family.

The telephone call was demoralizing. We felt ourselves to be genuine duds. The dissonance between the Christmas card message and the psychiatrist's news was perplexing and gave me the feeling of being caught in a dream. Mrs. Marker's cycle of self-abusive behavior began again in earnest. In the end she was sent to a residential treatment facility, and her husband moved away from the city. Neither of them ever made further contact with us.

We were never able to understand what went wrong with our treatment. Perhaps in our anxiety we talked too much with our professional neighbors. Had we enjoyed our agonizing too much? Had Whitaker's leaving to do a visiting professorship been to blame? As physicians had we somehow treated the husband too much as a colleague and thereby double-crossed the wife? Had we panicked them with our overinvestment?

In addition to being a failure, this case represented a defeat. We implemented every measure that we wanted, yet the family's situation did not improve as hoped. The involvement with this family defeated my (Keith's) omnipotence. I had heard about this impossible family long before they were referred. It was a perfect opportunity to demonstrate the effectiveness of family therapy with impossible families. Perhaps it was this overinflated purpose that caused our downfall. Grandiosity is a hidden danger.

When I learned of the outcome, my feelings were mixed. I thought about giving up on family therapy. On the other hand I experienced an odd exhilaration. I was reminded of Kahlil Gibran's (1969) poem "Defeat" (quoted in part):

> Defeat, my Defeat, my shining sword and
> shield,
> In your eyes I have read
> That to be enthroned is to be enslaved,
> And to be understood is to be levelled
> down,
> and to be grasped is but to reach one's
> fulness
> And like a ripe fruit to fall and be consumed.
>
> Defeat, my Defeat, my bold companion . . .
> You and I shall laugh together with the
> storm,
> And together we shall dig graves for all
> that die in us,
> And we shall stand in the sun with a will,
> And we shall be dangerous.

As Jacob was changed following his defeat by the angel, so I (Keith) felt changed by our struggle with this family. There is relief in the collapse of a delusion of grandeur. I think I now do better with big league families. I have failed grandly once, and I can stand to fail again. I am less intimidated by my own fear of failure. Although my omnipotence was shattered, I did not lose my caring. I approach families more casually and no longer need to force change.

Conclusion

Family therapists, like any adult, ought to know when, with whom, and how to be creative. Likewise, we need to know how to be adaptive and adequate and to have the wisdom not to be. Like parents, we walk through a terrain that has on the one side the possibility of failure, ineffectiveness, and despair and on the other the process of increasing maturity, discovery of new components of ourselves, and the joy of participating in the personal growth of our patients. A tension is present, which keeps us balanced yet threatens to upend us. There is no road, only a forest of measureless confusion and endless dilemmas. We cheer ourselves on by sharing tales of successes. When we talk about success, we may mean only that we had fun, a challenge was met, or something happened. If the therapist is creative and enlivened, then the treatment experience is at least a partial success. That component of our work should not be diminished. We think it is dangerous if the patient comes first.

Yet, we can know more about our work if we know more about our failures and find a way to discuss them more freely. This chapter is a bit of a failure: We still don't understand failing as well as we had hoped. It has to do partly with the nature of the problem; failure is a linear concept and does not fit with ecosystems. It also has to do with our way of thinking, which not only tolerates but respects and enjoys ambiguity in the interest of adding experience.

It is intriguing to think that we can only fail by not caring or by disregarding our integrity. It is intriguing to think of success as our having the power to give over to the family the responsibility for living whenever they ask for it. What is left if there is no success or failure? Just living—so we might as well make it creative. Take care, though: Living is also dangerous, and isolation makes it more so.

REFERENCES

Betz, B., & Whitehorn, J. C. *Effective psychotherapy with the schizophrenic patient.* New York: Jason Aronson, 1975.

Gibran, K. Defeat. In *The madman.* New York: Knopf, 1969.

Kipling, R. If—. In *Rudyard Kipling's verse, definitive edition.* Garden City, N.Y.: Doubleday, 1940.

Malone, T., Warkentin, J., Felder, R., & Whitaker, C. *The origins and growth of experiential psychotherapy.* Symposium at the American Academy of Psychotherapy annual meeting, Atlanta, 1978.

Whitaker, C. A., & Keith, D. V. Family therapy as symbolic experience. *International Journal of Family Psychiatry,* 1980, *1,* 197–208.

Whitaker, C. A., & Malone, T. P. *The roots of psychotherapy.* New York: Blakiston, 1953.

PART TWO

OUR FAMILY THERAPY FAILURES

2

The Surreptitious Power
of the Sibling Cohort:
An Echo of Sin and Death

SANDRA B. COLEMAN

> Those who restrain desire, do so because theirs is weak enough to be restrained; and the restrainer or reason usurps its place and governs the unwilling.
>
> And being restrained, it by degrees becomes passive, till it is only the shadow of desire.
>
> The history of this is written in Paradise Lost, and the Governor or Reason is called Messiah.
>
> And the original Archangel, or possessor of the command of the heavenly host, is called the Devil or Satan, and his children are called Sin and Death.
> —Voice of the Devil (William Blake, *The Marriage of Heaven and Hell*)

Introduction

As I reflect upon the Haverman family, I immediately become aware that this case still presents many haunting paradoxes that challenge my theoretical beliefs, my therapeutic stance, and my innermost core as a human being. The Havermans will always remind me of the contrasts conveyed in William Blake's prophetic work *The Marriage of Heaven and Hell*, and I cannot help but think that Blake must have known the Havermans at some point in time.

Treating the Havermans was always like doing a balancing act between Blakean Wisdom and Folly. Just when I thought I had accomplished a sagely therapeutic coup, I was catapulted into witnessing the extreme absurdity of such thinking. Even though there were moments of undeniable success, the final outcome suggests that the periods of achievement were just temporary "finger-in-the-dike" experiences. But regardless of the judgment surrounding their treatment or the disappointment at the end, the Havermans were a special kind of family, the kind that just stays with you, piquing memories of tenderness and caring—the bottom line of what therapy is perhaps all about.

Sandra B. Coleman. Family Guidance Center of Bucks County, Yardley, Pennsylvania; Department of Mental Health Sciences, Hahnemann University, Philadelphia, Pennsylvania.

Theoretical Frame of Reference

General Theoretical Model

The treatment of the Haverman family was essentially structural–strategic, rooted in a "systems" or "communication" model (Stanton, 1981a). Although there is currently a strong force in the family therapy field to develop a cogent theory integrating the major tenets of both structural and strategic approaches, as Stanton (1981a) notes, this has not yet been accomplished. At the time that this case was being treated, the combination of structural and strategic therapies was in its earliest phase of development. Thus, the treatment was derived from a model that had a paucity of literature from which to draw when one was "stuck."

Several basic principles of treatment provided a foundation for the Havermans' therapy. These concepts represent both structural and strategic schools and an integration of both. The basic elements of these models are described originally by Minuchin (Minuchin, Montalvo, Guerney, Rosman, & Schumer, 1967; Minuchin, 1974); Minuchin, Rosman, and Baker (1978); and Haley (1973, 1976). Later reviews by Aponte and Van Deusen (1981) and Stanton (1981a, 1981b) offer additional information. An elaboration of these schools will not be attempted here and the reader unfamiliar with these principles is referred to the original sources. The key concepts are briefly mentioned because of their particular relevance to the case.

The central approach to treatment was derived from systems theory, within which the family's structural dimensions were initially given major attention. Understanding the family included exploring issues of power, proximity and distance, and boundaries and alignment. The major techniques included those designed to allow the therapist to use the family's own interactional patterns to facilitate change, that is, structuralization, enactment, task setting, joining, restructuring, and so on (Aponte & Van Deusen, 1981).

Later, strategic methods were integrated with structural therapy, which, in contrast focus on the symptom and the sequence of family behaviors that serve to maintain or reinforce it. Symptoms are viewed as the family's unsuccessful attempt to resolve their problem (Watzlawick, Weakland, & Fisch, 1974), which is most apt to be a result of some untenable circumstances (Haley, 1973). This often occurs at a transitional point in the family life cycle. Rather than focusing on structural inadequacies with their concomitant faulty alignments, boundaries, and struggle for power, the strategic therapist explores issues pertaining to symptom-related patterns. Change is felt to be accomplished by the therapist's goal-oriented intervention techniques, which are specifically designed to change symptom-maintaining interactional sequences into symptom-free behaviors. Methods associated with strategic therapy include paradoxical interventions with strategies originally described by Rohrbaugh, Tennen, Press, White, and Raskin (1977) and reviewed by Stanton (1981b). Prescribing, restraining, and positioning strategies are most representative. Positive connotation or reframing techniques are also commonly used, while more detailed methods for working paradoxically are described by Weeks and L'Abate (1979); Madanes (1980); Selvini-Palazzoli, Boscolo, Cecchin, and Prata (1980); and Andolfi (1980); and reviewed by Stanton (1981b).

One of the essential differences between structural and strategic methods is that the strategic therapist prescribes tasks for the family to do between sessions as opposed to the within-session task orientation of the structural therapist. Thus, change is expected to take place away from the therapist's environment, which underscores the clinician's stance that the family can heal itself.

Stanton (1981a) offers three general rules for using structural and strategic methods concurrently. Although the Havermans' treatment began and ended before Stanton (1981a) wrote his article on the integration of structural–strategic approaches, my use of the two treatment methods correlates precisely with his suggested sequence. They therefore are briefly cited here.

• *Rule No. 1:* The initial treatment of the family is structural, using concepts as previously described, that is, joining, accommodating, boundaries, restructuring, and so forth. Stanton suggests that this is a more direct and more reasonable method, and its effectiveness has been well documented.

• *Rule No. 2:* A strategic approach should be used when structural methods are not working or not likely to work. Stanton's rationale here is based on several examples; the most applicable in the case of the Havermans is that the switch from a structural to a strategic approach is made when no change occurs or when there is no evidence that the change that has taken place is "second order" in nature. (Watzlawick *et al.*, 1974).

• *Rule No. 3:* The therapist should return from a successful use of strategic methods to structural therapy again in order to enter the final or "restructuring" phase of treatment. Here effort is concentrated on working with family members' individual development in an attempt to deemphasize the role of the identified patient.

A few additional comments regarding theoretical reference points bear noting. First, in conjunction with my students' needs for a schematic model to assess families and to plan treatment strategies, I recently developed a brief evaluative inventory for use after the initial family session. The *Coleman Family Life Cycle Assessment Scale* (Coleman, unpublished) determines (1) the developmental stage of the family life cycle, (2) the structural components of the family, (3) the dysfunctional or problem area(s), and (4) the treatment design. The latter involves a four-step procedure establishing the treatment approach. Step 1 is an explicit delineation of the symptom; step 2 requires formulation of the hypothesis(es) regarding the function of the symptom for the family; step 3 establishes the family's treatment goals; and step 4 involves the therapist's plan(s) toward helping the family to achieve those goals. Thus, in addition to the structural–strategic model, I use an assessment technique to further understand the family and clarify the direction of treatment.

Specific Theory: A Substance Abuse Model

Finally, because the Haverman family presented with a drug and alcohol problem, my own specific theoretical view of addictive processes shares space with the more general family systems theories. More will be said about the role of the incomplete mourning theory (Coleman, 1975, 1980a, 1980b, 1981; Coleman, Kaplan, & Downing, 1981) in the case analysis, and only a review of the major issues is presented here.

Within the context of family systems theory, compulsive drug use is viewed as a function of intrafamilial transactional patterns. From this perspective drugs play a significant role in maintaining family balance or homeostasis. By adapting the major tenets of family systems theory to the drug abuse field, several authors cogently explain how the family encourages, reinforces, and sustains drug-seeking behavior (Klagsbrun & Davis, 1977; Stanton, Todd, Heard, Kirschner, Kleiman, Mowatt, Riley, Scott, & Van Deusen, 1978; Steinglass, 1976; Stanton & Coleman, 1980). For an elaboration of these constructs and concepts, the reader is referred to the publications cited. The focus here is on one particular dimension of family life— death, separation, and loss—which appears to have a significant etiological effect on drug abuse, given the necessary addiction-producing elements of family behavior. Specifically, the incomplete mourning theory of drug abuse (Coleman, 1980a, 1980b; Coleman & Stanton, 1978) suggests that addictive behavior is related to an unusual number of traumatic or premature deaths, separations, and losses that occur within critical or transitional stages of the family's developmental cycle and are not effectively resolved or mourned. The homeostatic family processes and interlocking transactional patterns make drug abuse a likely response for coping with overwhelming stress associated with the loss experience. Drug use also serves to keep the abusing member helpless and dependent on the family, a process that unifies and sustains family intactness. Within the complex set of interpersonal relationships is an overall sense of hopelessness, despair, and a lack of purpose or meaning in life.

The early foundation for the theory lies in a pilot study that discovered an unusual prevalence of premature or untimely deaths among 25 recovering heroin addicts and their families (Coleman, 1975). Additional clinical evidence for the significance of death and death-related issues in addict families was found while working with siblings (Coleman, 1978, 1979).

In addition to separation caused by real death, any type of disengagement is particularly difficult for addict families. Stanton *et al.* (1978); Stanton and Coleman, (1980); and I (Coleman, 1978, 1979) have written extensively about the conflictual elements of separation, expressing doubt that it is mere coincidence that drug use becomes intensified during adolescence, when separation conflicts are at a peak. As Stanton *et al.* (1978) point out, drug abuse is a "paradoxical resolution" to growing up and leaving the family. The drug permits the user to leave as a means of establishing some independence, but it also facilitates the return to the hearth when it is time to "crash." This perpetuates the cyclical pattern of leaving and not leaving, keeping the addict straddled between home and the outside world of drugs. The profound conflict that separation presents for these families has been discussed extensively in other publications and will not be repeated here.

Akin to exploring the role of death in addict families is the investigation of the function of what I call "religiosity" (Coleman, 1981). I view a religious or philosophical belief system, that is, a "purpose in life" (Frankl, 1963) as the major interface between death and the family's adaptive behavior. A sense of faith may either alleviate or exacerbate the sorrow, rage, and guilt that accompany or follow the loss of a loved one.

Recent research examining patterns of loss across the family life cycle of addicts, psychiatrics, and normals (Coleman *et al.*, 1981; Coleman, Kaplan, & Downing, 1985) indicates that the clinical findings are supported by statistical evidence that the incidence of death differs significantly across groups with addicts having a more distinct orientation to death, being more suicidal, and having more premature and bizarre death experiences. During childhood they have more family separations and develop a unique pattern of continuously separating from and returning to their family. Further, they are also less likely to have a clearly defined purpose in life.

Thus, in addition to all the clinical studies, there is finally systematic, empirical research to support the incomplete mourning theory. This gives credence to the view that the etiology of drug abuse is due to both unpredictable, unexpected experiences of death and loss, as well as to structural or functional imbalances in the family. The idiosyncratic orientation of these families toward death and loss makes it extraordinarily difficult for them to complete the mourning process. Thus, death and loss become integral parts of a homeostatic pattern that keeps the drug-abusing member helpless and dependent on staying at home with the family. Within the complex set of feedback mechanisms involved in the drug-sustaining cycle of family interactions lies an overall sense of family hopelessness and lack of purpose or meaning in life.

In this manner the initiation of drug abuse cannot be ascribed to a linear, cause-and-effect model. Rather, drug abuse can be best understood from the standpoint of the "new epistemology" or from a cybernetic model that would view the family's relationship patterns and feedback system as essential to the addictive symptom.

Background

The Havermans were referred to me at a time when I was deeply involved in a federally funded research project. As Principal Investigator of the grant and director of the drug program's research department, I had not permitted myself to do any clinical work at all, largely because I knew the potential of clinical cases to absorb time and energy. In March 1978, Dr. Stevenson, the medical director of our large inner-city treatment program, asked me to consider treating the Havermans. He felt that he could not sanction Mr. Haverman's Methadone treatment unless Harry Haverman, his wife, and children participated in family therapy. Dr. Stevenson knew that I was reluctant to do any direct treatment. He clearly understood that although I had treated hundreds of addict families throughout the past, I was now more interested in discovering addict family life-cycle patterns than I was in trying to change them. Despite all this, Dr. Stevenson presented me with a challenge that intrigued me and after I listened to the details of the case, the Haverman family hooked me.

My interest was really three-fold. First, the abundance of obstacles associated with the case intrigued me. Mr. Haverman was 51 years old, suffered from heroin and alcohol abuse, and had a multitude of medical problems. His history of addiction began in World War II, when as a 19-year-old soldier in Europe he first used morphine. Shortly after the war he started using heroin on weekends while also engaging in regular use of other narcotics and barbituates. His drinking began somewhat later, when his sales job necessitated frequent travel.

Harry had a long treatment history to accompany his drug portfolio. He was hospitalized in a well-known addiction treatment center for 4 months in the late 1940s, only to return there two or three times following his initial discharge. Visits to the inpatient unit at the VA hospital were frequent, and outpatient treatment contacts at local drug centers were numerous. Clearly Harry was an inveterate drug addict. He also had a host of medical problems largely associated with the physical deterioration caused by so many years of chemical abuse. He was a borderline diabetic, had relatively severe peripheral neuropathy, increasing problems with a cirrhotic liver, and hypertension. Harry was also hard of hearing and had frequent bouts of narcoleptic-like behavior. The inventory of legitimate drugs required to nurse his physical ills was almost as long as the illegal list.

Although he was not on parole or probation at the time of this referral, he had a history of earlier arrests and a few incarcerations. During one jail sentence he received his high school equivalency diploma, having had less than 8 years of formal education.

Harry was the fourth born of five, having two older brothers and one older and one younger sister. His family had remained intact until his mother's death many years previously. Although Harry had some contact with his aged father, in recent years he rarely saw his siblings. There was no known drug abuse or alcoholism in his family history.

For 14 years Harry had been married to the only child of divorced parents. Connie's father had recently died after living with Harry, Connie, and their two children for several years. Her mother, remarried for many years, lived with Connie's stepfather 2500 miles away. Connie rarely indulged in drug or alcohol use but suffered from an assortment of emotional disorders including a severe phobic reaction to being alone at night in the dark. She had been hospitalized in the psychiatric unit of a large general hospital almost every summer and claimed that she had been diagnosed as schizophrenic. The history of her symptoms suggested however, that her annual "craziness" was more consistent with hysteria. Connie was tall, attractive, and appeared more secure and in control than her mental history conveyed. She was employed in a dress factory as an evening supervisor requiring her to be away from home from midafternoon to nearly midnight. Her salary was essential to the family's support, as the only other income came from Harry's disability.

Harry and Connie had two adopted youngsters, Kathy, a 12-year-old girl, and Robert, an 11-year-old boy. Both children were adopted at birth and were obtained through a licensed adoption agency. It appears that Harry had been abstinent for the first 10 years of marriage. During that time he worked as a sales manager for his brother's business, earned a good income, and presented a responsible picture. He and Connie owned a home in a suburban neighborhood and gave evidence that they could provide a secure environment for children.

Approximately 3½ years ago, after more than a decade of sobriety, Harry again began to abuse drugs. At about the same time when his brother's once successful business was forced into bankruptcy, he lost his job. Reinitiation of drug use now included heroin, alcohol, and a daily habit of 20–25 mg Dilaudid. Harry had recently gone to the VA outpatient drug treatment unit where it was suggested that he enter family treatment. One unsuccessful and very brief experience in family therapy at another clinic led Harry to decide to transfer to our outpatient Methadone unit. Initial screening led the medical director to stipulate family therapy as a requisite for Harry's daily Methadone.

The second reason that I agreed to take the case was associated with the staff at the drug clinic. Although most of the counselors had graduate degrees and were well trained in traditional therapies, few had family therapy training; out of necessity, however, they did see a considerable number of couples and families. There was a great deal of interest in such training, but their overwhelmingly large case responsibilities afforded little time for extramural education. As part of the inservice training program, I occasionally gave a theoretical seminar or presented a tape of an interesting or well-conducted session. I had always been distressed when students were bombarded with tapes demonstrating the brilliance of an expert doing a one-time consultation, even though I had a habit of doing this also. How different is the tedious week in and week out struggle of families and therapists wrestling with change. If I took the Haverman case, it would offer an opportunity for the staff to view a continuous case, allowing them to view what really happens in on-going treatment with very difficult family problems.

Finally, there was staff pressure to have me demonstrate my expertise. I was the only staff member who was actively involved with senior-level professionals on a national level, which gave me a mixed dose of respect, awe, and skepticism. Sometimes I was also given resentment. Perhaps by joining the staff on this case adventure and by exposing myself, we could eliminate some of our distance. This essentially describes the scope of family information and the staff environment as I began my journey with the Havermans.

Diagnosis and Treatment Plan

Before meeting the Havermans I decided to be more of a structural purist than I normally was. I felt that the structural teaching model would be most consistent with the behavioral and reality-oriented methods used by the staff counselors. The reading list would also be straightforward, and since the staff was always extraordinarily challenging to any lecturer, especially me, I assumed it would be more effective and efficient to avoid confusing them with my more typical intergenerational model[1] of structural therapy. I also decided to leave the strategic methods out of initial presentations, hoping that the Havermans would benefit from a strict structural model.

My first encounter with the Havermans was in mid-March 1978. The following exchange took place approximately 10 minutes into the session after our initial social exchange. The discussion had centered on the children's age, grade, school performance, and so on. Turning to the parents, I asked:

> DR. C: Are you proud of them?
> HARRY: They make me feel good, they do.
> DR. C: Harry, you seem to want to talk because I noticed you try to get a word in and maybe everybody's talking and not listening, so go ahead, why don't you tell me.

---

1. The previously described incomplete mourning and loss theory is integrated with an intergenerational structural model.

HARRY: They make me feel good.

DR. C: You're proud of them.

HARRY: Very very proud.

DR. C: Do you think they're proud of you?

HARRY: Do I think they're proud of me? I don't know, I hope they are—I don't think—I have a funny feeling that they're not and that bothers me very very much.

DR. C: Why don't you ask them? That would be something very important to talk about.

HARRY: I don't think I spoke to them about the way I really feel. Kathy, I love Kathy so much. I've always, my whole life—and I feel that Kathy don't like me as much as I like her, nowhere near where I like her. I don't know why I just feel that Kathy don't like me. She probably has a reason for it although I'm not too sure what it is, but I hope that Kathy maybe would tell me.

DR. C: Okay, I would like to work on that for a few minutes. Kathy is right here, and I'm here to help.

Harry attempted to withdraw from the potential encounter, but my repeated encouragement led him to finally face Kathy:

HARRY: Hi, sweetheart.

DR. C: How do you feel about what he said?

KATHY: It's true.

DR. C: What's true.

KATHY: What he said. Well, every summer I get sent away because something happens around the house with him. This summer I got sent away because he went after me with his fist, like our cat had kittens, and he threw the chair on the cat because it got in the way, so I jumped up and grabbed the kittens, and then I went downstairs and came back and told my Mom, and he came after me with his fists yelling, "liar," at me. And almost every night he sneaks out of the house because he's real mad at my Mom, and then he comes back singing and dancing.

DR. C: So he goes away upset, and when he comes back he's singing and dancing.

KATHY: Yeah. And when he comes home he just dozes off, and we have to make excuses to our friends and not tell them the truth, and he dozes off, and it looks like he's going to fall off the chair and dozes into his dinner.

HARRY: This makes you angry at me or ashamed of me? Are you ashamed of me, or what?

KATHY: I'm both.

HARRY: Both?

KATHY: Every time, he picks fights with my Mom, and there's a big argument, and then my Mom goes upstairs and lays down and falls asleep.

And my Mom doesn't want him driving because she doesn't think he's in good enough shape, and he sneaks out in his car, and he's not supposed to, and then he comes back singing and dancing and all whoozy. I think he goes out and gets something to drink, because Robert and I have already gone down the cellar and found booze in his desk.

Dr. C: Did you ever ask him where he goes when he goes off and comes back singing and dancing?

Kathy: Yeah, but he says he goes to the market but they're closed sometimes when he goes out.

Dr. C: Why don't you ask him where he goes when he goes out and comes back singing and dancing?

Kathy: Do I have to?

Dr. C: Yes, sure you have to, how are we going to find out, maybe he's on the stage, maybe he's in vaudeville, I will help you if you have trouble.

Like her father, Kathy attempts to retreat from pursuing this any further, but with persistence she finally asked:

Kathy: Where do you go when you go out?

Harry: Sometimes you're accurate. Some of the things you say are accurate, but it's not always. There are times when I go out, I don't always go to the store. An incident happened two days ago with the frozen steaks, remember Robert, that really upset me very, very much? The way I understand it, I went to the store to exchange or get money back because, Robert, you know you didn't want me to go, but I went anyway and the store was closed. There were people still in the store at the time but they wouldn't open the doors, they were closing. I came right back, I don't think I was gone 5 minutes.

Kathy: Twenty-five minutes!!

Harry: The way I understand it you told Mommy I was gone 25 minutes.

Kathy: It was that long!

Dr. C: Do you know what the problem is, you sound like you have parents here. She sounds like your mother and he sounds like your father.

Connie: He [Robert] didn't want him to go because he knew the store was closed.

Dr. C: That's incredible!

Kathy: And there's another thing, he always yells at my Mom and says she's brainwashing me but she's not. I can see this and he doesn't understand.

Dr. C: I want to get back to who is the parent in the family. Go ahead . . .

Robert: Kathy, you don't know what time it is because every day you come home from school and fall asleep. Then you wake up and see Daddy's not home and you go, "He's been out drinking."

KATHY: I do not.

ROBERT: He went to the store . . .

KATHY: I was too, "My Three Sons" was on channel 6 at 5:30 and 6:30, 6:00 . . .

DR. C: Harry, do you see what's going on here?

HARRY: Robert's defending me.

DR. C: Does he do that a lot? [To Robert.] You don't think your father should listen to Kathy?

ROBERT: No, she's bossy and she always makes a lot of noise of everything, over just little things she makes a big racket over.

KATHY: [Interrupts angrily.] Mom, do I do that?

CONNIE: Yeah, we're all pretty vocal.

ROBERT: And Kathy that incident you were talking about, that was a long time ago, about a year and a half ago.

KATHY: No it wasn't.

ROBERT: Yes it was.

KATHY: No it wasn't. [Eyes become tearful, face reddens.]

ROBERT: [Becoming agitated.] Kathy, you think you have the biggest memory.

DR. C: What's wrong Kathy? Do you want to talk about it?

KATHY: Nothing.

DR. C: Are you sad?

KATHY: No, I want to go home!

CONNIE: Come sit with me. Can she sit with me?

DR. C: No, I want Kathy to sit right where she is.

KATHY: Mom, I want to go home.

CONNIE: Yes, sweetie.

DR. C: She's okay. Do you want to talk about it?

KATHY: No!

The session continued with work focusing consistently on the theme of shifting the parental function to Connie and Harry.

The assessment of the family is best described from verbatim notes written after the Havermans' first session:

(3-16-78) The family consists of Harry, 51 years (IP), Connie, mid-40s, and siblings Kathy, 12 years and Robert, 11 years. Initial session revealed that Connie and children are in coalition with Harry being triangulated. Dyads consist of Connie and Kathy; Harry and Robert; and Kathy and Robert whose dyadic relationship appears to be an attempt to manipulate parents. This is an enmeshed family with loose generational boundaries. There is a prevailing role reversal with children serving executive function as parents. Restructuring of family seating arrangement resulted in major theme that parenting function is much in need of change. Kathy became severely upset when her role as wife–mother became threatened by my intervention. Goal of session was to begin to shift executive function from children to parents.

Harry attempted to "parent" Kathy but quickly reverted to "begging," "pleading" as if he was a victim of her unrequited love. Session concluded with parents being asked to help each other in carrying out leadership role.

My choice of a treatment model seemed well supported by the family transactions that took place during the initial session.

In reviewing this first structural map of the family, however, I am somewhat amazed at the missing pieces of the assessment. Because this will be discussed later in the chapter, it is merely noted here.

Process of Therapy

One addition was made to the Haverman case prior to the second session; a cotherapist became involved. A staff counselor approached me after my first meeting with the family and requested working with me. I knew this would further increase my responsibility, yet I always welcome trainees, and I knew Gregory Adams could offer something important to the family. Although he had limited experience in psychotherapy, having only recently completed a Master's degree in counseling, he had recycled a successful career in bioengineering and was bright and capable. He was a few years older than I, had graying hair and would present a mature picture. Also, his manner was soft-spoken, which would be an interesting contrast to my more intrusive approach. Greg was terribly interested in families and promised to conscientiously attend weekly supervisory sessions with me. Because his engineering experience was an excellent resource for understanding systems, I decided to go with his request—it seemed like we might be a viable team.

Greg joined me in the second session with Harry and Connie alone. The following case notes are taken verbatim—except for the change in names—from the Haverman file. The notes describe the results of what took place and indicate that there is some early evidence that the restructuring attempted the previous week carried into the home. Both parents really were trying to fulfill a much-needed executive function.

(3-23-78) The couple started the session by presenting an episode which had occurred during the week. Kathy had said that she would not return for further therapy sessions. When Connie told her that she would have to attend according to requirements, Kathy proceeded to state that she would commit suicide first. Connie responded by telling her that she'd probably get very sick and have to have her stomach pumped; Kathy retorted that she'd run away and find the caseworker who knew her biological parents; again Connie told her that she could do that if she wanted but she'd still have to attend the session. Kathy concluded by saying that she'd go if she had to but would take her sewing. Connie was supported for doing a good job of parenting.

Session further revealed that Connie's father, who had lived with them for several years, had died a few months previously. He too was an alcoholic. Harry complained about not feeling well psychologically. I asked him to select a goal of life or death and stated that I would be away for 2 weeks but upon my return he was to make a decision regarding future therapeutic focus. If life, we'd have a birth to celebrate and this choice must be accompanied by a visit to AA [Alcoholics Anonymous]. If death, we'd have a funeral during the next therapy session. Connie's attendance at Al-Anon was to also occur if Harry and she chose to "live."

It was interesting that, despite all the years of treatment for assorted addictions, Harry had never attended AA meetings. The closest he came was on one occasion when, as he reported, "I stood in the hallway" and "peeked in." Because Harry's drinking appeared to be the most serious and life-threatening of all his problems, I was adamant about him joining AA and going to regular meetings. When I returned from my trip I was quite pleased to learn that Harry had gone to AA.

(4-13-78) Harry and Connie report that Harry attended several AA meetings for the first time in 34 years of addiction. Connie, however, has not gone to Al-Anon yet and was prepared with multiple excuses, one of which included Kathy spraining her ankle on the evening that Connie was to go. Connie became upset, stating that she was "going crazy." When I questioned her further, she talked about the loss of her father, crying strongly about his death. She was able to express her love and her anger toward him, and questioned if he loved her at all. I relabeled his caring for her auto, home repairs, and so on, as "loving" her. Connie felt that Harry "is acting like my father now," wearing his clothes and so on. She believes in parapsychology and suggested (covertly) that the father in some way is now acting thru Harry. I told her to continue to mourn him [her father] and to cry every time she felt like it, behavior which she stated was not acceptable to her family of origin.

(4-20-78) Harry had his first relapse of drinking this week. He had abdominal pains and had decided to self-medicate by eliminating Antabuse. Connie continues to avoid going to Al-Anon, becoming angry at me for suggesting that Greg buy Harry a bottle since it was apparent that this was the decision she had made. Harry stressed that they really needed to learn to communicate more with each other. He stated that neither one heard what was said by the other. He related an incident that had taken place on Sunday when he decided to take Robert fishing. Connie got upset, felt left out, became depressed, and retreated for 2 days to her bed. Interestingly enough, this was the first time Harry had ever gone fishing, and not only did he take Robert but he included Robert's boyfriend. This appeared to be a good attempt at parenting behavior. Children were invited to attend next session.

(4-27-78) Prior to session Harry had been drinking again and had come into program for help with children's refusal to come to session next day. They were told to just come in with everyone. It is apparent that a crisis (which was anticipated) was occurring. Family had to wait as it was planned that they would observe their initial tape while being taped on another video system in order to record feedback effects. When Kathy attempted to block out all participation by reading a book, video was turned off while parents were asked to take over their function. Mother pleaded (similar to Harry's first attempt to parent Kathy). No success was obtained until Connie bribed her. Therapists intervened and Harry stated that he did not like what was happening. Robert interrupted and became angry at Kathy himself. When I asked him to limit his complaints to his own problems he became hysterical and fled into hall. Parents spent a good bit of session getting him to return to therapy room, but this was only after both therapists looked at them, claimed impotence, and waited for them to take over. After Robert sobbingly returned stating that this NEVER happens, family was given assignment of making a behavioral chart to record daily child behavior and resulting parental intervention. Harry commented at the conclusion of session that "I've learned what I've been doing—pleading, begging. It doesn't work. By doing that I let the children control the situation."

After the session I [coincidentally] met the family in a local store and mother asked if people really get better when they've had patterns for so many years. I replied, "Only if they want to." Connie also reported that she had spent an entire day cleaning out her father's things from Robert's room. The next day she looked outside, saw the sun, and recalled that her father would have been outside gardening. She allowed herself to cry, which this time did not drive her into bed.

(5-4-78) Family arrived together looking like an intact, well-organized family. Harry cheerfully presented chart covering entire week. Almost all days were marked with stars for both children. Sessions focused on helping them to deal with trouble spots, particularly Robert's staying out beyond the dinner hour. Also spent time making rules regarding homework, and so on. Children participated nicely, but it was clear that parents were taking charge. Task of restructuring executive function appears to be taking shape. Also, there is more evidence that Harry and Connie are in parental alliance. Harry continues to attend AA (at least once a week). Connie has not gone to Al-Anon.

In early June Connie became extremely upset and asked to be committed to a mental hospital, claiming that she was beginning to feel the same way that she always felt right before she was hospitalized. Her symptoms, which she described as "hallucinations," were really acute anxiety attacks with alternating states of depression and crying. Harry supported her desire to go to the hospital, yet did not interfere when I reframed Connie's request by calling it "her need for a vacation." Little more was said about the hospital as Connie began to ponder the possibilities of taking a few days off from work to relax. Harry offered to take care of her if she would stay at home in bed. He said that he would serve her meals and bring her medicine to make her better.

Following this, Harry became upset and arrived at the next session asking us to put him in the hospital. Here was the system seesawing its way up and down with no one ever hitting hard enough to really feel the "thud." We remarked that Connie and Harry had a real dealer–junkie relationship; they took turns at selling each other a substance to take away the pain. We suggested that what they really needed was to find another way to take care of each other; they needed to bury the drugs. In the next session we had a funeral service for the drugs, and shortly thereafter Connie started going to Al-Anon meetings while Harry regularly attended AA.

Gradually things seemed to improve for everyone in the family. Harry had one bout of drinking after he started going to AA, which was predictable and happens to most people during their early days of abstinence. When this occurred, Harry agreed to undergo detoxification as an inpatient, which greatly accelerated his return to the family, sobriety, and AA meetings. Again things appeared much better and with a certain amount of confidence, in late July I left for a 2-week vacation. The Havermans knew that I would be gone and said that although they would miss me, they had Greg Adams whom they would continue to see regularly.

Greg had been sincerely attempting to work with the family. He never missed a session and was dedicated to the case in every way. His cotherapy role was largely supportive, and, although I never suggested that he assume a passive position, he just seemed to feel more comfortable doing so. He did not work at cross purposes with me, and because I am naturally active I accept a cotherapist's need to find his or her own comfortable position. What did give me difficulty was Greg's tendency to use my words echolalically. We worked on this in supervision, but Greg had a habit of doing it anyway, especially when he was anxious. Short of hitting Greg over the head with a baseball bat, there was little I could do to stop it. Of all the behaviors he had, this bothered me the most because I felt the Havermans needed to see him as a strong and separate individual. This mattered much more than who was active and who was supportive—we all know that in cotherapy the one in the foreground is often just a "front" for the real power in the rear. In our case, however, this did not seem to be happening. I welcomed my vacation not only for the usual reasons, but because it would give Greg an opportunity to assert himself with the family while I was totally removed from the scene.

When I returned from vacation I was almost bowled over by the medical director bellowing at me to get to Greg immediately—"The Havermans have really taken a turn for the worse!" Before I could even unlock my office door that morning, Greg arrived, out of breath with anxiety. "Things are terrible," he declared, "wait until you see the tape of the session. . . . I'm so glad that you're back. I'm not sure that family therapy is working."

During the time that I was gone, Greg experienced a rather traumatic episode with the family. In the therapy session, which Greg rapidly replayed for me in the video room, Harry and Kathy became embroiled with each other; Harry lost complete control of himself and physically beat her in clear view of the camera. The following segment describes the sequence of events associated with their interaction:

CONNIE: [Connie opened the session with a complaint about Harry. She was concerned about him driving the car at night because of his narcoleptic-like behavior.] . . . I am very concerned about him driving; he cannot walk right, he cannot talk right, he cannot hear, he sleeps all the time. I won't go into all the things he's been yelling at me about, but last night we really had a bad hassle; as usual I'm responsible for everything that happens. He was going to go to AA last night but his car battery was dead. I would have driven him but he would have slept the entire evening.

GREG: That's okay, as long as he's there.

CONNIE: Well I had things to do, Greg, and he wasn't capable of driving himself. He wanted to go to the one in Grove Mills which is far from us.

GREG: Find one near him.

CONNIE: He doesn't want to go to a nearer one.

GREG: Harry, if Dr. Coleman was here what would she say to you now?

HARRY: She would say, "Go to whichever one I want to go to."

GREG: What would she say about not going?

HARRY: That I would have to go.

GREG: We're not going to continue doing therapy for you if you don't do your part.

HARRY: But I—but the thing is I wasn't—I wanted to go just to be out of the house, but I wasn't in no condition to go anywhere; I don't think I could have stayed awake.

GREG: It doesn't matter as long as you are there and you have a sponsor.

CONNIE: But how is he going to get there, Greg?

GREG: You'll have to drive him.

CONNIE: Well I have to go to work. I took Tuesday night off. I have to go to work tonight, tomorrow night, and Saturday night. I have to work or we won't have money to eat and that's the truth. Now I said to him, because I heard it at Al-Anon meetings, that he could pick up the phone and call AA and someone will drive him.

GREG: Yes.

CONNIE: He refuses to do that. He insists on driving the car.

The discussion continues and family tensions mount as Connie and Harry debate the issue of which AA meeting to attend and how Harry is to get there.

GREG: Wednesday you can go there, and the other days you go elsewhere. You call and if necessary tell them to put you in contact with somebody who can give you a ride. I know damn well next week when Dr. Coleman is back if she finds out you haven't been going she's going to be one angry young lady.

KATHY: [Interrupts and chides her father for paying more attention to *where* he goes rather than to the fact *that* he goes.] You don't care if you go to AA . . . You only want to go where your junkie friends go.

GREG: Kathy's right but that's not your place to say.

KATHY: Shut up Robert. [Responds to brother's humming at her.]

GREG: Kathy . . .

KATHY: I'm allowed to say to him what I want to say to him.

GREG: Hold it, wait a minute . . .

KATHY: He's my brother I can say what I want to him.

CONNIE: Let's not start.

KATHY: I ain't starting.

GREG: Kathy, what you did to your father is the same thing Robert did to you, and you didn't like it done to you.

KATHY: Well too bad if he don't like it.

GREG: [Banter between Greg and Kathy continues until Greg changes subject and refers to previous issue about Harry's reluctance to get a necessary prescription.] What about this medication, what's going on?

HARRY: I don't have the money.

GREG: You find the money, Harry.

HARRY: What.

GREG: Find it.

HARRY: I don't have it.

GREG: Run up a bill at the drug store.

CONNIE: I paid for it.

GREG: Do you have money for a funeral?

Discussion continues to focus on family's goals until Harry interrupts by claiming . . .

HARRY: I said, I don't know what you're saying!

KATHY: It's not about you.

CONNIE: I don't know why . . . I'm sorry, Harry.

HARRY: Three times I said to you I don't know what you're saying and yet you just talk right over my head.

CONNIE: I'm talking about losing my temper, and get off my back.

HARRY: I don't know what you're saying, Connie.

GREG: Are you having trouble hearing her or understanding her?

HARRY: Hearing her.

GREG: You can't hear?

HARRY: Yes, I can't hear her.

GREG: Okay, can you talk a little more loudly so Harry can hear, why don't you sit over there, it will be closer? [Points to seat near Connie.]

HARRY: If she don't want me to hear then I don't want to hear it. [Resists suggestion to move closer to his wife.]

GREG: Harry, it's difficult to talk to somebody who has a hearing problem. She was saying that she's having difficulty controlling her temper.

HARRY: Let her say what she wants to say.

CONNIE: (a) I am not talking about you; (b) I am talking about my relationship with the kids.

HARRY: Well, don't it concern me?

CONNIE: If you would like to hear it why don't you do like Greg said and move a little closer to me?

HARRY: Because you don't want me to hear it.

CONNIE: This is what it's been like 24 hours a day.

Family members continue to complain about each other. Connie reports that the children are not cleaning up the kitchen after eating, and that her anger toward them is increasing. Finally, Kathy breaks in saying:

KATHY: I don't ever want to come back to this place again, it's ruining my summer.

GREG: It's ruining your whole summer?

KATHY: Yeah.

GREG: Wow!

CONNIE: How is it ruining your summer?

KATHY: Because I have things to do.

CONNIE: Kathy for the past week you have been in bed 'til 1:00 P.M. every day.

KATHY: See, that's what I mean—it's ruining my sleep.

CONNIE: Are you being serious or are you being a child?

KATHY: Yeah, I like to sleep 'til 12:00, and I am a child.

CONNIE: You are 12 going on 13; you are not a baby.

KATHY: Yeah, so I'm still a child, so I can be myself.

CONNIE: When you're an adult you can be yourself, but you can have respect and have manners and use your brain once in a while.

GREG: Kathy what were your goals? [Changes subject in attempt to stop unproductive behavior.]

KATHY: I don't remember.

GREG: You have two.

KATHY: Want to make a dollar bet, Dr. Coleman told me to change it. It's the truth.

CONNIE: Do you act like that in school?

KATHY: Me?

CONNIE: Yes, and I want an honest answer.

KATHY: Not to the teachers.

CONNIE: Well then I expect the same kind of respect to Greg that you give to your teachers.

KATHY: I don't have to.

CONNIE: I demand it, all right?

KATHY: Doesn't mean I'm going to give it.

CONNIE: Well then . . . this is it, man.

GREG: Go on, Connie.

CONNIE: Well, then you will pay the consequences.

KATHY: Then I'll suffer them.

CONNIE: Then you'll suffer them.

GREG: Are you afraid to come and see me?

KATHY: No I'm not. I don't want to come. I lose time in school, I lose marks, it ruins my summer. How would you like to go to school and say, "Hey teacher I am going to a shrink because my father is a drunk and a dope addict." How would you like to tell that to your teacher? You go in and say it to them.

CONNIE: How many times have you lost school as a result of other things besides coming here?

KATHY: That's when I'm sick.

CONNIE: Besides being sick, oversleeping?

KATHY: I hardly ever lost school. I lost it two times on that.

CONNIE: How many times did you lose school coming here?

KATHY: When did we start March?

CONNIE: You didn't come every week.

KATHY: Okay we started . . .

GREG: You came here two or three times.

KATHY: How much do you want to make a dollar bet?

CONNIE: I'll make you a dollar bet.

HARRY: It doesn't serve any purpose.

GREG: Right on Harry!

HARRY: It doesn't serve any purpose.

KATHY: Oh, who cares?

CONNIE: I care.

KATHY: Then you care. I don't care—I don't listen to him anymore.

GREG: Okay let's go to Robert. Robert?

Greg proceeds to ask Robert about his goals, but Robert quickly shifts back to Kathy blaming her for the mess in the kitchen.

KATHY: I didn't spill the crackers.

ROBERT: I know, I'm just saying that you took them up to the bedroom.

KATHY: Polly [a friend] told me to, and anyway I already told Mommy, *tattletale*!

ROBERT: [Mimics Kathy's voice.] Tattletale.

GREG: Kathy.

KATHY: Brat!

GREG: Kathy!

KATHY: Hold it, I'm not through with him yet.

GREG: I am through listening to this, I am through listening to this.

KATHY: I don't care, I'm just getting back at you for what you did to George [a friend].

ROBERT: [Mimics Kathy more by humming.]

GREG: Kathy!

KATHY: . . . and you told George to say to me . . .

HARRY: You better start caring or I'm going to let you have it.

KATHY: Yeah, you let me have it and I'll run away from this house for a long time.

HARRY: And you can do it!

KATHY: I don't want to.

HARRY: I'm going to give it to you right here, right here and now.

KATHY: You touch me and I'll . . .

[Harry starts hitting Kathy.]

GREG: Harry, once is enough.

HARRY: I'm going to give it to you. [Throws her down on couch and starts punching her repeatedly.]

GREG: Harry, that's enough! Harry, Harry . . .

CONNIE: Harry! Harry! Harry!

GREG: That's enough.

CONNIE: Harry . . .

KATHY: If you touch me again, so help me I'll kick you.

CONNIE: Harry . . .

KATHY: Get away from me.

CONNIE: Harry, Harry . . .

HARRY: [Inaudible comment.]

CONNIE: Get out Kathy, get out!

[Kathy flees screaming. As she runs past Robert, he puts his foot out, trips her, and she falls to floor. No one else notices this action, and Kathy quickly gets up and leaves room.]

HARRY: [To Kathy.] Don't you do that to me again.

GREG: Stop it.

HARRY: [To Kathy.] You're not going to do that to me again.

GREG: Sit down, Harry.

HARRY: You leave me alone. I'm going to find her Greg.

GREG: No you're not. She'll be all right.

HARRY: Are you going to find her or am I going to find her?

GREG: She'll be all right.

HARRY: I said, "Are you going to find her or am I going to find her?"

CONNIE: Sit down.

GREG: Harry, sit down.

They continue to repeat themselves with Harry ignoring Greg's attempts to reassure him of Kathy's safety. Finally, Harry stops perseverating and orders Connie to find her.

HARRY: I'm ordering you, you better get up.
GREG: Connie, go downstairs and bring her back.
CONNIE: Bring her back?
GREG: Bring her back. Sit down, Harry.
HARRY: I'm sick and tired of her disrespect for you Greg.
GREG: Don't worry about me, sit down.
HARRY: I can't take it anymore.
GREG: Good, but there are other ways of not taking it, this is not a very effective way.
HARRY: I didn't hurt her one bit.
GREG: I know that but it doesn't work, there has to be other ways of dealing with it.
HARRY: I can take her disrespect for me all she wants, but she's not going to be disrespectful to you.
GREG: I'm not her father.
HARRY: No, she don't have to be disrespectful to you.
GREG: Robert, what do you think about this?
ROBERT: It's normal, not really normal, but I never see that.
GREG: I did remember that time . . .
HARRY: Greg, Greg, Connie told everybody on my street, everybody except one family about me, all about me and it reflects on Kathy.
GREG: Sit down, Harry.
HARRY: It reflects on Kathy. Every family on my street Connie has told about me, and I'm sick and tired of that, because it reflects on that kid, and that kid has to take all kinds of crap on account of me, on account of her. She'll deny it up and down. [Looks over at Robert.] He'll tell you it's the truth.
GREG: Harry you've never been this awake and this angry.
HARRY: She told every family on my street about me.
GREG: Relax Harry.
HARRY: I'm—I can't live on that street. I want to move from that street. She'll deny from here to—from one end of Princess Avenue to the other, but she told every family on the block about me.
GREG: What did she say about you?
HARRY: I'm a drug addict and an alcoholic.
GREG: Why do you think she might have said that?
HARRY: Revenge—I don't know why she does anything, I don't know why. I haven't the slightest idea why. She shouldn't have done it.
GREG: She shouldn't have done it . . .

HARRY: I didn't abuse her ever. I never touched her.

GREG: You came awfully close just now.

HARRY: I came awfully close, but I didn't do it. It took a lot of willpower not to do it. I'm sorry about this, and if you want to get rid of us I wouldn't be a bit surprised, because you don't have to put up with it, Dr. Stevenson [the medical director] don't have to put up with it, nobody has to put up with it. As far as my Methadone, I can get my Methadone from the VA hospital so anytime you want to get rid of us you can get rid of us.

GREG: Harry, I'm not sure if you're angry or you want to cry.

HARRY: I'm sick and tired of it. She don't want to go out and get Connie [uses wife's name, but means Kathy] because she's scared of Connie. She's scared of Connie.

GREG: Who's scared of Connie?

HARRY: Connie bullies her and everything else.

GREG: Who bullies who, Kathy? . . .

HARRY: Kathy bullies Connie. Kathy bullies everybody in the house, including Robert, and I'm tired of it.

CONNIE: [Returns to therapy room.] She's sitting on the stairs. She's too frightened to come in. She's shaking like a leaf Greg. She was outside crying her eyes out. She already left the building and everything.

HARRY: Where is she?

CONNIE: At the bottom of the stairs. She's right here at the bottom of the stairs.

GREG: [Goes to the phone and calls Dr. Stevenson for immediate help.]

Within the first 5 minutes of the session, it was obvious that an explosion was imminent. The family came in "gunning" for Harry. Connie was exasperated with him and regressed to her former way of treating Harry as a child. It was easy for Harry to accept this dependent position particularly when the children aligned themselves with Connie. Unless Greg could take charge and engineer a quick restructuring, chaos was inevitable.

The nonverbal cues were as significant as the verbal ones. In the initial portion of the session, Harry was seated next to his wife. As she chastised him, he moved closer to Greg, but when Greg joined Connie and the children, withdrawing any potential support from the therapist's camp, Harry moved completely out of the circle. At this point the camera's only evidence that Harry was still in the room was an occasional view of his foot.

Greg had no difficulty understanding what happened when he reviewed the session on videotape. He was appalled when he saw how he mirrored Harry's dependency by beginning the session with a reference to my power, that is, by saying "Harry, if Dr. Coleman was here what would she say to you now?" and later—when unsure of how to handle things— calling the medical director for help. At this point the symmetry between the cotherapy subsystem and the marital subsystem was glaringly obvious. Unless we changed and unless Greg became more assertive with the family, it was unlikely that Harry would change. Connie kept getting stronger and more adequate; without Harry achieving this, the marital system would remain askew and weak in its executive functions. Greg promised to really work on keeping aware of his position in the sessions, and I promised to try to hold back.

Greg and I made an honest effort to take note of our behavior with the Havermans. In supervision I moved into personal areas and explored Greg's experiences with his own family of origin, his feelings toward women, toward me, and so on. He was open to sharing some information, but this type of relationship was difficult for both of us. We were not treating the family in a psychodynamic mode, and since supervision generally follows the case model, this approach was not particularly helpful.

The Havermans, improved considerably, however, although Harry's physical condition became increasingly problematic. By autumn he decided he no longer needed his minimal amount of daily Methadone, and within a short period of time he was totally drug-free. He was still attending AA meetings several times a week, and there was no evidence that he was about to resume drinking. The children seemed more under control, and since Connie had been able to avoid hospitalization for the first time in many years, the parental subsystem demonstrated its grip on responsibility.

Before Thanksgiving Kathy got a job babysitting and began saving money for Christmas. Robert was doing well in school and had stayed out of trouble. Greg and I began to relax and feel that we had overcome some pretty major hurdles. By the first of the year, it was evident that the family was ready for a vacation from therapy. After Harry lived through the holidays without booze or drugs, we decided that the Havermans deserved to experience their lives without us. We agreed to a gradual move toward discharge with follow-up visits scheduled at regular intervals for at least 6 months.

For the next several months, we saw the family every 4–6 weeks. Harry was able to maintain drug-free status for approximately 1 month. After that he began to slip and requested Methadone again. As a preventative measure he was put on a relatively small daily dose. Greg agreed to monitor his progress weekly and family work continued on our reduced schedule. Both Harry and Connie worked hard on fulfilling their parental tasks and their relationship strengthened. They even resumed sleeping in the same bedroom, and although Harry was sexually impotent they were affectionate and caring toward each other. In a session without the children, Greg and I were amazed at their mutual silliness and warmth. Connie said that she felt a resurgence of her former love for her husband because, as she explained, "I know he's really trying."

While others at the clinic waited for the other shoe to drop, I sustained my confidence in the Havermans' ability to improve. The major problem as I saw it was Harry's physical health, which was rapidly deteriorating. He was frequently edemous; at times he could hardly put on his trousers because his ankles and legs were so swollen. Although he had not been drinking, we knew that if he did he would face life-threatening consequences.

Approximately 6 months after our initial attempt to set the Havermans loose, things were going well. Three months later, things were not going so well; Harry kept showing up with increased physical pain. When admitted to the local medical center with severe "pains in his legs," the diagnostic impression was (1) depression; (2) inadequate personality; (3) alcohol and drug abuse; (4) cirrhosis; (5) peripheral neuritis; and (6) diabetes. Upon discharge, 1 week later, the diagnosis included (1) alcoholism; (2) depression; (3) cirrhosis; (4) polyneuropathy; (5) pneumonia; (6) hypertension; (7) diabetes; (8) narcotics addiction; and (9) immature or inadequate personality.

Harry's hospitalization was in late January. By May (14 months after we had initiated family therapy) things improved again. A follow-up medical visit and lab report from the consulting physician stated, "Harry looked great! Stopped most of his meds on his own. . . ." We began to feel good again, a feeling which continued until after the summer.

By September, however, it was clear that Harry had started to drink again. Connie became terribly upset, and the children were in trouble in school several weeks after classes resumed. Greg and I realized that we were losing ground and that the entire family was now in a serious state. Something more radical had to be done. In attempting to decide what to do next, I reviewed the progress and regression that had taken place. To a large extent we had maintained a consistent structural approach, encouraging Harry and Connie to take charge of their children who were always struggling to regain their power. Although an overview of the case revealed a degree of continuous improvement, closer scrutinization indicated that the changes were largely "first order" (Watzlawick et al., 1974). Following my own theoretical map, hopefully leading to more permanent change, that is, "second-order change," I decided that a more strategic intervention was now indicated. This was also based upon Stanton's (1981a) "Rule No. 2" (see "Theoretical Frame of Reference" in this chapter). The strategy that emerged from my thoughts was one that would jolt the entire system while simultaneously helping Harry to face his self-destructive drinking. Both moves were absolutely essential. Either one alone had little chance of working, yet a strategy integrating both had some potential.

I took charge by calling a special session. After devising this plan I told Greg what I was going to do. There was really minimal discussion with him—someone had to do something and it was clear that I was the designated one. At this point Greg had largely withdrawn from any active involvement with the case.

In the hallway, prior to the start of the session, Kathy told me that she was sick and thought she might "barf" in the session.

DR. C: I brought you here because I'm having a little problem.

HARRY: [Slurs his words and has obviously been drinking.] You're having problems?

DR. C: I have a problem and I need your help. [Looks at Kathy.] This will make her barf for sure. Can you help me? I helped you when you had a problem, what do you think?

CONNIE: It sounds like we're being invaded.

DR. C: That will stop.

CONNIE: [Looks at daughter who is acting ill.] You might be more comfortable in this chair.

KATHY: I'll be comfortable when we're out of this place.

HARRY: I'm sorry to hear about your problem. Something serious?

DR. C: Yes, it's very serious, and I want you to help me. My problem is, I don't know why we're working with all of you.

HARRY: You don't know?

DR. C: Why are we working with all of you? I can't figure out why we're working with you. I was away and I came back and I was talking to Greg and things weren't going too well.

HARRY: He said what?

DR. C: Things weren't going too well.

HARRY: No.

DR. C: So I thought I would ask you to come help me because I don't understand. I don't understand . . .

HARRY: Well I . . .

DR C: Well, you're the king[2] of the family?

HARRY: I'm not the king in the family.

DR. C: Sure you're the king in the family, everything centers on you; you're the king.

HARRY: Centers around me, but I'm certainly not the king of the family.

CONNIE: Kathy, will you turn around?

DR. C: I bet everybody else thinks you are.

HARRY: No they don't.

DR. C: Why don't you ask them?

HARRY: They don't.

DR. C: Kathy is smiling she must agree with you. Is he the king?

KATHY: No.

---

2. The reference to Harry as a "king" is a metaphor used strategically by Maurizio Andolfi in exaggerating the IP's role.

DR. C: He's not the king? He acts like the king.

HARRY: I act like the king?

DR. C: You said everything centers around you.

HARRY: The problems do . . .

DR. C: [Kathy begins to squirm, rubs her stomach, etc.] You better give her the barf bag mom, she wants to take over as the queen. She doesn't want Harry to get all this attention.

KATHY: Mom, tell her to leave me alone.

DR. C: Why don't you tell me?

KATHY: Leave me alone. I don't feel good.

DR. C: Okay, consider yourself left alone. I really needed you today Kathy, I needed you to help me.

KATHY: I don't care, leave me alone, my stomach hurts.

DR. C: I know.

KATHY: And I do feel like I'm going to barf.

DR. C: Well, we have a bag for you or a toilet or basket. It's very sad, I don't know what to do so I brought you in to help me decide what we're going to do. We've been working a long time. It seems like Kathy is still sad, Connie looks mad, Robert looks . . .

HARRY: I . . .

DR. C: I don't know what I can do.

HARRY: I can't stop drinking.

DR. C: No, I think you should keep on drinking.

HARRY: What?

DR. C: I think you should keep on drinking.

HARRY: Do you think I want to?

DR. C: I don't know if you want to or not, but I don't think you should try to stop.

HARRY: I want to, I want to stop.

KATHY: Then why do you keep drinking if you want to stop and you're on the Librium too?

HARRY: I'm taking the Librium to help me stop.

KATHY: Yeah, but you're still drinking down the cellar, I caught you. Mom, I want to go home.

DR. C: So the family is the same. Is that what you're saying Kathy?

KATHY: Keep me out of this.

DR. C: Well, you're part of the family.

KATHY: Well, I don't want to be here.

CONNIE: Show respect please.

KATHY: I don't care. I don't want to respect her.

CONNIE: Kathy!

DR. C: It looks bad, I guess we're going to have to throw in the towel.

CONNIE: Oh, Jesus Christ.

DR. C: It's sad, isn't it Connie?

CONNIE: It's—you know, he can do anything he wants, and you're not supposed to say anything, or we don't most of the time say anything or do anything, or if you do one thing that he thinks is out of line, you always get, "he's been drinking. . . ." Well he's been drinking day and night for weeks now, and yesterday he decided not to drink, and he took Librium, which I was not aware of. Now, I am not a doctor, and I don't know the difference when I look at somebody who is smashed, whether they're smashed on booze or on Librium, and he was like really out of it, he started a conversation and I said, "If you don't mind I'd rather not discuss it when you're drunk."

DR. C: So what are we going to do? The meeting is not to find out whether Harry is drinking; we know that. What are we going to do? Shall we say good-bye?

CONNIE: I'll tell you something. I don't think I should come here anymore, because it's not accomplishing anything. I'll tell you something. I have a guilt thing right now, I really do, and I'm not home very much. I'm working 40 hours—or at least trying to anyway—for reasons, otherwise I'll be dropped off what they call "full-time" employees. And I'm spending a lot of time driving him back and forth here, and as a result of that I'm not home. I'm not with the children that much. Harry is with the children a lot, and they've been having a pretty rough time, the kids with Harry. I feel that— people have said to me that it's all right for me to put up with it but they're kids.

DR. C: I want to get back to my problem. My problem is I don't know why we're seeing each other.

CONNIE: I don't know either, because nothing is different. I mean, if we're working at it, we're working at it, but if we're still drinking we're not working at it.

DR. C: I guess the whole family is still drinking.

CONNIE: Not the whole family is still drinking, but if somebody in that house is drunk and disruptive the rest of the family—I don't give a shit what AA says—cannot proceed normally to do what they're doing when somebody is falling, not falling down, but arguing all the time or doing something that you think they're going to hurt themselves, using electric drills all the time when they're drunk.

DR. C: So what should we do, say "good-bye"?

CONNIE: I'll be frank with you, I don't feel like coming here.

HARRY: You don't feel like what.

CONNIE: Coming back here anymore. I really don't.

DR. C: Well Kathy doesn't want to come, how about you Robert?

CONNIE: Well I had a thing with Robert today to get him here.

DR. C: Yes, I can tell he's not very friendly. And Kathy isn't very friendly to me. So I guess this is sort of like the funeral that Greg was talking about. We're sort of saying good-bye, I guess Harry is going to die soon, and then you won't have to worry.

CONNIE: That's Harry's choice.

HARRY: My choice for what?

CONNIE: For whether you want to live or die.

DR. C: Well kings can make that decision to live or die. How will it be for you, Kathy, when your father dies? Will it make things better for you? How about you, Robert?

ROBERT: I don't care. He's not going to stop. He knows it, so what is he lying to us for?

HARRY: I still want to stop.

ROBERT: Yeah, you want to but you're not going to try. I want to get good grades in school but I fool around.

HARRY: You fool around, I don't understand . . .

ROBERT: I want to get good grades in school, but I have to work at it to get them. If you want to stop drinking you have to try and stop.

HARRY: I have to work at it.

ROBERT: Yeah, which you've said you've been doing for 2–3 years now.

DR. C: You know Robert, I think what you are probably saying is that you think it's hopeless.

ROBERT: Yeah.

DR. C: That Dad's going to continue to drink 'til he dies. So if he were laid out in this room, what would you be saying to his dead body?

ROBERT: It's his fault, it's nobody else's fault. [Becomes tearful.]

HARRY: [Says something inaudible.]

DR. C: You're the only man who can go to his own funeral. You really are king, Harry. You know you got everybody jumping around here Harry. You got Greg all worried about you, you got your family worried about you. You're king.

HARRY: I don't want to say good-bye.

DR. C: I think we have to say good-bye.

HARRY: I . . .

DR. C: Look at your family.

HARRY: I've been trying to get off Methadone; they won't take me off.

DR. C: Harry, look what's happening, everybody is giving up.

HARRY: They're all giving up on me. They all gave up on me.

DR. C: I think it's like it's really your funeral.

HARRY: They all gave up on me.

DR. C: I can see that.

HARRY: I'm very depressed today.

ROBERT: So he goes out and drinks some more.

HARRY: I'm very depressed. Everybody gave up on me.

ROBERT: You made it like that, we didn't do it.

HARRY: I didn't say you did.

DR. C: How will it feel?

HARRY: I want to undo it. And I don't know how to undo it.

DR. C: Leave them.

HARRY: Huh?

DR. C: Leave them.

HARRY: They won't let me, I can't, they won't let me.

DR. C: Will you let him go?

HARRY: No, no, no.

DR. C: Would you let him go, Connie?

CONNIE: Under certain conditions.

DR. C: What would be those conditions?

CONNIE: That when he went, he went, that he didn't call in 2 days and say somebody rolled him and took his money and he's broke and he's coming back.

HARRY: What's that?

DR. C: Well you don't have to go get him; you can say too bad, good-bye.

CONNIE: Then he just knocks on the door.

HARRY: What was this?

CONNIE: If it's not done legally he can come in.

DR. C: We'll help you to do it.

HARRY: Wait a minute, I can't hear a word.

CONNIE: She said would I stop you from going? I said, "no," but if you went it would have to be under certain conditions.

HARRY: Why?

CONNIE: Because I don't want you to go and say 2 days later you pick up the phone and call me and say, "Somebody rolled me and I have no money and no place to sleep. I'm coming home." I don't want to get into that scene.

HARRY: No, now wait, in other words it would be a bitter thing.

CONNIE: I'm not saying it's bitter, but final.

HARRY: If I went away I would only go away to try and straighten myself out.

CONNIE: Harry, in other words you're going to get better on your own terms right?

DR. C: Harry let them go. I think you need to leave them, because if not I think there's going to be a funeral of four people. Do you know what mass suicide is?

HARRY: She takes my money. I don't have anything to go with.

DR. C: We'll help you to go.

HARRY: Huh?

DR. C: We'll help you to go. You've got to get out.

Connie and children become very tense and question whether or not they can manage alone. Robert expresses his anxiety by becoming agitated.

ROBERT: Oh sure, and what are we supposed to do?

DR. C: You can manage, the three of you can manage fine.

ROBERT: Oh sure, yeah.

DR. C: That's the bind he's in; on one hand you tell him to go away and you pull him back with the other.

HARRY: I can't come back.

CONNIE: You can come back if you're Harry Haverman but not if you are Harry Haverman drug addict or alcoholic.

HARRY: I wouldn't want to come back under those conditions.

DR. C: How soon can you be ready to go? What time tomorrow can you be here?

HARRY: I can't come. I have nothing . . .

DR. C: Will the three of you help him to go? Because up to now you really haven't helped him to go.

ROBERT: What do you want me to do, give him a lot of pennies?

DR. C: No.

ROBERT: What am I supposed to do?

DR. C: Say good-bye to him. How would you say good-bye to him?

ROBERT: Good riddance!

HARRY: [Inaudible comment.]

DR. C: Harry, you have to leave, it's not healthy for you to stay here.

HARRY: I feel everybody dislikes me.

DR. C: That's right, they dislike you, and you need to go. And I think you dislike them.

HARRY: Well, I don't know where to go.

DR. C: We'll help you.

HARRY: I'm not going to no Y. I'm still a sick guy, I still got a lot of medical things that . . .

DR. C: We'll see that you get medical care.

HARRY: You'll see that I get medical care?

DR. C: Absolutely, we will help you, we won't desert you, but you can't continue to live this way.

HARRY: No, no, no. I don't want to leave and turn around and find out I'm left in a lurch.

DR. C: We'll find a place—it might even be out of the state, but we'll find a place. Maybe in another state. You'll be protected and safe, because there's no safety here in this family Harry, and there's no safety for them. And they're all dying, the whole family is dying. And if this is our final session as a family . . .

HARRY: I don't want the family to die.

DR. C: Well they're dying; look at them, look at them, through your drunken eyes, look at them; they're dying. So if you mean what you say, then leave them, because if you love them you'll leave them. If you really mean what you're saying, we won't desert you; we'll help you find a place for yourself. But all these people are going to die, their funeral is going to be right along with yours.

HARRY: No it isn't.

DR. C: Yes it is. I have a fantasy of you sitting there when they're all dead. Look at them. I never saw three such depressed people in my life.

HARRY: I want to do something about it.

DR. C: All right, then leave them. Let them go. Will you help him to pack?

CONNIE: He's got most of his clothes out.

DR. C: What's left?

HARRY: I got nothing. I can't do it tomorrow.

DR. C: When can you do it? What day this week would you choose?

HARRY: I want to be detoxed.

DR. C: We'll do it as a package.

GREG: Once you leave we'll get the detox papers signed, and they'll be no problem.

HARRY: I don't understand what you mean.

GREG: Dr. Coleman said we'll make it a package.

HARRY: What's that mean?

DR. C: A package?

HARRY: Yeah.

DR. C: A package is like your airfare, meals, continental breakfast, rental car. That's the whole package.

HARRY: Where am I going?

DR. C: I don't know, we'll find a place. I can think of a couple of places. I know one place in—I think it's in—Minnesota that's really good.

HARRY: Minnesota?

GREG: That's a nice state.

HARRY: What's the package got to do with that?

DR. C: The package is you're going to save three people. You're going to be a hero, you're not even going to be a king now, you're going to be a hero and save these three people.

HARRY: What about the Methadone?

DR. C: We'll take care of it, it will be part of the package. Have we let you down?

HARRY: I've been trying to get off of Methadone. What kind of papers do I need?

GREG: You got it backwards Harry.

HARRY: You get me off it and I'm gone.

DR. C: Backwards, you heard what the man said, the other way.

HARRY: I don't, you mean I leave, and then you get me off?

DR. C: Yes, that's the package. What day this week will you be ready?

HARRY: About the end of the week.

DR. C: Thursday!

HARRY: I don't know where the hell you're going to send me.

DR. C: I don't know. You can help find a place, you can be a consultant, but you can't continue to live with people who are dying. You've got to save their lives, you're not going to save yours, you're going to save theirs. Harry, at least you can look down from heaven and say there's Robert my son, he's now 25 and is in business and doing well; there's Connie, she's a lot older now but she's making it and she found herself a nice boyfriend who's taking care of her; and there's Kathy, she's 26, she's got a nice husband, and she's a very beautiful woman. Now, won't you feel good because you would have saved them. If you don't do that, do you know what the other picture is? You're going to have a son on drugs, a wife who's sitting in a rocking chair crying, and a daughter who's a prostitute. If you love them and want the other picture you better get the hell out.

HARRY: I'll get out. I don't want to live like this forever either.

DR. C: Okay then. Can you let him go Connie?

CONNIE: I guess.

HARRY: You know it's a family—do they have anything to say?

DR. C: It's a dead family Harry.

HARRY: Do they have anything to say?

GREG: Why don't you look and see what they're telling you, Harry? You don't have to be able to hear to see what they're saying, there's nothing wrong with your eyesight.

HARRY: No, there's nothing wrong with my eyesight.

GREG: Then why don't you look? Connie isn't telling you anything. Look at Kathy she's not telling you anything. Look at Robert he's not telling you anything.

HARRY: [Inaudible comment.]

GREG: Well maybe you ought to look again. Maybe you ought to look at yourself in the mirror too, and see if you get that message.

HARRY: That message I have.

GREG: What does it say?

HARRY: It tells me to straighten the hell up, and I want to do it and I need help. I've tried and I've failed and I'm not afraid to say I failed. I failed a lot of times. But other people have made it, and if other people can do it I can do it.

DR. C: This is your chance.
HARRY: I'll tell the truth, I don't want to go.

The family continues to hesitate and raise obstacles, questioning everything.

KATHY: Will we have to visit him, like when you get a divorce?
HARRY: But Kathy likes me.
DR. C: But Kathy has to live, that's more important.
HARRY: When you say you'll help them out, what do you mean?
DR. C: Well, if they're sad and they need to cry they can come in and cry. We have lots of tape, and if they want to see you on tape we'll play the tape. They can see you when you were drunk and when you were sober; they can visit with you by TV. We'll keep your spirit alive with the family.
HARRY: Keep my spirit alive don't mean a damn thing, what's going to happen to them?
DR. C: They're going to live, they're going to survive.
HARRY: No, no, you said you're going to help them.
DR. C: Yes, we'll help them.
HARRY: What do you mean, show them movies?
DR. C: Maybe, sure.
HARRY: What the hell is that going to do for them?
DR. C: I don't know, as long as they're alive . . .
HARRY: What about my medical benefits, how about my medical benefits?
DR. C: Greg, do you notice how Harry's cutting me out?
GREG: Why don't you listen to the lady, I just came in at the last minute.
HARRY: Yeah, I'm cutting you out because I'm looking for a way to get out.
DR. C: I don't think you're going to get out, because it's one life or three deaths. [To Greg.] Is this the funeral you were thinking about?
GREG: Yes, this is it.

Within a week Harry packed a suitcase and admitted himself to a 90-day inpatient alcoholism program. Family therapy sessions were on an "as needed" basis, but Connie called us regularly to let us know how things were progressing. She talked about her feelings of strength, not being afraid of staying alone at night, and wanting to develop a new feeling of family with just the children, who she reported were doing well. Harry was also making excellent progress and was beginning to make plans for where he would live when he was discharged. There was no evidence that either he or Connie and the kids intended to live together.

Approximately 70 days into his program, Harry's benefits ran out. The hospital called Connie and told her to take him home immediately. She quickly informed the caseworker that he could not be returned to her and that other arrangements would have to be made. Without further notice at 2 A.M. that morning Harry was delivered to Connie's doorstep. Fortunately, they were all determined to do it differently, and this time they did. Harry was admitted to a day-treatment program and came home only to sleep. He attended AA meetings regularly and was doing very well.

In late January he called to let me know how things were going. He said, "I finally am beginning to believe what you knew all along; I really am a valuable human being who deserves to enjoy life sober. You always knew that about me—that I could do it. You believed in me. I don't think anyone else ever did. But now I believe in me too. Thanks for all your help. You've really done a lot, both you and Greg."

That was my last conversation with Harry. He died suddenly in March, 2 years after we had originally met. At the funeral Kathy wore a silk dress, and her hair was pulled to the side with a bright flower. She smiled when she saw me, and I tried not to interpret it as an expression of dominant glee.

Harry's death, though predictable, seemed somehow untimely. He had been doing so well, so consistently. I was not surprised, just disappointed when I learned what precipitated Harry's final drinking episode.

Kathy had become seriously involved with a boy several years her senior. Both Connie and Harry were unhappy about the relationship and controlled the amount of time Kathy spent with him at nights and on weekends. They could not, of course, help what happened during school hours. Evidently Kathy and her boyfriend were becoming more sexually involved, and Kathy left some notes from him in her jacket. When Connie did the laundry, she discovered them. The messages were all sexual in nature. When Harry read them, he became distraught. Then Connie, worried about his depression, got embroiled in a physical battle with Kathy. Harry returned to his most familiar method of coping—the bottle. But this time he not only lost control of his newly gained abstinence, he lost control of his life.

I saw Connie alone a few weeks after Harry's death. She reported that ". . . things are good at home." Yet, she was still worried. Kathy was staying home from school too frequently for minor physical aches and pains. She worried also about Robert's tendency to be destructive with household property. She was trying to encourage him to participate in sports but felt that the chances for success were minimal. Robert was quiet, yet pretty determined.

Connie talked a little about missing Harry, stating that she had moments when she cried. She and Robert were able to talk about him. She recalled Robert saying that ". . . all my friends told me Daddy was a great guy." Connie explained that the kids liked him because he drove them anywhere they wanted to go. Kathy, she felt she would never understand. "I guess she has a shell around her or something." When I asked Connie if she thought that Kathy felt guilty, the following interchange took place:

CONNIE: No, I don't think so, because she said to me when I yelled at her, when he first started to drink, *"Did I put the glass in his hand?"* She said a couple cool things to me. We were downtown and it was Wednesday and there was a pastry shop there. I said, "Kathy I could go for a chocolate eclair." And she said, "I want to go home." Kids are like that—when they do their thing they're done, they want to go, they don't want to do anything you want to do. I said, "Come on Kathy, I really feel good today, like the first day I really feel good! My mother and I used to get chocolate eclairs together and it was fun." And she said, "What do you mean you feel good today? You just got off of 2 weeks' vacation." I said, "You got to be kidding. Your father died, and you call this a vacation?" Well, "It was," she said. That was the first thing and the other thing was—it was Saturday night. Anyway, she wanted to sleep at her girlfriend's and I said, "No way." I said, "First of all I don't want anybody sleeping out until my nerves are under control." She said, "Look Daddy's dead and he's dead and he ain't coming back, and you're trying to keep him alive." She said, "Why don't you just let him die? Dr. Coleman said you got to get used to being by yourself, can't keep having me around here all the time."

DR. C: You're worried about her aren't you?

We continued to talk about additional episodes involving Kathy. Later, Connie talked about the events leading to Harry's death. I then asked:

DR. C: So who do you think is going to pick up Harry's tradition?
CONNIE: What? Do you mean the way he acted around the house? Probably Kathy. Kathy has been vying for that all along, you know, I mean it's nothing new with her.

That was the last I saw of Connie or any of the Havermans. She called me several times to tell me she was managing okay and that the children were being fairly good. She had accepted my suggestion to have Kathy see a therapist at one of the neighborhood mental health clinics. I thought it best for her to stay away from the drug center, and since she had never really connected with either Greg or me, a new therapist, exclusively hers would probably be more successful. She agreed to go and Connie reported that it seemed to be working. Robert refused to have anything to do with therapy.

In March 1983 exactly 5 years after I first met the Havermans, I called to find out how things were. Because I was writing this chapter, I summoned up the courage to question further the results of what was a very disappointing case finale.

Connie was glad to hear from me and very willing to share the details of their lives. Kathy's baby was due momentarily, and Connie seemed delighted about welcoming an illegitimate grandchild into her life. Kathy had been in a great deal of trouble for several years, which led to Connie being charged with child abuse. All this was due to an episode after she found Kathy "dead drunk on the front lawn" and had "smacked her across the face." When questioned by her teacher, Kathy blamed her black eye on her mother. The teacher reported the incident. Connie was put on restrictions and was court ordered to be home with the children at night. Connie's mother, whose second husband had recently died, moved across the country to live with her and help with the children.

Kathy's behavior did not improve after this incident, however, and Connie reported a long series of frustrating experiences. Kathy had alternating bouts of physical illness and drug and alcohol misuse. She had been court adjudicated to an inpatient drug treatment center which was only temporarily helpful. After she began to date the boy who ultimately fathered her child, there was some change in her. She began to work and then returned to school in a work–study program. Connie said that although the relationship ended without any commitment to marriage, Kathy was working "compulsively" and suddenly doing well. She refused to even consider giving the baby up for adoption.

She described Robert as "passive and lazy." She said that although he scored in the "highest percentiles" in all of his tests, he had to repeat a grade because of his lack of motivation. She felt he was unusually angry, and she was especially worried because he had recently been suspended from school for smoking pot. He had come home drunk the night before, and she said her mother predicted that he was going to be a "crazy driver" because he drove a car way above the speed limit.

Connie said that despite all these disappointments she was still doing what she learned to do in family therapy, "taking care of myself." She was taking courses at the local community college and had received an "A" in biology. She thanked me for calling and concluded the conversation by remarking how ironic it was that I called at this particular time and that Kathy's baby was due "just 3 days after Harry died."

> Life must be understood backwards. . . . but . . . it must be lived forwards.—
> Soren Kierkegaard

Analysis of Failure

For some time I viewed the Haverman case as a success. With Connie's permission I continued to use the family videotapes for professional meetings and training. When I asked Connie if I could continue to use the videotapes that she and Harry had previously given me permission to show to professional observers, she readily agreed. She said it would be worth it if even one addicted person could be helped by his or her therapist learning something from her family's experience. She further noted that she knew Harry also would have supported such an educational process.

Although two of the tapes are unusually provocative—the one where Harry decompensates and beats up Kathy and the strategic final session—I nonetheless showed them in the context of successful treatment. Students and colleagues agreed. After all, there were many positive changes. Connie became far more competent. She avoided being hospitalized for the first summer in years. She stopped being afraid of staying alone in the house at night. Her parenting behavior became a bit more consistent, and she seemed to know very definitely what she should do even when she did not do it. Despite Harry's unfortunate death, he too had displayed more adequate behavior. For the first time in almost 35 years of addiction, he attended AA meetings; toward the end he went very regularly. This was nothing short of amazing to me. He certainly felt better about himself; in our final conversation he shared that with me. He developed more independence than he had had in the past. He was able to leave the family and stay in treatment; that too had never happened before. He always aborted the inpatient treatment program except for his first hospitalization. He really seemed on the right track at the end, at least until his final drink.

As a couple, Connie and Harry had also improved. They renewed their relationship, slept together again, and displayed a great deal of healthy interpersonal warmth. One of their videotapes shows a lovely interaction between them that tends to make observers tearful. It seemed that so many changes had occurred that even though Harry died in the end, I never thought we failed.

It was apparent that the children still had many problems, but I felt that some of their difficulty was related to adolescent stress—not everything could be attributed to the family. If the parents truly took charge, these problems could be overcome.

At about the same time that Harry died, I was developing my idea to publish a book about cases that were failures. I never once considered the Havermans for my illustrative case. Then, one day as I was presenting to a class I watched a segment from their very first session. I was stunned! The sibling subsystem had never changed; at the end they were just as they were in the beginning. And if they had not changed, any other shifts were merely first-order changes—not true systemic changes. Even my final strategic move had not produced the desired effect. It was not a case of, "the operation was successful, and the patient died." Rather it was a case of, "the operation was a disaster, and the patient died."

Once I began to look at the Havermans with a different lens, several interrelated factors came into sharp focus, and the failure became a function of them all colliding with each other. There were significant issues related to the referral situation itself, the case assessment, theoretical oversights, and therapist and family factors.

Referral Variables

From the beginning the Haverman case was a set up. Not only by the staff but by me as well. Although I had been working at the drug clinic for more than 18 months, the clinical staff rarely saw me. Every once in a while I would show up at an inservice training meeting as a presenter. I was never too well received, partly because the therapists viewed me as too academic and partly because I aligned myself with the administrative staff. The latter was necessary due to my position but the former was actually my choice. I really wanted to confine my therapy to private practice and keep my research and clinical skills separate. I needed all the time I had for my study, and if I became too involved with the therapists I was afraid I would lose my quiet sanctuary, where I needed to think and write.

When Dr. Stevenson, the medical director, asked me to take the case, he said, "I really have *some* case for you!" He and I were friendly, and I believe that he was sincere in wanting the Havermans to get the most experienced therapist to handle their many problems. He also wanted me to get closer to the treatment staff, and I never had. He too always viewed me as being in an ivory tower, and I did little to dispel this—I wanted my space, and I knew from previous experiences that when I became too personable with staff, my research suffered.

Obviously Dr. Stevenson wanted to pry me loose. At the same time that he was urging, I was beginning to feel the effects of being so isolated. Because I was not fully engaged in my next project, I thought I could eke out the time for one clinical teaching case. I anticipated that it would be concluded within 6 months, before my major research responsibilities would preclude this kind of involvement. The case itself was quite fascinating, which made it relatively easy for me to acquiesce. I had no way of knowing the extent to which that decision would affect the next 2 years.

A final factor associated with the circumstances surrounding the referral issue was the pressure I felt from Dr. Stevenson to be concrete and nonesoteric in the treatment of this family. He knew that if the staff would ever accept any training from me it would have to be on that level. Thus, before I ever met the family the treatment model was cast in stone.

Assessment Variables

The Havermans were assessed using a structural model. The behaviors evidenced in the first few sessions were examined and explained according to the theoretical constructs presented in the beginning of this chapter. The cross-generational alliances were obvious as was the powerful coalition among Connie and the children. It seemed very clear that the coalition had to be dissolved and that Connie had to join Harry and demonstrate their effectiveness as parents. Harry had to stop drinking—that was the most significant and uncompromising change that must prevail above and beyond all others. For the most part this was the essence of our assessment phase and this was the framework within which we worked.

Retrospectively, it seems impossible that the rest of my assessment schema (as previously described in the theoretical discussion) was not used. Worse than that, it was ignored. Of special interest is the fact that I am a very strong advocate of looking at life-cycle issues, and my developmental psychology background always hovers over my work. Even my research was designed within a family life-cycle paradigm. The Havermans were at a definite transitional point in their family life. Both children were reaching adolescence. They would, if circumstances were normal, be leaving home in a few short years. A clear family life-cycle factor was evident, but no hypotheses were generated to account for it. Nor was there any related speculation about the fact that Harry's own drug use had sprung forth during adolescence, making this period potentially more threatening for his children.

In addition to avoiding the life-cycle factors, I also overlooked other significant issues. I never explored the context within which Harry had started to drink again. It had to be more than coincidence that Harry, who maintained sobriety for 10 years, began to drink again at the same time that his brother's business declared bankruptcy. Along with Harry's loss of a job, were his loss of income, status, and so forth. These issues affected all the family members. They are also theoretically significant and will be discussed again in the next section.

Because I was so parochial, I abandoned any attempt to investigate family of origin parameters, which would have helped to develop better hypotheses about the current situation. I never learned about any of Harry's several siblings, and the only thing I remember him saying about his mother was that she said she would put her head in the oven if he did something, but I am not certain what he would have to do to affect her like that! Even though he had an aged father who was still living, Harry's relationship with him was not explored. Of course it would have been important to understand what was occurring in Harry's family of origin when he was Kathy's age. I do not think I ever ignore this with any family; with the Havermans, however, who had so many complicated problems, I not only did therapy in a strict "here and now" mode, but my initial assessment shows similar constraints.

The gravest error of all, however, is the linear way in which I assessed the family. It was clear in the very first session that the children's behavior was intimately connected with setting Harry up to drink. The systemic issues in the Haverman family were continuously being demonstrated; one of the best was Robert's foot surreptitiously slipping out to trip Kathy as she flew screaming from her father's clutches—all the time while Connie became suddenly inert and unable to break the chain of family violence. In this family the cybernetic paradigm hit you in the face; how then could I have missed it?

Theoretical Variables

One of the most significant concepts in understanding systems *vis-à-vis* a structural model is that of power. To overlook a power issue could gravely affect the process and outcome of a case. In structural family therapy Aponte (1976) describes power as "the relative influence of each [family] member on the outcome of an activity." Further, he (Aponte & Van Deusen, 1981) views power as not being absolute but "relative to the operation," that is, a powerful member may be less influential under varying conditions. Aponte also states that "power is generated by the way family members actively and passively combine, enabling the intention of one or more of the members to prevail in determining the outcome of a transaction" (p. 313), that is, the need of one parent for the other to uphold a decision, and so on.

The power of the siblings in the Haverman family was overwhelming. Kathy and Robert were a force that was at once pernicious and totally invasive. Their team work, had it been constructive, could have been responsible for some brilliant endeavor. Unfortunately, they only engineered destructive family movements. The weakness of the parental subsystem provided the gap for the sibling subsystem to enter and take control. Despite the strength of the cross-generational alignments, Kathy and Robert were the truly powerful piece that gave the system the steam that blew the parents' apart. They were invincible. Our original goal of strengthening the parents' executive function was too limited because the system could never allow Harry any individual power. Whenever he grasped it with sobriety, the children intervened and coerced Connie, he then began to drink again, the parental stronghold weakened, and the hierarchy with the children in power prevailed. This was the major circular feedback loop within which the system operated.

Theoretically, we were working on the right track by trying to get the parents in the executive position, but we overlooked how effective Kathy's and Robert's unbalancing techniques were; they were more strategic than we, more dedicated, and more clever. Every time their Dad was sober, they seduced him into taking another sip, and their mother held the glass. Almost all the literature on power focuses on adult structures and substructures, the basic tenet of which is similar—strengthen from the top. I have no argument with that; it is obviously sound and logical. However, despite Connie's efforts to handle situations more effectively—and she often did—Kathy and Robert were more resilient and could draw her back. Their system needed unbalancing and it never happened. They were unfortunately able to maintain their stronghold until the end.

An experience related to the issue of sibling subsystems bears mentioning. In the early 1970s I noted that younger siblings in drug addict families were grossly overlooked. Even in family therapy sessions, much of the focus was on the abusing older sibling rather than on the "good" younger one(s). I began holding group therapy sessions for the younger siblings and found that they were not nearly as "good" as they appeared in their family constellations. They actually had a great deal of covert influence on what happened in the family. After 2 years of experience with these youngsters, I decided to share some of my findings. Publication in a leading family therapy journal was blocked, however; one of the major criticisms was that I was most remiss in working with the least powerful, weakest, and most ineffectual subsystem in the family. Ultimately, I did publish these sibling group experiences (Coleman, 1978, 1979), but I never forgot that reviewer's message. Despite the fact that my follow-up data were quite encouraging and the support from parents of participating youngsters was outstanding, I carried the view of the siblings "weak" position in my work from the time that the first manuscript was rejected. It was as if the voice of that unknown reviewer's authoritative knowledge was to become a conscience from then on. I worked hard to always play it "from the top," and in this case the effect was unfortunate. Kathy and Robert needed more attention, and their capacity to ripple through the rest of the system should have been dealt a stick of dynamite long before it acquired so much control.

Another theoretical oversight relates to my own theory of incomplete mourning. The host of loss issues that were imbedded in this family were enormous. My ahistorical approach precludes my citing previous intergenerational losses, but those that are known include Harry's loss of job and its concomitant loss of status with self and family, the loss of income and interest, and perhaps even the loss of being able to depend on his brother. For Connie, we did help her mourn her father because that was a current issue at the beginning of therapy. We did not, however, look at any of her previous losses nor did we look at the effect of her mother's geographical move, which separated them immensely, or her step-father's imminent death from cancer. Perhaps even more astonishing is how we totally ignored the children's adoptive issues. Although they were both adopted within the first few days of birth, this was a critical separation and loss for them. Kathy continually threatened to run away to the social worker who gave her to Connie and Harry. There had to be substantive material here and it was left unexplored. In my efforts to be a structural purist, it seems I did not even attend to my own theoretical stance.

The final theoretical issue derives from the original research by Steinglass, Davis, and Berenson (1975), whose findings suggest that alcoholism is adaptive and functional for the system. Thus, in order to remove drinking behavior, one must first determine its behavioral rewards to the system. In the families studied by these investigators, there was a marked increase in family communication during states of inebriation while sobriety invoked isolation. This characteristic was also evident in the Haverman household. Whenever Harry drank everyone got involved. The metaphor of him "singing and dancing" is a good one (see transcript from initial family session). When we helped Harry to give up his booze we forgot to find something else to make him sing and dance.

Therapist Variables

There were several therapist-related factors that contributed to the failure. The primary one was the cotherapist issue. Greg and I were the wrong pair for the family. There was just too much symmetry between us and Harry and Connie. No matter what I did, Greg came off looking inadequate; Harry needed a much stronger male figure. This became paramount after the session I call "The Chaos Session" (the one where Harry beat up Kathy). Despite the fact that our imbalance as a cotherapy team was made crystal clear in that session, our recognition of it still did not alter our behavior. Greg remained passive or repeated what I said; I designed all the interventions and led us all into battle. We were as stuck in our system as the family was in theirs, and there was no evidence that this would ever change.

On an individual level, the case continued for many more months than I ever anticipated, and it began to interfere with my research time. More and more I wanted Greg to take over but I never could help him to feel that it would work without me. Harry was incredibly attached to me, and on a nonverbal level, Connie showed how much she wanted my support. She began to quote me and even began to dress more like me. One day she came to a session in a full peasant skirt and blouse and said, "I know that I'm not built right for this outfit but I love the way you look in some of these things, and I decided to get really daring." I believe that the family liked Greg a lot but after he deserted Harry during that critical session, Harry never seemed to regain confidence in him. Greg's alliance with Harry was shakey, and he could not quite understand how I could almost scream and carry on like a banshee with Harry without him ever losing the strong sense of caring and concern that I had for him. Somehow Greg's warmth always seemed "canned." This alliance factor kept me in there, and although the intensity of my care for the family did not change, I felt that it distracted me from what I needed to do.

A final issue was my attempt to explore personal data in Greg's supervisory sessions. He never said that he would prefer leaving some of these things alone, but his passive–aggressive response to my interpretative comments suggested it. I was certain that the Havermans evoked powerful responses in him, but I could never get anywhere and I probably should have abandoned my efforts. It never helped our relationship, which remained tenuous at best. As I think about it now, I realize how significant this factor is, for all my previous cotherapy experiences resulted in strong and inspiring relationships.

Family Variables

The Havermans brought some very large obstacles to therapy that had to intrinsically contribute to the failure. A history of more than 3 decades of drug and alcohol abuse does not portend remarkable success. Harry's laundry list of medical dysfunctions were not likely to significantly improve. They were a multiproblem family and probably needed 1 year of inpatient treatment together or a permanent live-in therapist. They had intractable kinds of problems, and it is questionable how much one could expect in terms of second-order change. Although the failure obviously was wrought largely by the previously discussed factors, a certain piece of the outcome must be attributed to the difficulties inherent in a family like this.

Hypothetical Reconstruction toward Success

There are many ways to speculate about the meaning of success and failure in working with families like the Havermans. One can explore them both esoterically, philosophically, pedantically, or logically, yet in my mind there is really only one basic criterion for success in working with substance abuse problems—the substance abuse must be eliminated and failure "doth prevail" when it is not. All the other intrafamilial changes are not without meaning, but if drugs or alcohol are still being used, the therapy has not been successful. Understandably some will refute this uncompromising position; but it cannot be argued that if Harry Haverman had been able to remain sober he might have been capable of stopping Kathy's outrageous behavior. He was effective in joining Connie in disciplining the chilren when—and only when—he was sober. Also, Kathy and Robert had little room to chide a father who was staying straight. Because there was affection and caring within the marital system, the lack of alcohol could only have enhanced and strengthened the entire system. Thus, if I had to do it again, all interventions would have been constructed with the object of keeping Harry drug free.

When I question how to accomplish this, the factors discussed in the previous section became salient. First, I would consider my own method of approaching a case as more important than the demands or expectations of those who might be viewing it as students. My assessment would include all the historical and life-cycle information necessary for the formulation of sound hypotheses about the symptom. This would certainly help me to understand more fully why the family needed an alcoholic member. Information about Connie's family of origin and the effect of being a participant in an alcoholic family during her adolescence would be sought. Also, every effort would be taken to provide the children with information about their own natural parents. After they were given these data, I might hold a "birthing" and "christening" to loosen the hold of the biological ghosts and to strengthen Connie's and Harry's parental bonds. In every way the sibling subsystem would be integrated into the treatment process. I would not take it for granted that if you change the parents, you help the children. The children are part of the change process, and too frequently their pervasive systemic role is misunderstood.

Most of all, if I could not reconstruct any of the previous episodes I would have included the children in the strategic move that pushed Harry toward his final and nearly successful treatment. The strategy lacked one major object—it did not include a vehicle for detouring the children's route to the bar. It was alright to send Harry away from the family, but this left Connie too vulnerable to the clever antics of Kathy and Robert. This was the wrong time to terminate treatment—the work was incomplete and needed more intervention than the telephone could provide. The seesaw had hit ground and it should not have been allowed to ascend again. By removing ourselves at that time, we committed the fatal flaw and placed the power right back in the creative paws of those nearly feral children.

Final Reflection

The follow-up suggests that Harry's legacy is still intact. Connie seems okay, and Kathy may be temporarily sober and responsible; they can allow that, because Robert is quickly demonstrating his ability to keep the ritual alive. If Robert should be remiss, now there is a new generation to inherit the sins of the fathers.

> Mock on, mock on, Voltaire! Rousseau!
> Mock on, mock on: 'tis all in vain!
> You throw the sand against the wind,
> And the wind blows it back again.
> —William Blake (*Mock On*)

REFERENCES

Andolfi, M. Prescribing the families' own dysfunctional rules as a therapeutic strategy. *Journal of Marital and Family Therapy*, 1980, *6*, 29–36.

Aponte, H. J. Underorganization in the poor family. In P. J. Guerin (Ed.), *Family therapy: Theory and practice*. New York: Gardner, 1976.

Aponte, H. J., & Van Deusen, J. M. Structural family therapy. In A. S. Gurman & D. P. Kniskern (Eds.), *Handbook of family therapy*. New York: Brunner/Mazel, 1981.

Coleman, S. B. *Death—The facilitator of family integration.* Paper presented at the meeting of the American Psychological Association, Chicago, September 1975.

Coleman, S. B. Sib group therapy: A prevention program for siblings from drug addict programs. *International Journal of the Addictions*, 1978, *13*, 115–127.

Coleman, S. B. Siblings in session. In E. Kaufman & P. Kaufman (Eds.), *Family therapy of drug and alcohol abuse.* New York: Gardner, 1979.

Coleman, S. B. Incomplete mourning and addict family transactions: A theory for understanding heroin abuse. In D. Lettieri (Ed.), *Theories of drug abuse.* National Institute of Drug Abuse, Research Monograph 30, Department of Health and Human Services Publication No. ADM-80-402. Washington, D.C.: Superintendent of Documents, U.S. Government Printing Office, 1980a.

Coleman, S. B. Incomplete mourning in the family trajectory: A circular journey to drug abuse. In B. Ellis (Ed.), *Drug abuse from the family perspective.* National Institute of Drug Abuse, Office of Program Development and Analysis, Department of Health and Human Services Publication No. ADM-18-31. Washington, D.C.: Superintendent of Documents, 1980b.

Coleman, S. B. Incomplete mourning in substance-abusing families: Theory, research and practice. In L. R. Wolberg & M. L. Aronson (Eds.), *Group and family therapy.* Brunner/Mazel, 1981.

Coleman, S. B., Kaplan, J. D., & Downing, R. W. *Heroin   A family coping strategy for death and loss.* Final report prepared for the National Institute on Drug Abuse, Grant No. DA-02332-01, 1981. (Document available through National Institute on Drug Abuse Library, Rockville, Md.)

Coleman, S. B., Kaplan, J. D., & Downing, R. W. *Patterns of loss across the life cycle of addicts, psychiatrics and normals.* Manuscript submitted for publication, 1985.

Coleman, S. B., & Stanton, M. D. The role of death in the addict family. *Journal of Marriage and Family Counseling*, 1978, *4*, 79–91.

Frankl, V. E. *Man's search for meaning.* New York: Beacon Press, 1963.

Haley, J. *Uncommon therapy.* New York: Norton, 1973.

Haley, J. *Problem solving therapy.* San Francisco: Jossey-Bass, 1976.

Klagsbrun, M., & Davis, D. I. Substance abuse and family interaction. *Family Process*, 1977, *16*, 149–173.

Madanes, C. Protection, paradox and pretending. *Family Process*, 1980, *19*, 73–85.

Minuchin, S. *Families and family therapy.* Cambridge, Mass.: Harvard University Press, 1974.

Minuchin, S., Montalvo, B., Guerney, B., Rosman, B., & Schumer, F. *Families of the slums.* New York: Basic Books, 1967.

Minuchin, S., Rosman, R., & Baker, L. *Psychosomatic families: Anorexia nervosa in context.* Cambridge, Mass.: Harvard University Press, 1978.

Rohrbaugh, M., Tennen, H., Press, S., White, L., & Raskin, P. *Paradoxical strategies in psychotherapy.* Symposium presented at the meeting of the American Psychological Association, San Francisco, 1977.

Selvini-Palazzoli, M., Boscolo, L., Cecchin, C., & Prata, G. Hypothesizing–circularity–neutrality: Three guidelines for the conductor of the session. *Family Process*, 1980, *19*, 3–12.

Stanton, M. D. An integrated structural/strategic approach to family therapy. *Journal of Marital and Family Therapy*, 1981a., *6*, 427–439.

Stanton, M. D. Strategic approaches to family therapy. In A. S. Gurman & D. P. Kniskern (Eds.), *Handbook of family therapy.* New York: Brunner/Mazel, 1981b.

Stanton, M. D., & Coleman, S. B. The participatory aspects of self-destructive behavior: The addict family as a model. In N. Farberow (Ed.), *The many faces of suicide.* New York: McGraw-Hill, 1980.

Stanton, M. D., Todd, T. C., Heard, D. B., Kirschner, S., Kleiman, J. I., Mowatt, D. T., Riley, P., Scott, S. M., & Van Deusen, J. M. Heroin addiction as a family phenomenon: A new conceptual model. *American Journal of Drug and Alcohol Abuse*, 1978, *5*, 125–150.

Steinglass, P. Family therapy in alcoholism. In B. Kissin & H. Begleiter (Eds.), *The biology of alcoholism* (Vol. 5). New York: Plenum, 1976.

Steinglass, P., Davis, D. I., & Berenson, D., *In-hospital treatment of alcoholic couples.* Paper presented at the American Psychiatric Association Annual Meeting, May 1975.

Watzlawick, P., Weakland, J., & Fisch, R. *Change: principles of problem formation and problem resolution.* New York: Norton, 1974.

Weeks, G. R., & L'Abate, L. A. A compilation of paradoxical methods. *American Journal of Family Therapy*, 1979, *7*, 61–76.

3

On Window-Shopping or Being a Noncustomer

LYNN SEGAL AND PAUL WATZLAWICK

Introduction

Perhaps the least expected and, therefore, most puzzling discovery that therapists are likely to make early in their careers is their clients' ambivalent attitude towards change. On the one hand clients may clamor for help in changing some painful and perhaps even life-threatening problem, on the other—almost as if the right hand did not know what the left hand was doing—they either resist change altogether or, if and when it takes place, complain that the cure is worse than the disease.

Well known as this seeming perversity of the human mind has been since the days of individual therapy, it is particularly noticeable in couple and family therapy. Families that come into treatment almost invariably signal in one way or another, "Take us back to the point in time before the problem arose, when we were all happy." With this impossible goal the stage is set for disappointment and failure.

Theoretical Frame of Reference

From the study of interaction, we know that natural systems have "individualities" of their own whose characteristics are more than and different from those of the individual organisms composing the system. But very much like any subsystem habitually referred to as an individual, systems fight for their survival *qua* system; that is to say, they actively resist any change of their structure. Hence the paradoxical demand, "Change us without changing us," even when this stubborn maintenance of the structure can only be achieved at the price of acute suffering or dysfunction of one or more subsystems.

In other words clinical experience suggests that systems are willing to go only through those changes from one internal state to another that do not require a change of their structure or of their behavioral and experiential

Lynn Segal and Paul Watzlawick. Brief Therapy Center, Mental Research Institute, Palo Alto, California.

repertory. Elsewhere we have referred to them as changes of the first order. However, when these first-order changes do not contain within their *domain*—as the mathematicians would put it—the necessary resolution of the problem, the system then runs over and over again through its entire repertory without ever arriving at a solution. It is then caught in a "Game without End" (Watzlawick, Beavin, & Jackson, 1967), in which more of the same unsuccessful "solution" leads to more of the same problem.

This is the situation which is most likely present in the overwhelming majority of the families that come for help, while it is very improbable that families capable of taking care of the problem by the simple everyday expedient of a first-order change should even consider therapy.

The usual situation underlying a request for help is therefore a "Game without End" for whose change only a restructuring of the system itself—and not merely one out of a number of available choices—can lead to improvement. This change is of a higher level, that is, of the second order. It is this change that the system may strenuously resist.

The following is the description of a typical case in which the three family members composing the nuclear system were not "customers" because they were not willing to let a second-order change take place. The identified patient completely refused treatment, while his parents professsedly wanted change, but only on their own problem-perpetuating terms. They were—to use professional slang—only window-shoppers.

We have chosen this case as an illustration of therapeutic failure, because it would be so easy to explain away this failure by using the time-honored argument that the severity of the pathology and the resistance of the family made them unfit for treatment. However, as Don D. Jackson used to say, "There are no insolvable cases, there are only inept therapists."

Background

The D family consisted of Mr. D, a 74-year-old retired engineer, his wife, Mary, a 65-year-old housewife, and their only child John, age 19, the identified patient. The D's were seen for seven 1-hour interviews, which took place during a 3-month period in the Spring of 1980. All sessions were held conjointly, except for the 6th hour of treatment when Mr. D was seen alone.

Mr. D, a tall, slim, dignified-looking man, reminded one of a gentleman farmer from Maine. He spoke in a slow, deliberate, low-keyed manner, participating minimally and only when addressed directly. He appeared undistressed and emotionally removed from the interviews, openly deferring to his wife on all matters. This impression was validated by his own self-description, "I'm a quiet, passive individual. Not the pushy type. I'm not aggressive; I take things as they come."

Mrs. D, a short, pudgy woman, was much less meticulous in her dress and appearance and presented quite the opposite picture. She was anxious, easily excitable, defensive, and generally took an oppositional stance in treatment. Although she was obviously quite bright, exhibiting a vocabulary befitting her 5 years of college education, Mrs. D had a remarkable ability to become confused and uncomprehending, particularly when asked to clarify her statements or to take some action *vis-à-vis* her son.

John, who was never seen because he refused treatment, was described by his parents as a very bright young man who coasted through high school with a minimum of effort. Mrs. D volunteered the information that John had had a difficult time growing up because she and her husband were such inadequate parents. She explained that early in John's life she and her husband had a major disagreement about parenting, because she felt her husband was too strict with John. Subsequently, much to her chagrin, Mr. D renounced all of his parenting responsibilities by giving her full charge on such matters. She stated that she had not been ready to take on total responsibility for raising a child; she said she knew nothing about parenting and, in addition, was struggling with emotional problems of her own, which she attributed to a stormy menopause.

When John was 8 years old, Mrs. D became concerned that he was increasingly withdrawn and placed him in individual psychotherapy with Dr. Jones, who saw the boy for 2 years. Although John improved, treatment was terminated prematurely because Dr. Jones was leaving the area, necessitating a referral to another therapist. Mrs. D stated that John "never could relate to his new therapist," so she stopped treatment and did not pursue the matter further.

For the next 8 years, John was able to function marginally, getting by in school and showing no major psychiatric symptoms. Most people would have described him as a shy, withdrawn individual. Then, at age 18, he unexpectedly dropped out of junior college and essentially became housebound. He refused to speak with his parents, took his meals alone, refused to bathe or to clean his room, and spent most of his time sleeping, watching television, or playing billiards on the family pool table. He rarely left the home and his only social contacts were a few friends he had known since grade school who came to the home once or twice a month and played pool or Monopoly® with John.

Mrs. D reported that after John continued to act this way for 3 months she became so depressed that she sought treatment with Dr. A. Describing her emotional state at the time, she stated, "I cried a lot, scratched myself, and I didn't do any housework." Dr. A worked with the D's for a period of 9 months, seeing Mrs. D both alone and conjointly with her husband. During this period of treatment, Mrs. D's emotional state improved slightly but John's behavior remained the same. Dr. A made a number of attempts to involve John in treatment, but John turned down all invitations. About a month prior to the termination of Mrs. D's treatment, responding to her insistence that something had to be done for John, Dr. A suggested two possible referrals: Soteria House, a nontraditional, residential treatment setting for young adults diagnosed as schizophrenic, and the Brief Therapy Center at the Mental Research Institute (MRI).

Approximately a month after their last session with Dr. A, Mrs. D called the Brief Therapy Center for an interview. When she informed us that treatment was for her son John, who was unwilling to come to the sessions, John Weakland, our Associate Director, suggested that we could begin by seeing her and her husband.

At the time of the first interview, the therapists knew only that a Mr. and Mrs. D were coming to treatment because their son was having problems. He knew that they had seen Dr. A about this problem, and that Dr. A felt that further treatment was needed, therefore referring them to the Brief Therapy Center. During their first interview, the D's described their problem as being John's reclusive asocial behavior, which began when he dropped out of junior college.

Diagnosis and Treatment Plan

The brief therapy approach at MRI utilizes a different set of premises regarding the nature of human problems. Unlike many therapies that operate from a model based on psychopathology or deficiency, the brief therapist works on the premise that the interaction between a problem and its attempted solution forms a self-perpetuating, interactional loop; problems are viewed as being maintained by their attempted solution. Thus, the brief therapist is concerned with how problems arise, how they are maintained, and what, at the very least, is needed to resolve them.

Seen from this perspective, patients are simply stuck in a closed interactional loop rather than being sick or lacking in some way. Patients frequently make logical errors in problem solving. Like the proverbial man caught in quicksand, the more he struggles, the more he sinks; the more he sinks, the more he struggles.

Accordingly, there are a number of basic diagnostic questions that guide the brief therapist during the initial interviews. These questions are: (1) what is the problem or presenting complaint; (2) how have the patient and significant others been dealing with the problem—what is their attempted solution; (3) what is their frame of reference regarding the nature of the problem and its treatment—that is, what are their positions on these issues; and (4) what are their goals of treatment?

The relationship between diagnoses, data collection, and the planning of therapeutic strategies boils down to the following question: Given the presenting complaint and the way in which the patient and family have been handling it, what would be the smallest, most easily achievable change in the way they deal with the problem, which would interdict the attempted solution and result in positive change? Since we want to work rapidly, we do not try to change the attempted solution by first teaching the patients to understand their problem from our theoretical point of view. Rather, we attempt to work in and around their own frame of reference or existential reality, utilizing their own belief system as a rationale for our suggestions and directives.

Diagnostic Data

For the most part, the D's agreed that the presenting complaint was John's behavior. Their attempted solution might best be described as a policy of *accommodation and encouragement*. Mr. and Mrs. D put no pressure on John to find employment, return to school, pay room and board, bathe, do chores, or eat dinner with them. Mrs. D always prepared dinner for three, so John could have a hot meal. From time to time the parents would suggest projects such as building a home computer or following the stock market, in the hopes of reawakening John's interest in normal life. They also encouraged others to do this. For example, they invited other families who had children of John's age to come to their home in the hope that John might be more willing to relate to people of his own age.

Mr. and Mrs. D held significantly different positions regarding the nature of John's problem. Mrs. D believed that John was suffering from a serious mental illness. For instance, she stated that John would not communicate with her or her husband "because it was too painful for him." He did not leave the house or get on with his life "because he is too fearful of the world to leave the house." Throughout the interviews, her language consistently revealed this view of John's problem.

Mr. D held a very different position. He claimed, "John escapes from problems. Life is very satisfactory for him. He knows we have an independent income, so he feels very little called upon to put himself out. He doesn't want to become independent and take care of himself." Mr. D explained that John dealt with his problems by avoiding them, which he could do quite nicely because he could take advantage of his mother's irrational concern and fear for his well-being. He implied that since his wife was "neurotic" and became easily distraught, and he was "a passive individual," he was helpless to do anything about the situation other than go along with his wife.

The D's also held radically different positions regarding treatment. By the end of the first interview, it was clear that Mr. D was only attending treatment interviews to placate his wife. He implied that John would simply grow out of his problem, and this made treatment unnecessary. On the surface, Mrs. D appeared to be motivated for treatment but pessimistic about the outcome. Upon closer examination, however, it was clear that she avoided making any direct statement about her own desire or need for treatment. For example, when questioned directly about what she expected to accomplish in coming to the Brief Therapy Center—especially since she was asking for treatment of an admittedly serious and long-standing problem, in a setting limited to 10 sessions—she would only say that Dr. A had referred her. She added that he would not have done so if he had not believed that brief treatment would be of some help. At no time did she state that she wanted our help in dealing with John's problems.

Strategy

Our general strategy was to work with the parents, rather than making it a condition of treatment that also John must attend the interviews. We accepted their view that John was the patient rather than attempting to convince them that they had a family problem. In keeping with this strategy, we framed our questions and statements in a manner that implied that the D's were our helpers and cotherapists who, since they were at home with John, would be in a useful position of helping us help him. Another way of describing this strategy would be to say that we worked within the D's own frame of reference rather than challenging it.

During the first 2½ hours of treatment, the therapist collected essential data and occasionally reflected back to the D's what they were saying about their son's problem. This phase of the work culminated in asking the D's to have a conversation about John, at a time and place he could overhear them. Mrs. D was to express concern to her husband about John's worsening condition, which Mr. D was to discount. This assignment was framed to the D's as a method of gathering diagnostic information; at the same time, it allowed us to maintain our maneuverability by not taking a position about the problem. Our aim in making such an intervention was threefold. First, we wanted to assess Mrs. D's compliance to directives that asked her to do something different. Second, we wanted to assess how closely John was listening to his parents' conversation. If he were to react to such a conversation, we might use this information at some future point in treatment. Third, the assignment echoed the D's own difference of opinion and therefore directed them to make this difference explicit. Such an assignment might have the effect of motivating Mr. D to speak up about this in treatment, possibly motivating him to take a different stance with John despite his wife's objections.

By the fourth interview we had learned that the D's had not carried out the asssignment because Mrs. D feared that such action might upset John and make him worse. Mr. D did not protest his wife's lack of compliance nor did he attempt to persuade her to follow our directive. Mrs. D made it clear that she was not about to do anything that made her nervous or uncomfortable, stating that Dr. A had told her that she would not have to do anything that made her feel this way.

Based on this negative response to our assignment, our second major strategy, used throughout the remaining sessions, was to actively assume a strong position of pessimism regarding John's improvement. The D's were told they unfortunately had the best of all possible worlds; hospitalization would only be detrimental for John, and he was not ready to live independently. Therefore, they must learn to live with the problem.

Process of Therapy

The first three sessions were primarily devoted to data collection, and led to the therapist's request that the D's have a conversation about John's worsening condition (see preceding section on strategy). Mrs. D became flustered and confused when asked to do this and repeatedly asked for clarification about exactly what she had to do. Mr. D, on the other hand, looked as if he understood what was being asked, at times helping the therapist clarify the assignment to his wife. He appeared quite willing to go along with the suggestion. This 3rd hour of treatment was terminated on the note that both parents were willing to carry out our suggestion.

Preceding the next interview, the therapist and his colleagues received a number of phone calls from Mrs. D. At first the calls were for the purpose of clarifying what she had been asked to do. But, as the week progressed and she had not carried out the assignment, her contact and tone became more argumentative. She desired more explanation of the task, arguing that, in her opinion, what we had asked them to do might make John worse. Finally, she was told that if we had asked too much of her, we had made an error and were sorry. We would take this issue up during the next interview.

Mrs. D was quite hostile and argumentative during the 4th hour of treatment. She had not carried out the assignment and actively invited the therapist to "argue" with her about the merits of such an assignment. After all, she contended, she and her husband could give us all the data we needed.

The therapist declined such a debate, apologizing for making demands on her which were too upsetting. This was followed by the therapist sitting back, taking a wait-and-see attitude. Mrs. D responded by wanting to know what other ideas he had. The therapist said that he was not sure what to do next, especially since the other ideas were guaranteed to make Mrs. D even more nervous than the first assignment. Mrs. D countered that Dr. A told her that she would not have to do anything that made her uncomfortable. The therapist stated that he did not think she would be able to do anything that made her uncomfortable and asked what additional ideas she or her husband might have for dealing with the problem.

Mr. D suggested that John might go on a trip with him to visit relatives back east. Mrs. D became irate, criticizing her husband for bringing up suggestions that would not work. She stated that she had asked John about this a long time ago and John had said, "Why would I want to visit relatives?" The therapist then asked what else the couple had tried to do in attempting to solve the problem. At that point Mrs. D became very pessimistic, stating that they had tried everything and nothing had worked.

The therapist excused himself so that he might confer with his colleagues in the observation room. When the interview was resumed, the therapist explained that his colleagues felt that they had been overly optimistic about what might be done to help John and had inadvertently misled the D's into getting their hopes up. Based on what we had learned to date, it was now our consensus that the D family had made an optimal adjustment to a bad situation. The dangers of hospitalization or forcing John to leave the home were reviewed as a prelude to taking up in detail the many sacrifices the D's must prepare to make in learning to live with such a difficult situation. They were asked to return in 2 weeks.

The choice of this strategy was determined by the structure of the interaction that had developed between the D's and the therapist. As already with Dr. A, they first accepted a treatment plan, then decided that it was not what was needed and came back asking for other and better help. This established an escalating symmetrical interaction. Now, as Bateson has repeatedly stressed in his writings, the most effective way of dealing with a symmetrical runaway is the introduction of complementarity. What is meant by this is that in the face of a message implying "change the situation, but do not try to change us," it would be quite useless for the therapist to insist on a change in the patients' attempted solutions. Rather, what is indicated is the utilization of the resistance in the service of its own correction. This is done by the therapist taking a complementary one-down position, insisting on the inadvisability and even the dangers of change and supplying as many cogent reasons as he or she can think of in support of his or her contention that the patients should not change. This leaves the patients with only two possible reactions: either they accept this viewpoint and must therefore stop their problem-perpetuating behaviors, or they reject it—in which case it is they who now claim that change is possible. This form of intervention is now known as *positive connotation* (Selvini-Palazzoli, Cecchin, Prata, & Boscolo, 1978).

Mr. D showed no visible reaction to our dour pronouncement, smiling as if to say, "You can't intimidate me." Mrs. D, however, seemed angered. She had wanted to travel with her husband, and this was one of the things that would not be possible under the present circumstances. As she walked out of the interview, she caustically remarked that it seemed like the observers had reversed their prognosis rather quickly.

The 5th hour was spent reviewing our pessimistic outlook and describing in painful detail what parental sacrifices would be necessary in order to care for John. As predicted, Mrs. D found this line of advice to be more and more irritating. At one point, she stated that John would be better off dead than just lingering in his present condition. The therapist commiserated with her while persisting with the theme that John was "their cross to bear" and that for Mr. and Mrs. D parenting would never come to an end.

About a week after the fifth interview, we received a phone call from Mr. D who stated that his wife was considering the possibility of making John live somewhere else; he wanted to discuss this with us. We asked Mr. D to come in alone on the supposition that if he was accurately reporting the present state of events, we might have a chance at coaching him on how to amplify his wife's motivation for taking such action.

During the 6th hour Mr. D explained that Mrs. D had received a letter from a friend who had a vaguely similar problem with her own son. After many unsuccessful attempts to deal with him, the friend had thrown her son out of the family home. Mr. D said that according to the letter, this action had resulted in the young man "buckling down," finding a job and an apartment, and pursuing a relationship with a young woman. Mr. D told us that this letter had given his wife some hope that a similar course of action might work with John. However, if such a plan were to be activated, Mr. D said he would have to be the one who would put John out of the house because John would simply not listen to his mother.

The therapist cautiously questioned Mr. D as to why he requested this private session. He replied that he had called at his wife's suggestion because she wanted to know what we thought about the idea of throwing John out of the house. She also reportedly wanted to know what possible dangers might lie in store for John if they did take such an action. When asked if he had any additional reason for coming in alone, Mr. D replied that he did not. He was only doing what his wife asked. However, he did take the opportunity to ask the therapist what he thought about this plan. The therapist replied that while the idea might have merit, Mr. D was being overly optimistic on two accounts. First, John would not go willingly and there would probably be quite a struggle to force him to leave the home. Second, the therapist predicted that at the first sign of John's distress, Mrs. D would intervene and put a stop to the entire plan. Mr. D laughingly agreed with this prediction, but added that there might be a chance his wife would follow through. One of the observers then entered the room, repeating the prediction that he was being overly optimistic and suggesting that he could test this out for himself. He could do this by selecting one small thing he would like John to either start doing or stop doing and see what success he might have. The observer predicted that John would not comply, and his wife would intervene even in something very small and inconsequential; a test of this nature would make it much clearer how terribly difficult, if not impossible, it would be to get John to leave home.

The 7th and last hour of treatment began by exploring what, if anything, the D's had discussed regarding the idea of putting John out of the house, and their feelings about it. Mrs. D stated quite forcefully that she had never wanted to do this. She said, "This is Mr. D's feeling in the matter, and while I have to honor his feelings, I can't go along with it." She reiterated how John was too immature to leave the home, and subsequently showed the therapist a new book she was reading that made her believe that John was suffering "from a very deep depression." The therapist responded by claiming no knowledge of the book and then waited quietly for either of the D's to continue the interview.

Mrs. D then inquired how they might determine what John was capable of doing for himself. She drew an analogy between her own child and one who was retarded. The therapist then returned to taking a pessimistic position, stating that she was being overly optimistic. He reiterated how things would not change, and again described the many sacrifices and adjustments she and her husband must make in order to provide a safe and protective environment for their son. When Mrs. D seemed to be the most resistive to these pronouncements, one of the observers entered the treatment room and suggested that the argument was academic and Mrs. D could easily conduct a test which would prove that we were right. When she asked what this would involve, she was told to stop preparing extra food for John's dinner unless he joined her and her husband at the table. She was to tell John that if he wanted a hot meal he would have to come to the dinner table and eat with the rest of the family. She was to tell him this only once. The observer predicted that if she were able to do this, he believed that John would not come to the table, go on a hunger strike, and simply wait her out until she relented and went back to the present way of doing things. The session was ended on the note that Mrs. D was to think this over and call us after she either tried the test or decided not to do it.

Approximately 4 weeks after this session, the therapist received a phone call from Mrs. D. She explained that she had carried out the test with the following results: John had not come to the dinner table so she only prepared enough food for her and her husband. In response to this John started making his own food, most of the time drinking milk and eating peanut butter sandwiches. In her view, this proved that John was not capable of taking care of himself. He was not eating balanced meals which reawakened her suspicion that his problem might be nutritional. So she resumed cooking food for three so that John could take his meals alone in the kitchen.

Termination

Termination took place by phone during the conversation described in the preceding paragraphs, which followed the last hour of treatment. Mrs. D stated that she could see no purpose for continuing treatment with us and that her husband concurred with this. The therapist replied that the only help he could give would be further instructions and suggestions as to how they might learn to better live with the problem. While most of these issues had already been covered, it was suggested that at some future date they might want to use any of the three remaining sessions for more counseling and support aimed at helping them cope with the never-ending responsibility of caring for John. Mrs. D was told that if she wanted to use any of these three remaining sessions she would simply need to make a call to our Associate Director, and she and/or Mr. D would be scheduled at the next free treatment hour.

Analysis of Failure

The D family was selected for this chapter because they clearly illustrate one of the most fundamental assumptions in the brief therapy model: If family treatment is to have any chance of being successful, at least one member of the family *must* be a *customer* for treatment. A "customer" is one who communicates three basic statements: "(1) I have a problem regarding the behavior of myself or another, which distresses me; (2) I have tried to solve this problem, alone or with the help of others, and these problem-solving attempts have been unsuccessful; (3) I am asking for your help."

In retrospect, no one in the D family was a customer for treatment, and having failed to adequately deal with this issue, we proceeded to make interventions that were doomed to fail. While it was clear that Mr. D was not a customer, it was more difficult to assess his wife's position, because she fulfilled two of the three basic conditions for being a customer. She had a problem that she was clearly distressed about; she had tried a number of solutions—both alone and with the help of professionals—which had failed to solve the problem. However, she never clearly stated that she wanted our help. At best she was only willing to admit that she was attending the sessions because Dr. A had sent her.

The following dialogue between the therapist and Mrs. D is a transcript from the first session where the therapist attempted to take up the issue of customership but failed to do an adequate job:

THERAPIST: Let me get back to you, Mrs. D. Given how you see the problem, I was wondering what you were hoping for in coming in to see us, especially since you know that we only work for a maximum of ten sessions.

MRS. D: As I say, I saw Dr. A since last year, and I don't feel that the situation is essentially any different than when I first saw him. And *perhaps* if I were to look for some change—and *perhaps* I have made this clear to Dr. A and *perhaps* he also felt that some change might be brought about by our coming. I don't think we were looking for any particular change . . . almost any change at this stage would be okay. I would hate to feel it would be for the worse, but. . . . (*Stops in midsentence and pauses.*)

THERAPIST: I hear that you want change, but I'm still confused about what you were hoping for in coming to see us since we have so little time to work, only having nine sessions after today.

The therapist was attempting to have Mrs. D define what she wanted, which would force her to deal with the issue of customership. If she had stated what she wanted from us, we would then have discussed exactly how we fit into the picture, that is, what she was expecting we would do, and how. Mrs. D did not, however, answer the question about what she wanted other than to state that Dr. A had sent her. Further, she hedged on these statements by using the word *perhaps*, making everything she did say even less definite. The therapist took a one-down position by claiming confusion, while attempting to elicit specific content on the issue of desired change.

The therapist continued to explore her expectations for treatment:

THERAPIST: Did Dr. A explain to you that we meet for only ten sessions?

MRS. D: Yes.

THERAPIST: Well, I'm still confused as to what you were hoping for since you say the problem is very serious and we have such a short time to work. Have you thought about this before coming here?

MRS. D: Well, I guess if you or Dr. A would tell me that it cannot be helped in such a short time, then we will have to go back to long-time. [She had already stated that long-term work had not been of any use.] He has not indicated to me that this would not be inappropriate in these circumstances, and of course I can only lean on him to a *certain extent* for his professional viewpoint. If he felt that there was nothing to be gained, then I don't think he would have suggested it. Or even *if* I had said to him, "Do you feel this is appropriate?" I *could* have said no. I didn't say "yes, yes, yes." If he didn't think it was appropriate, I don't think it would have been appropriate for him to have kept silent and said "go ahead."

As the reader can see, Mrs. D had not answered the question. The answers that she did give were once again qualified by the words *if, I could,* and the like. Furthermore, she stated that she was not that eager to come to the Brief Therapy Center, explaining how she had not said "yes, yes, yes," to Dr. A's referral. There is a discrepancy between her somewhat cavalier attitude toward treatment and her report of feeling distressed and hopeless about the problem.

The therapist continued to pursue the nature of the referral:

THERAPIST: So you're saying that you came here because Dr. A suggested it and you thought it would be appropriate?

MRS. D: Well, I feel we have come to a dead end.
THERAPIST: You mean with Dr. A?
MRS. D: With everything and anything. We consulted Dr. J.

Again, Mrs. D had not answered the therapist's question. Instead, she stated that she and her husband were at a dead end with everything and anything. One might speculate that if she were a customer, she might have made statements along any of the following lines: "Nothing has worked but we can't let him go on this way. Isn't there anything you might do? Have you treated cases like this? Do you think there is anything that can be done?" Or, "I know we only have ten sessions but if he were only able to do X, that would at least be some small improvement." All of these statements would have indicated a strong desire for change and willingness to work on the problem. However, Mrs. D made no statements of this kind, despite repeated attempts by the therapist to elicit them.

The therapist continued to use a "one-down" stance of confusion in the hope of obtaining more information:

THERAPIST: You said that you have come to a dead end with everything. Bear with me—I'm confused as to where we come in. What were you wanting from us?
MRS. D: The only thing I can answer is that Dr. A said they will ask something specific you want to change, some specific recommendation. Well, I wrote down some specific things, but this is pure amateurism from what I can expect from somebody I feel is aberrant to a degree. Now, I have no way. . . . Even Dr. A made mention of the fact that this is not a time to dig a grave or hold a funeral service. On the other hand, he said "Your son is crippled, not completely."
MR. D: You did say that you took this up because you didn't see anything against it anyway.
MRS. D: Yes, you see some changes. You know, I have been in therapy and surely one doesn't see great changes, but maybe one feels a little better or a little worse, or feels he doesn't want to continue. You know.

Here, Mrs. D did agree with her husband that she came to the Brief Therapy Center because there was nothing against it. She then talked of change in treatment in a manner that made little sense: "You feel a little better or a little worse or terminate treatment." The therapist pursued the question one more time, making one last attempt at clarification:

THERAPIST: God knows, I don't want to be discouraging, but you're describing a problem you see as very serious, and you have tried everything and nothing has worked. John will not come to treatment, and we only have ten sessions. So, again, I think it might be of help to get some idea from you what you thought might happen or what you envisioned might happen when you came. Because, as you say, John won't come for treatment.

MRS. D: (*Appearing agitated, speaking in a loud voice.*) This is what I thought. When we started. You expect John to come in, don't you? Maybe you expected John to come.

THERAPIST: I don't know. That's why I'm asking you. What did you expect?

MRS. D: I don't know, you see. I could have asked Dr. A, but he doesn't know your methods, you see. Other than a few examples of your work.

THERAPIST: Yes, but that's Dr. A. [Therapist then interrupted by observer who suggested that therapist drop this line of questions and ask Mrs. D to read the list of "specific things" that she had referred to earlier.]

Mrs. D proceeded to read her list of goals, but the subject of how the therapist would assist in reaching them was not taken up during the rest of the interview. The therapist failed to deal with Mrs. D's commitment to treatment and what role and responsibilities she might have if we were to be of any help to John.

At the beginning of the second session, the therapist made another attempt to deal with the issue of commitment to treatment, but once again the issue was left vague:

THERAPIST: Since John will not come for treatment, can I take it that we can expect your help in bringing about a small change that you would like to see?

MRS. D: You can take it we will help, but the amount of help that we will be able to give you in relation to John if there is any contact involved is going to be minimal.

THERAPIST: Okay, I realize that at this point you're feeling fairly tied up or concerned as far as what to do with him.

MRS. D: It's not that; it's that he won't stay in the room to make any contact.

THERAPIST: Okay, so he runs away or avoids you, and I'm not sure just what, but I'm just making it a little more explicit that since he wouldn't come in for Dr. A or Dr. J, he won't come in for me. Therefore, the best chance we're going to have of doing anything is, as we collect more information and if we come up with some idea that might be useful, with you two being in the house with him, and being his parents you are still in a powerful position of being able to influence him. Maybe I should say you're in a better position than we are.

MRS. D: Yeah, I think we are in the lowest position of anybody actually, other than . . . there is one boy in the North West who has been able to talk to John, and his friends are just that—friends. If they ever tried to talk. (*pause*) . . . Well, they are not particularly insightful, as this other boy, his friend, is.

THERAPIST: Okay, there certainly are difficulties, but you are still in a better position than we are.

MRS. D: Yes.

THERAPIST: So, if there is a message to be delivered to John, you, being in the house, are in the best position to deliver that message. [Call from observers.] . . . That was our Associate Director, who was pointing out that since John wants to avoid you, run away from you, some things we may ask of you may be of a nonverbal nature.

MRS. D: That sounds like the most possible thing. We're just so ignorant about it. . . . Oh well, no sense expatiating about it. Go ahead.

THERAPIST: If we are clear on that, then I have a few questions.

The transcripts illustrate the therapist's error of pushing Mrs. D into being a customer rather than taking the more useful tack of getting her to push us to help her. The therapist frames his statements so she can say yes. The therapist's statements do not leave any room for Mrs. D to work at committing herself to treatment. Furthermore, in response to the yes/no questions she qualified all of her statements in the direction of minimal commitment. She said, answering for both herself and her husband, that they cannot do much because John would not stay in the room. When the therapist said, "Won't you agree that you are in a better position to influence him than I because you live with him?" she said "yes," followed by a statement of how she and her husband "are in the lowest position of anybody to influence him." Even her subsequent agreement that she might be in a position to deliver a message nonverbally is highly qualified. She said, "That sounds like the most possible thing." She did not say for whom it is most possible, and her nonverbal communication indicated that she was not engaged with the therapist on this issue. The therapist then compounded his error by stating, "If we're clear on that then I have a few questions." This statement closes the subject of customership as if it were settled and goes on to more data collection. It is as if the therapist proceeded on the assumption that even one "yes" by Mrs. D was sufficient to proceed with treatment. While this might be fine in another context, such as business sales where the primary aim is getting someone to sign on the dotted line, to proceed in treatment on such a flimsy basis is asking for trouble—either a difficult case to handle and/or a poor treatment outcome.

Given this lack of involvement in treatment, it is not surprising that the therapist had very little leverage or influence with the D family. When we asked Mrs. D to have a conversation about John, she felt uncomfortable and refused to do it, although she was quite willing to waste time arguing about the wisdom of such action. Our stance of pessimism had very little impact on her. In hindsight one might posit that for such an intervention to be effective, the client must *want* treatment. Without this want, therapeutic pessimism has little or no power to positively influence the client.

Ironically, when one of the authors (Segal) recently discussed this chapter with Dr. A, he learned that it was Mrs. D who had been skeptical of the referral to the Brief Therapy Center, while her husband thought they ought to give it a try. One wonders if her coming to see us might have been her way of respecting her husband's feeling while not going along with him.

Hypothetical Reconstruction toward Success

Analysis of the case failure indicates that the primary error was not an incorrect assessment of the problem–solution loop, but our failure to clarify and deal with Mrs. D's lack of motivation for treatment. Having made this error, our interventions, which might have had a beneficial effect under different circumstances, had no impact on the family. One might say that our error was one of timing and pacing. Therefore, in reconstructing the case, the therapist, having correctly assessed Mrs. D's lack of motivation, would refrain from making any interventions aimed at interrupting the problem–solution loop. Instead, his initial goal would be to convert Mrs. D into a "customer" for treatment. This could have been done during any of the initial data gathering sessions, although theoretically it is best done as soon as possible.

Given Mrs. D's defensive and oppositional behavior in treatment, the therapist might have approached the subject of her motivation for treatment more slowly and gently by exploring the nature of her last therapeutic experience. What made her decide to enter treatment then? How did she come to pick Dr. A as a therapist? What had she hoped to accomplish? What did she think was actually accomplished? If she did not get what she wanted, how did she account for this? Similarly, how did the subject of referral arise in treatment? Could she reconstruct some of the conversations about the referral? How was the matter settled? What did she think would happen or what was she hoping for in treatment? What led her to that belief? How did she decide to follow up on Dr. A's suggestion to seek brief treatment? Why did she decide against Soteria House?

By interviewing in this manner, a number of things might have been accomplished. First, the therapist would now be correctly pacing the treatment. Assuming you cannot treat a noncustomer, the interview process is now directed toward the issue of motivation rather than attempting to intervene directly in the presenting complaint. Second, given Mrs. D's defensiveness, exploring the previous treatment and referral in this manner could have slowed treatment down and made the therapist's inquiries and challenges much softer, much more indirect. This might have increased the chances of establishing rapport and increased her willingness to actively cooperate with the therapist. Finally, such a line of questioning might well have revealed that Mrs. D was quite skeptical about therapy and this might have been discussed. Most importantly, however, Mrs. D's responses could have been used by the therapist to take a pessimistic stance about *her capacity to do what was necessary*, that is, carry out therapeutic directives to help her son.

Assuming that her skepticism about treatment would then have been out in the open, the therapist would have had a number of choices as to how to proceed with the case. In essence, they would all have been based in one way or another on the *utilization* of her resistance, rather than on trying to bypass or even directly counteract it.

Addendum: Doctor A

I was the therapist who struggled for 23 sessions over 9 months with the D family, described in this chapter. My own orientation is "MRI-Eclectic," and this includes discussing subjective feeling states, talking about the past as affecting the present, focusing on interactional styles, and making suggestions including occasional "strategic" ones. Though not as clearly articulated as the Brief Therapy Center approach, my approach is nevertheless a reasonably consistent and effective one.

Given our different conceptual approaches to "problems" and "systems," I was impressed with how this chapter detailed problems that were quite similar to my own with this family. The authors failed in engaging Mrs. D into becoming a "customer"; I failed to use to advantage the motivations that brought the family to me. The authors seemed to be caught up in endless power struggles with their clients; these struggles closely paralleled my own with them. I also experienced quite intensely the struggles between the two parents and their efforts to pull me into the middle. My picture of the two is that they had a most unhappy marriage for many decades, and a major focus of their struggles was their son. In a somewhat parallel way, each one (the mother in a more obvious way) tried to engage me on his or her side, and I did not make appropriate use of that facet of their control battles with each other. I made suggestions, reframed statements, and made other types of interventions. Typically one or the other parent would pick up on my idea and the other would undercut it: the father by passively not following through (or conversely sometimes doing so too fast), and the mother by strongly criticizing the intervention or the father's ineptness. In hindsight, I did not adequately deal with these struggles.

Given the two different approaches, the quite different styles of the therapists who worked with this family, and the similar outcomes (including the therapists' own frustrations), one wonders to what extent major specific issues cut across different schools of therapy. For example, a common denominator, which was missing in both the Brief Therapy Center's and my work with this family, was the failure to establish an effective level of rapport, customership, motivation, or sustaining working alliance. These factors, while not sufficient, are necessary conditions for effective therapy.

A brief postscript: Ten months after our last session, I contacted the family and shortly thereafter received a note from Mrs. D. She reported that the son was now seeing a "young man" psychologist with whom he had a "good relationship," that her own health was bad, that her husband was "fine and taking care of" her, and that the couple had made two satisfying trips of a week or so each. The note was signed: "Happy New Year! From (mother, father, and son)." I have no idea if or how these developments were influenced by the Brief Therapy Center or my efforts, or if she was pinpointing my failure and/or thanking me for my help.

ACKNOWLEDGMENT

The authors gratefully acknowledge the helpful suggestions and criticisms of Lenora Yuen, PhD, University of California, Berkeley.

REFERENCES

Selvini-Palazzoli, M., Cecchin, G., Prata, G., & Boscolo, L. *Paradox and counterparadox: A new model in the therapy of the family in schizophrenic transaction.* New York: Jason Aronson, 1978.

Watzlawick, P., Beavin, J. H., & Jackson, D. D. *Pragmatics of human communication: A study of interactional patterns, pathologies and paradoxes.* New York: Norton, 1967.

4

Failure in Behavioral Marital Therapy

NEIL S. JACOBSON, ROBERT A. BERLEY,
KATHY NEWPORT MELMAN, RICHARD ELWOOD,
AND CAROLYN PHELPS

Introduction

Behavioral marital therapy (BMT) is one of the fastest growing movements within the field of family therapy. It has already been subjected to more thorough experimental scrutiny than any other approach to marital therapy, despite its short 16-year history (Gurman & Kniskern, 1978). At the time of this writing, its effectiveness has been supported by at least seven controlled studies (Azrin, Besalel, Bechtel, Michalicek, Mancera, Carroll, Shuford, & Cox, 1980; Baucom, 1982; Jacobson, 1977, 1978b, 1979; Liberman, Levine, Wheeler, Sanders, & Wallace, 1976; Turkewitz & O'Leary, 1981), and it is the only identifiable approach to marital therapy whose effectiveness has been clearly documented (Jacobson, 1978a; Jacobson & Margolin, 1979; Stuart, 1980). No less than three textbooks have appeared in the last 2 years presenting clinical techniques in unusual detail (Jacobson & Margolin, 1979; Liberman, Wheeler, deVisser, Kuehnel, & Kuehnel, 1981; Stuart 1980). Critical commentaries on BMT by both advocates (Jacobson & Moore, 1981; Birchler & Spinks, 1980; Weiss, 1980) and critics (Gurman & Knudson, 1978; Gurman, Knudson, & Kniskern, 1978; Knudson, Gurman, & Kniskern, 1979) have led to an expansion of the model as well as a series of clinical innovations (Birchler & Spinks, 1980; Jacobson & Margolin, 1979; Weiss, 1980).

By any reasonable standards that one would use to measure the vitality of a model of therapy, BMT is thriving. Yet, despite the optimism suggested by this literature, the problem of marital distress has by no means been eliminated. If one defines success as the substantial improvement in the quality of a relationship, failure rates vary from 10–40% depending on the study (cf. Jacobson, 1984; Jacobson, Follette, & Elwood, 1984). Some couples show evidence of positive changes in therapy and still divorce shortly after therapy is over. Others fail to improve at all. Still others actually deteriorate as a result of marital therapy. Evidence as to the determinants of success and failure in BMT is sorely lacking. At this stage of our knowledge, one can only

Neil S. Jacobson, Robert A. Berley, Kathy Newport Melman, Richard Elwood, and Carolyn Phelps. Department of Psychology, University of Washington, Seattle, Washington.

speculate, pending a more systematic experimental inquiry into this important problem.

Given our present state of ignorance regarding these questions, we decided that it would be more instructive to provide an intensive analysis of why one case did not work according to pretreatment expectations and then to generalize from this case as much as one can generalize from one case. What has emerged from such an analysis, we believe, is some insight into one particular kind of couple that is very difficult to treat, as well as some general statements about some of the hazards involved in conducting BMT.

There are many cases that we could have chosen as the focus of this chapter. We decided to choose a case where the outcome was surprising and completely unpredictable from pretreatment data. The couple described in this chapter came into therapy resembling in many ways the stereotype of the happily married couple. It was difficult to ascertain at first why they were coming to therapy. The problems that were identified seemed minor. In fact, this case was viewed initially as a case of marital enrichment rather than as a case of marital therapy. The developments that emerged during the course of therapy began to expose this couple as the type that had given us trouble in the past. Moreover, when it began to become apparent that the case was not developing according to our pretreatment expectations, a number of interesting clinical and conceptual issues emerged regarding the practice of BMT. Therefore, we think that of all of our failures, this case may be the most constructive in illustrating some of the pitfalls that challenge the technology of BMT and the ingenuity of the behavioral marital therapist.

This chapter begins with a brief introduction to BMT, so that the reader can understand the perspective we are adapting as we conceptualize the treatment of this particular couple. What follows will be a detailed discussion of this case, beginning with a description of the couple and continuing with a discussion of the course of therapy. Then we will describe our soul-searching in regard to the reasons why this case failed. We will use hindsight to talk about some of the client characteristics that contributed to failure as well as some therapeutic interventions that might have been misguided. The chapter will conclude with some general statements about success and failure in BMT that can be abstracted from the experience with this case.

Theoretical Frame of Reference

Behavioral marital therapy is an approach to treating relationship problems that is based on a social learning model of behavior (Bandura, 1977). Its principles are derived primarily from basic research in social and experimental psychology and in particular from the work of learning theorists in experimental and cognitive psychology and exchange theorists from social psychology (Skinner, 1953; Thibaut & Kelley, 1959). Behavioral marital therapy assumes that the quality of spouses' "outcomes" or transactions with one another is the primary determinant of their satisfaction with the relationship. When one or both spouses are dissatisfied with their marriage, the behavior therapist attempts to pinpoint and identify pleasing or potentially rewarding events that are missing (or occurring with insufficient frequency) and displeasing or punishing experiences that are occurring in excess. Although this analysis focuses on the overt behavioral transactions occurring in the relationship, there is also an attempt to ferret out the role of spouses' perceptions and cognitions about those behavioral transactions. Thus, a social learning analysis inevitably includes the attributions that spouses impose on their own and their partner's behavior, their standards for evaluating behavior and determining its impact, and the cognitive, information processing systems that each spouse uses to alter the meaning or the impact of the behavioral transactions. Thus, a behavioral analysis includes a determination of what behaviors each spouse pays attention to and how each evaluates and interprets those behaviors. In addition to being a social learning model, as Weiss (1978) has pointed out, BMT also emphasizes the importance of relationship skills. Implicit in the model is the belief that spouses need to master a series of skills in order to sustain a satisfying relationship over a long period of time. Examples of these skills include communication, conflict resolution, sex, and a variety of instrumental tasks. There is a presumption that distressed relationships often manifest deficiencies in one or more of the skills required for a successful long-term relationship.

Finally, a behavioral analysis attempts to trace the developmental history of the relationship in question This attempt to reconstruct the developmental history of the relationship reflects our belief that whatever the current level of positive and negative exchange, the evolution of the current pattern has important treatment implications. Moreover, in reconstructing the developmental history of the relationship, the strengths of the relationship can be better elucidated.

Our research has suggested that there are some common developmental failures that characterize the histories of distressed relationships. Two of the most common are the inability to deal effectively with conflict and reinforcement erosion. Deficits in conflict resolution or problem solving have been shown to discriminate between distressed and nondistressed couples in numerous studies (Birchler, Weiss, & Vincent, 1975; Billings, 1979; Gottman, 1979; Vincent, Weiss, & Birchler, 1975). This has led to an emphasis in BMT on teaching couples more effective strategies for dealing with conflict (Jacobson & Margolin, 1979). Reinforcement erosion describes the deterioration in spouses' capacity to gratify one another during the course of relationship development, a decline that is due largely to habituation. Many couples counter reinforcement erosion by providing for benefits in a variety of interactional domains and by continuing to grow and change in ways that maintain a high level of gratification. In the case of distressed couples, this corrective and collaborative experience has not occurred to a sufficient degree, and spouses have seen their ability to satisfy one another decline. This leads to an emphasis in therapy on training couples to become more effective at providing each other with the gratification they shared during courtship and their early marital history.

Behavioral marital therapy, as it is typically practiced by our clinical research team at the University of Washington, focuses on promoting a consistently high rate of positive shared experiences in the relationship. In addition, there is typically a focus on teaching couples more effective strategies for dealing with conflict. There is a dual emphasis on the "content" of the presenting complaints, and on "process," the learning of communication skills that are necessary to solve and prevent future conflicts. The procedures oriented toward instigating behavior change are generically termed "behavior exchange" (BE) procedures, and the strategies for teaching conflict resolution skills are generically termed "problem-solving training" (PST). This dual focus on content and process comprises the core treatment in our outcome research. In clinical practice there is considerable variability in the treatment regimen, depending upon the idiosyncratic concerns and characteristics of particular couples. Both components tend to be oriented toward training couples in particular relationship skills.

Behavior Exchange Procedures

Behavior exchange (BE) procedures are instigative in that the primary focus of the therapy sessions is on creating change in the natural environment. The treatment sessions are graded so as to gradually increase the demands placed on spouses. During the early treatment sessions, each spouse has a maximum amount of choice in deciding what behaviors to change, and high-cost, difficult changes are avoided. The commitment required during these early sessions is that each spouse must direct his or her efforts toward increasing the partner's day-to-day satisfaction with the relationship by any means that he or she chooses. During the sessions the spouses are taught the skills of a behavior analyst so that each can learn to pinpoint which of their own behaviors, if delivered more often, would be likely to foster the other's increased satisfaction with the relationship. Then these hypotheses are tested with homework assignments to increase the partner's daily satisfaction. In subsequent therapy sessions, the homework assignments are debriefed, and, to the extent that the spouses were unsuccessful in bringing about increased satisfaction, troubleshooting is conducted to examine what went wrong and to generate alternative hypotheses that can be subsequently tested at home.

As couples gradually master the ability to increase their day-to-day levels of marital satisfaction, the tasks evolve toward more central concerns in their relationship. This process, however, is a gradual one, since it is believed that if movement is too rapid, spouses are likely to resist the therapist's directives. There is a continuing emphasis in subsequent sessions on providing each spouse with a maximum number of options regarding how they want to change. Thus, while each spouse must commit himself or herself to the principles of compromise and behavior modification, he or she is allowed to regulate and control the process of change. For example, during our "request/refusal" exercises (Jacobson & Margolin, 1979), one spouse might make a series of requests for behaviors that he or she would like to see increased, while the other spouse listens and chooses to implement a subset of these requests. The instructions emphasize the "freedom" of spouse to "choose" which requests to affirm and which not to affirm. One spouse is providing the other with "information" regarding what would make him or her happier, and the other spouse, while committed to some degree of responsiveness, can refuse any particular request with impunity. The instructions not only sanction but require each spouse to refuse a certain percentage of requests. This minimizes the negative impact of any particular refusal.

Thus, there are two principles juxtaposed during BE—principles that have the dual benefits of requiring a commitment to accommodation and change, yet easing the sting of such changes by allowing each spouse to work at his or her own pace. At the beginning of therapy, each spouse makes the commitment to focus on himself or herself. The treatment sessions are structured so as to encourage—even demand—that the spouses adopt a self-critical and self-evaluative stance. Spouses are prohibited from either blaming their partners or expecting their partners to carry the burden of change on their shoulders. At the same time every effort is made to allow this focus on oneself to occur in a manner that does not violate the individual's own desires. When changes do occur within this framework, each spouse is more likely to interpret these changes in a manner favorable toward long-term maintenance. In short, the flexibility and control given to each spouse in regulating the process of change not only renders change more likely, but also increases the likelihood that the changes will be perceived as internally motivated.

The BE philosophy holds that intimate relationships do not simply take care of themselves. People do not "live happily ever after" once they "fall in love." We try to foster the notion that maintaining a satisfying relationship requires constant attention and a continuing willingness to be flexible and attentive to the needs of one's partner. The skills inherent in BE are the skills of monitoring, pinpointing, and remaining sensitive to and responsive to the impact that one is having on one's spouse. Our therapeutic tasks are designed to be incorporated into the relationship on an ongoing basis, so that a high level of relationship satisfaction is maintained by spouses' constant awareness of and attention to the marriage. If a couple responds successfully to BE, the technology of therapy becomes part of the natural quest to maintain intimacy.

Problem-Solving Training

In contrast to BE, where the therapy sessions are primarily instigative and the essential learning process takes place at home, PST places a greater emphasis on the events that occur in the therapy sessions. In PST couples are taught a structured set of strategies to deal directly and more effectively with inevitable relationship conflicts. Problem solving is a specialized mode of interaction that is best thought of as a supplement to already existing patterns of interaction; the goal is not to replace arguing, but simply to expand the couple's repertoire so that they have the skills to resolve conflict when they wish to utilize those skills.

The structure of PST necessitates a collaborative effort, and it requires that a conflict be viewed as a mutual problem. The commitment to collaboration is difficult for couples who have been dealing with conflict as adversaries up until the onset of marital therapy. Typically, each spouse enters therapy viewing the partner as the primary cause of the problems in the relationship, with himself or herself cast in the role of victim. These adversarial perspectives are not easily altered, and considerable clinical skill is required to foster a suspension of disbelief so that the collaborative approach may be given a chance to work.

Once couples approach the resolution of relationship conflict from the standpoint of collaboration, PST moves smoothly. The rules are designed to affect the style with which problems are discussed, by altering the behavior of both the spouse who has the complaint and the one against whom the complaint is directed. Concerns are stated in specific and in behavioral terms. Neither derogatory adjectives nor pejorative trait labels are allowed. The complaint is placed within a context emphasizing the positive efforts already made. The complaining spouse admits his or her role in maintaining the problem. Once spouses begin to discuss solutions, the complainer is sensitive to the importance of compromise and mutuality. The partner who is the object of the complaint must listen and attempt to understand the nature of the other's concern and resist efforts to countercomplain, justify, or defend himself or herself. In doing so he or she is neither admitting to being wrong nor agreeing to make sweeping behavioral changes. Rather, he or she is simply helping to define the problem as it exists from the perspective of the concerned spouse.

The skills-training approach utilized in PST is based on a model that has been applied to teaching a variety of interpersonal skills (Jacobson & Margolin, 1979). The highly structured program, based on behavior rehearsal with feedback provided by the therapist, is essential if couples are to learn the complex skills of effective problem solving (Jacobson & Anderson, 1980). They start by reading a manual (Jacobson & Margolin, 1979) and then practice the skills on hypothetical problems so that they have the opportunity to master them without being distracted by the emotionally laden content of major relationship problems. Then the spouses begin to use the skills to resolve relatively minor relationship problems, moving on finally to the major concerns in their relationship. Each problem-solving session is culminated by a written change agreement, where the changes to be made are specified in detail, and the change agreement is implemented at home. Between therapy sessions, couples are instructed to practice the skills on new problems. Each therapy session begins with a survey of prior agreements so that the therapist can monitor whether or not spouses are implementing them. Agreements not proving to be viable can be renegotiated. The therapist is very active during the acquisition phase of PST, but as soon as the couples approach mastery of the skills, the therapist's influence begins to fade. The focus shifts toward ensuring generalization and maintenance of these new behaviors subsequent to the termination of therapy. By the time the regularly scheduled treatment sessions end, the spouses have become their own therapists and are holding regularly scheduled "state of the relationship" sessions on their own. During these sessions, spouses survey the past week, check on the viability of all change agreements, and negotiate the resolution to any new problems that have developed.

SUMMARY AND CONCLUSIONS

When BMT works as it is supposed to, spouses progress through each phase with a greater sense of mastery over their own lives together. They learn ways to monitor their ongoing relationship satisfaction, discover the most important sources of gratification that each can provide for the other, learn new skills to maximize their satisfaction, inoculate themselves against the pernicious effects of reinforcement erosion, resolve their presenting problems, and acquire skills that they can use to eliminate future problems as they arise. As positive behaviors occur with greater frequency, spouses' attitudes change in desirable ways. As the changes become permanent, the spouses begin to trust one another again.

We know that BMT often produces significant positive changes in relationships. But we are not yet able to predict when these positive outcomes will not occur. When BMT fails we can only speculate as to why. An attempt to better understand the phenomenon of failure will occupy us for the remainder of this chapter.

Defining Failure in Behavioral Marital Therapy: Clinical and Research Dilemmas

The fact that BMT has been developed largely within a clinical research context has resulted in a tendency to oversimplify the criteria for success and failure. When therapy is conducted within the constraints of a group outcome study, standardized criteria for relationship improvement must be applied to all couples. These measures must be taken at predetermined points in time. These research criteria oversimplify the task of determining success and failure in at least three ways. First, marital distress is an amorphous construct; couples are highly variable in their reasons for seeking therapy, and in the clinically indicated criteria for a positive outcome. This heterogeneity is completely disguised by standardized criteria. Second, conjoint marital therapy always includes three clients: the husband, the wife, and the relationship. The criteria for successful outcome are seldom identical for all three clients. Measures focusing exclusively on relationship satisfaction ignore this important source of within-couple variance. Third, measures alleged to indicate success or failure, taken at a few points in time, fail to account for the temporal relativity inherent in the assessment of success or failure. All of these problems create befuddling dilemmas for researchers as well as for clinicians.

Since couples vary widely in their reasons for seeking therapy and in their choices of treatment goals, criteria for success and failure ultimately must be personalized for each couple. When a therapist or a researcher asks, "was treatment successful?", the question that logically follows is, "compared to what?" The availability of normative data on some of our assessment instruments lends a false sense of security to our efforts to determine success and failure. True enough, they add some perspective to our evaluation of therapy by allowing us to consider not only how much change has occurred since the onset of treatment, but also how couples compare with "nondistressed" couples in the general population. Such criteria can be helpful both to therapists, who might otherwise be tempted to demand an ideal outcome based on their own values (would I be satisfied with this relationship?), and to clients, who might have no other basis for deciding how much satisfaction they can reasonably expect to derive from their relationship. The pitfall here, and the challenge to the therapist's capacity to personalize treatment goals, lies in assuming that if this couple behaves like the average married couple in terms of statistical norms, they then join the ranks of the "nondistressed." The therapist must not become so data-bound that she or he cannot respond to the couple as they present themselves rather than as they are tabulated. Our determinations of success and failure must be based on the couple's potential for change, their wishes, their comparison level for alternatives (Thibaut & Kelley, 1959), and by a host of additional factors that vary from couple to couple. Neither norms for nondistressed couples nor changes in control groups can serve as an appropriate comparison group for all couples.

One of the most common oversimplifications in determining success and failure is to base one's evaluation solely on relationship enhancement. Treatment is considered successful if the quality of the relationship improves, and unsuccessful when such improvement does not occur. From a research standpoint this criterion has seemed essential. Group outcome designs demand standardized criteria, and it would make little sense to adopt alternative criteria such as divorce or failure to improve the relationship. Since BMT treatment packages are oriented toward increases in relationship satisfaction, if one criterion is needed, this must be it.

However, the individual functioning of each spouse tends to be ignored in this dyadic outcome assessment, which in turn biases our treatment packages toward ignoring the two spouses as individuals by focusing exclusively on dyadic change. Moreover, the identification of positive outcome purely in terms of enhanced relationship satisfaction ensures that our determinations of success and failure will include both "false-positive" and "false-negative" outcomes. A false-positive outcome occurs when dyadic measures indicate enhanced relationship gratification for both members, but this "enhancement" occurs at such great cost to one or both spouses that he and/or she is ultimately harmed, or at the very least the overall quality of life is not enhanced. A false-negative outcome occurs when dyadic measures indicate no change or deterioration in the relationship, but as a result of therapy one or both individuals have benefitted. For example, a couple may decide to obtain a divorce at the conclusion of therapy, and after the initial stress associated with divorce subsides, one or both individuals are happier than they were prior to therapy.

This returns us to a point made at the beginning of this section: the fact that conjoint marital therapy involves two individuals, as well as a relationship, allows for the possibility that a successful outcome for one or both spouses might conflict with what would be a successful outcome for the relationship. When therapy concludes, and one spouse decides to end what for him or her was a destructive relationship, and 1 year later he or she is happier, more fulfilled, and functioning more effectively, then for this spouse treatment was successful. But what about the other spouse, who remains depressed, suicidal, and continues to yearn for the partner? Clearly, no summative, monolithic determination of success and failure would adequately characterize this couple, or many other couples for whom there is a discrepancy between relationship enhancement and personal enhancement for one or both individuals.

A final issue complicating our efforts to determine success or failure will be graphically illustrated by our case study. With this couple, as will become apparent, treatment progress fluctuated dramatically over time, and our conclusions regarding success or failure varied depending upon *when* the assessment was made. Both clinicians and researchers tend to rely on summative evaluations of their cases at the time of termination. These termination summaries are arbitrarily and misleadingly time-bound. From the standpoint of clinical assessment and therapy, emergent and ongoing assessments that can guide future interventions are vastly preferable to such summative evaluations that can lead only to untestable post hoc speculations. Since the status of all ongoing cases at our center is reviewed each week, progress and regress are carefully monitored to maximize the possibility of capitalizing on an early assessment of potential failure. Despite our ongoing assessments, however, the therapist is not always prepared for subsequent events. In the case to be described, the couple's early positive response to treatment tended to dull the therapist's vigilance, and steps to prepare for a "relapse" were not taken. The therapist's rhythm was also disrupted by the couple's tendency to respond to severe crises by becoming instantly happy and nondistressed. Thus, even repeated measures of ongoing success are not sufficient; they somehow need to be considered within a broader, more general framework conceptualizing the couple's failure potential.

Discussion of the research dilemmas resulting from these ambiguities in determining success and failure and of their resolution is beyond the scope of this chapter (cf. Baucom, 1982). Perhaps not quite so obvious, but equally befuddling, are the dilemmas that such ambiguities impose on the clinician. The obvious caveat for the clinician is to remain flexible and idiographic in setting criteria for success and failure and to personalize treatment goals for each couple and for each spouse within each couple. But, given the plethora of possible ways to determine success and failure, the infinitely flexible therapist can unwittingly surrender his or her capacity for self-criticism. The extreme version of this unwitting self-serving bias is to define almost any outcome as successful. If the relationship improves, if the couple realizes that the marriage is hopeless and therefore divorces, if one spouse leaves therapy having expiated his or her guilt so that an extramarital affair can be resumed without conflict, or even if both spouses remain depressed and the relationship remains unchanged, but each realizes the "need" for individual therapy . . . all of these, and many other, outcomes could be viewed as successes. We suspect that many marital therapists capitalize on the ambiguity of the criteria for success and failure and thereby prevent burnout. Once this process begins the therapist ceases to be accountable to himself or herself and his or her colleagues and clients.

We offer no solutions to these definitional dilemmas. The purpose of this section has been simply to alert the reader to these ambiguities, despite our tendency to deemphasize them in subsequent discussion. In the next section we present a preliminary attempt to concretize some of the variables that interfere with successful BMT.

Factors Associated with Success and Failure in Behavioral Marital Therapy

Thus far, we have presented an overview of the rationale for and the basic techniques of BMT. We have described how BMT is supposed to work, indeed, how it often does work. The remainder of this chapter focuses on an attempt to understand why it does not work all of the time. Our discussion will focus on therapist characteristics and client characteristics that we believe are associated with failure in BMT. It may occur to the reader that a third source of variability in outcome is not directly discussed—limitations in the technological characteristics of BMT. This exclusion should not be interpreted as a conviction that BMT as it currently exists is the ideal treatment for all couples. Elsewhere, we, along with others, have considered some of the technological limitations of BMT, particularly when BMT relies excessively on the modification of overt behavior and ignores cognitive dysfunctions in distressed couples (Birchler & Spinks, 1980; Gurman & Knudsen, 1978; Epstein, 1982; Jacobson, 1984; Jacobson et al., 1984; Knudson, Gurman, & Kniskern, 1979; Weiss, 1980). We have simply chosen to focus our discussion in this chapter on failure *given* a behavioral approach. Within a BMT framework, what are the critical errors that therapists commit? What kinds of clients are particularly difficult to treat?

THERAPIST CHARACTERISTICS

The successful behavioral marital therapist must maintain a perpetual focus on two different levels. He or she is attempting to teach couples a set of skills designed to improve their relationship and at the same time to pay attention to a number of clinical issues that can ultimately determine whether or not couples will successfully *learn* and *implement* the skills they are taught. In our striving to refine and improve our treatment procedures, there is an attempt to constantly reduce the portion of the variance in outcome attributable to therapist characteristics. That is to say, we try whenever possible to overcome therapeutic pitfalls by building into the technology rules that guide the therapist's behavior. But try as we might, therapist variables continue to mediate outcome, and in any given treatment session therapists make numerous choices without the comfort of rules and guidelines.

In this section we present our hypotheses regarding the most important response classes of therapist behavior in determining the outcome of BMT. These classes were derived from an intensive analysis of cases treated at our clinical research setting by therapists in training. All couples treated in our setting are supervised by the senior author (Jacobson) in collaboration with participating staff therapists. Supervision is conducted primarily in a group setting. In addition to the group supervision sessions, Jacobson observes as many cases as possible and dictates comments onto a cassette. Transcripts of these comments are typed and distributed to therapists. These comments are then incorporated into discussions during the group supervision sessions. Minutes of each supervision meeting are kept by a research coordinator; these minutes are then typed and distributed to all therapists.

Thus, we have accumulated a huge stack of clinical tips, including an ongoing record of recurring therapist errors. These records served as our data base. Therapist errors were categorized, and from those categorizations critical dimensions were identified. These dimensions include the ability to structure treatment sessions, the ability to instigate effective change in the natural environment, the ability to teach, the ability to induce and maintain positive expectancies, the ability to provide emotional nurturance, the ability to modify cognitions that neutralize or interfere with behavior change, and the ability to balance alliances.

Structuring Treatment Sessions. Successful BMT requires highly structured therapy sessions with a directive, active therapist. In order to instruct couples in the requisite therapeutic tasks within the time-limited format, time must be used efficiently. Moreover, the therapist cannot expect spouses to collaborate at home unless collaborative behavior can be induced during the treatment session. Behavioral marital therapy includes rules that structure clients' behavior during the sessions. Therapists, however, vary in their ability to enforce rules. When couples take control of the treatment sessions, agendas do not get accomplished and destructive interaction patterns are perpetuated. A therapist can err in allowing destructive behavior to occur and not stopping it. When rules for in-session behavior are violated, spouses must be stopped. But simply stopping them is not enough. They must learn why they are being stifled, and the best way to foster such learning is to ask them, "Why am I stopping you?" Active involvement by the spouses in critiquing their own rule violations helps them maintain an awareness of the rules and teaches them to monitor and regulate their own behavior. Frequent prompts by the therapist are also helpful. For example, a therapist might remind spouses, prior to the beginning of a BE session, "remember to focus on yourself, and what you could have done to avoid this argument."

Structuring also involves maintaining vigilance across therapy sessions. The therapist must safeguard the clients' presenting problems and ensure that important issues are discussed. Although it is generally desirable for spouses to choose what problems they wish to focus on, at times the therapist will be part of this decision-making process, because spouses do not always make the best decisions. In the case to be presented, the therapist was lax in prompting the couple to focus on a major issue, and progress was retarded. A turning point came when the therapist insisted that the couple focus on this issue.

Finally, when clients do obey rules and work productively during a treatment session, they should be heartily reinforced.

Effective Instigation of Change in the Natural Environment. Ultimately, the success of BMT hinges upon the modification of interactional behavior in the home environment. The therapist who is successful only at producing desirable behavior in the therapy sessions is not successful in bringing about permanent changes in the marital relationship. In order to successfully generate change in the relationship at home, the therapist must effectively induce a collaborative set, conditions must be created to foster compliance with homework assignments, and generalization and maintenance of changes initiated during the therapy sessions must be programmed into the treatment programs.

Although there are rules to guide the therapist in all of these endeavors, their successful implementation requires considerable clinical skill.

Since distressed couples are seldom prepared to collaborate when they first enter therapy (Jacobson & Margolin, 1979), the therapist must undermine the adversary relationship by creating in both spouses a collaborative set so that therapy tactics have the opportunity to realize their potential. The development of a collaborative set is discussed in detail by Jacobson and Margolin (1979). It requires three basic sets of clinical skills. First, the therapist must provide spouses with a convincing conceptualization of their marital problems that defines them in terms of the relationship and implies mutual responsibility. Following from this conceptualization is a treatment plan requiring a bilateral commitment to behavior change, compromise, and most importantly, working together. Although it is not essential that both spouses immediately discard their adversary model in favor of this collaborative one, they must at least find it sufficiently convincing to suspend their disbelief. The therapist's model, first introduced at the conclusion of the pretreatment assessment, must then be followed consistently and resurrected whenever the spouses provide evidence that they are clinging rigidly to their adversarial perspectives. Second, the therapist must obtain from spouses a firm commitment to operate on the assumption that the therapist's model is correct. This means that spouses must behave collaboratively as defined by, for example, working to increase the partner's daily satisfaction or obeying the rules of PST. The critical component of this tactic is that therapists gain an active commitment from the spouses to adopt a collaborative repertoire, whatever initial reservations they may have about doing so. Having gained this commitment, enforcement becomes relatively easy, since noncollaborative behavior can be cited as a violation of their commitment. It is extremely important that the therapist acknowledge spouses' noncollaborative "feelings" while at the same time not justifying or excusing their noncollaborative behavior. Spouses often act as if these feelings automatically necessitate continued adversarial behavior. Some therapists have a difficult time countering spouses who excuse their behavior on the grounds that they feel mistrustful or angry. But we assume in BMT that spouses have choices in how they behave despite negative feelings. Acting on this assumption, and inducing spouses' acceptance of it, can make the difference between successful and unsuccessful therapy. Third, the therapist must ensure that positive changes occur rapidly, in the first few treatment sessions. This is the only way to effectively reinforce collaborative behavior. The early stages of BE are designed with this in mind, and the clinical skills involved are numerous (Jacobson, 1984a). Spouses must be effectively induced to provide the partner with higher rates of pleasing behavior. At the same time these behavior changes must not be perceived as costly or demanding, and a maximum amount of choice must be allowed in what behaviors are to be increased.

Pursuing and maintaining an "instigative" focus is another essential clinical skill in fostering interactional changes in the natural environment. Therapists can become excessively focused on discussing and analyzing past interactional deficiencies without producing new prescriptions. Although BE is oriented toward instigation of behavior change in the natural environment, therapists vary in their ability to maintain this focus. Distressed couples can be quite resourceful in expending time complaining and analyzing to the point where the session time has been used up without the production of a change agreement.

Homework assignments play a crucial role in BMT. Most of the important changes that occur are mediated by the enactment of homework assignments. The clinical skills involved here include the ability to choose appropriate assignments, explain these assignments clearly, gain a commitment from spouses to complete the assignment, and induce compliance with the assignment. Many therapists find it very difficult to foster compliance. In fact, their behaviors tend to encourage noncompliance. While there appears to be little evidence to support the notion of a schizophrenogenic mother, we have much reason to believe that there are noncompliantogenic therapists. A noncompliantogenic therapist presents assignments in an apologetic manner, gives only a brief and incomplete sketch of what is expected of the client, and readily accepts excuses when assignments are not completed. The following exemplify some of the tactics used by therapists who are effective in facilitating compliance: (1) Failure to comply with an assignment is treated very seriously; the therapist and client brainstorm about what interfered with task completion and about what can be done differently to insure completion of the task in the coming week. The remainder of the session is then cancelled and postponed until the following week. (2) Social reinforcement is given for effort, task completion, and skilled performances. (3) The therapist makes extensive use of the assignment during the subsequent therapy session. The therapist stresses the usefulness and value of each assignment. For example, as home data collection is first assigned, the therapist states "I'll be making a lot of use of this information. I find it functions like a seeing eye dog for me. I'm blind without it, so it is necessary that you complete the forms every day and that you do them carefully." (4) The therapist calls to collect assignment information during the week. (5) The clients can keep a notebook or diary that includes all of their assignments and progress. This functions like a personal record of the effort and changes they are making as a couple. (6) The therapist predicts in advance problems the couples will have in completing measures and assignments, thus anticipating and thereby neutralizing aversive reactions. (7) The therapist makes the contingencies clear; the next phase of therapy does not begin until the assessment is completed. (8) The therapist makes sure the clients understand each assignment. This is accomplished by having the clients describe their assignments to the therapist before leaving the session, as well as by writing down the assignments in their diary.

Finally, BMT is structured so that couples acquire the capability to maintain a satisfying relationship without having to reenter therapy in the future. Strategies for generalization are programmed. Nevertheless, a therapist is required to implement the program, and therapists differ in their ability to foster autonomy on the part of their couples. There seems to be a trade off between directiveness during the time of active treatment and the fostering of autonomous skill in couples that is sufficient to sustain progress subsequent to the termination of therapy. During the skill acquisition phase, the therapist is required to be directive, but the highly skilled therapist begins to fade his or her directiveness once the skills are acquired and focuses subsequently on generalization and maintenance. The clinical skills seem to manifest themselves in striking a balance between sufficient directiveness and in knowing when and how to fade the directiveness and remove couples' more effective functioning from the stimulus control of the therapist's influence. Specific maintenance–enhancement strategies are beyond the scope of this chapter, but they include fading, booster sessions, ensuring that the spouses extract general principles from the treatment sessions and are not simply responding to the therapist's behavior change prompts, and the establishment of "maintenance and enhancement" sessions in the home as a substitute for therapy sessions.

Teaching. In BMT the therapist is a teacher. The therapist who simply prompts interactional changes may be helping spouses in the short run, but is not adhering to the skill-training focus of BMT. When couples terminate from BMT, they should know how to problem solve effectively, be able to conduct a behavioral analysis to maintain the delivery of high rates of reinforcing behaviors, and be able to effectively pinpoint future problem areas—to list just a few of the skills that we hope become internalized during the course of therapy. In addition to the steps taken to foster generalization and maintenance, the BMT teacher is constantly moving from the specific to the general and back to the specific. As we mentioned in a previous section, when spouses are presented with feedback, this feedback should be connected with a principle. For example, "Okay, that was too vague. I want you to try and be more specific. Remember, it is always important to state your complaints specifically in behavioral terms. This leads to clear communication and it will also keep your spouse from becoming defensive."

Notice in the previous example that not only was a principle stated but a rationale was provided for the principle. Bad therapists are shy when it comes to repetition. It is easy to overestimate spouses' capacity to process information in the treatment session. Rules and guidelines, along with rationales for these guidelines, must be repeated whenever the opportunity arises. As we have already mentioned, active involvement on the part of spouses facilitates their acquisition of principles. For example, after the therapist has modeled a particular skill, it is often worthwhile to debrief the modeling episode, having the spouses produce the rationale for the modeled behavior and actively participate in the discussion of its advantages. As another example, typically at the conclusion of a problem-solving session, spouses are encouraged to reflect back on what they have learned about problem solving.

Like all effective teaching exercises, the BMT instructor must state things clearly, with a minimum of psychological jargon, and the interventions must be succinct. Although these reminders might seem elementary, we have found that they are among the most frequently violated of the guidelines mentioned in this section. Inexperienced or unskillful therapists are prone to engage in long-winded monologues that would be abtruse even to a colleague let alone our clients.

Inducing and Maintaining Positive Expectancies. If spouses are not optimistic about the ultimate outcome of marital therapy, they are unlikely to behave collaboratively during the therapy sessions, and they are less likely to adequately comply with homework assignments (Jacobson & Margolin, 1979). Many of the principles already discussed, if implemented properly, foster positive outcome expectancies. At the same time this ability is among the most subtle of all clinical skills in BMT, and we believe that this ability accounts for a great proportion of the individual differences in therapist performance. What makes this such a difficult skill is the necessity of simultaneously instilling optimism while at the same time tempering this optimism so that it is not unrealistic. If clients expect miracles, they may become passive and simply await the "cure." If therapy does not progress as smoothly as clients are led to believe, they may become demoralized.

As Jacobson and Margolin (1979) have recommended, verbalized optimism at the onset of therapy, buttressed by the brief mention of experimental evidence on the efficacy of BMT, is crucial for the establishment of positive expectancies. However, it must be made clear that positive changes are likely to occur only if the spouses adopt a collaborative set and dedicate themselves to a sustained effort to improve their relationship. It is bad therapy to foster the impression that the therapist is responsible for these potential benefits.

Along these lines, spouses must be prepared for the crises and downward spirals that often occur along the jagged path toward relationship enhancement. Progress is seldom linear in BMT. Unless the therapist provides spouses in advance with warnings regarding these typical "relapses," spouses are likely to discard their positive outcome expectancies when regressive periods occur. These downward spirals are particularly common when the focus shifts from BE to PST, since problem-solving skills are difficult to acquire and PST usually coincides with the tackling of central or core issues in the relationship. Especially when the early phases of therapy are successful, couples must be warned about the difficulty of PST and the likely reversal of progress at the onset of PST.

At times, in order to foster positive expectancies, the skillful therapist will make predictions that little or no progress should be expected in the short run. For example, when the focus in therapy is either exclusively or partially PST, and the first few sessions are spent acquiring skills using hypothetical conflicts, spouses should not expect improvement in their relationship during the early sessions. If they are not reminded of this repeatedly, they may become demoralized because no concrete relief from their suffering is being derived. Moreover, they also need to be reminded of the rationale for beginning PST with a focus on hypothetical problems. Otherwise, they may develop the view that therapy is not meeting their concerns. Let us reemphasize that frequent repetitions of these reminders are necessary; there is virtually no risk attached to overkill, but great risk attached to underemphasis. It should be added that often benefits do occur during this phase; the commitment to learning these new skills can in and of itself provide spouses with improved feelings about the relationship. If such improvements do occur, so much the better; however, in case no direct improvement occurs during this phase, positive expectancies will remain intact only if no improvement was expected.

It also pays to emphasize that no improvement should be expected during the pretreatment assessment. Although the distinction between assessment and therapy is clear to therapists, it cannot be assumed that it is clear to clients. Once again, improvements are often obtained during the assessment phase; indeed, the assessment is structured to foster improvement while information is being gathered. If improvement does occur, so much the better. Either way, positive expectancies are better fostered by a "counterdemand manipulation."

One particularly important facet of inducing positive expectancies concerns the level of enthusiasm manifested by the therapist regarding the approach. This aspect of therapist skill is particularly difficult to describe or teach, because it involves the nuances of interpersonal style. The therapist must sell the couple on the model of therapy, and his or her excitement and enthusiasm about the potential of the treatment program *for them* is an essential prerequisite to their "buying into" the paradigm. If the therapist does not display optimism, or if this optimism is not sufficiently resilient in the face of the normal ups and downs of marital therapy, spouses' optimism will surely waver as well. This optimism and enthusiasm for the approach lends an upbeat quality to the therapy sessions, and without it, the therapy sessions lose their vitality, and become "depressing" to all of the participants—spouses and therapist alike. This consistent enthusiasm includes an ability to effectively counter spouses' reservations about their progress or about the approach during the course of therapy. For example, spouses often equivocate around the mechanical nature of the therapeutic tasks. The therapist must remind spouses that these admittedly mechanical tasks, while in conflict with the romantic ideal of spontaneity that all of us strive for in intimate relationships, is a necessary expedient to relationship enhancement. Old habitual behavior patterns are not easily extinguished, and in the service of making the new, more desirable behaviors habitual and automatic, the seemingly mechanical approach is necessary. Most of our couples can be reassured by such cognitive interventions, but if the interventions are not forthcoming their absence is likely to create serious obstacles to the success of the treatment program. Along with enthusiasm and the active debunking of spouses' reservations, the ability to inject levity and humor into the sessions is highly facilitative. Therapy is hard work, and spouses are prone to approach the tasks with earnestness and sobriety. There is, however, often a lighter, more humorous side to marital problems, and the therapist who can induce some laughter can help mitigate the frequent negative emotional response to these important relationship issues being discussed.

Providing Emotional Nurturance. With a treatment regimen that is as highly structured as BMT, there is always the danger that the therapist will "overregulate." The dangers of "underregulating" notwithstanding, effective BMT requires that the therapist provide sufficient latitude and flexibility that the clients do not experience emotional frustration. The credibility of the therapist and the treatment program can be safeguarded only to the extent that clients are allowed affective expression. This expression includes not only a positive emotional response to the treatment procedures themselves, but also an opportunity to communicate to the therapist the depth and variety of feelings that each spouse has to therapy as well as to the partner during the course of therapy.

One major aspect of this emotional nurturance involves the frequent taking of each spouse's "affective temperature." Periodically during the course of therapy, the therapist should make contact with the clients to ascertain their degree of emotional involvement in therapy and their reactions to the changes that are occurring in therapy. First, during our roundtable or interpretive session, when the therapist presents to the couple his or her perspective on the problems in the relationship, these formulations must be carefully "cleared" with each spouse. In other words, the therapist must actively check out his or her perceptions with each spouse and be prepared to respond to their disagreements, reservations, and misgivings regarding what the therapist is saying. Second, throughout the sessions, the therapist must be attentive to the clients' nonverbal responses to the events of therapy. When the apparent affective response does not seem commensurate with the events, the therapist must do some probing. For example, one spouse remained relatively bland and unexcited despite the occurrence of an agreement that seemed to solve the client's major concern about the marriage. The alert therapist commented on the discrepancy between the importance of the event and the absence of an emotional response, to which the client admitted to incredulity regarding the effectiveness of the agreement. If the therapist had not been attentive to the client's emotional state, the agreement would have remained unaltered, and the client would have been dissatisfied, unbeknownst to the therapist. Third, the therapist must engage in frequent "search and destroy" missions, by frequently inquiring how each spouse is reacting to therapy. In this way concerns, reservations, and equivocal reactions can be ferreted out and subjected to cognitive interventions.

In addition to tracking clients' emotional responses during the course of therapy, the therapist must avoid repudiating or disqualifying a spouse's strong emotional reactions that are not conducive to collaboration. Here the therapist must, on the one hand, demonstrate that he or she understands the spouse's feelings while at the same time not allowing those feelings to serve as an excuse for noncollaborative behavior. One of many common examples of this dual role occurs when clients express anger and frustration and then attempt to justify noncollaborative behavior on that basis. If the therapist cuts off prematurely, or in other ways disallows the venting of these feelings, the client is likely to feel even more frustrated and may disengage from therapy. Feelings can be allowed adequate expression and then acknowledged by the therapist without detracting from the continued emphasis on collaboration.

Modifying Cognitions That Neutralize or Interfere with Behavior Change. Many of the specific clinical tips outlined in this section fall within the realm of cognitive restructuring interventions. Although there has been little systematic focus in the BMT literature on relabeling strategies, these strategies comprise an important part of the treatment program (Jacobson & Margolin, 1979). For example, spouses are often upset by their partners' behavior because of the meaning they ascribe to the commission or omission of the behavior, the causal attributions they impose upon it, or the motivational inferences they derive from it. In short, the problem often lies in the cognitive inferences about behaviors, rather than the behaviors themselves (Doherty, 1981a, 1981b; Epstein, 1982; Jacobson, 1978c; Weiss, 1980). Relabeling those behaviors in a more positive light can often serve a valuable therapeutic function. Once the client can generate alternative interpretations for a displeasing behavior, the behavior is often experienced as less displeasing. Moreover, even if the need for behavior change remains after such a cognitive explanation, there is often less emotional intensity attached to the behavior, and problem solutions are more easily negotiated.

We are now in the process of building a more systematic cognitive therapy component into our BMT treatment package. A cognitive therapy component allows for explorations of the meaning of particular displeasing behaviors. Within the context of a conjoint marital therapy session, the therapist can engage in a dialogue with one spouse to uncover the assumptions or perceptions underlying a particular behavioral concern. Once the underlying assumptions are exposed, they can be examined as to their validity. At this point feedback can be obtained from the other spouse regarding the accuracy of those cognitions. As we have already mentioned, such an exploration can often decrease the negative valence of a particular problem behavior. Cognitive strategies such as this one can also prove to be enlightening for the spouse who is listening to the dialogue, since he or she is aided in understanding the basis for the partner's concern about the behavior in question. In some cases such an exploration will preempt the normal problem-solving procedures. In other cases the exploration simply provides information to be taken into account in subsequent negotiations.

In general we are moving in the direction of trying to balance the focus on individual change with the focus on behavior change in the marital relationship. When one spouse is concerned about a particular behavior on the part of the other, the therapist and the couple have many options. Thus far, BMT has emphasized behavior change. But another option is for a balance between cognitive change on the part of the concerned spouse, and behavior change on the part of the transgressing spouse. There is nothing incompatible with dual goals of focusing on individuals and focusing on a dyad. After all, relationships are made up of two individual spouses, and effective marital therapy promotes only those relationship changes that are consistent with what is best for the two individuals making up the marital dyad.

Balancing Alliances. In our view it is both naive and unnecessary to strive for the avoidance of individual alliances with one spouse or the other. Inevitably, marital therapy involves shifting alliances and periods where one spouse needs particular support from the therapist. Alliances with one spouse are perfectly acceptable, and even therapeutic, as long as the balance is maintained across sessions. Therapists often err not by forming alliances, but by failing to insure that these alliances shift when appropriate.

Two examples in our recent case load help illustrate the importance of providing particular spouses with additional support from the therapist. In one case there was a notable discrepancy between the spouses in their ability to acquire problem-solving skills. The therapist dealt with this problem by temporarily aligning himself with the less-skilled partner (the wife). This alliance took the form of statements such as, "I often have problems being specific and sticking to these rules myself." In another recent case, a very distressed couple underwent a crisis during the course of therapy involving the husband losing his job. Their need for support shifted depending on the session. At times the wife appeared unsympathetic and unsupportive of the husband's reduced self-esteem subsequent to the job loss, and it became important that the therapist provide him with support. To do otherwise would have jeopardized the therapist's relationship with the husband, and it also would have deprived her of an opportunity to model the importance of being supportive during threats to one spouse's self-esteem. There were other times, however, when the wife was particularly frightened by the impending financial crisis, and she needed support from the therapist.

In summary, there is always a temptation for the therapist to align oneself with a particular spouse in marital therapy. It is rare that the sympathies of the therapist are mutually balanced between spouses. This is a particular danger when one member is in a one-down position. In this case our predilections are likely to lead to sympathy with the underdog. Therefore, it is important that the therapist track his or her own behavior carefully and make sure that the therapeutic alliance with both spouses is not jeopardized by a skewed focus on and an identification with one spouse at the expense of the other. With the therapist maintaining a truly dyadic focus, there is a greater likelihood that empathy with both spouses will be maintained.

Conclusion. This set of categories is not meant to be exhaustive, nor are the categories designed to be mutually exclusive; some dimensions are overlapping, and many of our specific therapist errors seemed to belong in two or three categories. The next step in our analysis of the relationship between therapist factors and treatment failure is to develop an observational coding system based on the preceding set of categories. Such a coding system will allow for sequential analyses of therapist–client interaction during therapy sessions, thus enabling researchers to study interactional therapy process as it relates to both emergent and ultimate outcome measures. The following section deals with client characteristics associated with failure in BMT.

CLIENT CHARACTERISTICS

Although there are very few couples who do not present challenges to even an experienced couples therapist, there are recurring patterns in client and couple characteristics that present hurdles to improving distressed relationships. At times a severe behavioral or emotional problem in one individual is the primary obstacle. In other cases, although there is no significant psychopathology manifested by one or both individuals, existing relationship patterns make therapy particularly difficult. Although the purpose of this section is not to provide an exhaustive list of client or dyadic characteristics that make relationship improvement more difficult to foster via BMT, we will mention some of the common patterns that have posed problems for us. They should be thought of simply as dimensions that create obstacles, and thereby are likely to be associated with negative outcomes.

Severe Behavioral or Emotional Problems in One Spouse. Marital relationships where one spouse is acutely psychotic provide serious obstacles to successful BMT. By acutely psychotic, we refer to acute schizophrenia, acute manic states, or severe, incapacitating depression. With regard to depression some important diagnostic considerations determine indications or contraindications for BMT. If one spouse is severely depressed primarily as a consequence of problems in the relationship, then marital therapy may be the treatment of choice. On the other hand, when the depression is either endogenous or attributable to factors outside the relationship, marital therapy is at best an adjunct treatment. That is to say, any severe psychopathology in one spouse has consequences for the relationship, and it is well known that marital distress is often a concomitant of such severe behavioral or emotional disturbances. However, the question here is whether BMT is to be the primary treatment modality. It is our view that BMT is to serve as the primary treatment modality only when an affective disorder in one individual is thought to be primarily a *consequence* of relationship problems.

Acute substance abuse problems in one spouse also contraindicate BMT in our view. Once again, although distressed relationships almost always accompany marriages where one spouse is a substance abuser, and therefore marital therapy is often indicated, the primary treatment for the individual in question will not be marital therapy. Until the substance abuse is under control, BMT will not or is not likely to progress as it normally would. Our typical recommendation in such an instance is individual therapy until the substance abuse is under control, followed often by marital therapy.

Finally, severe intellectual deficiencies in one or both spouses may contraindicate BMT. In our experience level of education is usually not a factor, although when couples have less than a high-school education we often have to tailor the program, particularly problem-solving training, to their more limited degree of intellectual sophistication.

Difficult-to-Treat Couples with No Significant Individual Psychopathology. Many of the factors that can be subsumed under the category "couple characteristics" militate against successful treatment. These factors do not necessarily render couples untreatable, but often pose particular problems to marital therapists and require some special modification of the treatment plan. One type of couple that is difficult to treat is the couple where spouses have differing agendas regarding the desirable outcome of therapy. If one spouse has already decided to end the marriage, BMT in the form described in this chapter is not viable. Behavioral marital therapy can be conducted when one or both spouses are uncertain as to the future of the relationship, but when one spouse has already decided to end the marriage, no amount of motivation on the part of the other spouse can overcome this decision. The best course of action with such couples is either individual therapy with the spouse who remains committed to the marriage, or conjoint divorce counseling. Unfortunately, at times such an agenda remains hidden despite lengthy individual and conjoint assessment sessions. Behavioral marital therapy that is conducted despite the discrepancies in the desirable therapeutic outcome is unlikely to be successful. A second category of couples who are difficult to treat with BMT are those in which one or both spouses simply refuse to buy into the philosophical underpinnings of the treatment program. We might add that this is a very rare couple: even couples who are negatively disposed toward a behavioral approach can often be convinced that treatment is worthwhile because it focuses on the present and therefore seems highly practical to them. At times, however, the world view of one or both spouses is simply antagonistic to our world view. Verbal exhortations notwithstanding, such couples tend to be highly refractory to successful treatment.

Behavioral marital therapy assumes that spouses have some reinforcement value for one another, at least in potential. Therefore, a third category of couples who are difficult to treat with BMT are those who have married despite possessing little reinforcement value for one another. With these couples the problem is not reinforcement erosion but rather that their reasons for coming together had little to do with their ability to gratify one another, even during the initial courtship phase of their relationship. There are many reasons for spouses choosing one another, and unfortunately not all of them involve either initial attraction or an ability to provide one another with gratification. One of our recent cases involved a couple where the partners married because the wife was pregnant, despite the fact that the two had spent little time together and had little basis for assessing their ability to sustain an intimate relationship over a long period of time. In previous generations couples often came together despite deficiencies in their ability to provide one another with gratification, and the social and legal constraints against divorce were often sufficient to sustain them over a lifetime despite this insufficient gratification. Nowadays, with the legal and social stigmas of divorce largely removed, couples are less inclined to remain in unsatisfying marriages. In these cases one could argue that successful marital therapy might involve the decision to separate, since the possibilities for happiness and fulfillment in both partners are likely to be enhanced in alternative relationships. But if one insists upon a definition of treatment success involving a significant improvement in the satisfaction level of both partners, this type of couple is high-risk for failure in BMT.

The fourth category describes couples who—despite a great deal of initial attraction and gratification—during the course of the marital life cycle change in directions that are incompatible with sustained marital satisfaction. At times these discrepant changes involve alterations in their individual goals for happiness in life, such that to stay together would mean that one or both would have to sacrifice these individual goals beyond a level that is tolerable to one or both of them. One fairly common example of this problem involves discrepancies regarding the desire to bear children. Spouses are often uncertain when they marry regarding whether or not to have children; if this decision-making process diverges within a relationship, and one spouse strongly desires children while the other comes to the decision that children are not desirable, it is difficult to resolve this discrepancy within a BMT model. Another example involves changing goals for the marital relationship. During the 1970s it was not uncommon for wives to grow dissatisfied with traditional marriages despite an initial marriage contract calling for a fairly stereotypic division of roles and responsibilities. With the onset of the Women's Movement, many women grew dissatisfied with these traditional marriage contracts and began to desire relationships where the sex roles were balanced and more flexible. Conflict was inevitable with such couples, and its resolution depended upon one or both partners adjusting their expectations to these changing values.

Related to this fourth category are couples who were initially strongly attached and attracted to one another, but during the course of their marriage one partner repeatedly engages in behaviors that are experienced as very painful and malicious by their partner. Over time, the "victim," often female, develops interpersonal distance and barriers to experiencing fond feelings. The hurt partner, while aware of not having lost the initial love, harbors intense past resentments that repeatedly interfere with progress in marital therapy but may facilitate personal growth and independence. One couple we recently worked with, Sally and Darrell, clearly fit this pattern. He had several secretive affairs during his working hours, some of which she discovered. During Darrell's most recent affair, his mistress convinced him to get a vasectomy and posed as his wife in signing related papers. When this affair ended she telephoned Sally asking how her husband was recovering from his vasectomy. To Sally the vasectomy was unforgivable, since she is young and having her own family meant a great deal to her. Another example of this fifth category involves a history in which one partner's change requests go unanswered. This partner, again usually female, also develops barriers and has difficulty accepting and positively receiving change efforts that begin during marital therapy. For example, the wife of one couple we are currently seeing has unsuccessfully requested specific changes—such as more foreplay before intercourse and more companionship—for 25 years. As the husband now expends considerable effort to change and be responsive, she has great difficulty lowering her barriers and trusting that his change is sincere and lasting.

A sixth category of couples who are difficult to treat involves those where there is a large discrepancy in optimal level of intimacy desired in a relationship. This problem is discussed in detail by Jacobson and Margolin (1979) and will only be briefly discussed here. The problem involves two spouses where there is a major and substantial difference in the extent to which reinforcement in life is provided through intimacy in a relationship. In the extreme case one spouse places a great deal of importance in interpersonal activities for the provision of gratification, while the other focuses on independent activities for the provision of gratification. Whether these are consistent personality trait differences or differences largely induced by relationship dynamics, these differences tend to be self-perpetuating and almost inevitably create severe conflict. Although these preferences are reversible, and spouses can be successfully treated within a BMT framework despite this problem, in some sense these couples provide a special case of the category in which spouses change in different directions. In this case one spouse desires a great deal more intimacy than the other, and one spouse's preference for a certain amount of distance is in conflict with the other's preference for more sustained closeness and intimacy. Thus, the goals for marital therapy within each spouse are often divergent, and therefore finding a successful compromise that will be satisfactory to both partners is difficult.

When the escalation of aversive control has reached the point where physical abuse has begun to occur in the relationship, a standard BMT treatment often encounters major hurdles. Although we do not believe that spouse abuse is a qualitatively different problem than any other presenting marital problem, the level of punishment is so great in such relationships that it is often irreversible. Moreover, once physical abuse has begun to occur in a relationship, the duties and obligations of a marital therapist often demand that the focus be on protecting the abused spouse (usually the wife) from the abusive spouse. Although one or both spouses may ultimately benefit from such a focus, the treatment often involves something other than BMT in its usual format (Jacobson & Margolin, 1979).

Finally, we have had occasion to treat couples with an accumulation of many years of marital distress. When couples have been married for over 20 years, have developed very stable patterns of aversive interaction, and perceive few alternative relationships available from which to choose, the patterns of interaction are difficult to impact. Such couples, often referred to as having "stable–unsatisfactory" marriages, seldom seek therapy. We manage to find such couples because of our outreach program and our frequent media advertising.

The characteristic of these couples that makes them so difficult to treat is their unwillingness to end the relationship, regardless of the outcome of therapy. They have often made the decision to stay together even if the relationship does not improve, and therefore they are lacking in the desperation so often found in younger couples who view themselves as having options.

This section has been a brief overview of some of the client and dyadic characteristics that present obstacles, although surmountable, to successfully working with distressed couples from a cognitive–behavioral perspective. Once again, it must be emphasized that we have successfully treated couples in all of these categories, and therefore none of them serve as absolute contraindications for BMT. However, they all present obstacles to treatment. Conjoint marital therapy is challenging with all distressed couples. Ultimately, what is needed are detailed clinical descriptions of efforts at struggling with the hurdles as well as an empirically based set of predictor variables involving demographic characteristics, behavioral profiles of individual spouses, and dyadic combinations, which collectively might remove ideas about treatability from the realm of speculation to the arena of experimentally validated facts.

We have chosen to describe the treatment course of Jack and Jane for a number of reasons. They were an ongoing case at the time this chapter was invited, and therefore we were given the opportunity to analyze prospectively rather than retrospectively. Second, they represent neither a clear-cut success nor a clear-cut failure, although a case could be made for either one, depending upon which criterion one chooses to adopt. Thus, this case illustrates some of the definitional ambiguities alluded to earlier. Third, the case illustrates the elusive nature of clinical prediction, since they initially presented none of the poor prognostic signs that typically arouse our pessimism regarding the outcome of a case. The difficult course of treatment was a surprise, although our retrospective analysis was able to accommodate the unexpected turn of events.

Background

Jack, 34 years old, and Jane, 28 years old, had been married for 3 years at the time they sought treatment. They were both intelligent, middle-class, and physically attractive. They seemed to have a basically happy, loving relationship, and most of the attention during the pretreatment assessment was devoted to ascertaining exactly why they sought treatment. On our pretreatment questionnaires their scores placed them in the normal, happily married range. They pinpointed very few concerns about the relationship. The data they provided based on their at-home interaction revealed mostly positive exchanges and uniformly high daily satisfaction ratings. During the early assessment and therapy sessions, they laughed and joked with the therapist, and were attentive and responsive to one another.

Their primary complaint was "a lack of communication." Jane complained, and Jack agreed, that he seldom disclosed personal feelings. When conflict occurred over day-to-day events, Jack tended to withdraw, while Jane would get extremely angry and "lose her temper." She felt rejected by his withdrawal and he was frightened by her anger. Secondly, Jane had felt lonely and isolated since they had moved to Seattle, which had been 1 year earlier. During the past year she had been a housewife and mother (they had a 3-year-old son, Willie) while he was employed in a semiprofessional position. This problem seemed on the verge of elimination since she began a new job just as therapy began.

Two additional issues emerged soon after she began to work outside the home. She began to complain that he was neither encouraging her nor showing interest in her new job. Although he denied this, he did express chagrin over the fact that her job "put them in a higher tax bracket." He also admitted to "turning up the stereo" when she would begin to relate stories to him about her day at work. Now that she was working, she expected him to share the household tasks with her. He expressed a willingness to do so but had not taken any initiative in that area. She insisted that he should not wait for her to tell him what needed to be done.

These presenting problems could be viewed in part as continuations of patterns that had begun in each of their families of origin. Jack's mother had a long-standing bipolar affective disorder characterized by recurrent manic episodes. As a result family life focused on her, particularly during her manic episodes, at which time she was extremely "hard to control" and "emotional." In the marriage, Jack was emotionally distant and extremely reluctant to express emotions; he was also afraid of Jane's emotional expressiveness. It is probable that both of those tendencies were based on early learning history, where emotional expressiveness was associated with chaos and disorganization and women were emotional and out of control, requiring both appeasement and subordination of his own affective tendencies.

The passivity exhibited by Jack in regard to taking initiative around the house was characteristic of him. There was a boyish vulnerability to him, and a maternal quality to the way Jane treated him. To give but one example, she would dry his hair for him, with an electric hair dryer, every morning. Jane was accustomed to being maternal. Her mother died when she was very young, and from that point on Jane assumed a maternal role relative to her brothers and her father. She viewed herself as having no choice in the assumption of this role, and she automatically fell into a similar position with respect to her husband. She resented having to take care of her husband and she tended to be hypersensitive to what she perceived as demands from him for excessive nurturance. Although her maternal role made her angry, and she made periodic protests accompanied by efforts to break out of it, she was also accustomed to it and comfortable in it.

Diagnosis and Treatment Plan

The pretreatment assessment led us to predict a relatively smooth path for Jack and Jane toward relationship improvement. Treatment was to focus on communication training, emphasizing both PST and helping Jack learn to disclose personal feelings. They seemed to be seeking an enrichment experience, and they stood in stark contrast to most of the couples who were treated in our clinic in that they appeared to be highly collaborative and basically committed to the marriage. Jane mentioned during the assessment that she had considered divorce or separation on occasion, but that these had only been fleeting considerations, and she seemed basically committed to the marriage. Although this mentioning of divorce seemed not to fit with all of the other data, we did not take it too seriously given that everything else suggested a good prognosis.

Process of Therapy

The first few treatment sessions had a distinctly upbeat quality to them. They came to the sessions in good spirits and both brought in data that suggested consistently happy days. Jack insisted that the commitment to therapy and the collection of data in the home had made them particularly aware of and attentive to one another. After spending the first few treatment sessions mastering the skills of PST, they began to tackle problems in their relationship. These were handled smoothly and collaboratively, with resultant change agreements that were, for the most part, successfully implemented.

Periodically, the therapist attempted to broach the issue of Jack being unwilling to express negative feelings. This discussion never progressed very far, as he would either deny that he had negative feelings or insist that they were irrational and best handled on his own. Similarly, during the early PST sessions, Jack's typical response to Jane's complaints was to immediately give in and agree to change in the way she wanted. Although the therapist would encourage mutuality and bilateral change, Jack continued to be cooperative almost to the point of docility. Indeed, he seldom complained about anything. As a result, therapy sessions were characterized by her bringing up complaints about him, and Jack agreeing to change. On those few occasions during the early sessions when he did venture a complaint, usually in response to therapist prompts, Jane tended to be *unreceptive*. On one occasion, he complained that she was "grumpy in the morning" and she countercomplained that she had too much to do in the morning for him to expect her to be "affectionate." In other words, she angrily tossed the problem back in his face, and he ended up agreeing to help Willie get up in the morning, without any commitment from her to convert "grumpiness" into "affection." A week later, he brought up her driving as a problem. She adamantly insisted that there was nothing wrong with her driving, and he ended up agreeing to cease his criticism.

The first eight sessions of therapy followed a relatively smooth course. For the most part homework assignments were being completed, change agreements were being reached, problem-solving skills were being acquired, and both Jack and Jane were reporting increased satisfaction. Beginning with the 9th treatment session, Jane enacted what was to be the first of a series of angry outbursts. There were three such outbursts: one during the 9th session, one during the 12th, and one during the 15th. In each case the outburst would begin in response to an apparently minor issue, but would quickly generalize to widespread and sweeping complaints about the relationship and about Jack. Finally, in each instance, Jane would conclude that he did not care about her, and that real intimacy between them was hopeless. During her outbursts he would remain sullen and withdrawn.

There was a striking cyclical pattern to the three incidents. The themes characterizing each crisis were similar, and each time the outburst was followed by an apparently complete recovery. All three crises were precipitated by Jack's behavior in regard to some third party. In each case Jane interpreted his behavior toward this third party as indicating that he did not care about her. All precipitating events involved Jack failing to assert himself to Jane's satisfaction. This would lead to her concluding that he cared more about others' feelings than about her own, and finally, that he did not care about her. Following each crisis, the couple would report to therapy the following week exhibiting signs of complete recovery. They reported that everything was fine once again, the significance of the conflict was minimized, and both partners seemed less than eager to discuss the crisis.

Rather than detailing the facts of each outburst, one example will suffice. The agenda for session nine consisted of deescalating the minor quarrels that seemed to occur about once each day. The focus was to be on developing a strategy for diffusion and deescalation. As an example they discussed a recent quarrel regarding Jack's co-worker, Bertrand. Jack had agreed to be best man at Bertrand's wedding, and in doing so turned down the opportunity to work overtime. Jane dislikes Bertrand, and was irritated that her husband was willing to forego work for Bertrand but not for a mutual friend who had been visiting them the previous weekend. The issue for Jane was not the money: To her this incident suggested that, "Jack chooses his friends over my feelings." The therapist was unable to divert her back to the process issue of quarrel escalation; whenever the therapist suggested that volatile issues should not be discussed at the scene of the crime but at prescheduled problem-solving sessions, Jane would respond, "putting off the discussion will not make the problem go away." The therapist attempted to point out that postponing the discussion was not designed to "make the problem go away" but to place them at some emotional distance from the problem so that when it was discussed they would be more likely to collaborate and use the rules of PST. Unfortunately, this point did not register with Jane.

Halfway through the session Jane burst into tears, crying out, "I don't want to have anything to do with Bertrand and I'm not even sure that I want to be around my husband anymore." She then proceeded to complain that Jack never showed interest in her work and was "afraid" of her becoming independent. She expressed bitterness that he responded to her career initiatives by complaining about the higher tax bracket. He answered her by insisting, "I'm a man. I have to be practical." The therapist reminded Jane that therapy was proceeding on the assumption that Jack could change, and that he had already provided considerable evidence of a willingness to change. But Jane replied, "I'm not sure I want to stay around that long." The session ended with the future of therapy uncertain and both Jack and Jane demoralized.

The following week they came to therapy as if nothing unusual had happened the week before. Jane had composed herself and had returned to her normal shy, cooperative therapy session style. The therapist simply put them back to work. No debriefing was done of the previous session. No inquiry was conducted to determine how Jack and Jane were feeling or how they had responded to the previous session during the interim period. The therapist allowed the spouses to determine the problem they were to discuss during the session. They chose the less volatile areas of household chores and child management.

The second crisis session followed an attempt on the part of the couple to terminate therapy. According to Jack, the decision was based on Jane being "in a bad place" right now. The therapist explained that even if they had decided to terminate, it was the clinic policy to discuss such a proposal "in person," and she urged that they have at least one more session to "wrap things up." Jack agreed to one more meeting. Later in the week the therapist also made contact with Jane, who insisted that her main reason for wanting to terminate was that "nothing was being accomplished." But she also agreed to come in for a "termination session."

At the onset of the "termination" session, the therapist learned that a second third-party crisis had precipitated the termination decision. The therapist was very straightforward with them, practically insisting that they not terminate: "I would be very concerned about letting the two of you go now. I think that it would be a big mistake, and I would not be doing my job if I simply went along with your decision." The therapist persistently countered Jane's complaints that "There's no communication: I'm taking all of the responsibility myself," by insisting, "The treatment program has not gotten there yet; you are quitting right at the time when this thing could have been helpful. It is an 18-session program and these last 4 sessions are the most important ones."

The therapist countered Jane's complaints regarding lack of sufficient change from Jack by pointing out that her expectations were unrealistic given that the most important sessions were still to come. Jane kept repeating the refrain that Jack had not changed, that he was not trying, that she was doing all of the work. The therapist seemed to accept Jane's indictment of Jack, but then went on to focus on one of her major, recurring complaints. The focus shifted to a direct confrontation of the "communication" problem, the most sustained and focused discussion of the communication problem that had occurred up until that time. Although no formal agreement was reached, many ideas were put forth specifying the changes that would need to be made before Jane would feel that Jack wanted to be intimate with her. The therapist dealt with Jane's concerns about any agreed-upon changes being "artificial" by pointing out that "Changes always seem artificial and forced at first. Only later after they become habits do they occur naturally." Moreover, the therapist told Jane, in a message that was directed toward Jack, that she should avoid taking responsibility for enforcing these new communication patterns, "Just watch him to see what he does. Let it go and give him a chance."

Jack worked very hard during the ensuing week, communicating with Jane in a way that was impressive to her. They entered the therapy session the following week reporting that they had been talking about her work, that Jack had been showing interest and support and "really listening" to her, and that he had been consistently implementing their change agreements. However, 2 weeks later, the third and final crisis session occurred. As in the previous crisis sessions, it was unclear to what extent Jack had actually "relapsed," and to what extent Jane was overreacting and drawing unwarranted inferences regarding the implications of Jack's behavior. The couple responded to this crisis as they had in past crises, with a renewed commitment by Jack and an apparently complete recovery.

It was at this point, following their third recovery, that the time limit for therapy had been reached (18 sessions). Although an extention of therapy was an option, Jack and Jane wanted to terminate. This time the therapist did not try to dissuade them. This last session was full of optimism and distinctly upbeat. Jack had been extremely responsive to Jane's requests for assertiveness during the third crisis. In addition he had begun to talk about his feelings, particularly satisfactions and frustrations that he was experiencing on the job. Jane was pleased that he had begun to talk intimately with her, and the only question remaining for her was whether or not these changes would continue.

There was a follow-up session 1 month later, and then a posttest 2 weeks after that. By the time of the follow-up session, 7 weeks had elapsed since the last crisis. No new problems had occurred. In fact, both spouses reported that the positive changes had continued, and Jane expressed renewed confidence that they would endure. These changes included the following: Jack was now expressing feelings regularly; he had become a better listener and, at least on a behavioral level, seemed much more accepting of her career aspirations; they had perfected and were utilizing their problem solving skills, so that instead of dealing with conflict by bickering and quarrelling they resolved issues as they arose in a constructive manner; change agreements had stabilized minor disputes in regard to child management and household responsibilities. Their discussions of the recurring conflicts regarding third parties had resulted in an understanding that had not really been tested since the third crisis. This third-party issue was Jane's main residual concern. Perhaps most importantly, Jack verbalized considerable insight into the importance of sharing feelings or concerns with his wife, and showing her that he cared about her as a human being independently of her ability to take care of him. This meant demonstrating empathy and support for her aspirations outside the home and potentiating her freedom to pursue such aspirations by relieving her of the full burden of domestic responsibilities.

Analysis of Failure

It would be very difficult to reach a definitive judgment as to whether this case was a success or a failure. In part, this determination can only be made on the basis of a long-term follow-up. We would consider either of two outcomes as constituting an ultimate success: If the presenting problems fail to recur and both spouses are more satisfied with the relationship than they were prior to seeking therapy; or, alternatively, if they were to separate and both experience greater life satisfaction apart than they did as a couple.

At the time of termination, their self-reports regarding both behavior in the natural environment and their subjective satisfaction with the marriage suggest that they benefitted moderately from therapy. Mutually satisfactory change agreements had been reached regarding all of their presenting problems, and these agreements were being followed. The couple was paying close attention to the state of their relationship and holding weekly meetings to monitor their progress. Jack understood exactly what Jane wanted from him and professed a willingness to provide it. They both claimed to have learned a great deal about their relationship as a result of therapy, in addition to the behavior changes that had come about. A simple pre–post assessment strongly suggested a successful outcome. Moreover, they came to therapy for communication training, and they left with the skills that they wanted. As consumers they were satisfied.

A longitudinal perspective on the entire process of therapy leads to a less sanguine appraisal. The recurring cycles of crisis followed by recovery suggest that the couple's apparent state at any one given time may be misleading and extremely transient. Insight and behavior change exhibited during recovery periods rapidly disintegrated during crisis periods. It was impossible to determine whether or not their appearance at the time of termination reflected changes that would be permanent and lasting or simply another ephemeral recovery period.

Jack and Jane exhibited a dyadic multiple personality. They were either in crisis or they were recovered, and on the latter occasions they presented themselves as a nondistressed couple. Their appearance at the pretreatment assessment during a recovery phase made it difficult to ascertain why they were in therapy, although the reasons became clear during times of crisis. We will attempt to elucidate both the basis for these crises and the rapid recoveries. We will also attempt to pinpoint some therapeutic maneuvers that may have facilitated a smoother course of treatment. Finally, we will attempt to pinpoint some characteristics of this couple that made them difficult to treat.

Although the first crisis appeared to be sudden and relatively unprovoked, its seeds were actually planted during the early phases of therapy, when all appeared to be well. Although Jack was behaving collaboratively and cooperatively and seemed dedicated to satisfying Jane's misgivings about the marriage, he was also doing things that contradicted his apparent motivation. These acts were subtle but they had a cumulative impact on Jane. She was requesting both a more intimate and a more egalitarian relationship, and although Jack complied with each specific manifestation of her wishes, he did other things to communicate a wish to maintain the *status quo*. Jane's cognitive set elaborated on Jack's manifestations of ambivalence, and she negatively tracked the distancing behaviors, ignoring or minimizing the importance of the changes he was making.

First, there was Jack's complete satisfaction with the relationship as it was, as manifested by his absence of complaints. In part this reflected a genuine preference for the *status quo*; but it also reflected his avoidance of emotional expressiveness, both his own and whatever emotional response she might have to his complaints. Jane interpreted his claim that he had no complaints as an indication that he did not care about her. Her reasoning was as follows, "I am unhappy because there is not enough intimacy in our marriage. He has no complaints. Therefore, he is satisfied with no intimacy. He must not want to be intimate with me." Because of her interpretation of his behavior, his behavior changes were essentially ignored. This became apparent only during the crisis session.

As we mentioned previously, at times her desire for his expression of feelings conflicted with her other major wish, that he share domestic responsibilities with her. When he finally did complain, she was unreceptive because the content of his complaint (her grumpiness in the morning) impinged upon what she viewed as excessive domestic responsibility. Thus, Jane gave her husband good reason to fear her response to his complaints.

Second, although Jack adhered to the homework assignments and was very agreeable to any changes which Jane requested, she was the one to initiate all therapy-related transactions in the home. She prompted him to implement his behavior-change agreements, and she reminded him that it was time to practice problem solving; she, in other words, retained unwanted control over the "executive functions" of the relationship. Jack thereby undermined his own behavior changes by delivering behaviors that appeared to contradict the spirit of these changes.

Finally, during the first eight sessions the major problems were not discussed. Jack was still not communicating with his wife in those areas in which she most wanted communication. Although this was not unexpected given the phase of therapy they were in, Jane interpreted his continued avoidance of intimate communication as a sign that he did not want to change the relationship.

All of these concerns were kept secret from the therapist until they exploded during the first crisis session. Let us consider what the therapist could have done during this first phase of therapy to prevent this process from developing.

Hypothetical Reconstruction toward Success

One major therapist oversight during the first phase of therapy involved the failure to provide Jack with sufficient support. Specifically, when Jane was unreceptive to Jack's rare expressions of dissatisfaction, the therapist should have confronted her. Her lack of receptivity contradicted her own stated wish that he share feelings with her. But not only was Jane not confronted, the therapist did not even notice this contradiction until weeks later. This issue was finally dealt with in the midst of one of the crisis sessions, but the failure to deal with it earlier meant that therapy was reinforcing his belief that the expression of feelings was dangerous. More generally, the therapist could have acknowledged the difficulties that Jack must have been having in responding to such sweeping requests from Jane. Although Jack never acknowledged such difficulties and may not have admitted to them had they been suggested by the therapist, such a suggestion would have constituted a therapeutic demonstration of support, strengthened the alliance between the therapist and Jack, and also been helpful in getting Jane to consider the possibility that Jack is not malevolently withholding from her. Jane tended to view Jack's distancing behavior in the worst possible light, as a demonstration that he did not care about her.

In truth Jack did care about her but had great difficulty providing her with what she wanted, due to inhibitions and fears about closeness and intimacy. The therapist did little to foster discussion of such inhibitions.

The failure to notice and confront Jane's lack of responsiveness to her husband's expressive overtures and the failure to provide Jack with emotional support both stemmed from the therapist's selective identification with the wife. After all, here was a woman struggling to break the shackles of a rather traditional marriage, countered by a man who had at least some investment in that model. To compound matters, Jack was not very likeable: He was meek, afraid of his feelings, and tended to intellectualize. In addition to limiting the amount of empathy expressed by the therapist toward Jack, this overidentification led the therapist to pay attention to the content of Jane's complaints to the exclusion of important process issues; thus, the therapist ignored Jane's responses to Jack's expressions of feeling and focused on her "legitimate" gripes about the specific concerns. Instead of adopting the normal tactic of addressing her failure to collaborate, the therapist let Jack withdraw and validated Jane's unwillingness to focus on herself.

Two other intervention strategies might have helped arrest the process that culminated in the series of midtherapy crises. The first falls under the category, ability to induce and maintain positive expectancies, discussed in the section on our theoretical frame of reference. As we mentioned, therapists must repeatedly remind couples during early therapy sessions that it is too early to expect major changes to occur. Jane thought that therapy was not working because her husband was not changing in areas that had not as yet received attention during therapy sessions. In fact, it was to be expected that changes occur only in those areas where attention was being directed. But unless couples are reminded of what to expect and not to expect during each phase of therapy, their expectancies are liable to be excessive, and they will become demoralized when these expectations are not met. Jane had unrealistic expectations, and she did become demoralized. The therapist failed to "search" for and "destroy" those unrealistic expectations.

The second error of omission involved insufficient probing, or "taking the affective temperature" during early therapy sessions. The therapist was too eager to accept the report, mostly emanating from Jack, that everything was fine. Given that Jane seldom initiated these glowing reports and given nonverbal cues (a noticeable lack of enthusiasm), which were discrepant from those reports, the therapist might have commented on these phenomena, thereby eliciting from Jane some of the concerns that eventually erupted into crises.

In session 9, the first crisis session, Jane finally broke free of the static calm that Jack had enforced on the earlier sessions. This was the first opportunity for the therapist to witness the acute distress that periodically characterized their quarrels at home. Just as she occasionally did at home, Jane reacted strongly to an apparently minor incident by threatening to end the relationship. Just as it occurred at home, the passage of time quickly led to a subsiding of her reaction, and a return to the *status quo ante bellum*. There was no integration, no resolution, and no change. The first crisis in therapy followed this familiar pattern. Jack withdrew and said nothing. The therapist looked on, feeling helpless, surprised, and demoralized. When they returned to therapy the following week acting as if nothing had happened, the therapist simply accepted the recovery without any kind of inquiry. No questions were asked regarding their process of recovery, no mention was made of the previous session, and the therapist simply began where they had left off before the previous session. It was obvious that both Jack and Jane wanted to ignore the conflict of the previous week, and the therapist colluded with them. Then, instead of suggesting that they use PST to tackle one of the major issues mentioned by Jane the previous week, the therapist allowed the spouses to determine what problem they wanted to discuss. They chose a trivial problem, and therapy was back on course. To Jane, this was more evidence that therapy was not going to help her in the areas that were of most concern.

The issues that had triggered the first crisis and the two subsequent crises involved Jack's refusal to adopt his wife's suggested course of action regarding third parties. In each case she requested some sort of assertiveness from him. When he balked she concluded that he was showing that he cared more about the other person's feelings than he did about hers. She connected this apparent lack of concern to all of the other unresolved problems, some of which were now revealed for the first time: his failure to initiate the completion of homework assignments, his disengagement from intimate communication, and his apparent satisfaction with their current lack of intimacy. None of these major issues were dealt with until after the second crisis following their attempt to terminate therapy. The fact that they almost terminated is hardly surprising.

Thus, in the therapist's initial response to the midtherapy crisis, the therapist treated both the outburst itself and the equally surprising recovery as if they were random events. Yet the recovery was part of the problem, not a sign that the problem had been solved. When Jane was complaining, the therapist at least had some real marital distress with which to work. But when her complaining ceased, so did the apparent need for change. In retrospect it appears that Jane's rapid recoveries had both respondent and operant components. On an emotional level she was highly "reactive" to Jack's immediate behavior. When he behaved in a way that displeased her, she became very upset, and we have already described the cognitive processes involved in exacerbating her reaction. When he showed the least signs of accommodation, however, she was easily appeased and genuinely relieved, albeit only for a short time. From an operant standpoint, the cycle of crisis–recovery reflected an elaborate "aversive control" pattern that had developed between them—a pattern that was reinforcing in the short run but in the long run simply maintained the *status quo*. Certain behaviors on Jack's part, behaviors which suggested to Jane a lack of love or caring, were followed by an emotional outburst from Jane, the cessation of which was contingent upon some short-term changes on his part. She thus punished him for transgressions and then rewarded him for compliance. Unfortunately, although her "negative reinforcement" suppressed the transgression, it did not decrease its frequency. Thus their habitual mode of behavior control had not been supplanted by PST, and the problem of how this couple coped with major conflict continued despite many sessions of therapy.

In addition to colluding with the couple in avoiding major issues during the recovery period, the therapist failed to focus sufficiently on Jane's dysfunctional attributional processes. Jane was clearly upset because of the causal attributions she invoked to explain Jack's behavior. Jack was ambivalent about change, had trouble being assertive, and was afraid of expressing feelings. He was trying, however, and attributions regarding his lack of caring were inappropriate. Therapy failed to draw attention to her dysfunctional attributions. Neither Jane's nor Jack's cognitive processes were relabeled, acknowledged, or explored.

The decision to terminate was an impulsive one. Jane was demoralized because in her view sufficient changes had not occurred despite 12 sessions of therapy. Jack was growing increasingly concerned that Jane's reactivity might drive her from the relationship. Therefore, although her dissatisfaction with him was obvious, he colluded with her and in fact welcomed the respite from emotional turmoil that termination might provide.

But in the therapist's response to the threatened termination, the therapist began to marshal the alternative forces manifested by Jack's collaborative behavior and Jane's anger. We believe that a turning point in therapy began during the second crisis session, in which the therapist refused to allow them to terminate. It would have been unthinkable to let them stop therapy at this point. Up until now, therapy had simply stirred up fears and other strong feelings that needed to be resolved. To stop now would have meant at the very least a therapy-induced resignation on their parts that no real change was possible. The therapist had one more chance to direct them toward a resolution of their major presenting problems, and the therapist did so with skill and persistence. The therapist was much more effective at confronting Jane when she complained about insufficient change from Jack. By directing them toward a change agreement in regard to the "intimate communication" issue, the therapist demonstrated that there was some value to continuing therapy. The therapist also communicated to Jack the importance of not waiting for his wife to prompt him toward compliance with the change agreements. During the session Jack committed himself to sharing the "executive functions" of relationship maintenance.

The session would have been even more effective if the therapist had initiated some cognitive interventions with Jane. For example the therapist might have examined the accuracy of Jane's perceptions of her husband's commitment to change, by perusing prior change agreements to determine the extent of his overall compliance. Jane had been ignoring or minimizing some rather substantial changes on his part, and a demonstration of her selective tracking would have forced her to give Jack the credit he deserved. In the process, Jack would be receiving needed support. By not responding in this way, the therapist seemed to accept Jane's indictment, and the therapist perpetuated the alliance from which Jack had been excluded throughout therapy. Although the subsequent course of treatment was clouded by a third "outburst" from Jane 2 weeks later, there was some evidence that the changes were becoming permanent. When Jane complained about Jack's assertiveness during the final crisis session, he was responsive and did perform to her satisfaction during the subsequent week, whereas in the past he simply made token gestures of appeasement and waited for her to calm down, without significantly modifying his behavior. Except for this final incident, Jack was apparently giving her what she wanted.

To be sure, there was more work that could have been done with this couple. In particular, Jane's tendency to catastrophize and engage in dysfunctional attributions was never dealt with. The third crisis suggests that this couple remains vulnerable to further crisis, because little was done to neutralize her tendency to overreact to Jack's transgressions. In general there was insufficient atte₁tion paid to the preventative aspects of BMT, which, with this couple, would have better prepared them for future stressful situations. They needed to learn strategies for controlling and neutralizing their tendencies toward escalation, particularly when Jack engaged in behaviors that were upsetting to Jane. Cognitive work would constitute an important segment of such training.

Thus, one could make a case for continued marital therapy for Jack and Jane. However, we hesitate to quarrel with the mutual decision on the part of the therapist and the couple to terminate when they did. All three of them were exhausted by the end of the eighteen sessions. It is extremely doubtful whether the couple could have been persuaded to continue, and—despite the fluctuating course of treatment as well as the ambiguities involved in assessing treatment outcome at the time of termination—there was some evidence of substantial progress.

Conclusions

Let us now summarize the factors in both the therapist's performance and in the clients that appear to be associated with the difficult course of treatment for Jack and Jane. In regard to the therapist's performance, it should be noted that skillful direction and persistence were ultimately responsible for changing the course of therapy in a more positive direction at the time of the second crisis. To a great extent the early oversights and omissions were rectified. It should also be noted that in our facility our failures are group failures, and our successes are group successes, since our supervision and treatment planning are conducted as a group. The therapist has to fend for himself or herself once the session begins, however, and no amount of preparation, even in a highly technologized form of therapy such as BMT, can protect a beginning therapist from the myriad of pitfalls that the script does not predict. This was the first marital therapy case for the graduate student therapist, and the mistakes she made were typical of those made by beginning therapists.

The therapist's mistakes were mostly errors of omission that impinge upon many of the categories identified in the earlier section on therapist factors. At crucial times, the therapist failed to direct the behavior of the couple in productive directions. This was reflected in a tendency to become absorbed in the *content* of issues under discussion and thus therapy failed to focus on certain key process issues that were occurring between the couple. It was also reflected in a reluctance to confront and relabel Jane's behavior when she deviated from a collaborative set. The therapist was at times insufficiently directive in guiding the couple toward a confrontation with major issues; instead of siding with the progressive side of their ambivalence, the therapist tended to collude with the couple in allowing them to focus on relatively trivial matters. When the therapist changed tactics and provided more direction, progress was greatly facilitated. These deficiencies impinge directly on two related factors: the virtual absence of a much-needed cognitive focus and the imbalance created by the therapist's exclusive alliance with Jane. The lack of cognitive work remains an unfinished, unsolved clinical issue that—more than anything else—detracts from a positive prognosis. The imbalance in alliances meant that Jane was often validated for destructive behavior, and Jack was deprived of needed emotional support. During the early sessions the therapist was too accepting of the superficially smooth course of treatment, and failed to conduct the kinds of probing and elicitation of affect (particularly from Jane) that might have identified her hidden dissatisfaction. Little was done to counter or even uncover Jane's unrealistic expectations by engaging in the precautionary counterdemand statements described earlier.

These omissions notwithstanding, one wonders whether a highly skilled and experienced therapist would have been able to significantly alter the course of therapy. Unlike most of the couples who presented themselves for therapy at our clinic, *Jack and Jane were initially unwilling to admit to any real marital distress.* Both of them censored a great deal of information. Although couples frequently fail to provide us with completely accurate information initially, almost invariably at least one spouse is willing to disclose his or her dissatisfaction. Thus, it is almost always possible to obtain some information from which we can make inferences about other aspects of the relationship. Then, once they began to show their distress, they did not sustain it for very long. They recovered quickly, and during recovery periods they showed little overt inclination for dealing with their major issues.

In other words one aspect of this couple that made them difficult to treat is that initially they offered us few inroads into the structure of their relationship. Although we were suspicious about their happy presentation of themselves, it was easy for the therapist to be lulled into complacency by the ease of the initial therapy sessions.

A second characteristic of this couple that made them difficult to treat was that, when they did show their distress, *only one spouse complained*. This is a more familiar pattern, but one which is no less pernicious despite its familiarity. The general pattern involves a history of one spouse (usually the wife) habitually discontent because of the partner's perennial withdrawal and disengagement. Since the level of intimacy prevalent at any one particular time is *always* determined by the partner desiring the most distance, the *status quo* favors the disengaged spouse. At some point the partner desirous of more intimacy becomes "extinguished" and threatens to terminate the marriage unless the partner makes sweeping changes. Armed with some sort of ultimatum, they enter therapy with the formerly disengaged spouse (usually the husband) overtly repentent and accepting responsibility for the problems in the relationship. He is cooperative and flexible during therapy, agrees to and does enact sweeping behavioral changes, and demands nothing of her except that she not leave him. He appears willing to do anything to keep her there with him. Therapy often progresses smoothly, but there is an obvious problem. Since he was satisfied with the *status quo* before therapy, he is likely to become less satisfied as he changes to conform to her desires for more intimacy. Moreover, he is likely to resent both the amount of change he is required to enact and the unilateral nature of the change, despite his preference for giving her what she wants in lieu of terminating the relationship. With some couples there is an additional problem. No matter how much he changes, the wife is not satisfied. Even if she gains everything that she has been asking for throughout the months or years of conflict, she may still decide to terminate the marriage. The reasons for this continued dissatisfaction are not completely clear, but two factors seem to be of primary importance. First, the more he changes, the more she is reminded of his months or years of intransigence. The extreme form of aversive control required to generate the behavior changes is received almost as a slap in the face; it seems to validate his selfishness, since he was unwilling to change simply because she wanted him to, but responded only to her threat to leave him. Second, in a very fundamental way her feelings for him have changed, and this change of feelings appears to be cognitively mediated. The same behaviors that seemed to have such reinforcement value for her at one time are no longer potent. In response to months or years of frustration and deprivation, she seems to cross an irreversible threshold where her view of him has been fundamentally altered, and she is no longer responsive to him.

Jack and Jane were on their way to becoming one of those couples. She is not as yet ready to end the relationship; it appears that the "threshold" had not as yet been reached. Their early entry into therapy may have prevented this process from continuing. But the skewed nature of their complaints, the inequitable distribution of dissatisfaction, was a subtle but not surprising obstacle to successful treatment. Our guess is that had they been further along in the process, we would have been unable to help them.

A third characteristic of this couple that made them difficult to treat relates to the ethical–political dilemma created for a therapist by the oppressive nature of this relationship for the wife. *Jane was clearly struggling to break free from the constraints of a traditional marriage formulated along sexist lines.* She was the oppressed spouse (although, we would assert, men are also oppressed by traditional marriages, albeit in more subtle ways), and mental health professionals are obliged to promote values that undermine sexism. One of the basic tenets of good marital therapy, however, is that the therapist should remain neutral and not form permanent alliances with one spouse. Thus, with Jack and Jane the therapeutic task was made exceedingly difficult by the necessity of supporting both spouses, on the one hand, and paying some special attention to Jane's laudable struggle to fulfill herself as an individual. One way out of this dilemma is to balance the alliances by promoting an egalitarian relationship, while at the same time offering sufficient support to the husband, which includes empathizing with the difficulties he might encounter in surrendering his "male-superior" position. It is very easy, however, to be insensitive to the male and intolerant of his ambivalence. Jack and Jane were ultimately treatable because Jack was amenable to behavior changes that were consistent with a more egalitarian relationship. With some couples, the dilemma is insurmountable without fostering a stance on the part of the woman that will ultimately lead to the demise of the marriage in the service of her struggle toward liberation.

Finally, this couple was difficult to treat because, despite Jack's behavior changes, *Jane's cognitions did not change in the manner predicted by BMT.* Despite numerous behavior changes on the part of Jack during the early phases of therapy, Jane still viewed him as not respecting her, not supporting her independence, and not caring about her. As we have already mentioned, there are a number of possible explanations for Jane's cognitions lagging behind Jack's behavior changes. He was, for one thing, somewhat inconsistent in his commitment to behavior change and was also undermining his behavior changes by, for example, not assuming any of the "executive functions" of relationship enhancement. It is entirely possible that Jane would have been more supportive of Jack's initiatives had he been more consistent. In addition Jack might have been more consistent had the therapist provided him with more support. A second factor that may have militated against

Jane's cognitive change was the lack of focus on issues central to her concerns until very late in therapy. Finally, the absence of systematic cognitive restructuring interventions may have been partly responsible for Jane's "cognitive lag." In the final analysis, however, the difference between success and failure in BMT often hinges on such cognitive changes, and some couples simply maintain their pretherapy cognitive sets despite successful resolution of behavioral concerns. Our success rate at changing behavior still exceeds the efficiency of our ability to modify cognitions, and it is the latter that usually indicates failure.

Jack and Jane failed to fall neatly into any one of our categories listed in the previous section on client characteristics. The Js do overlap with a number of categories, however. First, the Js had differing agendas regarding the optimal outcome of therapy, particularly in regard to the issue of how much intimacy there would be in the relationship. The general treatment obstacle embodied in spouses' differing agendas and the specific discrepancy in regard to each spouse's optimal level of intimacy place Jack and Jane in two of our categories of difficult clients. They also fit the category of couples who change in different and incompatible directions subsequent to marriage. At the onset the marriage contract was a fairly traditional one, and pressure from Jane to modify that contract served as a primary antecedent for the decision to seek therapy. Like many couples the J's struggle centered around the fundamental questions of how much intimacy and equality (sharing of roles and responsibilities) there will be in the relationship. Their long-term stability as well as their long-term satisfaction hinge on their ability to find levels on both dimensions that enhance the quality of life for each.

The illustrative case exemplifies some of the therapist and client characteristics that seem to be important in predicting and understanding the variability in couples' response to BMT. Somehow, the intricacies of each case will continue to defy our efforts to turn the study of marital therapy into a scientific endeavor. On the other hand it is hoped that more rigorous descriptive analyses of such intricacies will reduce the chances that cases such as this one will be left to fail.

ACKNOWLEDGMENTS

Preparation of this chapter was supported by Grant #5 R01 MH 33838-02 from the National Institute of Mental Health. The authors wish to acknowledge the help of Nicole Bussod, Janice Katt, and Mary Kolpakoff in preparing and critiquing early drafts of the manuscript.

REFERENCES

Azrin, N. H., Besalel, V. A., Bechtel, R., Michalicek, A., Mancera, M., Carroll, D., Shuford, D., & Cox, J. Comparison of reciprocity and discussion-type counseling for marital problems. *American Journal of Family Therapy*, 1980, *8*, 21–28.

Bandura, A. Self-efficacy: Toward a unifying theory of behavioral change. *Psychological Review*, 1977, *84*, 191–215.

Baucom, D. H. A comparison of behavioral contracting and problem-solving/communications training in behavioral marital therapy. *Behavior Therapy*, 1982, *13*, 162–174.

Billings, A. Conflict resolution in distressed and nondistressed married couples. *Journal of Consulting and Clinical Psychology*, 1979, *47*, 368–376.

Birchler, G. R., & Spinks, S. Behavioral systems marital and family therapy: Integration and clinical application. *American Journal of Family Therapy*, 1980, *8*, 6–28.

Birchler, G. R., Weiss, R. L., & Vincent, J. P. A multimethod analysis of social reinforcement exchange between maritally distressed and nondistressed spouse and stranger dyads. *Journal of Personality and Social Psychology*, 1975, *31*, 349–360.

Doherty, W. J. Cognitive processes in intimate conflict: I. Extending attribution theory. *The American Journal of Family Therapy*, 1981a, *9*, 5–13.

Doherty, W. J. Cognitive processes in intimate conflict: II. Efficacy and learned helplessness. *American Journal of Family Therapy*, 1981b, *9*, 35–44.

Epstein, N. Cognitive therapy with couples. *American Journal of Family Therapy*, 1982, *10*, 5–16.

Gottman, J. M. *Marital interaction: Experimental investigations*. New York: Academic Press, 1979.

Gurman, A. S., & Kniskern, D. P. Research on marital and family therapy: Progress, perspective, and prospect. In S. L. Garfield & A. E. Bergin (Eds.), *Handbook of psychotherapy and behavior change: An empirical analysis* (2nd ed.). New York: Wiley, 1978.

Gurman, A. S., & Knudson, R. M. Behavioral marriage therapy: I. A psychodynamic-systems analysis and critique. *Family Process*, 1978, *17*, 121–138.

Gurman, A. S., Knudson, R. M., & Kniskern, D. P. Behavioral marriage therapy: IV. Take two aspirin and call us in the morning. *Family Process*, 1978, *17*, 165–180.

Jacobson, N. S. Problem solving and contingency contracting in the treatment of marital discord. *Journal of Consulting and Clinical Psychology*, 1977, *45*, 92–100.

Jacobson, N. S. A review of the research on the effectiveness of marital therapy. In T. J. Paolino & B. S. McCrady (Eds.), *Marriage and marital therapy: Psychoanalytic, behavioral, and systems theory perspectives*. New York: Brunner/Mazel, 1978a.

Jacobson, N. S. Specific and nonspecific factors in the effectiveness of a behavioral approach to the treatment of marital discord. *Journal of Consulting and Clinical Psychology*, 1978b, *46*, 442–452.

Jacobson, N. S. A stimulus control model of change in behavioral marital therapy: Implications for contingency contracting. *Journal of Marriage and Family Counseling*, 1978c, *4*, 29–35.

Jacobson, N. S. Increasing positive behavior in severely distressed adult relationships. *Behavior Therapy*, 1979, *10*, 311–326.

Jacobson, N. S. The modification of cognitive processes in behavioral marital therapy: Integration of cognitive and behavioral intervention strategies. In K. Hahlweg & N. S. Jacobson (Eds.), *Marital interaction: Analysis and modification*. New York: Guilford, 1984.

Jacobson, N. S., & Anderson, E. A. The effects of behavior rehearsal and feedback on the acquisition of problem solving skills in distressed and nondistressed couples. *Behaviour Research and Therapy*, 1980, *18*, 25–26.

Jacobson, N. S., Follette, W. C., & Elwood, R. W. Outcome research on behavioral marital therapy: A methodological and conceptual reappraisal. In K. Hahlweg & N. S. Jacobson (Eds.), *Marital interaction: Analysis and modification*. New York: Guilford, 1984.

Jacobson, N. S., & Margolin, G. *Marital therapy: Strategies based on social learning and behavior exchange principles*. New York: Brunner/Mazel, 1979.

Jacobson, N. S., & Moore, D. Behavior exchange theory of marriage: Reconnaissance and reconsideration. In J. P. Vincent (Ed.), *Advances in family intervention, assessment, and theory* (Vol. 2). Greenwich, Conn.: JAI Press, 1981.

Knudson, R. M., Gurman, A. S., & Kniskern, D. P. Behavioral marriage therapy: A treatment in transition. In C. M. Franks & G. T. Wilson (Eds.), *Annual review of behavior therapy* (Vol. 7). New York: Academic Press, 1979.

Liberman, R. P., Levine, J., Wheeler, E., Sanders, N., & Wallace, C. Experimental evaluation of marital group therapy: Behavioral vs. interaction–insight formats. *Acta Psychychiatrica Scandinavia*, 1976, Supplement.

Liberman, R. P., Wheeler, E. G., deVisser, L. A. J. M., Kuehnel, J., & Kuehnel, T. *Handbook of marital therapy: A positive approach to helping troubled relationships.* New York: Plenum, 1981.

Skinner, B. F. *Science and human behavior.* New York: MacMillan, 1953.

Stuart, R. B. *Helping couples change: A social learning approach to marital therapy.* New York: Guilford, 1980.

Thibaut, J. W., & Kelley, H. H. *The social psychology of groups.* New York: Wiley, 1959.

Turkewitz, H., & O'Leary, K. D. A comparative outcome study of behavioral marital therapy and communication therapy. *Journal of Marital and Family Therapy*, 1981, 7, 159–170.

Vincent, J. P., Weiss, R. L., & Birchler, G. R. A behavioral analysis of problem-solving in distressed and nondistressed married and stranger dyads. *Behavior Therapy*, 1975, 6, 475–487.

Weiss, R. L. The conceptualization of marriage from a behavioral perspective. In T. J. Paolino & B. S. McCrady (Eds.), *Marriage and marital therapy: Psychoanalytic, behavioral, and systems theory perspectives.* New York: Brunner/Mazel, 1978.

Weiss, R. L. Strategic behavioral marital therapy: Toward a model for assessment and intervention. In J. P. Vincent (Ed.), *Advances in family intervention, assessment and theory* (Vol. 1). Greenwich, Conn.: JAI Press, 1980.

5

A Truant Family

LYMAN C. WYNNE AND ROBERT JAY GREEN

Introduction

We began to review the case example described in this chapter because we were troubled by probable shortcomings in our therapeutic approach. As we proceeded with this self-examination, we also became aware that our difficulties may well be shared not only by other family therapists but also by those in social agencies who venture to make psychosocial interventions with certain elusive, "truant" families. This family was more difficult for us to treat than families that symptomatically have much more severely disturbed identified patients, for example, the families of florid schizophrenics. Initially, we believed that this family offered some prospect of therapeutic engagement. Ultimately, its members drifted away from treatment separately and collectively in a pattern that had been repeated for years in the community—a pattern we failed to interrupt.

Theoretical Frame of Reference

During the years since early 1976 when we met with this family, we both have modified and substantially diversified the techniques we use in therapy. At the time of this writing, it is quite difficult to explain to ourselves, or to others, how our treatment approach bore much rational relationship to our theoretical frame of reference. Our major concepts and constructs have not undergone very much change during this time interval; a major aspect of our failure with this case was our difficulty and, yes, ineptitude, in translating our concepts into effective, workable techniques.

Given this dissociation between our theory and our techniques, only the briefest sketch of our concepts should suffice. Then, as now, our theoretical framework can be characterized as ecosystemic, structural, problem-oriented, and concerned with the current actualization of enduring family roles, rules, and myths. Especially relevant for this family is the systemic concept of a family boundary in the form characterized as a "rubber fence" by Wynne,

Lyman C. Wynne and Robert Jay Green. Department of Psychiatry, University of Rochester School of Medicine and Dentistry, Rochester, New York.

Ryckoff, Day, and Hirsch (1958). The members of such families are poorly differentiated from one another as individuals and share externalizing myths that harassment, blame, and responsibility for misfortune exclusively arises from sources external to the family. This externalizing mode of constructing and constricting their experience turns nonfamily members into adversaries. Hence, the family works as a unit to elude outsiders and conceals, or remains unknowlcdgcable about, the physical and psychological whereabouts of those family members who are being pursued or attacked by others. These maneuvers contribute to the elasticity but continuity of the rubber fence. Then, when avoidance becomes excessively difficult, another class of shared family mechanisms may be invoked: appeasement, especially through temporary incorporation of others into the family system, without changing the family rules or patterns. The rubber fence is especially likely to be stretched to include benign accepting therapists. It should be noted that this kind of family boundary problem was originally identified as being especially vivid in the families of certain acute schizophrenics. However, such boundary problems are not, of course, limited to families with a member identified as schizophrenic.

Background

Our first knowledge of the T family came to one of us (Green) through a call from a resident in pediatrics. (In this case Green and Wynne acted as cotherapists, though Wynne was the family therapy supervisor.) This resident had seen the identified patient (a 13-year-old boy, Floyd) together with his mother. The resident stated that they had come to him on referral from a hospital cardiologist who had seen Floyd 9 days earlier for a routine checkup of a congenital heart defect that had been troublesome in earlier years, but now had significantly improved. According to the cardiologist the mother asked that Floyd be referred for "counseling" because he had "lost interest in gym and become more introverted." The cardiologist responded by referring them to the Adolescent Clinic in Pediatrics where the resident saw the mother and son together once. He concluded that the problem was part of a broader family difficulty, particularly involving Floyd's 14-year-old brother, Tommy. The resident recommended family therapy to them and called one of us (Green) in the Family Clinic in the Department of Psychiatry. Green agreed to call the family when he returned from a 5-day vacation (the referral call was made late in the afternoon on Christmas Eve).

That same evening before Green had direct contact with the family, a further "communication" occurred. While the rest of the family were opening their Christmas presents, Floyd went to his room to "test" a tape recorder of his 11-year-old sister, Sally. A little later when she played the tape in front of the family, the content, as later reported by the mother, was a "good-bye" to the family because he was "tired of living." He said on the tape that he could not handle arguing with his brothers and sister any more, he could not stand thinking about past misdeeds that he had told his mother about a few weeks before, and, finally, that he was afraid his dad was sick again (history of heart trouble). Two days later, on December 26, the parents brought Floyd to the hospital emergency room where he was seen by the same resident in pediatrics who had met with him in the Adolescent Clinic. He was then referred to the psychiatric emergency service, from where he was hospitalized as an "active suicidal threat." The resident in pediatrics also informed his counterpart in psychiatry that the family already had been referred to the Family Clinic.

Upon returning from vacation, Green was surprised to receive from the resident in psychiatry an urgent message that read, "Your patient, Floyd T, was admitted to the hospital over the weekend. When can you see him today?" By that time, Floyd had been in the hospital for 4 days. Green arranged that the resident would continue to take treatment responsibility during the brief hospitalization and that Green would begin family evaluation after discharge.

Green then sent a note to Wynne—"Re: Case for us to see." We had indeed planned for some time to see a case together as cotherapists, but it is nevertheless of interest that this *particular* case was selected for cotherapy. After describing the referral and hospitalization in his note to Wynne, Green added, "There was a lot of confusion as to who would take charge."

In the hospital Floyd was given a diagnosis of depressive neurosis and adjustment reaction of adolescence. After initially being sullen and uncommunicative, he conveyed to the psychiatric resident that he had wanted to communicate something important to his family through his "suicidal threat." Both he and his mother spoke spontaneously and positively about the prospect of having family meetings. Quite rapidly, Floyd's depression lifted and he was discharged after 5 days, on December 31. With Green's agreement the resident scheduled the first appointment with the whole family to take place in the Family Clinic a few days later.

The above account describes the events of the referral that were known to us when we first met with the family. Concealed from us initially was a second, nonmedical pathway to family therapy referral that already had been activated. This channel involved the school system and the Child Protective Unit of the County Department of Social Services. Eventually, we were able to reconstruct the following background that led up to the eventual referral. For a number of years during which this white, Anglo-Saxon family had lived in a series of urban dwellings, the parents had quarrelled vigorously, with the mother particularly complaining about the father's drinking. Both parents worked long hours, the father as a building custodian and the mother as a machine operator. For several years Floyd had been assigned the role of supervising the home behavior of his siblings, his older brother, Tommy, and his two younger siblings: his 11-year-old sister, Sally, and 9-year-old brother, Gary. During the year or so before the referral, Floyd increasingly stayed home from school. Tommy was much less at home and also was truant from school; he wandered around the neighborhood with whereabouts that were only vaguely known to his parents. Because of the truancy, the urban school authorities threatened, during the preceding spring, to put the two boys on probation or to suspend them from school. In response, during that summer, the family moved to a new school district in a suburb.

At the same time that the family was making this move, the mother threatened to divorce her husband unless he stopped drinking; he reportedly complied, at least for a while. During the same period when these changes between the parents were taking place and the family had just moved, Floyd lost contact with a girlfriend who had become important to him. This left him quite melancholy. In the suburban school system, the boys' truancy resumed in September in an unchanged form. According to the school reports that we obtained later, several school authorities became progressively more frustrated because numerous threats to the parents and the boys had no apparent effect on the truancy. In late October when a school attendance teacher made a visit to the home and found Floyd in charge, she concluded from the appearance of the home that the evidence of "neglect" was sufficient to call in the County Child Protective Unit. At the same time this teacher asked the school psychologist to evaluate all the children of the family and to tell the mother to go to the family clinic at a university teaching hospital for family therapy. A month later, when little further change had taken place despite "faithful promises" by the parents, they were warned that a court petition would be filed jointly by the school and the Child Protective Unit unless they complied with orders to cease the truancy and to set up an appointment "*that* day" for "family therapy and counseling for Floyd at the hospital." When Floyd came to the Cardiology Clinic for his routine checkup 6 days after this threat of a court petition, the mother made the request for counseling to the cardiologist without mentioning the urgency and the pressure from the school and county.

Diagnosis and Treatment Plan

All six family members physically came to the initial interview but were uniformly apathetic and disinterested in the meeting, with the partial exception of the mother who was the tired spokesperson for the family. There were occasional instances of sniping between Floyd, the 11-year-old daughter (Sally), and the 14-year-old son (Tommy). The 9-year-old brother (Gary) made a few disruptive comments. The father listened passively while his wife described her feelings of being burdened, her concern about her husband's chronic heart condition, and the history of Floyd's cardiac defect. We also learned that the family had moved to the suburbs to escape threats and pressure from the city school system about Floyd's and Tommy's truancy. The mother rather vaguely expressed the hope that in the new suburban setting the boys would attend school. We tried to discover if this was the problem for which they were now coming to us. Floyd's suicidal threat and depression were entirely out of their current focus. When we wondered whether the sniping that took place among the children during the meeting was also a problem at home, the family shrugged their shoulders in unison.

As we struggled to identify a presenting problem, the children picked up enthusiasm when they arrived at a consensus that they did not have any real difficulty. Rather, the problem lay, they agreed, in the school's disciplinarian (vice-principal) who was said to be hated and feared by "all the kids in the neighborhood."

We concluded the initial meeting with a working hypothesis that this family looked toward external, environmental changes to produce changes within the family and its members. Indeed, it appeared that the school, rather than the family, was distressed by Floyd's lack of attendance. Furthermore, we believed, from their passive, uninvolved participation in the session, that the motivation for treatment resided primarily in the therapists.

Although we had a free-floating discussion about the presenting problem and our strategy after the initial interview, we did not explicitly formulate a treatment plan. Rather, we were still trying to assess what was the problem, or problems, about which we could join with the family in a shared effort. Although this assessment process is described throughout this report as "therapy," this term is applicable only if one takes the viewpoint, as we do, that assessment and therapy are inextricably interwoven. The scope of our initial assessment was oriented predominantly to the intrafamilial structure and relationship patterns. We quickly defocused from the emphasis of the inpatient stay on the depressive symptomatology of the identified patient, Floyd. Instead, we gave more attention in our thinking to the parentification of Floyd and the imbalance in the participation of mother and father. We formulated a structural view that helping to build a collaborative parental coalition should be both an intermediate treatment goal and a prerequisite to a change in the overall family system. We had passing thoughts about whether it would be desirable to see the parents as a couple without the children in order to discuss their difficulties in setting limits for the children. Perhaps because the children seemed to be the activators of whatever lively interchange occurred, we never took steps to implement this thought about seeing the couple alone.

Because the referral process through Pediatrics and the inpatient psychiatric services had so emphasized Floyd's distress at home, and because we did not hear about the active intervention of the school and Child Protective Unit until later, our initial assessment plan focussed upon intrafamilial issues.

Process of Therapy

The Family-Therapist Interface

Our notes about difficulties in scheduling subsequent sessions suggest that the family was reluctant, or unwilling, to engage in a relationship with us. No doubt this was a two-way difficulty in which we were clearly uncertain about whether a treatment contract was possible. For reasons that are now unclear, the second meeting was scheduled 2 weeks later. (Usually, when a treatment plan has not been worked out, our custom is to meet again in a week or less.) Our expectations and those of the family for the second meeting appear to have been vague. For example, we assigned no tasks for the interim period. It appears that we merely stated that we would need to meet again in order to see whether there were any family problems for which we could be helpful.

The next scheduled session was cancelled; our notes are unclear as to whether the cancellation was initiated by the family or by us. The second session was rescheduled and held 3 days later, followed by two more sessions in the next 10 days. These meetings, and those subsequently, through a total of 14 contacts over a period of 4 months, were characterized by major difficulties in scheduling the time of the appointments, in working out who would be present, and whether the session would proceed in the absence of some family members. In short, the "battle for structure" was never won, if indeed it was ever truly joined (Napier & Whitaker, 1978).

In the next three sessions after the initial meeting, we continued to focus upon the parental difficulties in forming a coalition, especially in setting limits about the truancy of the two boys and in changing their delegation of authority to Floyd in supervising his siblings. It became apparent that the fighting among the children produced a more or less continuous uproar that seemed to go on with little change when the mother was present. The father's authority was much more effective in quieting this dissension, but he only rarely used this authority, tending to sit by passively even when he was at home.

A broad family pattern—paralleling the son's truancy—began to emerge. A central feature was that the father was frequently truant from the home and from the therapy, arriving near the end of the meeting times or not at all. Ostensibly, he had great difficulty getting to the sessions, even though they were held at the same time he usually arrived home from work. In fact, the sessions were held closer to his place of work than to his home.

There were other sessions in which the father arrived at our meetings on time from work, but then the mother was unable to get one or both of the older sons to come and would bring only the younger children. On another occasion, Floyd did not come but did tell his mother that he was supposed to attend. She erroneously told him that we had requested her not to bring him, and she did not telephone us to check out this difference of opinion with Floyd.

When either the father, or the two older sons, were absent, the mother felt helpless to change the situation and tended to excuse their behavior. In effect, the family members seemed to be in an unspoken collusion with one another not to have the whole family meet together.

Another facet of the T's family life was a sort of game in which the father and one of the older boys would mysteriously disappear from home early in the morning (around 5:30 A.M.) without giving the rest of the family advance notice of their departure, their whereabouts, or when they would return. The father and sons took great pleasure in this repeated activity; the fun explicitly derived primarily from the "playing hookey" aspects of the event and Mrs. T's subsequent irritation. In retaliation, Mrs. T and her daughter had once played hookey from the rest of the family to "show them" what it felt like.

The family theme of running from responsibilities and obligations to others and "bucking" their expectations and authority played a major role in generating family excitement and fun. This theme pervaded the family members' relations with one another and with the therapists. We were convinced that progress would be very slow and difficult if we were unable to get both parents and at least both older sons to attend the sessions simultaneously.

We tried a number of tactics to structure the sessions and elicit full attendance. In an effort to support the parents in their authority roles, we said we would begin meetings only when both parents were present. This approach met with some success for a while. The mother began successfully pressuring the father to attend after she and the children spent several whole meeting times waiting for the father to arrive. However, then the sons began protesting about coming and, following father's example, made themselves scarce when mother would try to get them to go. The mother, trying simultaneously to excuse her husband's behavior and get compliance from the children, felt helpless to influence the situation. She conveyed both to the therapists and to the school an air of being well-intentioned but helpless, alternately blaming and excusing the boys and her husband for their actions. The therapists more and more gained the impression that the father set the tone for much of the truancy of the older sons, that mother's helpless passivity was collusive, and that father's cooperation was crucial for progress to be made.

Truancy in this family also was accompanied by alcohol abuse. In earlier years the father often came home from work very late because he would stay out drinking. Upon his return he sometimes was verbally abusive and usually uncommunicative. A year or so before they began therapy, mother threatened divorce if father continued his excessive drinking. The father then substantially reduced his drinking, but it seemed that the sons then began (at the ages of 12 and 13) to "pick up where father left off."

On several occasions the boys became intoxicated, rowdy, and were arrested by the police. Thus the legacy of father's drinking was followed by increasing alcohol abuse on the part of the sons. The identificatory aspects of this phenomenon were clear in a conversation that Mrs. T overheard between the oldest son (Tommy) and one of his friends. When the friend asked if Mr. T got mad when Tommy drank, Tommy responded, "No! Why should he? I don't get mad at him when he drinks."

In the face of massive family "resistance" to treatment, as in the T case, it is useful to understand this family's ability to keep the therapists invested in treatment. The therapists were reinforced by hints of change. The mother, especially, indicated that some gains were accruing from family therapy, albeit temporary ones. She believed that she was more able to set limits on the sons' behavior, and she experienced some short-lived success in influencing her husband to attend the meetings. Prior to the Christmas suicide threat, she had been working full-time. After Christmas, she took a leave of absence from work to see if she could prevent Floyd's truancy and be available when the school authorities were checking on his whereabouts. Briefly returning to work 1 month later, she then arranged to get "laid off" from the job so that she could "solve the problems at home" and still receive unemployment benefits. She also made efforts to help Floyd with his studies, although she had great difficulty with the schoolwork herself.

The therapists strongly encouraged father to support mother's authority over the children consistently because his directives seemed to have more clout. In fact the parents attempted to follow the therapist's suggestions, and during a few meetings it looked as if some progress was being made toward forming a more effective parental coalition.

The Family-Community-Therapist Interfaces

During the first four meetings, we heard increasingly about the pressures and threats from the school system, and we also began to learn that the Child Protective Unit of the county had been involved. We deduced that our experience may have been paralleled by that of a series of community agencies, each of whom had become sequentially exasperated in trying to work with this family over the years. In order to share information and work out a consistent treatment plan with school officials and protective service caseworkers who were currently involved, the therapists called a meeting of representatives from these agencies—what we now were calling the "helping network."

Five weeks after our initial interview with the family, four school personnel and a caseworker from the Child Protective Unit met with Green in our clinic. Later, the school superintendent, who was not present at this meeting, but who identified himself as an "interested party," said that in this network meeting "each explained their perceptions of Floyd T's problem to Dr. Green." That statement seemed fairly accurate in the sense that the meeting, from our standpoint, served the purpose of information gathering about what we regarded as a confusing situation. A narrative unfolded that documented the rapidly diffusing involvement of more and more school and county personnel, including several others who were not present at this first network meeting.

In reviewing this meeting we began to hypothesize that the various school and community officials passed responsibility from one to another in a way that was complementary to the shifting of responsibility from one family member to another. Within the school system we could not find out who was most knowledgeable about (and who was most administratively responsible for) educational planning for Floyd. We also realized that we did not explicitly clarify our responsibility and authority in relation to the other participants in the meeting nor had they done so with one another. This point was highlighted when the school attendance teacher wrote a letter to Wynne (who had not been present) saying that the school superintendent (who had not been present) wanted "some recommendations" that he "could use in rendering a decision." However, another school official, who also had not been present, called to tell us that the school "really" wanted to use our services to obtain a "psychiatric exception" (i.e., legal expulsion) of Floyd from the school system or to have him placed in a residential treatment center until he reached age 16.

In a letter responding to the superintendent, we expressed concern about "apparent conflict of activity" of the various professionals. We urged consideration of an alternative occupational training school program for Floyd. Without waiting for our letter, the superintendent established an after-school tutorial program for Floyd to fulfill the school's legal obligation to provide an education for him. Floyd began attending these tutorial sessions regularly and seemed to be developing a significant relationship with his tutor; also, now early in the 3rd month of therapy, the family was attending with only moderate confusion about scheduling.

Meanwhile, 1 month after the network meeting, the school psychologist, knowing that Floyd was still not attending school but not aware of progress in tutoring and family therapy, reviewed the problem with a school Committee on the Handicapped. This Committee recommended that Floyd be taken from the home and placed in a residential center for unmanageable children. The psychologist then held a conference with Mrs. T and Floyd and "encouraged" (i.e., threatened) them with the out-of-home placement plan. Earlier, another person in the school system had threatened court action unless the family continued in therapy and Floyd continued tutoring. Because they now were complying with this directive, the new intervention by the school psychologist was perplexing to the therapists, to the Child Protective Unit caseworkers, and even to other school officials (e.g., the principal) who had not been consulted in advance. We wrote the school and country officials and requested another network meeting. We expressed dismay over the "lack of collaborative efforts" in the work with this family. The superintendent of schools fired back a letter expressing "concern" about this statement and giving a list of dates when contacts had been made with us and with the Child Protective Unit.

Meanwhile, the children began asking their parents and the therapists what the consequences would be if the family dropped out of treatment. Following a demand from both parents that Floyd and Tommy attend, Floyd went out and was picked up by the police for drunkenness. The parents joined together and grounded him, and father, with mother's support, ordered Floyd to go to his room. However, Floyd climbed out of his bedroom window, managed again to be picked up by the police, and complained to the patrolman that he ran away to avoid a beating from his father. Soon, to his parents' surprise, Floyd was at the front door (instead of in his room), and the policeman with him was warning the parents not to use such severe punishment. A few days later Floyd telephoned one of the therapists, saying, "My mother told me to call you and tell you that I don't want to go to sessions anymore and won't come." When the mother was asked to come to the phone, she described the incident with the police. She said she would try again to get the kids to the family meeting, but she sounded pessimistic and demoralized. (Only she and the two younger children appeared for the next meeting.) Our perception was that the police reprimand to the parents had undermined their authority, as well as their energy and motivation to work together in limit setting. Thus, the family was being given contradictory messages by multiple components of the treatment network.

A week later the second network meeting was held at the Family Clinic, this time with both therapists, the school attendance teacher and school psychologist, and two caseworkers and a supervisor from the county Child Protective Unit. The latter group expressed annoyance with the school, saying that the county agency, not the school, had the "ultimate responsibility" and were "surprised" at the recommendation of residential placement. They added that the school's suspicion of neglect and possible "abuse" in the home had not been sustained; on the other hand, the caseworkers said that they had difficulty in knowing what to do and looked to us in the Family Clinic for help. We noted that we felt handicapped by our inability to achieve regular attendance by the family. Very much in the gloomy tones expressed by the mother to us, we said that we would "try again."

Termination

Three more appointments were scheduled, with the mother arriving for all of them, the father for none, and the children in a variable pattern. For the final meeting the mother and all four children arrived and waited in the lobby for the father. After 45 minutes we came to them and said that we were unable to work under these circumstances and that we would let the county court system and schools know of our decision. The 9-year-old son jumped up and down exuberantly and shouted, "We won! We won! We don't have to come anymore! Yeah!"

The mother said little about termination, then reported that the family had just been evicted by their landlord along with some other families who were making too much noise and causing too many calls from the police to be tolerated by the suburban, middle-class community to which they had moved only 7 months earlier from a more urban part of the area. She said that the family was now planning to move back into the center of the city in the hope that this change would relieve their problems (the same problems that only the preceding summer had led them to leave the same city).

In a spontaneous call to the clinic a few weeks after termination, Mrs. T stated that therapy had given her the courage to set stronger limits on the children, even though Mr. T was still less supportive and active with the children than she wished.

Four years later the hospital received a request saying that Mr. T gave permission to release Floyd's medical records so that his enlistment in the US Army could be processed. Meanwhile, no one in the family had sought or been referred for psychiatric services in the hospital outpatient or inpatient services. The family had moved again, judging from a new city address. Still more recently, 2 years later, none of the family could be located in a follow-up effort.

Analysis of Failure

A major source of our treatment difficulties was our failure to have a comprehensive picture of the context of the presenting problem—how it came about and who was involved. Indeed, it was only in the course of preparing this paper, long after the case was concluded, that we succeeded in piecing together the relatively coherent story of the events described above, which at the time were conveyed to us and experienced by us in a highly fragmented fashion. In particular, during the actual contact with the family, we were constantly obtaining information about events that would have been helpful earlier. To be sure, all therapy is characterized to some degree by the need to act despite limited or even inadequate information, but, in this case, the available information was misleading, not simply lacking.

From a theoretical standpoint, our difficulties in establishing a useful therapeutic relationship can be understood as a failure to recognize boundary issues, especially the psychological rubber fence enclosing the family. At the time of the referral process, the cardiologist was pulled within the rubber fence and became the family's agent for unknowingly meeting the school's demands for family therapy. Thus, the family was, for the time being, secure from further external harassment.

During the inpatient stay of Floyd, the problem was located in Floyd, the identified patient. So long as he was the focus (scapegoat), the family as a system was protected both from attack and from the need for change. During the initial family interview and for much of the work that followed, we probably were highly disconcerting to the family because of our inquiry about the family as a whole. The mother invited us to shift the focus from Floyd to herself, but we continued to ask about a presenting problem for the family as a whole.

These various boundary difficulties have been described by Selvini-Palazzoli, Boscolo, Cecchin, and Prata (1980) as "the problem of the referring person," who is apt to be absorbed unknowingly by the family system while trying to help one or more family members to change or, in the case of the school officials and the T family, to force them to change. However, when it becomes apparent that the family pattern is being perpetuated rather than changed, then the person refers the family for therapy out of sheer exasperation and frustration. In the case of the T family, the school referral persons did not inform us of the fact that the referral had been made. Hence, our difficulties were increased in discovering that the school personnel, not the family members, were "hurting." Nevertheless, if we had inquired initially in more detail about the circumstances of the mother's request to the cardiologist, we could have uncovered much sooner the fact that the school had initiated the referral and that the family's complaints about the school were not merely projections. Additionally, we failed to take stock of the family's shared complaint about the school as an *eco*systemic issue. That is, by our preoccupation with the family system, we failed during the early meetings to regard the school as not merely context for the family but also as a system in its own right and one with whom we should make contact.

Thus, part of our treatment failure can be attributed to our overemphasis upon the family system and our belated and ineffectual work with the community systems of the school and the Child Protective Unit. We would have been better able to understand the shifting boundaries of the family if we had appreciated and worked more fully with the systems with which the family was interacting. These agencies, and increasingly we ourselves, tended to be in a complementary relationship with the family, a relationship that tended to perpetuate the longstanding family pattern rather than to induce change.

Like the school and county agencies, we were able to make contact with a constantly changing portion of the family but not with the family as a unit. An analogy that is similar to the rubber fence is of the family as an amoeba. Different segments of its membranes contact and adapt to external agents so that, for an observer at any point on the perimeter, it presents an ever-changing appearance. Nevertheless, as an organic whole, the amoeba itself remains unchanged. Thus, we were repetitiously dismayed by the uncertainty as to who would appear for the family therapy meetings, just as the school authorities were frustrated in their attempts to track down either the truant sons or their parents. In a systemic sense, beyond the individuals, one can think of this as a genuinely truant family.

When we belatedly began to make contacts with the community agencies, our discovery of their complementarity with the family left us frustrated and often annoyed because, as with the family, we could not find out whom to deal with in these agencies. Upon each contact, we seemed to discover a new or different person who was involved. Still later, at the time of the second network meeting, we discovered that there was a similar lack of communication between the school and the county Child Protective Unit. During the therapy, and even in reviewing the data more recently, we found ourselves scapegoating various persons in the community network. In effect, we had lamented: If these people only had been doing their jobs more adequately, then we would not have had these treatment difficulties with the family. However, a more comprehensive and sober overview suggests that our blaming was simply one more isomorphic example of the same process that we viewed more easily in the family and community.

In the network meetings we appear to have been expected to serve as consultants to the school and Child Protective Unit. Instead, we tended to limit our function to that of information gathering. Thus, we lost the opportunity to take a leadership role and to use this to win the battle for structure— not only with the family but also with the community agencies.

It also is likely that our difficulties in establishing a workable therapeutic structure with the family and the agencies were increased because we did not sufficiently clarify the structure of our relationship with each other as cotherapists. Without making an explicit plan for our respective roles, it appears that Wynne took the leadership within the meetings with the family and Green took the early leadership for contacts with the family and community agencies between the family meetings. Later, our notes reveal that Wynne was being contacted by some of the school officials and was writing to them, so that the earlier, more clear division of roles became blurred. This split undoubtedly made contact with us more difficult for the family and community agencies who may not have been quite sure with whom they were dealing. This muddy perception of us would have been the reciprocal of our not knowing with whom we were dealing in the family, school, and county agency.

Hypothetical Reconstruction toward Success

If this family were referred to us today, we would not begin with such a loose cotherapy arrangement. The relationship between Wynne and Green at the time of this therapy was that of supervisor and supervisee (Fellow). Wynne now would want a more structured relationship, most likely with the family therapy Fellow doing all of the therapy and Wynne serving as a live supervisor or consultant—either observing through a one-way mirror or entering the room only part of the time to help out with specific issues. With a supervisee who was a novice, which Green was not, Wynne might take primary therapeutic responsibility, with the trainee present but clearly in a secondary role. On the other hand, with a more experienced therapist as a colleague (as Green would be today), Wynne might advocate reversing the roles, with Green serving as a consultant supervisor. Having a second person involved in the role of colleague–consultant is especially helpful with families who are confusing and perplexing, such as this one. This approach also reflects the influence of the Milan group in working as teams of colleagues and reversing roles with a series of families (Selvini-Palazzoli, Cecchin, Prata, & Boscolo, 1978). Another approach to the cotherapy roles that was partially used with this family and has been recommended by Aponte (1976) is to have one therapist take primary responsibility for the work with the family system and the other therapist for work with the school.

One of the hazards of a loosely structured cotherapy relationship is that it is all too easy for the therapists to evade dealing with differences and responsibility about what should be done. Each therapist can unwittingly assume that the other will take the responsibility, resulting in a lack of effective leadership by either. In effect, the avoidance of the divergence constitutes a pseudomutual cotherapy relationship (Wynne et al., 1958). Thus, the first step toward improved results would be to structure more clearly the cotherapy relationship.

When a family such as the Ts is highly pseudomutual in its bland way of dealing with difficulties and differences within the family and externalizing them all onto the environment, the therapists need to be well-differentiated in their relationship with one another and in their game plan. The support that we each gave the other as cotherapists helped us to tolerate the frustration of the "therapy" as long as we did; if either of us had worked with this family on a solo or more clearly primary basis, he probably would have been more anxious, more frustrated, and more energetic in defining the problem and in changing it.

In the initial interview with this family, when we discovered that the family saw the problem as being with a school official, a start toward a more successful outcome could have been made by our raising the question of whether the school official should be present. Such a family–school interview, preferably at the school, would follow the model recommended by Aponte (1976). Ideally, this three-way meeting should constitute the first contact with the family. Given the concealed referral process, this could have been arranged only after much telephone discussion, but, even after a delay, such a joint meeting probably would have been useful.

When explicitly suggesting that the school people should be participant, we probably would have started hearing more quickly about the legal pressures being applied to the family. It is striking that it was only shortly before termination that we learned that the real legal responsibility lay with the Child Protective Unit and not with the school. Before establishing a regular appointment schedule with the family, we should have clarified explicitly the formal relationships between each of the community agencies, between each of them and the family, and our potential role with each of them—beginning, if possible, with the Child Protective Unit.

Such explorations could lead to a consultant role for the family clinician. As a consultant to those persons with legal and educational authority, leverage may be more strategically utilized to effect change. With externalizing families, consistent extrafamilial pressure often seems necessary to generate sufficiently motivating intrafamilial distress. When many helping persons are involved, the external pressure may be nullified by their incompatible treatment goals and strategies. With the T family, the family consultant might have helped centralize the treatment responsibility in the hands of the Child Protective Unit worker assigned to the case. In this way, knowledge *and* authority could have been utilized together in treatment, rather than having these two sources of leverage working at cross-purposes. From this perspective, the family consultant helps with the "problems" of the "on-line" worker.

A different approach that might have been useful would have been to accept initially the family's externalization of responsibility for the problem onto the community. The therapists are then in a position to help the family members with an acknowledged family dilemma—how to have their needs met (e.g., for education) and yet to interact with what the family views as an unfair or prejudiced community in such a way as to stay out of trouble. This approach could involve much more meaningful joining with the family in a shared task. Then, a variety of paradoxical maneuvers could be introduced as well as Whitaker's (1976) psychotherapy of the absurd. The malevolence of the community could be fantasized by the therapists as so great that even the family would laughingly question where reality begins and ends.

Another approach that accepts some of the externalization in family systems selects only one or a subset of family members who seem most accessible for change. Following systems theory, a change in the behavior of one family member produces corresponding changes in the entire family system so that it may not be necessary to have the entire family attend sessions (Weakland, Fisch, Watzlawick, & Bodin, 1974). In the case of the Ts, it may have been sufficient to see only the mother who, after all, was the organizer and spokesperson for the family, and to coach strategically her efforts to change the family system.

Still another alternative, which we would be apt to utilize today, is a paradoxical intervention of the following form and after a few sessions when essential data were available: Tell the family that no intervention should be made or change undertaken at this point because the family is not ready. Praise the family's unity against outsiders and discuss the dangers of change in terms of a threat to family stability. Point out how much fun the family members have with their individual truancies and that these need to be protected for the time being by each of them covering up for one another. Then, after concluding that no therapy is needed, schedule another session. In dealing with community agencies, an abbreviated report of this presentation may suffice so long as one emphasizes that therapy is not recommended although some consultations have taken place.

A variation of the full-fledged paradoxical intervention is to know when you are licked and get out as soon as possible. Here one simply accepts at face value the externalizing family's statement that it has no problem. In announcing his or her exit, the therapist expresses perplexity about whether or not the family actually has a problem and merely states that he or she has heard from the family that no family problem requiring therapy exists. On the basis of this statement by the family, the therapists take the initiative to discontinue the treatment (Selvini-Palazzoli *et al.*, 1978). It is important to recognize that in certain situations, this alternative is not advisable or even possible (e.g., in the case of suspected child abuse or other family violence, and in certain professional settings where the provision of treatment is legally mandated).

With the T family we terminated with the statement that we could not work "under these circumstances." For this pushed-around family, this may have been a positive move. At least we have no reports that matters became publicly *worse*. Earlier and more strategically planned expressions of our impotence probably would have been useful.

In conclusion it can be questioned whether clinical efforts of any type are feasible and appropriate for this kind of family. The therapists had moments of both optimism and pessimism throughout the course of therapy, and it is possible that the optimism was self-generated rather than based on a realistic assessment of the potential for change.

It is our experience that cases such as the T's are frequently avoided by family therapists or not pursued at such great length. They are more likely to be followed sporadically by caseworkers in county social service departments who typically work with the mother alone and occasionally make home visits. Although the entire "therapy" was stretched out over about 4 months, the number of sessions in which we actually met was few—many meetings were aborted when various family members did not arrive. The family's central pattern of externalizing responsibility for change from the family onto various components of the community was repeated by each of the professional groups involved in the case—from the school to the Child Protective Unit to the therapy team and back again.

REFERENCES

Aponte, H. J. The family–school interview: An eco-structural approach. *Family Process*, 1976, *15*, 303–311.

Napier, A. Y., & Whitaker, C. A. *The family crucible.* New York: Harper & Row, 1978.

Selvini-Palazzoli, M., Boscolo. L., Cecchin, G., & Prata, G. The problem of the referring person. *Journal of Marital and Family Therapy*, 1980, *6*, 3–9.

Selvini-Palazzoli, M., Cecchin, G., Prata, G., & Boscolo, L. *Paradox and counterparadox.* New York: Jason Aronson, 1978.

Weakland, J., Fisch, R., Watzlawick, P., & Bodin, A. M. Brief therapy: Focused problem resolution. *Family Process*, 1974, *13*, 141–168.

Whitaker, C. A. Psychotherapy of the absurd: With a special emphasis on the psychotherapy of aggression. *Family Process*, 1976, *14*, 1–16.

Wynne, L. C., Ryckoff, I. M., Day, J., & Hirsch, S. I. Pseudo-mutuality in the family relations of schizophrenics. *Psychiatry*, 1958, *21*, 205–220.

6

Five Factors of Failure in Structural-Strategic Family Therapy: A Contextual Construction

HOWARD A. LIDDLE

> Give me a fruitful error any time, full of seeds, bursting with its own correc-
> tions. You can keep your sterile "truth" for yourself.—Vilfredo Pareto

Introduction

It is not often discussed in graduate school course work on psychotherapy, nor in the freestanding institutes training postdegree professionals in the difficult art of family therapy. Not one of the more popular items of collegial discussion, it is similarly not something family therapists prefer to dwell on in their solitary moments. Still, this mostly ignored topic, which endures as chiefly unpleasant, is constantly confronted by therapists of both sexes, every orientation, and every age and stage of career development. It represents an inevitable aspect of the experience of being, becoming, and remaining a family therapist. Yet this crucial commonality remains one of the least overtly and least critically treated topics in a field still struggling for its niche in the world of psychotherapy. We refer here, of course, to the matter of therapeutic failure—heretofore a topic of literally unspeakable proportions.

> Our traditional American response to failures is to reject them, to consign them, metaphorically or actually to the refuse heap where they are expected to decay and disappear into our tolerant environment like all of our wastes and useless by-products. We tend not to recycle our failures and process what may be valuable in them, to examine the conditions under which they occur so as to make appropriate adjustments in our procedures. (Graziano & Bythell, 1983, p. 406)

In psychotherapy and in particular in family therapy, it is unfortunate that such recycling—a process that would redefine failure as informationally

Howard A. Liddle. Division of Family and Community Medicine, University of California School of Medicine, San Francisco, California; Mental Research Institute, Palo Alto, California; Family Institute of San Francisco, San Francisco, California.

useful feedback for the redesign and recalibration of our therapy models—has not yet occurred. This kind of movement seems unlikely, however, without significant value shifts. The procedure of reframing, long known to family therapists, might help in this regard.

> Errors usually have their good reasons once we penetrate their context properly and avoid judgement according to our current perception of "truth." They are usually more enlightening than embarrassing for they are signs of changing contexts. . . . The study of inspired error should not engender a homily about the sin of pride; it should lead us to a recognition that the capacity for great insight and great error are opposite sides of the same coin—and that the currency of both is brilliance. (Gould, 1980, p. 243)

Our fashion magazines of the day, broadcast and print media, and numerous representatives of modern chic culture have declared, especially to women, that thin is beautiful. Just as the magazine models set unrealistic standards by their mere presence, the family therapy field has its counterpart of utopian goal propagation. Several factors seem culpable in this regard. First the family therapy field was largely founded on the impressive clinical artistry of several charismatic pioneers. Over the years a proliferation of conferences and workshops have allowed therapists to witness the Great Originals (Hoffman, 1981) perform their therapeutic magic. Eventually, slickly edited training tapes of the masters became more visible to the developing therapists who could review the experts' moves over and over again.

A generation of therapists has been raised on the notion that tapes such as these represent both how therapists should act and how therapy routinely should be done. It is somehow easy to forget the many years of experience and personal development contributing to the skill of the master therapist idolized on the video monitor. Nonetheless, examples of this kind of ultra high-level therapist functioning—which can be simultaneously helpful as a model, yet harmful as a perpetuator of utopian myths about clinical wizardry and therapeutic magic—continue to flourish in the family therapy field. Videotapes are analogous to a Greatest Hits record of powerful interventions. It would be uncommon indeed to have appear a training tape of the masters' outtakes or Greatest Failures. Thus the culture of family therapy has continued to exist, indeed flourish without a systematic, thoughtful treatment of the topic of clinical failure. In this sense we have lagged behind other subsystems in the psychotherapy field—such as behavior therapy—that have been significantly more forthright in addressing what is for most therapists a frankly unpleasant subject.

This chapter addresses at a broad level the implications of introducing new values and attitudes about failure into the field of family therapy. By posing what might be considered a prototype schema useful for others examining this topic, the chapter argues for a contextual definition of failure through an examination of five interrelated factors of failure as they applied to a structural–strategic theoretical position. Finally, this chapter is an attempt to offer some conceptual and pragmatic guidelines for those working to build an integrative structural–strategic family therapy.

Theoretical Frame of Reference

The conceptual framework employed with the clinical case in question was a structural–strategic model of family therapy—an approach only recently developed in the literature (Fraser, 1982; Stanton, 1981a, 1981b). It must be noted that the model attempted when the case was seen (over 8 years ago) was distinctly less integrated than the present version (Liddle, 1984).

The topic of how distinct approaches to family therapy can be integrated in practice is currently a popular and important topic in the field (Gurman, 1981; Liddle, 1982; Pinsof, 1983). Two important aspects of this integration issue are (1) the degree to which models are theoretically and/or technically compatible and (2) the extent to which the models truly blend to become a single, unified approach, or merely coexist side-by-side in their original forms. These aspects of the matter of integration are addressed later in the chapter, as factors in an unsuccessful implementation of a structural–strategic approach to family therapy.

Basic Concepts of Structural–Strategic Therapy

The essential ingredients of structural–strategic therapy can obviously be found in the original work of Minuchin (1974) and Haley (1976). Additionally, more detailed analyses of the distinct advantages of structural and strategic therapies can be found elsewhere (Aponte & Van Deusen, 1981; Liddle, 1981, 1982c; Stanton, 1981c) as can a comparison of structural and strategic therapies with each other and with several other contemporary schools of family therapy (Liddle, 1982b). Although there are many branches of what has become strategic family therapy in various stages of development, the present structural–strategic model defines its strategic components along the lines of Haley's work, although the work of the Brief Therapy Center group of the Mental Research Institute (MRI) has also had conceptual and pragmatic relevance.

Although a working knowledge of structural and strategic therapies is assumed, a brief summary and review here of the basic operating principles of these viewpoints should assist in reading the case material to follow.

ORGANIZATION/STRUCTURE OF THE FAMILY

Not seen as a static entity, the ways in which a family is organized are deduced from the repeating acts, *sequences*, which are observed in the session and elicited through self-reports. The structure is the sum of the rules of interaction. The therapist perceives the family as internally organized, and as comprised of a series of interdependent yet distinct subsystems (individual, sibling, parental, and marital). Families maintain themselves by generic or universal rules, such as hierarchical organization, as well as by idiosyncratic rules. The therapist probes for a picture of the family's rules of organization (e.g., patterns of redundancy) along several dimensions of family functioning:

1. negotiation of proximity and distance of relationships (fostering belongingness while preserving individuation);
2. clarity of boundaries (defined as the rules governing participation) within and between subsystems;
3. autonomy and interdependence of subsystem functioning;
4. the family's flexible adaptation to natural development and transitions;
5. the family's accommodation to unforeseen needs for change (fortuitous life events);
6. the family's relationship to broader systems of influence (work, community, ethnic, cross-cultural factors).

The therapist is interested in the interactional sequences that surround the presenting problem. These sequences are revealed through verbal description, the self-reports of family members, as well as through observing the way family members interact in an interview. The therapist then can move beyond the individual, linear versions of reality presented by each family member, that is, beyond a conversational to a more experiential form of in-session process. In this fashion the family's typical ways of responding and behaving can be assessed by encouraging the presenting problem to be brought into the interview room. Doing so provides the therapist with a new and valuable source of interactional, experientially derived observable information not obtainable through the serial delivery of self-reports.

Enactment—the art of asking family members to deal with each other in the therapist's presence—is not only an assessment tool, but it is also seen as a means of creating a context from which new possibilities can emerge. The family members then have a setting in which experimentation with new ways of relating can be tried.

The therapist's role according to the structural–strategic viewpoint embodies elements of both in-session and out-of-session theories of change. The therapist uses himself or herself as an instrument of change during the interview. Through a skillful blending of support and challenge, family members are helped to experience new relational realities and perceptual and behavioral alternatives during the session. In addition, however, the therapist employs directives (between-session tasks), reflecting an assumption that the seeds of change are not only sown in the therapy room. Devising and assigning a family a task to carry out between sessions intensifies the relationship with the therapist. These tasks are always informationally useful whether or not they are followed and, most centrally, are ways in which the problematic, repeating sequences that maintain the symptomatic behavior can be altered. Directives, in and outside of sessions, are one way of moving toward the basic goal of therapy, "to get people to behave differently and so to have different subjective experiences" (Haley, 1976, p. 49). Directives can thus introduce the possibility of greater complexity, and provide concrete opportunities to extend and solidify the newly forming relational pathways forged through in-session enactments.

Background

Mary Lou, a 40-year-old single woman, telephoned the university-based community mental health clinic seeking help with what she called her "compulsions." For the previous 8 years, upon entering a grocery or department store, she would feel overwhelming impulses to buy or sometimes shoplift mass quantities of inexpensive items she did not really need. During the first telephone contact Mary Lou indicated that she lived with her 77-year-old mother, Mrs. M, and although Mary Lou had been in individual therapy intermittently for many years, her mother had never been requested to take part in any of these therapeutic endeavors.

Later in the telephone intake and during the initial interview with mother and daughter (Mary Lou's first response to the request to bring Mrs. M to the first session was completely positive), Mary Lou revealed more extensive aspects of the presenting complaint. Along with the compulsive behavior that had assumed significant proportions 8 years ago, Mary Lou had been collecting and saving these purchased items, along with a large assortment and quantity of magazines and newspapers. The items were placed mostly in large paper shopping bags, the kind with cloth handles to ease their carrying, and spread throughout their modest one-bedroom apartment. There were, however, more than a few bags strewn about the premises—the apartment was literally a sea of the white bags. Every room of the pair's dwelling was thus cluttered with chest-high piles of the collectible-filled shopping bags—each bearing the distinctive royal blue seal of the same store from which they were obtained. Accommodatingly, paths were cut and in the main maintained—reminiscent of those narrow pathways that might be needed to allow movement through drifts of snow. Incredibly, the collecting and compulsions had existed for the previous 16 years, growing especially unmanageable and voluminous during the last half of that time.

"Well, I'm—you know, nervous" captured Mary Lou's basic description of herself. Her extensive experience in numerous forms of mental health care in the city (individual therapies, group, milieu, and the ever-present drug therapy) made her a kind of self-styled consumer expert on local psychotherapy possibilities. Despite this impressive parade of treatments, all were reported as failures; none had successfully cured the presenting problem of compulsions and hoarding. Significantly, and sadly as a comment on our mental health care system and degree of family therapy influence, the other family member with whom she had lived for more than 20 years was not once included in any of these multiple therapeutic efforts.

Mary Lou's degree of socialization into the culture of a career patient was impressive—one aspect of which was her own and her mother's financial and emotional dependence on Social Security Income (financial aid for those certified by the state as mentally disabled). Mary Lou was not only a vociferous consumer critic of mental health care in the area, but also an avid reader of the latest psychology-oriented books for the public. Early in therapy she volunteered insightful, book-review variety commentary on two recent self-help volumes: one on separating from one's parents, the other on overcoming compulsive habits. Her previous therapy "training," along with this independent study of mass-market literature led Mary Lou to have a highly developed capacity to psychologize much of her time away. Thus, although from a certain viewpoint, a patient's and family's ability to conceptualize abstractly with psychological–social awareness is defined as an asset, Mary Lou probably was overorganized in this regard.

Mrs. M, Mary Lou's mother, had just turned 77 at therapy's onset and had recently retired from a salesperson position in a large, prestigious downtown department store. Mrs. M was successfully employed at the store for many years and was receiving a modest but needed pension check along with Social Security. Mr. and Mrs. M had been separated for 20 years, he having long since returned to his native England, also the birthplace and childhood home of Mrs. M. It was hardly the vast distance alone which led to the lack of contact between the father and his wife and daughter. The report from both Mother and Daughter about the marriage coincided—it seemed to be a distant relationship with basic disagreements in many areas. There was another daughter, 18 months older than Mary Lou, who lived on the opposite coast. The older sibling left home stormily at age 18 and got married several years later. She is still married and has one child. Like Mr. M, the older sibling rarely saw or contacted Mary Lou and Mrs. M over the years.

Diagnosis and Treatment Plan

Over the past 2 decades, Mrs. M and Mary Lou had created a context that would be uninhabitable by most of us. It was a highly circumscribed island of their own design. They were isolated from other family members and although Mary Lou and her mother had mutual friends, each rarely saw someone else without the other. Most of Mary Lou's social network over the years had been with mental health professionals.

At the time of the telephone intake, as with most referrals, it was possible to hypothesize a fair amount about the interactive nature of the presenting problem. In this case especially, the simple fact of the family's composition, ages, and the nature of their living situation could not help but lead to clear hypotheses. The family's degree of overinvolvement, in relation both to the hoarding as well as in many other areas, was curtailing each member's potential functioning. When a family consists of only two people:

> The therapist can guess that these two people probably rely on each other a great deal. If they are mother and child, the child may spend much time in the company of adults. She [the child] may have advanced verbal skills, and because of a high percentage of interaction with adults, she may become interested in adult issues before her peers and appear more mature. She may spend less time with peers than the usual child, having less in common with them, and she may be at a disadvantage in physical play. The mother is free, if she chooses, to give the child more individual attention than would be possible if there were a husband or other children to be concerned with. As a result, she may be very good at reading the child's moods, satisfying her needs, and answering her questions. She may, indeed, have a tendency to over-read the child, as she has no one else on whom to concentrate. She may have no one with whom to check her observations. The result can be an intense style of relating which fosters mutual dependence and mutual resentment at the same time. (Minuchin & Fishman, 1981, p. 51)

This description, although describing a mother and younger child's organization, is strikingly reflective of the family under discussion.

From the present theoretical viewpoint, then, issues of boundary blurring and subsystem dysfunction seized our immediate attention. Operating at the enmeshed side of the continuum of boundary functioning, the interpersonal boundary (rules defining who participates in which subsystems and how) was considered quite diffuse. Mary Lou, in especially overt ways at least, had little identity outside of the one as a chronic patient who acted as an inseparable member of a dyadic holon. The pair, despite their protestations to the contrary, acted as if it were not possible for each to exist as separate individuals. Indeed, from a family life-cycle perspective, the dyad's exclusionary tightness took precedence over the formation of other developmentally appropriate relationships.

While a problematically diffuse boundary existed between Mother and Daughter, a rigid boundary was maintained around them in relation to their world at large. Their high degree of mutual dependence and reliance on the other for everyday concrete and emotional needs was evident from the first contact. Hierarchically, Mrs. M and Mary Lou often related more at a sibling than intergenerational level. Seeing them together, we often wondered what the quality of each's life without the other would realistically be like.

Both Mother and Daughter were in clear and severe emotional stress at the time of intake. Consistent with Minuchin's definition of families with preferred transactional styles of enmeshment, this family responded "to any variation from the accustomed with excessive speed and intensity" (Minuchin, 1974, p. 55). This high degree of interpersonal reactivity was apparent from the initial interview.

In addition to being a clearly defined patient in their limited social world, Mary Lou was also very much in an incompetent position in relation to her mother. While Mrs. M had successfully worked for many years, Mary Lou had had several jobs—all of which led to an identical outcome. In Mary Lou's own words, "Sometimes I think my mother's got ESP—that she's psychic. I lost six jobs. She told me I'd be fired and I was—from all six of them."

This brief statement captures the extent to which Mary Lou attributed (i.e., gave) power to her mother. In the initial session Mary Lou went considerably beyond her original (telephone intake) definition of the problem as hoarding and compulsive urges. "My mother tends to be a very domineering and powerful person . . . but then, that's just the way she is—she can't help it, really."

This sequence, Mary Lou's criticism of Mother followed by a softening and absolution, was one which we would see isomorphically again and again in the course of therapy.

Not surprisingly, Mrs. M's main complaint was the condition of the apartment. She stated that she did not have access to many of her clothes and personal belongings, as the sheer volume of bags blocked all storage areas. Mrs. M bitterly complained about not being able to gain entry into a certain closet to retrieve a needed table fan for over 2 years! In the mother's words: "I'm in a prison, a cage. She domineers me with the bags." When pressed as to why she did not simply move the bags herself, Mrs. M replied that when she had tried to do so Mary Lou became hysterical and would likely "beat me for touching them." Interestingly, each accused the other of a dominating demeanor, and it was not difficult to quickly obtain a picture of how this reciprocal control (or at least attempts at control) was acted out.

Mother complained that when she was not being "tortured by that situation in the house," her daughter was demanding that *she* go into the stores and buy the unneeded items, "She wears me down with lists. She gives me lists of things, silly things, she wants me to buy. After I buy them, she puts them into the bags."

Mary Lou enlisted and gained her mother's full, but overtly grudging complicity in the perpetuation and amplification of the symptom. Mother was thus actually purchasing items that she knew would become part of Mary Lou's permanent collection.

The interactional nature of the symptom began to emerge: Mary Lou's hoarding behavior, from her vantage point, was in response to her mother's overcontrolling nature. Mrs. M indicates that her daughter needs help for her "nervous condition," bitterly complaining about "being completely domineered by the bags." Over the years, the symptom of collecting and hoarding seems to have become more firmly established with the dimension of Mary Lou's *fear of entering stores.* In her words this latest problem began as an attempted solution, an adaptive mechanism "to try and stop my compulsions." From this point, Mother becomes an obvious active agent, a coconspirator in the accumulation and collection process—all the while steadfastly and vociferously complaining about her daughter's "problem."

Treatment Plan and Therapeutic Strategy

At the beginning of therapy, treatment objectives were categorized according to ultimate (long-term) and mediating goals (short-term, necessary steps in the achievement of longer-term objectives). The ultimate objectives with the M family were envisioned along the following lines:

1. Family life-cycle goals. Mother and Daughter could live separately and be capable of living more productive, satisfying, developmentally appropriate lives. In the absence of this degree of separateness, Mother and Daughter could have more functional, less constricting lives—an existence, for example, in which Mary Lou could feel more able, and reciprocally be permitted to have some productive aspects of her life that would be distinct from her mother.

2. Individual goals beyond asymptomatic functioning. Goals for Mary Lou included alteration of her persistent image of herself as an incompetent, helpless patient, whose only perceived means of coping with the relationship with her mother was to collect and defend what she felt to be tangible extensions of herself. Additionally, we had hoped to involve Mary Lou in the world of relationships and work. Alternately, initial goals for Mother included her increased capacity to truly permit and assist in the promotion of independence and competence in her daughter. Further objectives of course included assisting the mother in managing her own life-cycle issues—the difficulties of loneliness, isolation, and declining health in her advancing years.

3. Symptom amelioration of the identified patient. Ultimate goals with Mary Lou included a cessation of her compulsive hoarding and fears of compulsive behavior. Mediating goals were to achieve an in-session, week-to-week change of the transactional style of the mother and daughter. That is, for the aforementioned longer-term objectives to be reached it was felt that the boundary issues needed to be solved—evidence of which could be observed in the session. The therapist would first need to join with and support the family members, establish a workable interpersonal base for the problem, and work in the sessions to prompt new patterns between Mother and Daughter. The therapist would need to shape the in-session enactments to challenge existing rigidities and explore new, alternative ways of relating. Between-session directives would build upon and further the changes begun during sessions. Enactments would work at the level of the minute-by-minute sequences between the pair, while the between-interview tasks would intervene at more broadly defined units of sequence that were more difficult to track in sessions.

Process of Therapy

This section summarizes the major themes developed during therapy with the M family. Its intent is to portray the flow and sequence of therapy. A point-by-point analysis is reserved for the next major section of the chapter, the five factors of failure.

There were three distinct stages to our work with the M family. The first lasted 7 months and was comprised of 15 sessions. This proved to be the lengthiest and most intense contact with the family. There were two themes of concurrent focus during this phase:

> 1. The presenting complaint of Mary Lou—her compulsive behavior of collecting and hoarding bags.
> 2. The problematic relationship of Mother and Daughter.

Early in therapy it became relatively simple to focus on the metaphoric aspects of the bag collection in the dyad's relationship. Mary Lou discussed the ways in which she felt controlled by her mother. Her interpretation of why the bags were present was reminiscent of an anorexic's description of one outcome of refusing to eat, "Okay, mummy, you say I'm domineering about the bags? Yes, maybe that's the only thing I have to be . . . to hold on to . . . to make me somebody who says—no, you can't control me anymore."

Despite this articulateness about the function of the symptom in their relationship, the situation of Mary Lou's collecting behavior changed very little during the course of therapy. Although the volume with which she collected did diminish, the old materials and new purchases were still saved, despite a variety of attempts by the therapists, and eventually her mother, to have her gradually dispose of the bags. Along these lines, we worked quite directly on the issue of what Mary Lou would substitute for the bags. In this way we hoped to be able to introduce new possibilities into the mother-daughter relationship.

As a teenager and developing young adult, we learned that Mary Lou had always been extremely timid and subservient to her parents (especially, of course, to her mother). We thereby were able to introduce the theme of Mary Lou's lack of appropriate developmental progression; that she and her mother as well had missed a crucial aspect of maturation.

The bags' existence was redefined as a necessary boundary-maker between Mother and Daughter. In their bedroom the two twin beds were separated by an ever-present row of bags. They were also framed as a manifestation of the parental rebellion that Mary Lou, unlike other adolescents and young adults, had neglected in her earlier years. This rebellion was defined as a natural and necessary stage in the independence process. A major theme therefore became the mother's and daughter's capacity to redo an aspect of their own family life cycle. This encompassed their ability to allow Mary Lou's development as a competent, separate individual, and to permit her mother more freedom from the burden of caring for a grown-up child.

The therapeutic focus emphasized plans to help Mary Lou replace the hoarding with new ways of responding to her mother and life. Sessions, both with Mary Lou and her mother individually and together, directly addressed the form this new relationship would take as well as the implications for change for both Mother and Daughter. Here the therapist worked both a structural and strategic posture of change. In the former case in-session dialogue between Mrs. M and her daughter was fostered on themes of how togetherness and distance could be negotiated.

As Mary Lou began to be more appropriately assertive in relation to her mother, the expected concomitant distance began to appear in their relationship. Predictably, Mary Lou served as a barometer of this therapy-induced crisis and became symptomatic. However, the timing and nature of her symptoms were in this case not only predictable, they were fully understandable in light of the emerging process between Mother and Daughter. Mary Lou began to experience tremendous isolation, depression, reported frequent suicidal thoughts, and began to show extreme dependence on the therapist as a source of support, telephoning several times a week to report her distress. Additionally, she began to call the local crisis/suicide prevention services with similar frequency. At this time and others in which the consequences of relationship change were clearly in evidence, the therapeutic stance included more strategic components, specifically those addressing the consequences of change. The paradoxical challenges ("Perhaps working on your competence in this relationship is not the proper thing to do. It's causing you too much upset. As you yourself have said, Miss M, until there is something to replace the bags, they probably should remain where they are") were worked mainly through Mary Lou, although some were offered through her mother as well ("She's been with you all these years, so loyal. If she became normal, she'd have to do what everyone else does—go out and live life away from their parents, grow up, and be on their own. That would be a tremendous loss—a change for you as well").

The major change during this first phase was a shift in the relationship between Mother and Daughter. As Mary Lou put it, her "coming out" was indeed different, yet the symptom (or the metaphor, depending on one's perspective) remained. The bag collection never appreciably diminished during these 7 months of therapy. Mary Lou did, however, become more assertive and forceful in relation to her mother. These changes encompassed both her *reactions* (especially in terms of her mother's criticism) and her capacity to *initiate* nonprovoking dialogues with mother (expressing clearly her expectations about what she wanted in life and how she would like to be treated by her mother). These kinds of changes were observed in and reported as occurring between sessions. In the last phase of this main phase of therapy, Mary Lou relayed a story which to her exemplified the nature of this change. The incident includes Mother, Daughter, and William, one of their mutual friends, with whom they would frequently meet for lunch.

All three of us were together, sitting on a bench in the park. I was feeling good—you know, happy on that day. I started to, well, laugh a little bit—I got up and danced a little too. Then my mother—I could tell—got mad at me. She said, "I'm embarrassed by you." All three of us then went to the restaurant for lunch. My mother turned William against me—making fun of what I did. But what I did after that was different. I decided that it wasn't going to get me down. She doesn't realize what it feels like for 40 years to not be considered valid, as a person.

During this period Mrs. M's behavior shifted somewhat as well, yet not drastically. She was less apt to engage her daughter in symmetrical struggles during sessions. By the end of the 15 sessions, the mother too displayed a good deal of cognitive clarity about the inflexible nature of their relationship.

MRS. M: (*To Mary Lou.*) I think I made a big mistake years back. I should have let you go on your own years ago.

MARY LOU: You never let me grow up in my own way.

MRS. M: I know I've done the worst thing. I've protected you too much. I've done the wrong thing all these years. Protected you? Yes—because you told me how nervous you were. I should have, little by little, let you go on your own.

Although Miss M was more active outside of her relationship with her mother—she interviewed for jobs, volunteer work, and tried to make social contacts—her improved intentions in this sphere were not matched by improved outcome. Mary Lou did not find a genuine job or volunteer situation. She was attempting more social contacts and was mildly successful in this regard. By the close of therapy, she appeared to have more self-confidence, a sharper definition of her own worthwhileness apart from a member of a dyad with her mother, was able to challenge her mother more directly in sessions, and to be clear about the kind of relationship she might like with her. However, the issue of the presence of the bags and the fears associated with their removal persisted. There was no appreciable change in their daily schedules of togetherness-filled activities or their use of time. The escalating arguments between Mother and Daughter diminished but did not end. In a sad way, each seemed to act as if they were now resigned to a fate of living together for the remainder of their lives.

This resignation and despondent feeling was shared by the therapist who initiated therapy's termination on the verge of the 8th month—believing that enough had been tried that proved unsuccessful. Termination was actually framed to the family along the lines of a break in the therapy. The rationale was a wait-and-see stance—it dealt with the issue of whether time outside of a therapeutic context might amplify some of the small changes made during therapy. The therapeutic situation was apparently effective to some extent, with in-session changes and some out-of-session change reported. The therapy was not successful, however, in terms of significant symptom alleviation outside of the interview context.

Another session was set for 2 months from the time of the 15th interview. When this next session was held, there was still no appreciable difference reported. The improvements that had been achieved were maintained, but the bags remained along with a belief system that a move by either the mother or daughter to discard them would result in interpersonal chaos. Three sessions in all were held during this brief second phase.

Almost 1 year to the day after this third interview and just prior to a scheduled follow-up telephone call, Mary Lou called in a crisis. She would not indicate the exact nature of the crisis over the phone, only that it was extremely urgent and that her situation was in dire need of immediate attention. Her request to come in for this session alone was granted and she was seen by the author in a few days (the PhD student cotherapist was no longer in the geographic area). Mary Lou reported that since the family therapy had ceased, she had sought individual treatment in a renowned behavior therapy center. She complained about the methods prescribed for treating compulsive behavior, as well as about the lack of relationship developed with the therapist during her brief try at a strict behavioral approach. She reported that the treatment failed and was distraught over another unsuccessful therapeutic venture, but at the moment was much more upset over a new, externally imposed, crisis.

Amazingly, it seems that in Mrs. M and Mary Lou's apartment building there existed two other sets of tenants with their apartments in a condition similar to their own (piles of papers, bags, etc.). Mary Lou related the tale of the "Hamilton sisters, whose place was in the same kind of shape as ours, until the manager found out." After being discovered the sisters were faced with eviction or an immediate clean up of the collection. Under this pressure the sisters' apartment was rearranged according to the manager's specifications, and they were permitted to stay. Through the doorman Mary Lou learned about an elderly, single man who lived down the hall and also hoarded things. (She briefly peeked into his place through the front door.) The manager had not yet found out about this gentleman's apartment, but had learned about the collection of Mary Lou and her mother through an unknown source. Just a few days before, the manager had informed Mary Lou in no uncertain terms that she had 2 weeks to "clear out the junk in that apartment. It's a fire hazard," or face eviction.

Mary Lou was panicked. She began to clean up some of the apartment on her own, concentrating on items that she felt were less personal than boxed and bagged articles of her own and her mother's clothing, for example, which she found very difficult to disturb. Our individual session lasted over 2 hours and focused on Mary Lou's alternatives: to engage in an activity that had been unaffected by many years of therapy, or be cast out of one's home of over 10 years. The therapist alternately assumed a straightforward problem-solving stance (how much could be moved by when, who might serve as resources to help, would Mary Lou speak to the manager again before the inspection date, etc.) as well as a more indirect posture toward change (was there enough newness in Mary Lou's relationship with her mother to replace the bags, since they had been such a central aspect of their lives over the years? Could Mary Lou really get rid of them?). This interview thus covered the steps involved in the change threatened by the imposition of a severe new rule, as well as the personal, emotional, and relational consequences of this change. Not surprisingly, Mary Lou appeared at this session quite sick with the flu. She spoke freely about "how sad and depressed I am and how tremendously traumatic this whole ordeal had become. When I throw stuff out, I feel that I'll never get anything again." One got the feeling that Mary Lou was talking about giving up an important part of herself; it was as if she were losing some familiar companions. She was only too aware that without them, there would only be herself and her mother.

Somehow in the following 2 weeks, Mary Lou managed to discard most of the clutter and actually enlisted her mother (and William, their mutual friend) to help in the process. Although the apartment was not totally in order, it was sufficiently cleared out to avoid eviction—the manager's inspection was passed. Mary Lou reported that the relationship with her mother was about the same as at the end of therapy 1 year ago. She was not working or looking for work, was not making plans to move out, was, however, increasingly worried about her mother's health; yet she did not feel that additional therapy at that time would be beneficial. The therapist agreed and reminded her of the opportunity to return to therapy at any future time.

A telephone follow-up 5 years after this final contact began like this:

THERAPIST: Hello, is this Mrs. M? This is Dr. Liddle, your old therapist from the clinic at Temple University; I'm calling to see how you and Mary Lou are doing.

MRS. M: Oh my my goodness! You're going to have a shock, you're going to have quite a shock.

THERAPIST: (*Fearing the worst.*) What's happened?

MRS. M: Mary Lou's married!!

Mrs. M gleefully relayed the news that 6 months prior to this follow-up call, Mary Lou had married a man she met in their apartment building (not the person down the hall with the matching symptom). Mrs. M expressed how happy and relieved she felt now that her daughter was out of the house and on her own ("I'm free!"). The condition of the house never returned to the level it reached during or prior to family therapy. Ironically, it was the intervention of the apartment manager and not therapy that broke the symptom of the bags.

Analysis of Five Factors of Failure

This section details a retrospective construction of five variables that, in their own and in synergistic ways, could be said to have contributed to the unsuccessful outcome of family therapy with Mary Lou and her mother. It should be emphasized that these factors must be considered as interdependent, mutually influencing processes—as interconnected verbs, so to speak, rather than discrete nouns. This analysis is scarcely the type where we can partial out how much variance can be accounted for with each one, nor should we necessarily hypothesize about one or two factors being *the* crucial, causative culprits. In the realm of the following discussion, we deal much more at the level of probability and correlation than with if–then, pretherapy–posttherapy certainties. The serial presentation, and more basically, the partialing out of each factor in this presentation is accomplished for heuristic purposes. Additionally, the following five factors are not intended as an exhaustive compilation. Rather, after contemplation of the case and the thorny topic of psychotherapy failure, it was decided that the multidimensioned experience could reasonably be covered under these headings.

There remains yet another significant dimension to consider before our content discussion commences. This aspect, perhaps it might be termed a *metafactor*, concerns the arbitrary, nonobjective, constructive, and ultimately personal nature of the enterprise of case reportage. The reconstruction of these factors was accomplished largely through the author's extensive review of the videotapes of the original sessions. It is one thing to review tapes about which one has positive recollections, and quite another to do the same procedure with a series of sessions one deems unsuccessful. In this case, however, it was felt that the tape review now accomplished with the advantage of an increased conceptual–therapeutic sophistication, as well as with the asset of the passage of time, could yield a fruitful analysis. Still, the end product is far from a detached, scientific synthesis of therapy with the M family. Finally, there are the inevitable constraints imposed by the written word (as well as, of course, any author's own limitations of expression) and, of course, the highly impressionistic, constructive nature of the hindsight phenomenon.

The five factors considered to be operational in the analysis of this case are:

1. Family factors
2. Model factors
3. Therapist factors
4. Context factors
5. The emergent factor: beyond illusions of understanding

Family Factors

Inherent in this set of variables is the question: Can we identify the family types or forms that are more difficult to help? Upon the mere posing of this inquiry, however, we must qualify the question in at least two ways. First, there is the matter of family typologies or classification schemas *per se.* The difficulties, in the form of potential rigidities of perception and reification of process, have been developed elsewhere (Liddle & Saba, 1983). Suffice it to say here, however, that the simple act of thinking in terms of classifying clinical families on degrees of difficulty must be accompanied by a reminder of the potential for oversimplification of extremely complex, multidimensional interactional phenomena. Second, there is the matter of always needing to place the question of difficulty in context. That is, what represents for one therapist (of a certain orientation, age, experience level, personal background) an unappealing or difficult clinical encounter may be quite the contrary for the next clinician. Further, there are context determinants in regard to the setting in which the therapy occurs. In sum, the pseudocertainty of comprehensive understanding often provided with a family typology as well as such context markers as the person of the therapist and clinical setting will clearly interact in one's determination of the question of degree of difficulty.

THE GENERIC DIFFICULTY VARIABLE

With this in mind, it might be useful to consider the factors involved in specifying particularly difficult clinical families—families that are more likely to be involved in a nonsuccessful therapeutic experience. Just as therapists can be helped to sharpen their clinical thinking through the process of an epistemologic declaration (Liddle, 1982c), the act of specifying the kinds of clinical families and situations that each of us finds particularly troublesome can be a similarly rewarding venture. In fact, thinking along these latter lines probably helps the process of clarifying our individual epistemologic foundations as well. For instance, is the idiosyncratic degree of difficulty increased by a certain type of presenting problem and/or interactional style of the family? Are there factors of family composition, or ethnic–cultural background issues that come into play? Or, is our major determinant the illusive "chemistry" that develops, or fails to do so between ourselves and the family with whom we must work? Just as certain kinds of therapeutic interventions can be identified as having more "generic difficulty" than others (Liddle & Schwartz, 1983), the same could be said of clinical families. There are probably families that most therapists will find generically difficult.

HOPES, DREAMS, AND THE HUMAN SPIRIT

From the earliest days of psychotherapy outcome research, the area of *expectations* (both patient's and therapist's) has been thought to play a significant role in the determination of therapy's impact and results. In this regard the early work of Frank (1973)—signifying the importance of a patient's hope or positive expectation of outcome and the concomitant mobilization of this hope by the therapist—still has relevance and importance today. The M family could be considered an example of a family that, at least during the course of therapy, did not exhibit much genuine hope for significant change. The mother and daughter were disillusioned with each other and with therapy and therapists. At the same time, the daughter exhibited an overreliance on helpers and helping agencies. In some cases, after repeated frustration with social service systems that fail to meet patient and family needs, help-seekers often conclude that the problems might best be solved without external intervention. In these situations people often discover personal and familial resources, which had been previously ignored or untapped. Unfortunately this was not the case with Mary Lou and her mother. Their frustration with the extrafamilial resources did not help them conclude that things might best be solved on their own. They continued to seek help, carrying with them a perceptual–attitudinal set, however, that the newest therapy would probably be no more useful than the previous brand.

One reason for family therapy's success that must be considered is its emphasis on the activation of the family's own resources for change and growth. In structural–strategic therapy, emphasis is placed on the redefinition and relabeling of problems and processes and on the therapist's ability to accentuate the family's strengths and underutilized problem-solving mechanisms. The idea of creating workable therapeutic realities through reframing and resource mobilization begins with the therapist's perceptual–conceptual–attitudinal stance. To say that a family always has unused, but available, alternatives is as much a construction as a more negatively oriented conclusion—it represents a half-full versus half-empty posture toward people and change. This is not to suggest that either of these therapeutic stances is incorrect. It is merely that the view emphasizing alternatives can often lead to more alternatives, while the pathology-seeking vision similarly tends to produce more of its own kind of perceptions. The essential point here, however, lies in the perspectivistic issue of whether or not the M family had the resources to change their own life course. The therapist's interpretation and assertion that they do is not only based on an assessment of resources. Rather, it is an *a priori assumption* that they along with all other families inherently possess such possibilities. The conclusion is less in the domain of family assessment than in the realm of a philosophy about families and life.

In the case of the M family, however, let us examine some facts. Mary Lou had a very poor work history, was entrenched in a societally reinforced definition of herself as incompetent, as a mental patient, and was clearly dependent on her mother (as was her mother with her) for social contacts. Mary Lou and her mother intentionally cut themselves off from contact with other family members—they did not define them as potential resources. Further, they each felt certainty that the other was not only incapable of serving as a resource for change, but moreover, they each defined the other publicly as an irritant whose ways should be changed. Thus their own constructed resource realities excluded each other, other family, extrafamilial, and themselves as individuals as capable of effective positive change. (The ways in which the therapist became inducted into this reality is detailed in the section entitled Therapist Factors.)

DIFFICULTIES IN LETTING BYGONES BE BYGONES

The recent trend in the family therapy field to reexamine the concept of time and the role of history should be welcomed by all schools of thought. The theoretical tradition of family therapy has been markedly ahistorical. This thrust itself, of course, should be viewed in historical context. Family therapy (and behavior therapy for that matter) in part evolved in contradistinction to those schools of psychotherapy that emphasized a redoing or reworking of past psychic hurts. The new view, with its epistemologic roots more in the communication and cybernetic theory tradition, focused the therapist on the present interactional phenomena of family life. Yet, part of the recent reconsideration of the role of a family's historical antecedents must be construed as our realistic accommodation to a basic aspect of life, whether we choose to consider that aspect as being central to the therapeutic task or not. We are here referring to the fact that people do have a past, that there are certain events, and probably more accurately, cumulative- or accumulation-effects that stay with us throughout our lives. This is not to suggest of course that our affective memories are not highly selective and distorting. It is, rather, a reminder of the inevitability of the influence of the past on our present. For our present purposes, however, this mere reminder is insufficient. We must now add the layer of individual and familial differences to the previously stated principle. Certainly traumatic events and long-term negative interactions happen in a wide variety of families. Still, different families have far from a standard reaction to what might be similar events. Some, like the M family, seem to hold on to these past transgressions and bring the former hurts and disappointments into the present, everyday life. History then transcends its mere report value and becomes an element or modus operandi of interpersonal warfare in the present.

Let us approach this same issue—the role of the past in the M family—from a slightly different vantage point. Recently, while watching a television show in which the survivors of the Nazi Holocaust were being interviewed, one could not help but be struck by the depth of the individuals' experience and the profoundness of their anguish and pain. I asked myself, is there anything that can help these families cope with an experience of this magnitude? For example, how much and in what ways could therapy help, if at all? Are there kinds and degrees of human tragedy that are so powerful as to adversely affect families' lives forever?

In the M family there is not a single-event theory of what has gone wrong; the elements of how repeated transactions over time affect current behavior, as well as the dimension of human forgiveness, are very much in operation with Mrs. M and her daughter. In the M family we must strive to understand how a long period of interpersonal struggle (yet isolation) and a definition of one of the family members as an incompetent patient contributed to the demoralization and lack of hope expressed by both Mother and Daughter. We can say that history is not or should not be important, yet for many families, their daily lives are filled with recollections and affects of the past, not unlike some of those Holocaust families. For many people the passage of time or other means of coping do not erode those painful memory traces. This certainly seemed the case with the M family. The past was not only acted out and reproduced in the present; it was the present.

Although they were able to have some happy and close times together, Mrs. M and her daughter spent many of their disagreements covering old territory.

MARY LOU: Why haven't you let me grow up, Mummy?
MRS. M: You didn't want to—you always stayed close to me. You went away with a man for a week and you would call every day.

MARY LOU: I was worried about your health then—remember, you were getting sick then.

MRS. M: You called me *every* day. (*Turning to therapist.*) Every day!

Much of their lives consisted in replaying arguments and reformulating worn recriminations. A family of this kind plays tricks on itself with time—virtually acting as if time has stood still and the future (if it exists at all) can only play variations on all too familiar themes.

DRAWBACKS OF AWARENESS

In some respects, there was an unhealthy degree of insight with the M family. This high degree of understanding was a periodic temptation for the therapist. In Mary Lou's words: "I know why those bags are there—you don't think they're there for no reason, do you?" We often wished that we could help the family develop some much needed amnesia about their past life, despite its formidableness. A related difficulty concerned the degree to which their level of psychological sophistication was employed in the service of escalating conflict with the other. Perhaps it was not the articulateness alone that was problematic. The extent to which this was used as a weapon must also be considered a compounding difficulty.

Early on in therapy these mutually triggered, past-focused blaming bouts were rampant. This was a family preoccupied (at least overtly) with the negative aspects of their experience together. Although Mary Lou would often criticize her mother for not having accepted her, Mary Lou appeared to act identically in relation to Mrs. M. There were few positive cycles of interaction in the sessions; mutual supportiveness did not appear very often (Mary Lou: "There are some people who can't give you self-praise—my mother's one of them. I'll have to find a way to give it to myself"). Yet as a pair, they were sometimes able to have fun together, both in- and outside of the interviews. During an early session when the therapist had excused himself to consult with the observing group, Mother and Daughter playfully teased the therapist and the entire treatment context:

MARY LOU: I know this stuff [about the bags] must sound fantastic [in the sense of incredible] to you. I've seen quite a few therapists over the years.

MRS. M: Have you ever seen—treated anything like this before? It's something, don't you think?

The dyad's togetherness was thus often demonstrated at times like this, and at other times when the absurd aspects of their living situation emerged.[1]

1. In many respects mother and daughter were a study in sameness. Until the very end of the first 7-month period, they would dress very much alike, wear articles of each other's clothes and jewelry, and each would invariably appear at every session sporting what became their trademark at the clinic—a similar hat or cap that would be worn throughout each interview.

(In thinking about a 77-year-old woman with her 40-year-old daughter living together in a small one-bedroom apartment *filled* with bags, it was difficult not to let the absurd—and not in a disrespectful sense—ingredients of that context emerge into consciousness.)

Finally, another interrelated family factor seemed to contribute to our lack of success. Ironically, it was a variable that usually we would not judge to be a problem. In fact, with many families we often find ourselves in an opposite dilemma. This situation could be summarized by saying that personally Mrs. M and her daughter were quite engaging, lively, and entertaining—almost, depending on one's viewpoint, to a fault. They were, as the saying goes, characters in the truest and best sense of the word. Many would describe them as, in the main, lovable, rather than cranky eccentrics. This kind of family, on the one hand, certainly enhances a therapist's interest and spark about a case; yet this ironically had overall negative correlates in this case (see the discussion of context factors).

This family, because of their individual and collective selves and the sensational nature of the presenting problem, created a novel kind of figure-ground dilemma. With some families, we find it strained and awkward to find aspects of certain members with which we can relate. It will always be easier to join some families and not others. With the M family one felt almost too comfortable,[2] and unfortunately too often a participant in their drama. At the same time, their antics *were* so genuinely entertaining that one also often felt like an observer—an investigator on an anthropological journey exploring the captivating idiosyncrasies of a strange, yet wonderful culture. (How the therapist and therapeutic context became inducted in this process is addressed in the sections entitled Therapist Factors and Context Factors.)

Model Factors

This section addresses issues idiosyncratic to the particular model used with the M family that seemed related to the outcome of therapy. That is, taking into account the problems of implementation in the section entitled Therapist Factors, can we identify process and outcome variables related to the model as it was defined with this case?

The theoretical stance of the structural–strategic approach used with this family has been detailed in an earlier section. To recapitulate, however, it is a model that deals both with the presenting symptom in a direct problem-solving way and with the organizational aspects of the family. The approach does address domains of the family's functioning that are not necessarily observably related to the presenting problem, such as subsystem functioning.

2. Again, there are parallels here to what often happens with an anorectic, "All-American" family (Minuchin, Rosman, & Baker, 1978).

The model includes both in-session enactments and between-session directives, for example, as elements of its theory of change and role of the therapist.

In discussing model factors related to the structural–strategic approach, we cannot fail to address issues of integration in general, and in particular those that relate to the model in question. Model integration is a complex, sophisticated, and challenging enterprise, even for advanced clinicians, despite implications to the contrary (L'Abate, in press). Much of what passes for integration constitutes a mere wholesale blending of two or more models, with insufficient concern for the potential confusion and inconsistency of epistemology or intervention. In practice, model integration often gets translated as sloppy eclecticism at worst and at best as a technical eclecticism that minimizes theoretical issues. Nonetheless, there is a strong, continued impetus among clinicians for efforts of integration. Although some of this energy might be related to utopian expectations about any one therapy model's possibilities, the branch of this movement that seeks more complex paradigms in order to help a greater variety of families must be honored.

Structural–strategic therapies have been at the forefront of family therapy's model integration attempts. Haley's Leaving Home model integrates a basic structural framework with his strategic therapy approach, which was developed in collaboration with Milton Erickson (Haley, 1973, 1976). Stanton and Todd's (Stanton, Todd, & Associates, 1982) work on the drug addicts and families project successfully adapted the Leaving Home approach in their own structural–strategic family therapy. Additionally, Stanton's work in the area of structural strategic marital and family therapy has produced some clinical guidelines for the concurrent use of these approaches (Stanton, 1981a, 1981b).

Let us examine the specific operative model factors in this case. First, there is the issue of the overall stage of development of the therapy model one is attempting to use. Indirectly, this matter reflects the development of the family therapy field as well as the whole of psychotherapy. It is related to the principle of contextual influence and constraint. The belief that the prevailing intellectual, epistemological, and social–cultural contexts in which therapy approaches exist cannot help but affect model evolution. Thus, as in therapy and in our understanding of families, we are inevitably guided and constrained by the rules and evolutionary level of contexts.

The integrative structural–strategic model used in this case had inherent problems in construction (as well as problems in implementation). There was more of a serial or sequential application of first structural then strategic methods. This did not lead to a true integrative model or a unified theory, but more to an interpretation of integration that resembled *two* approaches being glued or stapled together side-by-side. In retrospect there was an overemphasis on technique and technique selection. It has been found that proceeding in this way is a working from what we could call the "bottom–up." When we overemphasize techniques, the major premises upon which the techniques rest easily can become obscured and forgotten.

The problem of becoming a "technique junkie" seems curable by working from the "top–down"—developing an attitude or perceptual set that assumes the specific technical operations will flow naturally and easily from one's basic premises about change, the role of the therapist, and therapy in general. Thus, the clinician brings to therapy broadly sketched but specific conceptual overlays or transparencies—templates in the mind's eye of the therapist that are explicit reminders about one's essential epistemologic leanings, rather than laundry lists of possible interventions. Working more consistently at this theory of change level gives the therapist more freedom to spontaneously interpret and create interventions (letting them happen, as it were) than is possible when one is attempting to reproduce techniques that we ape from the great masters' videotape interviews.

There were related difficulties in the important area of *reading feedback* in this version of structural–strategic therapy. One issue in this regard was the oscillation and inconsistency in over- and underattending to the family's feedback.

Feedback is defined here as the therapist's attentiveness to the constant flow of information and reactions about his or her own presence, style, and certainly, interventions. Detailed guidelines for reading feedback in family work is a frontier area of development. In the least it can be said to be a difficult but inevitable task of the therapist, a function that is indispensable in recalibrating one's therapeutic efforts.

Still, reading feedback is tricky business. It is often simple to forget the constructive, attributive, and selective nature of assessing reactions we define as being "out there," as being other people's reactions. When a therapist declares, "The patient can't tolerate any more stress, I'd better let up," another translation of the same event might be, "*I* can't tolerate it, so I'd better let up."

The typical course of events includes our intervening in a definable way and then reading the feedback from our intervention. This latter action—the conclusion we draw, the clinical judgment we make about it—must be cast in its proper personalistic, impressionistic context. Reading feedback (drawing inferences and conclusions) is ultimately a relativistic, nonobjective endeavor, not comparable on an absolute scale. That is, events that trigger a certain clinical decision for one therapist may not do the same for another. The second therapist, even if operating within the same theoretical orientation, may not be similarly activated until much later, perhaps not until the sequence has reached his or her threshold or until a different kind of sequence unfolds.

The two model variables mentioned thus far interacted to produce the following situation with the M family. There was an oscillation between the techniques of structural and strategic therapy that often seemed activated by a sequence of over-, under-, then oversensitivity to the family's feedback. In this case when a course of reasonable action was selected, we did not persist long enough to accurately gauge the longer-term (rather than more immediate) results. One problem in this regard was the overemphasis on technique, which can often lead to such "technique-flipping" sequences in structural–strategic therapy. When the therapeutic stance of unbalancing seemed stuck, for instance, there was too rapid a switch to indirect techniques, without enough attention to the probable prompting of such a move (e.g., therapist discomfort), or consequences of this inconstancy (such as insufficient time to build pressure for change). A therapist-related variable in this regard is the matter of belief in the model of therapy. Trusting the model, of course, cannot be considered separate from trusting and believing in oneself as a therapist, which is another topic meriting further exploration.

The technique oscillation is also related to the previously mentioned difficulties in working up from the level of techniques, rather than down from the presuppositional level. Perhaps in particular with structural–strategic therapy, there is the tendency to miss the interconnection of direct (challenging) and indirect (paradoxical) methods. When working too exclusively at a technique level, the direct and indirect methods are difficult to blend into a unified model that interlinks these positions toward change. When a therapist can operate at the level of premises about change, for example, it is easier to conceptualize the "paradoxical" aspects of a therapist's unbalancing challenge ("I don't think you will let her grow up"), as well as the challenging aspects of indirect messages ("Perhaps it is best that you do not change in this regard; you probably could not tolerate the consequences"). A therapist who understands these remarks as exemplifying possible *stances* about change can more easily view these *postures* as merely two sides of the coin of reality. These interventions are thus seen, not as emerging from a grab-bag of clinical tricks, but as the logical outgrowth or manifestation of two interdependent, complementary perspectives comprising a unified whole.

There is a further, more generically troublesome problem related to an overemphasis on technique. Sometimes, because of both semantic traps and conceptual lapses, we can begin to see therapeutic techniques as discrete procedures that are performed on clients and families, much as a surgeon employs surgical methods in an operation. What gets lost in the techniques-as-things conception is the bidirectional, cyclical quality of a therapist's interventions. These techniques are never done in interactional isolation; they are modified and recalibrated, as we have mentioned, as the system's feedback is registered and taken into account.

Yet, even a circular, cybernetically oriented explanation that advances us beyond linear description falls short in this regard. As Haley (1981) has pointed out, systems theory has not been helpful for therapists in the sense that, originally at least, it was a formulation not about change, but about how stability is maintained. Replacing the notion of a therapist applying a model or technique to a patient-family is the still-developing idea of therapist and patient-family as a coevolving, changing system. That is, therapist and family in the course of their therapeutic contact (and perhaps beyond) constitute an organic system, and it is the functioning of this therapeutic system that changes—in rules, structure, organization, and so on—in therapy. Naturally what therapists and outcome researchers usually examine in terms of change(s) is the family's degree of differentness. We must remember that to cite change as occurring in a linear, cause-and-effect way, and only in the domain of the family is to arbitrarily punctuate or draw a distinction (Bateson, 1979) for a certain set of purposes and from a certain perspective. The proposed alternative is still in its formative stages, but for now, it can be said to be intimately related to conducting therapy, as I have termed it, from the level of epistemologic premises down to the level of technique. Further, the therapist's attitude becomes one of realizing that techniques are coparticipatory experiences that can be arbitrarily chopped into beginning (intervention) and ending (outcome) sequences. But they are preferably construed as manifestations of a coevolving process—the movement of therapist and family through time, each pulling and being pulled by the other in a coevolutionary spiral.[3]

Several other model-related variables are important to mention here. There was an inconsistent focus on the issues of how and when to use the symptom as a lever to change the M family's relationship system. Similarly, in the area of goals there was an undue degree of inconsistency. Initially, our goals were probably overly ambitious (help Mary Lou move out of the house as soon as possible) and as therapy progressed they in all likelihood became too tame.

The issue of time as it relates to continuous and discontinuous theories of change was not adequately conceptualized at the time of the model's implementation. Indeed, this matter, which includes such troublesome issues as the readiness[4] of change, is far from resolved. The continuous-discontinu-

3. Time is the newest dimension to be reconsidered in family therapy. It has allowed us to transcend the closed-loop conceptualizations of: A leads to B, which then recursively folds back to A. Several authors (e.g., Penn, 1982, and Hoffman, 1982, in the area of systemic therapy; and Liddle & Saba, 1985, in press, in the area of training and therapy's coevolutionary relationship) have attempted to develop the perspective of this rediscovered lens.

4. The whole notion of the organism/system's *readiness* for change is a potentially useful and additive concept to make our ideas about change more appropriately complex, if it can be cast in a nondeterministic way.

ous change debate has been taken up in another context (Liddle & Saba, 1983) and need not be repeated here.

The age of the identified patient (Mary Lou was 41 years old) presented a novel situation. On the one hand, the situation dictated a Leaving Home model (Haley, 1981), since that indeed was one clear way of defining the problem interactionally. Conversely, to unequivocally, firmly, and consistently back Mrs. M at the outset of therapy as required in this approach would mean negating or at least not attending (for a time) to Mary Lou's valid and accurate complaints about her mother's behavior.

Finally, there was the matter of the therapist's level of organizational sequence focus. What kinds of data/information should be elicited and dealt with at any particular point? What level of interactional pattern should be the locus of intervention and change? Several possible levels of pattern, depending on theoretical perspective, dominate the focus of the family therapist. The therapist can ask about and/or attempt to elicit a family's transactional style at the following levels:

1. Cross-cultural/ethnicity background.

2. Multigenerational/intergenerational—family life cycle over several generations.

3. Family as part of other contexts—what Koestler (1978) has termed the "integrative" functions of organisms; the family's linkage with community, religious, school, friends, other families, and so on.

4. Family as whole—compare Koestler's (1978) "self-assertiveness" concept; defined as the traditional nuclear family and includes the family life-cycle transitions of that family as a whole unto itself; includes information about other symptoms in the past and other occurrences of the present symptom/problem.

5. Family as whole, events around therapy—deals with longer-term cycles (e.g., more of interaction around the presenting problem than are observable in the therapy session). In the Leaving Home paradigm, for instance, Haley (1981) has carefully tracked the broad, out-of-session cycles of problematic interaction of the identified patient's improvement: the parents increase their conflict, the young person relapses and the parents pull together to rescue the problem person, and so on. Such sequences should be differentiated from family-in-therapy.

6. Family-in-therapy—deals with in-session and between-session sequences that can be elicited through enactment and self-report of the immediate past.

7. Subsystem pattern—deals with interaction at the subsystem level; includes self–self interactions (in distinction to self–other) in which individuals perpetuate perceptions, belief systems, and the like through a consistent message-giving to oneself, and an equally consistent filtering

of information that would produce a dissonant or conflictual view. This domain has unfortunately not been adequately addressed by family therapists.[5] As we know, it is not that a family therapist only sees families, it is more a thinking, conceptualizing process that differentiates him or her from other psychotherapists.

Had it been formulated at the time, this degree of conceptualization of the levels of possible therapeutic focus might have minimized the conceptual confusion and intervention switching from one level of system function to another.

Additional guidelines need to be developed regarding how clinical decisions on these many foci might be determined. This area begins to address not only the consultation of others in their recommended manner of decision making, and indeed what these decision points are, but also touches on the way a therapist individually defines and translates his or her own idiosyncratic version of structural–strategic therapy or any therapy. This is not a willy-nilly eclecticism. It is the development of a personal, evolving model of therapy (PEMT), based upon one's knowledge and experience with certain, established therapeutic approaches. The construction of a PEMT counters strict doctrinal interpretations of the therapy of our field's charismatic master therapists as well as unsystematic, grab-bag eclecticism. It represents a thoughtful, experimentally grounded (i.e., emphasis on outcome) building of a personally workable, internally consistent, and reproducible therapy approach. A PEMT is, realistically, a life-long career goal, and certainly not obtainable at the conclusion of a training or graduate program. At best, it represents a process that teachers of therapy might be able to facilitate during a training experience, so as to cultivate the kinds of professional values necessary to make this effort a career-spanning project.

Therapist Factors

This variable pertains to the inseparability of a therapeutic framework from the translator of that model—the person of the therapist. Like the samurai warrior and his sword, a model of therapy and the self of the therapist must be considered inextricably connected (Minuchin & Fishman, 1981). There is much research to suggest the crucial nature of therapist expertise in relation to therapeutic outcome (Hadley & Strupp, 1976; Garfield & Bergin, 1978; Gurman & Razin, 1977; Gurman & Kniskern, 1981). This factor offers an interpretation of the therapist's contribution to the outcome of therapy with the M family.

5. The cognitively oriented therapies of Beck (1976; see also Beck, Rush, Shaw, & Emery, 1979) and Ellis (1973), however, are representative of those points of view in psychotherapy that make extensive, effective use of self–self interactions.

There were two therapists involved in the direct treatment of Mary Lou and her mother—the author and a PhD student trainee. After the initial contact and telephone intake, the author judged the case to be a difficult one, more than one could reasonably expect a trainee to handle, even with a high degree of monitoring and live supervision. Thus, two factors led to the decision to have the family be seen collaboratively by myself and a student. The first was the issue of the complexity and difficulty of the case, and the second was the, at that time, still unsettled matter of cotherapy[6] (supervisor and trainee) as a training method. In retrospect it is clear that this experience was an instrumental and formative one in my ultimate decision to abandon this technique as a viable teaching format. The specific ways in which this procedure proved to be more problematic than its gains are detailed below. Although in the position of the supervisor-senior therapist in the case, I had, at the outset of therapy with the M family, only 5 years of family therapy experience. Further, and perhaps more significantly, I was beginning the second half of 2 years of postdoctoral training in structural and strategic family therapy at the Philadelphia Child Guidance Clinic. Previous doctoral and internship training in family therapy was of an eclectic orientation, with structural and strategic being only two of several models emphasized. Thus, the developmental stage of the therapist(s) must be considered crucial to our discussion. At the time, now over 8 years ago, I was clearly in a heightened transitional phase. Being involved in an intensive training experience in two similar theoretical orientations provides high degrees of conceptual input and challenges old belief systems and preferred ways of working. It is hardly a time when one can feel expert in the new ways of thinking and behaving clinically.

Additionally, there was the issue of the theoretical orientation being simultaneously learned in one setting and applied and taught in another. The 1st year of the training program was primarily structural in emphasis, while the second was strategic with a focus on the therapeutic stances of symptom prescription and positive connotation as mechanisms of change. The case was thus begun on the cusp of a change within a change. On this level was the recent intensive supervision/training in a structural mode and the shift to a new and not yet complementary (given the stage of model and therapist development) therapeutic posture. At a more general level, there was also the issue of how this kind of training destabilizes the intellectual and personal therapeutic confidence and functioning of a therapist. Along these same lines the factor of the degree (or lack thereof) of consolidation of training input and learning must also be considered. This encompasses the process variable

---

6. Cotherapy is used more descriptively than literally here. Therapy with a trainer and trainee is quite different from the cotherapy of two colleagues of relatively equal experience, skill, and so forth.

of the *time* needed for generalizable and independently reproducible new conceptual and behavioral patterns to take hold.

In the section on family factors, we briefly examined the lively and captivating personal style of the family. This was the kind of family that one might love to see again at a family reunion; they could be devilish and fun and very engaging. This observation, of course, had clear interactional components in relation to the therapist's behavior. It was often easy to be carried by the family's mood in a session. This was especially so if it was a demonstration of their appreciation of the absurd aspects of their living situation. They were often so entertaining that during some of these sequences the therapist was tempted to sit back and take in their antics, thereby becoming part of a counterproductive pattern—in this instance the diffusion of intensity and focus through laughter or absurdity.

Along these same lines of pattern induction, there developed an interesting isomorphic transaction between mother and daughter, and family and therapist. Especially pronounced early on in therapy, Mary Lou would begin to relieve pressure for change by criticizing her mother in one sentence, then in the next excusing her and absolving the mother of blame.

MARY LOU: (*To therapist.*) She'll never let me grow up, at least not in my own way. To the way I dress, to the way I look, to the way I act, to the way I speak, to who I call—it is never right. (*Turning to therapist.*) This is my mother's way, it's not her fault—she cannot help it. She is just an extremely powerful and dominating person.

Just as Mary Lou diffused the intensity of her challenges to her mother, the therapist replicated this pattern of unbalancing and then backing off, becoming distracted, simply not following the challenge through, or frequently by changing tactics. In response to feedback from her mother or Mary Lou that these challenges were difficult and quite stressful as well as feedback that the unbalancing was producing a deadlock, the therapist often switched to an indirect, symptom-prescription or positive connotation stance.

In this regard there seemed to be two levels of problems. First, there was the personal dimension of it being easier to challenge Mary Lou rather than Mrs. M. The daughter could be openly conflictual and antagonistic with the therapist while the mother generally remained more placid and calm. It was simply more difficult to challenge the distinguished-looking, sweet, white-haired 77-year-old mother with the charming British accent than it was her daughter, who was so adept at convincing others of her patienthood.

The second level of problem was the unfortunate oscillation of the therapist between direct and indirect requests for change (Rabkin, 1977). The therapist did not have sufficient experience with each approach alone, or with these models in tandem to have developed the necessary personal guidelines for clinical decision making about such difficult matters as how to vary and alter a challenge while not abandoning it altogether. Further, there were the personal stylistic issues of how much conflict and stress the therapist could tolerate as the therapeutic crises built. One factor in the oscillation between crisis induction through unbalancing enactments and an indirect pressure-building stance is thus our own threshold for tolerating the systemic fallout of pushing and holding a conflictual holon past its accustomed, preferred range of interaction. Further still, there is the issue of knowing what to do (e.g., when to participate in continued unbalancing, how to shape the enactment in a productive direction) with a therapy-induced crisis once it has begun. All of these overlapping issues seemed to be in operation in our work with this case.

An interesting, yet at the time perplexing, paradox developed in our work with the M family. On the one hand, I felt overinvested in the family's change and overinvolved in the case. Conversely, as time went on, I began to hear messages about a lack of joining, especially from Mary Lou. Carl Whitaker's adage about the therapist respecting the family's assumption of their own initiative for change (that the therapist must not "take away" their tension/initiative by being overcommitted to their change) has relevance here. There was an impatience felt with the family which was, to the degree that it was experienced, novel for the therapist at that time. Therapy felt less difficult and was more effective with other cases. As the therapist and still new therapeutic model failed to achieve immediate dramatic change (admittedly, also a problem of utopian expectations), frustration grew.[7] Here we approach the interrelationship between the unrealistic impatience for sweeping change and the lack of joining. Overfocusing on the dramatic interventions to realign relationship boundaries, for example, while underemphasizing those behaviors that lay the foundation through which the stressful pattern dislocation can be tolerated, is a common, yet problematic tendency. Operating in a vacuum of not consistently appreciating the essential nature of solid joining (e.g., not merely seeing joining as only a beginning therapy necessity), the therapist thus operated in a vacuum of not consistently appreciating the essential and ongoing nature of joining and that this operation is necessary throughout therapy. In this situation, then, we were presented with a family who themselves heightened the nature of their crisis by emphasizing past therapeutic failures. The therapist was thus unduly organized by what was interpreted to be a dramatic, painful need for immediate help.

Finally, two related issues regarding a therapist's reading of systemic feedback need to be addressed in this section. Early on in therapy, I unfortunately did not read the correct metaphoric content of Mary Lou's statements, ostensibly referring to her mother, "I'm not supported." Haley's (1976) work has been particularly helpful in reminding us about the indirect and subtle analogic aspects of therapeutic communication. As the sessions progressed and the structure of the therapy itself was altered (split sessions with Mother

---

7. Context factors, discussed in detail later, were also clearly at play here.

and Daughter together for 45 minutes to 1 hour, then each alone for 30 minutes) the issue of support and joining became less problematic. Mary Lou's messages were eventually correctly seen as referring also to the therapeutic context and therapist.

As this issue became less of a difficulty, another matter related to reading feedback from systems we are simultaneously part of and attempting to help change became problematic. As Mary Lou, in particular, began to act more competently in relation to Mrs. M, Mother, predictably, escalated some of her old ways of dealing with her daughter (criticism, dismissal). However, especially later in therapy, Mary Lou persisted in these sequences and was able to achieve new ways of relating to her mother. The stress resulting from these newly forming, unfamiliar pathways and patterns, however, was formidable. Interestingly, at the periods of the most noticeable gains in the mother–daughter relationship, Mary Lou tended to return to a noticeable patient status. She would criticize the therapy and vociferously reemphasize the condition of the house, demanding that "you people do something to help me with my problem with the bags." Observation and participation in this sequence (Mother criticizes, Mary Lou improves, Mother escalates criticism, Mary Lou reclaims patient role) was often confusing to the therapist who, alternately, became over- and underresponsive to its appearance. This sequence (feedback) should have been read as a natural, predictable manifestation of change. Here again emerges the matter of isomorphic transactions at different system levels—therapist reactivity and direction/focus overcorrection replicates a similar pattern in the family as well as between the family and therapist.

Context Factors

This section acknowledges and traces the contextual influences and constraints that seemed to operate in relation to the M family. It assumes that the setting (private practice, institute, training center, etc.) in which the treatment occurs will be a variable in the ongoing definition and process of that treatment and its outcome. This factor thus clearly presupposes that, as Bateson has put it, "context fixes meaning" and more basically, that context can be thought of as "pattern through time" (1979, pp. 14–15). Just as we appreciate a patient's context in assessing and intervening into problem situations, so also do we continue to use this contextual sensitivity in relation to our treatment settings.

With the M family, as mentioned previously, the treatment context was a training clinic, designed to serve a mostly poor, urban population. It was a community counseling clinic of a counseling psychology doctoral program approved by the American Psychological Association. The theoretical orientation of the clinic was structural–strategic family therapy, a point of view not wholly syntonic with the general orientation of the doctoral program (Liddle, 1978), which was more individually centered and eclectic. An average of six students met for a total of 10 hours each week, of which 2 hours consisted of a didactic and case seminar. Supervisory methods relied on the integrated use of live and videotape delayed supervision, as well as on the development of the observing group as a treatment team and source of peer consultation. A detailed description of this training setting has been presented elsewhere (Liddle, 1980).

Traditionally, training contexts have difficulties in balancing the interacting and interrelated demands of *teaching* and *service* to the clinic's intended population. In fact, one reason for the initial development of the training procedure of live supervision was to minimize the negative impact of inexperienced therapists on the clinical families, while simultaneously providing an excellent context of immediate learning. Thus training settings are inherently more complex than pure service contexts. In the training context in which the M family was seen, several aspects of this complexity contributed to the therapeutic outcome.

First, there was the decision to accept the family into treatment. At the time of the initial contact, there were not clearly established guidelines about the kinds of clients the training clinic should see. Although it is often difficult to determine beforehand the true difficulty of a given client or family, the M family was not one of those situations. From the beginning it was clear that Mrs. M and her daughter would constitute a formidable clinical challenge. In light of this consensus as well as the lack of criteria about the kind of client situations that were suitable for our therapists and clinic, the case could be made that the M family should not have been seen. The question of what constitutes ideal, acceptable, and poor training cases has yet to be substantively addressed in the training literature, either in- or outside of the family therapy field.

Another contextual dimension was the issue of the dual role of the senior therapist-author in the case. At the time I served as the director of the clinic in which the M family was seen. The duties of this position included administrative responsibilities (e.g., generating, maintaining referral sources, overseeing record-keeping and evaluation, as well as straightforward clinical supervision[8] and teaching the didactic seminar). The decision was made that due to the probable difficulty of the case, the clinic director–supervisor should be involved in working with the family. However, due to the multiple time and functional demands on the supervisor and because the clinic had a primary training function, a cotherapist PhD student who was enrolled in the clinic at the time would also have significant clinical responsibility. This addition, of

8. An advanced 4th-year PhD candidate served in an associate director capacity, assisting in these duties.

course, now added the dimension of complexity of trying to train a relatively inexperienced therapist to work with a difficult family, while simultaneously struggling with one's own questions about the use of a still-developing therapeutic model. Along these lines, there were two points during our work with the family that the supervisor-senior therapist was pulled from involvement with the case due to clinic responsibilities. Although this happened when the therapeutic strategy and particular lines of interventions had already been generated for the cotherapist to follow, this inconsistency seemed disruptive to both the student and the family.

Along these lines the M family must be considered a case in which all of a context's therapeutic and personal resources must be coordinated for there to be any hope of a positive outcome. The use of therapeutic teams have been a developing hallmark of the family therapy field in recent years. Indeed, the M family matches those characteristics of families treated by such therapy teams—a record of previous therapeutic failure, a severe, dramatic symptom, and a familial situation defined as chronic. In this case, then, use of an observing team of beginning family therapy trainees as a therapeutic resource could obviously not be considered as beneficial as a group of experienced therapists, accustomed to working in this way. Here again we are faced with the overly complex role of the supervisor-senior therapist. The difficulties of balancing clinical responsibility with a challenging family, along with supervisory responsibility to a student cotherapist and teaching duties around this and a dozen other active cases proved to be an overwhelming task.

Many cases probably fail due to insufficient therapeutic attention. We have all had the experience of losing interest in a case, for reasons from being overworked to relationship problems with the client or family. In the case of the M family, however, the opposite dilemma was probably operational during most of our contact with them. Mrs. M and her daughter became, in fairly short order, the stars of the clinic. Their personal styles, unusual living situation and presenting problem helped to captivate the entire staff of the clinic with the week-to-week reporting about their lives.

In the group supervision meetings, we would often find ourselves referring disproportionately to the M family and our struggles to be of help. This pattern persisted largely undetected at the time, again probably due, at least in part, to the weekly drama supplied by this engaging family and our frustrated attempts to deal with their situation. Although unfortunately probably more covert than overt, there seemed to be more of an anthropologic or explorer mentality around the M family than other cases seen in the clinic. The follow-up data (6 months after treatment) supported acceptable therapy effectiveness in our clinic and therefore this situation could not be considered a pervasive phenomenon. Yet there was an impressive degree of overorganization that occurred around our attentiveness to this case. That is, the entire context became one that communicated this high degree of fascination with the family's culture and perhaps gave this message more loudly than clear expectations about realistic change.

A common theme throughout this section has been the consequences of conducting therapy in a context that attempts to satisfy two demanding masters—training and therapy. This complex yet crucial issue is an underdeveloped one in the training field of family therapy as well as in the psychotherapy profession as a whole. Family therapy is in a unique position to contribute clarity if not solutions in this regard because of its philosophic underpinnings of a context's importance in understanding and changing human behavior.

The Emergent Factor: Beyond Illusions of Understanding

In a paper designed to counter the developmental determinism of socialization theories that "tend to view life patterns as largely the product of childhood socialization," and stage theories that "portray development in terms of an invariant succession of distinct stages," Bandura (1982) introduces the refreshing idea of fortuitous, unforeseen, and unpredictable events as intimately shaping the development and life paths of human beings (p. 747). This final factor is posed in the same spirit of Bandura's view that, among other things, human encounters involve varying but significant degrees of unpredictability.

Evolutionary theorists, of course, have utilized the concept of the effect(s) of randomness for some time now. Bateson (1979) and Gould (1977, 1980, 1983) are among those who have successfully reframed and described the manner in which "randomness" in nature does not only act in generating variation, but is also an important agent of evolutionary change at all levels of life. One problem related to the incorporation of randomness as a valid variable in our thinking is the extent to which we negatively connote randomness as somehow unscientific, and worse, as synonymous with chaos, disorder, or incomprehensibility. Gould (1983, pp. 332–342) has sharply censured this narrow view of randomness as misinformed and misinforming. His position asserts that randomness does not imply complete unpredictability, lawlessness, or chaos. Random processes can yield a highly complex order, although not of the variety or degree to which we might (unrealistically so) be accustomed to expecting. From this view:

> Chance may well describe a sequence of events without implying that each individual item has no cause. Take the classic random event, a coin flip or the throw of a die. I imagine that each flip has a determined outcome if we could (and we cannot) specify all the multifarious factors that enter into it—height above the ground, force of the flip, initial side up, angle of the first contact with

the ground, for example. But the factors are too numerous and not under our control; an equal chance for each possible outcome is the best prediction we can make in the long run. (Gould, 1983, p. 341)

Here we approach the crux of this final factor's thesis. Just as Gould pinpointed the folly of any attempt to articulate the multitude of factors comprised in "causality," so too can we make this point in relation to the conduct of therapy. Similarly, "the factors are too numerous and not under our control," yet we can speak of prediction in some terms—perhaps probabilities will suffice. In our quest for surety, we must remember that it is not always possible to be sure; and in our desire to become more scientific about therapy, we must not succumb to a false scientism that tempts us into an overly empirical posture toward our work.

The emergent factor thus encompasses that realm of the therapeutic experience that lies beyond rational, logical analysis or statistical quantification. It deals with the synergistic quality of all human interaction, including of course, the psychotherapeutic encounter. As therapists we often interpret a family's premature termination or lack of engagement in therapy as our own failure in joining, and so on. The frame of therapist responsibility for such an outcome is useful in the sense that it can keep us honest; we are thereby reminded of the crucial nature of our behavior in successful outcome and are less likely to blame patients ("They were resistant"). Yet therapists must also be reminded that our attribution of failure is precisely that—an attribution, an interpretation constructed for particular purposes. From another, less unidirectional and more interactional vantage point, however, it could be said that the newly formed subsystem (therapist and family) had difficulty in becoming a workable unit. Thus the therapeutic alliance is a reciprocal affair, joining is not a technique therapists do *to* families so that the skids of therapy can be properly greased; it is a mutual, reciprocal process that, when in operation as a unidirectional phenomenon is not likely to produce good outcome. We do not expect to become friends (establish a mutual, complementary relationship) with all those people we meet in the course of our lives. We have certain preferences, biases, likes, dislikes, and so on in this domain of human interaction; why should a dissimilar process exist because we wear the hat of a professional therapist? Similarly, we would not expect any patient or family to react the same with all therapists. This is not to minimize the inherent problems that ensue when these human tendencies prevail. Rather my intent is merely not to deny their existence.

The essential message here is that some therapist–patient–family subsystems make it and some do not; not unlike that which could be said about all relationships. So in specifying the factors of failure or success of a complex human enterprise such as therapy, appropriate conceptual caution and restraint must be exercised. In this regard, let us consider the valuable counsel of Gould in his response to those who have offered reductionistic explanations of complex, multidimensional realities. He refers here specifically to early probability theorists' overly purposive conception of the world.

> This explanation may be comforting (and true), but I think we must face a second possibility. Perhaps randomness is not merely an adequate description for complex causes that we cannot specify. Perhaps the world really works this way, and many events are *uncaused* [emphasis added] in any conventional sense of the word. Perhaps our gut feeling that it cannot be so reflects only our hopes and prejudices, our desperate striving to make sense of a complex and confusing world, and not the ways of nature. (Gould, 1983, p. 342)

The Many Flavors of Truth:
Toward a Perspectivistic Epistemology

Aldous Huxley employed a graphic literary metaphor to teach the systems philosophy:

> Universe lies on top of universe, layer after layer, distinct and separate, like a Neapolitan ice [cream cake]. What's true in the chocolate layer, at the bottom, doesn't hold in the vanilla at the top. And a lemon truth is different from a strawberry truth. And each one has just as much right to exist and to call itself real as every other. (quoted in Davidson, 1983, p. 211)

Just so, this chapter, indeed this text, is comprised of many flavors of truth. The factors of the present chapter and the chapters of the book are not true (or True) in some ultimately verifiable, positively knowable sense. They are all constructions of reality and approximations of truth. To inquire at the level of the "real" reasons for failure or success in psychotherapy is to operate within a problematic or, if there is such a thing, a false epistemology. The factors of failure with the M family are idiosyncratic representations of what transpired; they are one person's images of reality.

Psychotherapists' discussion of failure is overdue. Yet the very partialing out of the topic of failure, although useful in a teaching sense, creates problems. Failure is but one branch on the tree of psychotherapy. Its introduction in our field is necessary, if only for the new value thrust that must accompany its examination. Like other cultures that have experienced positive value shifts, the culture and civilization of family therapy can be enhanced by maintaining our accessibility to a viscerally unappealing, yet ethically compelling and, in the long run, exciting topic.

The caveat offered through the emergent factor, however, should discourage those who strive to be sure of heart. As Heisenberg, Kuhn, and a host of other substantive thinkers have observed long ago, every theory or paradigm has its limitations of explanation. Like it or not, it appears we must be content with (as the experimentalists might put it) unaccountable portions of variance. Couched in other terms, perhaps we must, as the physicists successfully have, grapple with predictability of a different order—the slippery concepts of probabilities. To advance in this regard requires sincere answers to profound questions, some of which are beginning to be posed.

> Does not this kind of randomness offer sufficient comfort against the threat of chaos? Does it not even make for a more intriguing world? After all, it is chance, in this sense, that gives our own lives, and the course of human history, so much richness and interest. Call it by its older names of fortune or free will, if you like. Shall we deny a similar richness to the rest of nature? (Gould, 1983, p. 342)

REFERENCES

Aponte, H., & Van Deusen, J. Structural family therapy. In A. S. Gurman & D. Kniskern (Eds.), *Handbook of family therapy.* New York: Brunner/Mazel, 1981.

Bandura, A. The psychology of chance encounters and life paths. *American Psychologist,* 1982, *37,* 747–755.

Bateson, G. *Mind and nature.* New York: Dutton, 1979.

Beck, A. *Cognitive therapy and the emotional disorders.* New York: International Universities Press, 1976.

Beck, A., Rush, J., Shaw, B., & Emery, G. *Cognitive therapy of depression.* New York: Guilford, 1979.

Davidson, M. *Uncommon sense.* Los Angeles: Tarcher, 1983.

Ellis, A. *Humanistic psychotherapy: The rational–emotive approach.* New York: McGraw-Hill, 1973.

Frank, J. *Persuasion and healing.* Baltimore: Johns Hopkins University Press, 1973.

Fraser, J. S. Structural and strategic family therapy: A basis for marriage, or grounds for divorce. *Journal of Marital and Family Therapy,* 1982, *8,* 13–22.

Garfield, S., & Bergin, A. (Eds.). *Handbook of psychotherapy and behavior change.* New York: Wiley, 1978.

Gould, S. J. *Ever since Darwin.* New York: Norton, 1977.

Gould, S. J. *The panda's thumb.* New York: Norton, 1980.

Gould, S. J. *Hen's teeth and horse's toes.* New York: Norton, 1983.

Graziano, A., & Bythell, D. L. Failures in child behavior therapy. In E. Foa & P. Emmelkamp (Eds.), *Failures in behavior therapy.* New York: Wiley, 1983.

Gurman, A. S. Integrative marital therapy: Toward the development of an interpersonal approach. In S. Budman (Ed.), *Forms of brief therapy.* New York: Guilford, 1981.

Gurman, A., & Kniskern, D. *Handbook of family therapy.* New York: Brunner/Mazel, 1981.

Gurman, A., & Razin, A. (Eds.). *Effective psychotherapy: A handbook of research.* New York: Pergamon, 1977.

Hadley, S., & Strupp, H. Contemporary views of negative effects in psychotherapy: An integrated account. *Archives of General Psychiatry,* 1976, *33,* 1291–1302.

Haley, J. *Uncommon therapy.* New York: Norton, 1973.

Haley, J. *Problem-solving therapy.* San Francisco, Calif.: Jossey-Bass, 1976.

Haley, J. *Leaving home.* New York: McGraw-Hill, 1981.

Hoffman, L. *Foundations of family therapy.* New York: Basic, 1981.

Hoffman, L. A co-evolutionary framework for systemic family therapy. In B. Keeney (Ed.), *Diagnosis and assessment in family therapy.* Rockville, Md.: Aspen, 1982.

Koestler, A. *Janus: A summing up.* New York: Random House, 1978.

L'Abate, L. *Systematic family therapy.* New York: Brunner/Mazel, in press.

Liddle, H. A. The emotional and political hazards of teaching and learning family therapy. *Family Therapy*, 1978, *5*, 1–12.

Liddle, H. A. On teaching a systemic or contextual therapy: Training content, goals, and methods. *American Journal of Family Therapy*, 1980, *8*, 58–69.

Liddle, H. A. Review of J. Haley, *Leaving home*, and C. Madanes, *Strategic family therapy*. *Journal of Marital and Family Therapy*, 1981, *7*, 545–549.

Liddle, H. A. Review of S. Minuchin & H. C. Fishman, *Techniques of family therapy*. *American Journal of Family Therapy*, 1982a, *10*, 81–88.

Liddle, H. A. Diagnosis in family therapy: A comparative analysis of six schools of thought. In B. Keeney (Ed.), *Diagnosis and assessment in family therapy*. Rockville, Md.: Aspen, 1982b.

Liddle, H. A. On the problem of eclecticism: A call for epistemologic classification and human-scale theories. *Family Process*, 1982c, *21*, 243–250.

Liddle, H. A. Toward a dialectical–contextual–coevolutionary translation of structural–strategic family therapy. *Journal of Strategic and Systemic Therapies*, 1984, *3*, 66–80.

Liddle, H. A., & Saba, G. W. Clinical use of the family life cycle: Some cautionary guidelines. In H. A. Liddle (Ed.), *Clinical implications of the family life cycle*. Rockville, Md.: Aspen, 1983.

Liddle, H. A., & Saba, G. W. The isomorphic nature of training and therapy: Epistemologic foundation for a structural strategic training paradigm. In J. Schwartzman (Ed.), *Families and other systems: The macrosystemic context of family therapy*. New York: Guilford, 1985.

Liddle, H. A., & Saba, G. W. *Family therapy training and supervision: Creating contexts of competence*. Orlando, Fla.: Grune & Stratton, in press.

Liddle, H. A., & Schwartz, R. Live supervision/consultation: Conceptual and pragmatic guidelines for family therapy trainers. *Family Process*, 1983, *22*, 477–490.

Minuchin, S. *Families and family therapy*. Cambridge, Mass.: Harvard, 1974.

Minuchin, S., & Fishman, H. C. *Family therapy techniques*. Cambridge, Mass.: Harvard, 1981.

Minuchin, S., Rosman, B., & Baker, L. *Psychosomatic families*. Cambridge, Mass.: Harvard, 1978.

Penn, P. Circular questioning. *Family Process*, 1982, *21*, 267–280.

Pinsof, W. Integrative problem-centered therapy: Toward the synthesis of family and individual psychotherapies. *Journal of Marital and Family Therapy*, 1983, *9*, 19–36.

Rabkin, R. *Strategic psychotherapy*. New York: Basic, 1977.

Stanton, M. D. Marital therapy from a structural/strategic viewpoint. In G. Sholevar (Ed.), *Marriage is a family affair*. Jamaica, N.Y.: S. P. Medical & Scientific Books, 1981.

Stanton, M. D. An integrated structural/strategic approach to family therapy. *Journal of Marital and Family Therapy*, 1981b, *7*, 427–439.

Stanton, M. D. Strategic approaches to family therapy. In A. S. Gurman & D. Kniskern (Eds.), *Handbook of family therapy*. New York: Brunner/Mazel, 1981c.

Stanton, M. D., Todd, T., & Associates. *The family therapy of drug abuse and addiction*. New York: Guilford, 1982.

7

Systems Therapy of a Family Presenting with a Schizophrenic Member

W. ROBERT BEAVERS

Introduction

In a field so zealous for success, the opportunity to talk of failure is rare. From the vantage point of my 30 years in medicine, success and failure usually intertwine; rather than opposites, they are close kin, intimately related to the dimension of time. I hope that the telling of this clinical tale will illustrate the fluctuating market in success.

In all of the healing arts, the final defeat, death, awaits patient and doctor alike; success is further constrained or restricted by the unexpected. If a patient with a severe myocardial infarct at 35 years of age lives to be 65, most observers would agree that the doctor was successful. If a schizophrenic patient stays sane and productive for, say 5 years after psychosis, most would term the treatment a success, though patient and the family might disagree if in the 6th year the demon returns and takes permanent root.

The family presented here has an adult child who has been quite psychotic in two extended episodes. I chose to present this family partly because the ancient and awesome disease of madness originally brought me to systems theory and family work.

Early in my psychiatric training, schizophrenia intrigued and propelled me into the cauldron of family. I thought then, as I do now, that to understand schizophrenia would be to understand the human predicament, the shared question marks we all carry. What is this body of mine? How does it relate to me? Where did I come from and what relation are my parents and their parents to me? What is growing up? Does one ever leave home, or simply cleverly recreate shadows of the past?

As Al Scheflen explained in his final creative burst (Scheflen, 1981), schizophrenia can only be understood by considering many system levels, from society to neurotransmitters, and a good therapist will attend to all of

W. Robert Beavers. Department of Psychiatry, University of Texas Health Science Center, Dallas, Texas; Southwest Family Institute, Dallas, Texas.

them (eight, in Scheflen's reckoning). Just so, emotional and physical health can only be comprehended, touched (never grasped, I am afraid) by dealing with these same levels—society, institution, family, dyads, person, nervous system, dendritic proliferation, synapses, and neurotransmitters (Beavers, 1983).

I began my psychiatric training by moving across the medical school hall from the pharmacology department, where I had been a physiologist and a biochemist of sorts. At that time it seemed to me quite clear that I would continue to use those skills in psychiatry. However, I became fascinated with information coming from schizophrenic people and their families.

"My family murdered me," said a frail, 20-year-old woman as she repeatedly cut her wrists to see if she would bleed.

"If I move, Russia and the United States will destroy each other," said a 20-year-old catatonic young man whose parents were locked in conflict. And so on.

So, 25 years later, I approach emotional (and for that matter physical) illness from a systems standpoint (Beavers, 1981). In a given treatment situation, I expect to intervene at several levels and to help and get help from family members of identified patients.

Theoretical Frame of Reference

I believe a systems approach means perceiving illness and health at many biological and social levels, shifting from society to family, to individual, to tissue and back again, rather than approaching them at any one level, even at the family level. That is to say, "family therapy" is not systems therapy if it ignores or denies the importance of understanding illness from the biological and individual point of view as well.

Remembering this hierarchical aspect of systems concepts provides the opportunity to embrace a new paradigm while remaining coherent to other physicians and mental health professionals who continue to think in terms of individual disease or dynamics. A systems approach does not negate illness at the person level; rather, it adds dimensions to the understanding of disease that offer novel and more effective approaches to intervention.

Systems theory has, among many, the following basic assumptions:

1. Any individual needs a group, a human system, for individual experience of coherence and satisfaction.

2. Causes and effects are interchangeable.

3. Any human behavior is a result of many variables rather than one clear-cut single cause.

4. Humans are limited and finite. A social role of either absolute power or helplessness prohibits many of the needed satisfactions found in human encounter.

In a study of healthy families, I found that these systems concepts were integrated into the interaction of optimal family members (Beavers, 1977), which strengthened my belief that psychotherapists who attend to systems phenomena are probing a vital aspect of human functioning.

Space limitations prevent a review here of family systems theory, but some principles important to me and supported by research (Lewis, Beavers, Gossett, & Phillips, 1976) should be listed:

1. There is a correlation between the problem-solving capabilities of an individual in a particular family and the family itself.

2. Just as individual adults have different levels of maturity on a developmental scale of emotional and social growth and development, so do families show different degrees of adaptation, and of differentiation.

3. Less differentiated families are more apt to have identified patients in their midst, poorer morale, and more emotional pain.

4. Symptoms in family members are often the result of their frozen position in the family and their inability to extricate themselves from that family. The family itself is often at an impasse, unable to continue its expected movement through family life stages.

5. By improving the systems qualities of these families—especially the boundaries between members, the communicational clarity, member autonomy and sense of choice, and respect for each member's internal experiences and unique viewpoint—symptoms can be eliminated and further growth and development of individuals and family made possible.

Family assessment is as important as individual diagnosis in developing a treatment plan. My assessment schema was developed over many years and focuses largely on process evaluation of family competence and style. A more detailed description is found in previous publications (Beavers, 1981, 1982; Beavers & Voeller, 1983). Accurate assessment involves attending to the interactional processes of the family, the members' ability to deal with personal ambivalence and family conflict, and the family's ability to negotiate, solve problems, and perform tasks. A therapist can determine the developmental level of current family functioning, where it is blocked, and the function of the symptoms for the identified patient and for the family. Beyond assessing theses processes, two additional aspects of family functioning are critical: (1) how family members relate to each other and (2) how family members relate to persons outside the family circle. Once the assessment phase is completed, appropriate interventions are developed.

For example, intervention in severely dysfunctional families often requires dealing with profound despair, confused boundaries between members, absence of a shared focus of attention, and inability to have encounters that foster change and movement. A family rule usually found in these families is, "Loving means thinking and feeling alike," which places an irresolvable conflict into the family structure. Since everybody experiences the world differently, one can be accepted at the risk of being nobody, or be oneself at the risk of being rejected.

Less disturbed families, termed "midrange" in the assessment schema, have coherence and a shared focus of attention. Intervention with these families must usually be designed to cope with the enormous impasses related to control issues. A family rule common in this group is, "Loving means controlling," and various forms of intimidation are used to control spouses, children, and parents.

Treatment strategies are dictated by the family assessment. The family reported in this chapter was assessed to be in the group defined as severely dysfunctional, centripetal.

The term "centripetal" refers to the stylistic quality of a family in which members characteristically look to the family more than to the outside world for satisfaction. They handle ambivalent feelings toward one another by attempting to play up the positive and ignore and even deny the negative. "Centrifugal" families, in contrast, produce members who usually look outside the family for gratification. They handle ambivalent feelings by denying or ignoring warm and positive emotions and by promoting the expression of anger and rejection.

In severely dysfunctional families, *coherence* is a needed but elusive goal. Severely dysfunctional family members handle ambivalence poorly, and a vital part of intervention strategy is the encouragement and acceptance of expressed unresolved ambivalence. The therapist helps by modeling, by direction, by arranging a climate in which open, clear expression of feelings and desires is safe and rewarded. Therapeutic intervention must encourage successful coherent encounters between family members in order that family and individual developmental tasks can be accomplished.

Severely dysfunctional centripetal families fear the biological pull of children's growth and development. They regard much of normal family evolution—such as children growing up and leaving home—as disloyal, and rules that inhibit this movement frequently result in symptomatic children. Therapeutic strategies should help family members accept increased independence and individuation, redefining these efforts as loving and loyal. In short, for severely dysfunctional centripetal families (who typically are quite willing to attend sessions together) classical family therapy is an optimal technique.

Background

In April 1979, Mr. and Mrs. W brought their 24-year-old daughter, Donna, to me at the recommendation of a family therapist in another city. Donna had been psychotic for 3 months, hospitalized, and placed on a rather heavy dosage of an antipsychotic drug, haloperidol, along with an anti-Parkinson-ian drug, benztropine mesylate. The parents had actively sought her hospital discharge, wanting to bring her back to Dallas for outpatient treatment. They trusted the referring therapist, and since he strongly urged family involve-ment, they wanted to be a part of her therapy.

Donna looked a mess. Her hair was unkempt, she held her left arm stiffly, and her face was masklike. Mrs. W was a 40-ish, gray-haired woman with a pleasant face, neatly dressed, polite, but expressing some tension, pain, and urgency in her voice and facial expression. Mr. W, a powerfully built, rough-handed, weatherbeaten man, held himself erect and aloof. His polite-ness did not completely hide an underlying current of anger or even rage.

The family was economically upper middle-class; the father through his drive and shrewdness had pulled himself and his family up from a lower status. He was proud of his success, accustomed to direct solutions to problems, and baffled by the current family situation.

As in all families, there was more history than could ever be compre-hended, much less transmitted to others. The work began immediately, and the historical information was gleaned in bits and pieces during the next 3 months. I will capsulize the themes that seem most important to me.

Mother had had a puzzling and painful arthritic condition from 16 years of age, increasing to the point of near invalidism when Donna was 10 years old. Possibly because of this, and partly because of the recommendation of a psychiatrist who saw Donna when she was 12, Donna was sent to a boarding school several hundred miles away for the 7th grade. Mother's health im-proved dramatically and she remained well. After a year Donna, who learned about the use of illicit drugs and alcohol in this "restricted" environment, returned home, apparently because of her insistence and her mother's im-provement.

This started a peculiar "yo-yo" pattern. In the succeeding teenage years, Donna would become increasingly frustrating to her parents and angry with them, then precipitously leave home. After a time she would run out of friends and confidence and return, Donna and her parents would pledge their best efforts to do better, and the sequence would begin again. After several months of run-ins with Daddy, Mother's attempts to be peacemaker, and Donna's increasing drug use and defiance, off she would go.

A vivid series of sexual triangles evolved. Father was emotionally labile, especially toward Donna, alternating between seductive intimacy and pas-sionate denunciation of her behavior and character. Unresolved triangles included Mother, Donna, Father, and a series of boyfriends unacceptable to Father. After she was 17 years old, she always left with or went to a boy-friend. During this time Father seemed to have a highly emotional, sexually charged relationship with Donna. This was pieced together many months later through discussions with family members.

Donna did finish high school but was not much of a scholar in college. At age 20, she sustained head injuries in a car accident. She was hospitalized for several weeks and complained of a continuing left-side weakness which seemed to have cleared over several months.

Subsequently, Donna became even more moody, and the parents, especially her mother, worried and fluttered more. Donna then became a skydiver and broke a foot. She used large amounts of street drugs and took up with some questionable characters. While living with one of these in the winter of 1978, she became psychotic for the first time. Convinced that the boyfriend was influencing her thoughts, and that she was able to control the weather, she alternated between angry outbursts and sullen suicidal ruminations. Her delusions included the belief that she was crippled from her head injury and would never read or write normally again.

Diagnosis and Treatment Plan

The family showed a classical pattern of family-with-schizophrenic-offspring. The mother and daughter were enmeshed, and the father was disengaged from them both. He surveyed both his daughter's strange speech and her mother's blind solicitude with a superior distant air (though managing to betray hints of a puzzled wistfulness from time to time). I pictured him as a lion high on a grassy knoll looking down into a murky swamp.

It is important to note that the father's disengagement had been preceded by the previously mentioned steamy, sexualized enmeshment. The terms enmeshment and disengagement have been utilized by Minuchin (1974) to describe boundary phenomena; they can be conceptualized as dyadic relationship qualities found in dysfunctional families and representing a similar failure of family system differentiation.

Family members evidenced a significant amount of mind reading, of speaking for one another, and of direct invasiveness. Donna was preoccupied with her symptoms and her ability to control natural phenomena, and she made cryptic references to people outside the family who might hurt her.

The family, at the first interview, could be diagrammed as shown in Figure 7-1A.

This severely dysfunctional, centripetal family, with dramatic boundary problems, looked, however much in vain, for satisfaction within the family. Though the father was at present disengaged from his wife and daughter, he had no other consistent emotional support. Donna was, at best, a delegate to the outside world, doomed to return to the family from her forays into drugs, sex, or psychosis.

At the individual level, Donna provided adequate data for a diagnosis of schizophrenia. She was isolated, in poor emotional control, with eccentric

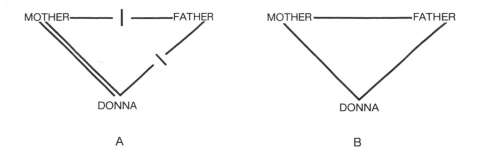

FIG. 7-1. Family dynamics at first interview (A). Family dynamics as projected in treatment goal (B).

and obscure language and thought content. She fluctuated from flat affect to sullenness, to depression, to agitation.

In this first episode, Donna's psychotic symptoms were documented for about 5 months. If her story was accurate, she had probably been psychotic for a total of 8 months. Donna's personal history was characteristic of the "stormy" type of premorbid personality of schizophrenia described many years ago by Arieti (1955).

At the neurological level not only was her ability to have left-brain dominance, hence linear thinking (Scheflen, 1981) impaired, but there was a question of organicity. Was this from the haloperidol? Or perhaps from the brain insult of 4 years previously? Was her face impassive from catatonia or from drug-induced Parkinsonism?

And at the neuronal, synaptic, and neurotransmitter level, was she on the right medication? Could I do better than haloperidol? Would the family relate to her more competently if she could look and act more like an attractive young woman, less like a soon-to-be-chronic zombie?

Before the treatment plan was finalized, I asked for a psychological consultation regarding Donna's neurological state. Was there any clear-cut evidence of irreversible organicity? I received a hesitant statement from the psychologist that Donna probably had not suffered organic damage other than that produced by the medication.

Process of Therapy

After the initial assessment interview, the focus was on structural realignment, that is, moving the family from A to B as shown in Figure 7-1. More attachment and sharing between parents was needed, less intense and murky

interaction between the mother and Donna was important, and more interaction between Donna and her father would be helpful if this were to be accomplished without reverting to the old enmeshed intensity.

Weekly sessions were instituted with goals to obtain clarity, firm up boundaries, and pull the father in closer. Donna's crazy imagery was utilized in guiding the family work. For example, her belief that she had caused tornadoes was related to the family's anxiety about Father's and Daughter's relationship once she had become a sexual young woman.

At the individual level, we needed a sane Donna who could begin to work on her problems and enjoy her possibilities with shared, rather than private, symbols. I agreed to see her individually once a week, with the emphasis on resolving ambivalence, increasing a sense of choice, and communicating in a fashion that we both could understand.

At the neurological level, I wanted to eliminate the Parkinson-like symptoms so that Donna could more easily relate to family members and friends, and so that she herself would be reassured that her body had not betrayed her. The haloperidol was discontinued, and a modest dosage of trifluoperazine hydrochloride was prescribed at a level which in my experience had not produced significant extrapyramidal side effects. After 2 weeks, the anti-Parkinsonian drug was discontinued, and drug management became quite a bit simpler. It is my clinical observation over many years that antipsychotic drug administration beautifully illustrates the reality and importance of thinking about illness and health on several levels. The drug dosage and the extent of supportive personal relationships are inversely proportional. That is, if a person is isolated and alone—on a ward or in a family—the drug dosage required to develop or maintain sanity is much higher than when the same person experiences some sense of sharing with others and a reduction in the isolation.

Initial Outcome: Success

After 10 individual and 10 family sessions, Donna was sane. The family was partially restructured, with Mother and Donna making more sense to each other and to me. Each was usually taking responsibility for himself or herself rather than each other. Father had been encouraged to problem solve with his wife and to expect her to be a partner with him. Mother responded to his increasing attention by reaching out to him and lessening her involvement with Donna.

Donna was well-groomed and had found a sense of humor. Gone were the mask-like face, the left-sided stiffness, and her fears of never being physically normal. She became interested in getting a job and did so, as a clerk in a dress shop.

Although I urged the family to continue treatment, they were so delighted with Donna's recovery that they wanted to take a vacation, and did. Everything went too fast.

Secondary Outcome: End of Success, Beginning of Failure

Donna continued for 3 months in individual treatment, becoming more erratic in appearing for her sessions, and in taking her medication. She began to have stomach pains that would go away with the medication, and she would take the medication only for this purpose. Finally she was able to get along without any medication. She moved out of her family's home and moved in with a girlfriend. She then fell in love and appeared to bloom. She left treatment with no symptoms, no despair, but was a cheerful, changed young woman. Too fast.

In the next 12 months, I saw her parents several times. They would come in fighting over some aspect of their relationship with Donna. Should they try to keep her from visiting some of the drug-abusing friends she had had before her breakdown? Should she be forced to use her own money to pay for treatment, for a car she had wrecked, or must her father pay for everything? From chaos when Donna was sick, the family structure moved to ineffectual efforts at dominating her when she was "well." Donna began to drink on weekends, and this provided an additional reason for concern. I encouraged the parents in each instance to work out a plan that they could agree on and that they thought would work. This usually reduced the father's tendency to attempt more control than he could actually accomplish.

Failure

I lost track of the trio for about a year. Then came an urgent call from the father. I must see the family right away. Donna was sick again. I was unable to offer an immediate appointment, but I struggled to make one available for a time 5 days later, and the father reluctantly agreed to wait.

When they arrived, Mother was absent, Father was terribly anxious and torn, and Donna was as crazy as she had been the first time. She was again controlling the weather, her feeling state alternated between hostility and suicidal depression, and she seemed thoroughly fed up with herself, her father, and her mother. Recent history revealed that she had lost her boyfriend, quit her job, and wandered around Texas. Finally, spent and out of emotional credit with anyone outside her family, she had come back home in a wildly psychotic state.

In this rather frantic interview, I obtained the update, tried to get a relationship started once again with Donna, attempted to support her father, wondered where her mother was, and instituted antipsychotic drug treatment.

Neither Donna nor her father could give me any coherent explanation of why her mother was not there. In Donna's metaphor of weather control, storm clouds gathered and lightning flashed. I gave the family the earliest appointment time available for 7 days later and urged all three to be there.

Though Father's and Donna's emotional responsiveness to me were cool, just "off" a bit somehow, I remained hopeful that with family work we could turn this around as we had done before.

Such was not to be. The following week, Donna was even more withdrawn and less coherent than on the previous visit. Father was stiffly distant. Mother was enraged; I have never heard anyone express more venom and remain coherent. She was adamant that she would not tolerate Donna at home; Donna needed to be in a hospital, and it was for Donna's own good that she would not allow her in the house one more night. In vain I tried to accept her suggestion to hospitalize Donna on the basis that she and her husband were overwhelmed and Donna's illness was a greater burden than they could handle. She would have none of this; she was fine; Donna was sick and must be in a hospital. I was convinced that continuing stubbornly to insist on family therapy as the modality at this juncture would have been stark disaster. Suicide would have been the most likely conclusion to the drama. Donna had run out of emotional capital with everyone in the outside world and with her mother. No longer a clearly observable enmeshment that a therapist could work with, the relationship now showed itself as blind rejection/ejection. The image evoked by the mother's tirade was of helplessly vomiting again and again to eliminate a poison. The family had redefined itself in a manner represented by Figure 7-2. Enmeshment was replaced by disengagement with a vengeance, and Father and Daughter were not a stable enough twosome to withstand Mother's active distancing.

Here we see the potential interchangeability of enmeshed and disengaged dyads within an overall family framework of inadequate differentiation.

With as much calm and dignity as I could muster, I called a fellow psychiatrist and arranged for hospitalization. (I do not do hospital work in my present practice style. It is not possible for me to do a good job of treating

FIG. 7-2. Family at second crisis.

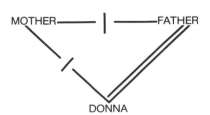

both inpatients and outpatients. In addition, the institutional restrictions of hospital practice produce more barriers to systems oriented intervention than I care to struggle with.) Donna then received the best traditional individually oriented treatment for psychosis—containment, medication (higher dosages of trifluoperizine hydrochloride than I had ever used), milieu, group therapy, and very occasional visits from her parents. She did well with this regimen, and remained in the hospital for about 3 months. I never heard from the family in all that time.

There it was—failure. Loss of rapport with the family and with Donna. Loss of my role in the family, rejection of the family treatment model, and a psychotic patient who had to be referred to someone else.

A New Start

After Donna had been out of the hospital for about 2 months, Father called me to arrange family sessions while my colleague remained Donna's individual therapist. This time around, we were less stressed and less hurried. I had more rapport with each family member, and they knew and accepted me to a greater extent. Mother had forgiven us all since Donna had gone to the hospital and the unbearable load was lifted. Donna was optimistic about being sane yet not alienated from her parents, and her father was convinced that the family relationships were important to Donna's emotional condition. I explored the parents' family of origin to help us all understand Father's need for power and Mother's denying herself. Mother spoke of her early memories of feeling that she had to please everyone in her family, and how she becomes disgusted with herself now for doing so. She was encouraged to assert herself with family and friends. Father had painful memories of his own father who paid no attention to his successes but only noticed when he failed. Both parents defined themselves more clearly and forgave themselves and each other for present failures that related to past learning.

The family roles were changing to allow for more autonomy; each member was speaking more clearly for himself and taking responsibility for individual actions. Donna began college once again with high hopes and less dependence on her parents. She found two girl friends with whom she was comfortable.

During this time Donna rejected her individual therapist and, after negotiating, she returned to alternating family and individual sessions with me. Donna finished 1 year of college, making A's and B's for the first time.

She continued medication and psychotherapy during this college year, for she was somewhat sobered by having had two psychotic breaks.

Nevertheless, after the successful year she left treatment, and her family to return to live with friends in an eastern city where I helped her find a therapist.

Is success or failure in store? Who knows? It will probably, as in the past, depend on when the pie is sliced; at what point in this ongoing relationship do we examine the "results"? Donna is in a highly vulnerable period presently; after two psychotic breaks, she is at risk to slip into chronicity. Yet she is functioning on a more consistent and more competent level with a better network than she has ever done before.

Carl Whitaker (1981) has commented that upon nearing 70 years of age he does not know whether he is a success as a parent: "Perhaps it will depend on how well the grandchildren turn out."

As one adopts a systems perspective toward psychopathology and emotional health, such a point of view about time and outcome evolves. Diagnosis and assessment of the individual identified patient and of the family system are essential; the dynamics of the family and the family members interrelate and influence one another. Pain and suffering are related to the diagnosis of individual illness, and the therapist is honor bound to attempt speedy and efficacious intervention to relieve that suffering.

Further, measures of outcome related to a time dimension are extremely important in determining whether one kind of systems intervention is better than another, if there is some kind of comprehensible assessment framework in which to put the family.

The outcome statement—success, failure, and dropout—is necessarily related to a time dimension, unless perhaps the outcome is death rather than dysfunction. This clinical vignette illustrates the varying fortunes of families, patients, and therapists. It suggests that though we can all improve our approaches to a given treatment situation, we may also be offered further opportunities to deal with the evolving family. Defeat and failure may be changed into success even though this in turn may be temporary.

A story I heard as a child has remained in my mind as an experience with circular as opposed to linear thinking. This was the tale of a small boy on a runaway railroad train. The boy fell off as the train angled up the side of a mountain. He panicked and felt sure all was lost until the sound of the train coming around the mountain a little higher made him aware that he could scramble up and jump on again. In the long view of family therapy, as in most other endeavors, "It will come 'round again," and failure is a relative phenomenon.

Analysis of Failure

When a practical physician is struggling to understand a "case" of schizophrenia, it is too much to explore all relevant factors such as ethnic background, the time of the family of origin's immigration into this country, current economic pressures, and the like, although many factors are powerful influences contributing to health or illness.

I would like to examine this failure from the standpoint of:

1. faulty termination, participated in the first time around by the therapist, the patient, and the family;
2. overestimation of the power of family intervention to achieve success without assistance from other systems levels, such as continuing individual work and drug treatment; and
3. the inadequacies of a conventional private practice model to meet the needs of families with an acutely psychotic member.

Let us take them one by one, although they all interact.

Faulty Termination

It has been my thesis that psychotherapists tend to fall into groups, the growers and the controllers (Beavers, 1977). Each approach has values and shortcomings, and each can work better if the customers and the vendors are thoughtfullly matched rather than arbitrarily assigned. I have a style that is predominantly egalitarian; I am loathe to be responsible *for* someone, but rather prefer to be responsible *to* my patients. This approach is quite useful in working with many families, couples, and individuals who desire, or find they can use, a nudge toward accepting responsibility for choice. A steady spotlight in family sessions on the ubiquity of ambivalence, the importance and difficulty of resolving mixed feelings, and the vital satisfaction in personal choice making, is often effective in changing individual behavior and family system rules. ("Loving means controlling," for example, can metamorphose into "Loving means respecting people's struggles to make up their minds.")

But the down side, the potential defect, of this therapeutic style is illustrated in this chapter's case example. Families who have an acutely psychotic member do not need to be convinced that they need help. When the psychosis clears, however, both patient and family frequently tend to declare victory and go home. (In my clinical work, this occurs in about one-half of families with psychotic members.) To keep the W family in treatment required more persuasiveness than I have. The problem of the acutely well patient is much more significant with psychosis. The seriousness of the illness encourages a focus on the identified patient rather than on family difficulties, and dramatic difference between illness and health with recovery encourages the denial of family problems. I was unable to hold the family in treatment, and Donna reverted to her moderately antisocial, drug-abusing style of coping. She was like Pinocchio as she laughed and played, oblivious to her increasing dependence on alcohol and drugs, sneering at sage advice that she considered unnecessary and inaccurate. As long as her symptoms of anxiety badgered her, she took the antipsychotic medication. When she fell in love, her anxiety left. She was swallowed up, possessed, by the enormity of her passion. In comparison, the treatment relationship was rather small potatoes. I felt like Jiminy Cricket bouncing along ignored and finally dismissed as a drag on Pinocchio's party.

Mother and Father had derived some lasting benefits from the family work focusing on boundaries and parental closeness. They did not, however, completely give up their perceptions of themselves as having trouble chiefly because of Donna. Their own problems were seen as related to Donna's but not overwhelmingly important in themselves. Therefore, as Donna left treatment, so did Mother and Father.

The success, in short, sowed the seeds of failure, as family members escaped from an obvious nightmare and went back to previous familiar patterns, secure in seeing Donna sane and happy. I wished at the time that Donna could have waited a bit before plunging into a consuming love. However, many experiences with such family situations have taught me that falling in love is often used by people to finesse needed work in separation and individuation.

Overestimation of the Power of Family Intervention

Another factor in the premature termination was an overestimation of the staying power of the family work to maintain the success without reinforcement at intervals, support from individual psychotherapy, and biological support from the antipsychotic drug. The family members certainly shared the overestimation, and in retrospect, I probably did also. It is difficult to distinguish between excessive optimism and bleak hope based on nothing but feeling helpless.

An excellent study (Goldstein, Rodnick, Evans, May, & Steinberg, 1978) reports the results of family treatment when added to adequate drug therapy in the aftercare of previously hospitalized first- and second-break schizophrenic patients. Their data indicate a dramatic and significant drop in recidivism that can be related to six carefully defined and prescribed family interviews. This study, however, looks only at a 6-month slice of time in the patient's life. There are no data that I am aware of to suggest how long such intervention might have a favorable effect. Mosher and Keith (1979), in a review article on psychosocial treatment of schizophrenia, called for research that would include 1–2 year posttreatment assessment of community adjustment and family interaction in such patients. Anderson, Hogarty, and Reiss (1980) provide valuable information on procedures in continuing work with families of schizophrenic patients discharged from hospitals, but their study does not specifically address the issue of what risk families take when they do not continue family treatment. These data will emerge and be valuable to therapists and family members alike.

Inadequacies of a Conventional Private Practice Model

Finally, after the prolonged loss of contact, when the family urgently called for assistance once again, my way of practicing failed me and them. An advantage of the private practice model is that people can develop a strong relationship with their doctor, who gets to know them well and can provide the special personal attention so important to despairing, isolated, demoralized people. There are disadvantages also; I am continually confronted with more demands from current and potential patients than I have time and energy to address. Though I am part of a group of practitioners oriented to family treatment, the W's did not accept referral to another therapist until the moment of despair. They wanted me, and I tried to provide help with an inadequate allotment of time.

I attempt to control this unfortunate possibility of a former patient's landing on my doorstep without warning by urging patients and families who terminate to contact me *before* they get into big trouble. This often works, but not with the W's, who did not provide me with the time cushion that I needed, and hence I was not able to respond adequately.

Reviewing this phase of the treatment failure has helped me to see that the institution of private practice has its own rigidity, comparable in many ways to the more obvious rigidity of institutions defined by brick and steel. I painfully acknowledge that I was as rigid as any institution; I was not so much in control of my life that I could quickly undertake a new big job. I would have to have more slippage, more leeway in my professional life to be that flexible.

I also did not pick up on the significance of Mother's not calling and not being there for the first interview of the abortive treatment episode. In retrospect, I should have reached out to her and invited her in. I do not, however, believe that refusing to begin treatment until all family members are present is defensible. Therapy can only work if somebody else is willing and able to be more flexible and to consider clients more hallowed than the method. I start with those family members who come, and I develop strategies to involve other family members or work without them. While I treated the biological level of the problem, reinstituting the antipsychotic medication, there was a vital week in which Mother was seething, feeling overwhelmed and abandoned. She developed a rejecting mind-set during that week that I could not melt. She was fed up with Donna, with me, and with a family approach to what seemed to her at that moment to be clearly an individual madness. It seemed definite to me that Mother believed her sanity, even her life, depended on eliminating Donna from the family at that time. She spoke of Donna's suicidal potential, and I believed her. I also had fantasies of Mother's being homicidal and suicidal, overwhelmed and believing that no one—not me, not her husband, not her extended family, and least of all Donna—was offering what she had to have to survive.

It is here I believe that a family systems approach was useful in dictating the abandonment of family therapy for Donna's psychotic state. With my head evaluating the network of available helpers and my gut determining the sense of urgency, helplessness, and loss of morale on the part of all participants (myself included), I decided that more troops were needed. For this reason Mother's desperate demand to hospitalize Donna was heeded, failure was acknowledged, and Donna was treated traditionally in her second psychotic episode.

From any perspective, failure is painful. Even with the long view regarding failure and success as time-related, the loss of a patient to what I now consider a foreign rigid medical model and the loss of the hard-earned confidence of the W family was a bitter pill.

Hypothetical Reconstruction toward Success

Routine success with a systems approach to psychosis requires great changes in treatment strategies, but equally great changes in the institutions of psychiatric care. The initial success with the W's was almost a fluke due as much to favorable surrounding circumstances as it was to any brilliance of intervention.

First, a traditional hospital environment had broken the fall and the sense of abject fear and hopelessness of the family, even though Donna was still psychotic at the time of entry into family therapy.

Second, Donna had already been placed on antipsychotic drugs, which had ameliorated some of the bizarre and frightening quality of her delusions, and therefore the family was a little more disposed to seeing her as one of them.

Third, the family had already become dissatisfied with the traditional approach to Donna's illness, and was emotionally ready to throw in with a therapist who was willing to treat her as an outpatient with the family.

The next psychotic episode required much more in the way of external structuring than I was able to do. Langsley, Pittman, and Swank (1969) reported, "When a patient decompensates for the first time, the family feels responsible and are more willing to consider their involvement as a group" (p. 272). On subsequent breaks, there is a greater tendency of family members to see the identified patient as different and separate from the family.

Those who have reported success in treating schizophrenic breaks on an outpatient basis, such as the Langsley group and Levenson, Lord, Serman, Thornby, Sullender, and Comstock (1977), have found it necessary to develop a specialized outpatient clinic format, in addition to a family systems orientation. Levenson's group described an intensive treatment setup that included seeing the identified patient daily during the psychotic episode until remission or transfer occurred. It seems clear that optimal family therapy of acute schizophrenia requires a setting that amounts to a crisis intervention center, with the available flexibility to handle family visits daily and/or unpredictably. Our group of famly-oriented therapists is currently exploring the economic feasibility of such a unit for private outpatients. One of the problems is, of course, the rigidity of third-party payers who may provide excellent financial coverage for emotional illness within a hospital, little or no coverage of the identified patient if seen outside the hospital, and no coverage for family therapy. Until these larger systems issues are adequately addressed, it will continue to be an exception, not the rule, for a systems definition of psychosis to be translated into consistent treatment strategies.

Nevertheless, I will try to increase the chances of success with such families by leaning somewhat harder on the family members to stay in treatment after a "miracle cure." I believe I can increase my ability to be authoritative without moving to an authoritarian position. I can offer a firm technical recommendation that will increase the chances of family system changes holding and progressing favorably.

In addition, I believe I have learned that equivocation when a family is desperate—in effect, offering a peanut when a steak dinner is needed, even demanded, does not have a good chance of success. I will either make room in my schedule for daily visits or throw in the towel immediately. It is quite likely that if I had given enough attention to the whole family quickly enough, the desperation would have been less and would not have proceeded to the point of the extrusion of Donna.

It was fortunate that the family gave me another chance, following Donna's discharge from the hospital. The results of this episode reaffirm the usefulness of the systems approach with psychotic patients. But the question of routinely handling acute psychotic episodes occurring in the lives of families without traditional hospitalization is far from clear. I will try (as all conscientious therapists do) to play my therapeutic cards the best I know how, and to learn from my failures.

REFERENCES

Anderson, C. M., Hogarty, G. E., & Rciss, D. J. Family treatment of adult schizophrenia patients: A research based psycho-educational approach. *Schizophrenia Bulletin*, 1980, *6*, 490–505.

Arieti, S. *Interpretation of schizophrenia.* New York: Brunner/Mazel, 1955.

Beavers, W. R. *Psychotherapy and growth: A family systems perspective.* New York: Brunner/Mazel, 1977.

Beavers, W. R. A systems model of family for family therapists. *Journal of Marital and Family Therapy*, 1981, *7*, 299–307.

Beavers, W. R., Healthy, midrange, and severely dysfunctional families. In F. Walsh (Ed.), *Normal family processes.* New York: Guilford, 1982.

Beavers, W. R. Hierarchical issues in a systems approach to illness and health. *Family Systems Medicine,* 1983, *1,* 47–55.

Beavers, W. R., & Voeller, M. N., Family models: Comparing the Olson circumplex model with the Beavers systems model. *Family Process,* 1983, *22,* 85–98.

Goldstein, M. J., Rodnick, E. H., Evans, J. A., May, P. R. A., & Steinberg, M. R. Drug and family therapy in the aftercare of acute schizophrenia. *Archives of General Psychiatry,* 1978, *35,* 1169–1177.

Langsley, D. G., Pittman, F. S., & Swank, G. E. Family crisis in schizophrenics and other mental patients. *Journal of Nervous and Mental Disease,* 1969, *149,* 270–276.

Levenson, A. J., Lord, C. J., Serman, C. E., Thornby, J. I., Sullender, W., & Comstock, B. S. Acute schizophrenia: An efficacious outpatient treatment approach as an alternative to full-time hospital. *Diseases of the Nervous System,* 1977, *38,* 242–245.

Lewis, J. M., Beavers, W. R., Gossett, J. T., & Phillips, V. A. *No single thread: Psychological health in family systems.* New York: Brunner/Mazel, 1976.

Minuchin, S. *Families and family therapy.* Cambridge, Mass.: Harvard University Press, 1974.

Mosher, L. R., & Keith, S. J. Research on the psychosocial treatment of schizophrenia: A summary report. *American Journal of Psychiatry,* 1979, *136,* 623–631.

Scheflen, A. *Levels of schizophrenia.* New York: Brunner/Mazel, 1981.

Whitaker, C. Personal communication, 1981.

8

A Conflict of Vows:
The Unconsummated Marriage
of an Ex-Priest

ILDA V. FICHER AND J. DOREENE KAPLAN

Introduction

All psychotherapists are familiar with the agony of cases that do not seem to go anywhere, with families who resist one's best interventions and frustrate all attempts to be helpful. There are some cases that one almost immediately knows will be extremely difficult and which one therefore approaches gingerly. However, I (Ficher) have treated many cases of unconsummated marriage over the years and have found them to be quite amenable to treatment.[1] It is a relatively straightforward dysfunction that is extremely responsive to treatment.

Jane and Peter were apparently an ideal couple for sex therapy. They were both bright, attractive, articulate professionals who were very cooperative and obviously shared a warm, caring relationship. I therefore anticipated smooth sailing with them and was most perplexed when the therapy faltered and failed. By the time I finally figured out what was going on, the case was lost. This couple taught me that you can never take success for granted—even the apparently "routine" case can fail.

Theoretical Frame of Reference

The last 20 years have brought an expanded freedom in our approach to sexuality. Taboo topics such as masturbation, once confined to whispers

1. The couple described in this chapter was seen in private practice by the first author, Ficher. The second author, Kaplan, was not directly involved in the treatment, but participated in analyzing the case and preparing the manuscript.

Ilda V. Ficher. Van Hammett Psychiatric Clinic, Human Sexuality Section, Department of Mental Health Sciences, Hahnemann University, Philadelphia, Pennsylvania.

J. Doreene Kaplan. Family Guidance Center of Bucks County, Yardley, Pennsylvania.

behind closed doors, are now discussed in great detail on national television. This proliferation and acceptance of sexual information is a clear indication that women and men are now claiming sexual satisfaction as a right and are both more aware of and less tolerant of sexual dysfunctions. In many cases they are turning to professionals for help in solving these problems. Concomitant with these societal changes, sex therapy has emerged as an accepted method of intervention for sexual dysfunction. Masters and Johnson's (1966) ground-breaking study of the effects of sexual stimulation on the body is generally cited as the beginning of the recognition of sex as a legitimate area of professional interest. Building on their findings, Masters and Johnson (1970) went on to develop a specific therapeutic approach for the treatment of sexual dysfunction. Their brief directed therapy emphasized exercises such as sensate-focus, mutual responsibility in the couple, and the use of male–female cotherapy teams. This model is still widely practiced and has been joined by other approaches, which may take a different theoretical orientation but incorporate many of the Masters and Johnson's techniques. Kaplan (1974) synthesized psychodynamic and behavioral approaches into a model that utilizes a blend of behavioral techniques, marital therapy, and psychodynamically oriented therapy. Treatment in the case presented here incorporates a combination of these approaches and will be described briefly.

Sex therapy with couples is seen as a part of marital therapy, and very often no clear distinction is made between treatment of sexual and marital dysfunctions (Ficher, 1982). The approach is multicausal, that is, the therapist looks for both the immediate and remote sources of the dysfunction. The immediate causes are explored within the context of the couple's ongoing relationship, and the connection between their relationship and satisfactory levels of sexual intimacy becomes the focus of treatment. Remote causes, such as unconscious intrapsychic conflicts derived from early family experiences of either partner, are brought into the treatment as necessary, when they are manifested through the therapy process (Ficher & Eisenstein, 1981, 1984).

There are several basic concepts and components which are an integral part of this approach to the treatment of sexual dysfunction:

1. Mutual responsibility. There is no such thing as an "uninvolved" partner. Each member of the couple is considered to be equally responsible for creating and maintaining the dysfunction and is therefore responsible for change and the solution of the difficulties.

2. Sexual education and information. Despite the "sexual revolution" and the proliferation of information in the media, a surprisingly large number of men and women are ignorant about sexual anatomy, functioning, and techniques. Therefore, a basic component of treatment is to provide clear, precise sexual information in an accepting, sexually encouraging atmosphere.

3. Attitude change. Throughout history the message from social control agents has been that sex is immoral, sinful, dangerous, and taboo. Even today there are many men and women who maintain a negative attitude toward sex and therefore have great difficulty in discussing it. One of the important goals of sex therapy is to provide a safe, supportive, permissive environment that can foster a change in these negative attitudes and allow an easier expression of sexuality.

4. Reduction of performance anxiety. By the time most couples come to sex therapy, they have developed a high level of sexual performance anxiety, which is extremely destructive to sexual functioning. Couples are therefore taught that sexual desire and performance cannot be forced or produced on demand. In the beginning stages of therapy, couples are discouraged from focusing on achieving a goal, and encouraged to focus on giving and receiving pleasure, and on becoming increasingly aware of physical sensations. The sexual situation that has previously generated anxiety is gradually reentered through a step-by-step process, which encourages new learning and greater comfort.

5. Improving communication between partners. Many couples have a great deal of difficulty with clearly and directly communicating their sexual desires, preferences, dislikes, and feelings. Such discussion is often seen as criticism of the partner and is therefore carefully avoided for fear of rejection or retaliation. The accepting climate of sex therapy breaks down these inhibitions and encourages the couple to talk about previously avoided topics. The therapist models an uninhibited attitude that facilitates communication between the couple.

6. Taking responsibility for oneself. An essential part of sex therapy is exploring and accepting one's own sexuality. The individual who does not understand his or her own sexual preferences cannot communicate them to the partner. In therapy each partner is encouraged to be "selfish" and to focus on his or her own pleasure. This is facilitated by the exercises, which are structured around taking turns.

When a couple presents themselves for sex therapy, they often have a combination of marital and sexual difficulties, regardless of the initial complaint. The first step in treatment therefore is to assess the dynamics of the couple's relationship to determine the link between marital conflicts and sexual disorder (Ficher, 1982). This step is crucial in selecting the appropriate initial focus of treatment. In choosing the optimum initial focus, Sager (1974) has identified three general categories of couples, based on an analysis of the extent to which sexual disorder is secondary to marital disharmony or *vice versa*: (1) When the sexual dysfunction produces discord in the marital relationship, sex therapy usually is the treatment of choice. (2) When couples have basically positive feelings toward each other but have some marital problems that impair sexual functioning, sex therapy usually is indicated because of their desire to improve their sexual relationship. (3) When couples have severe marital problems and basic hostility, sex therapy is not indicated, and treatment will focus on the marital relationship.

This theoretical orientation to sexual difficulties as related to the dynamics of the marital relationship, and not necessarily expressions of one partner's intrapsychic conflict, is a most significant advance in understanding and treating such problems. This approach to sexual dysfunction, along with the specific behavioral techniques that have been developed, is one of the reasons sex therapy enjoys such a high rate of success.

Background

Jane, a 29-year-old school counselor, and her husband, a 39-year-old physical therapist, were referred for sex therapy by her gynecologist because, although they had been married for 7 years, the marriage was not consummated. It was unclear at the time of the referral if the chief complaint was vaginismus, erectile dysfunction, or both. Jane and Peter reported that they were seeking help at the present time because of their desire to have a child. Both Jane and Peter were Catholic, and Peter had been a priest up to the time of their marriage.

Diagnosis and Treatment Plan

Evaluation Procedure

The couple was seen for a four-session evaluation prior to formulation of a diagnosis and treatment plan. Initially, a conjoint interview was conducted during which the couple was questioned about the history and current status of the marital relationship. Both partners were asked how they saw the presenting problem, how it started, and why they were seeking treatment at this time. They were also queried about the life cycle of the marriage, how they met, what attracted each partner to the other, the process of the courtship, difficulties in the early years, and what had since transpired. The goal of the first session was to acquire an impression of the quality of the marital relationship through the content and process of the couple's interactions.

The second and third sessions consisted of individual interviews with each partner. An extensive individual history was obtained with a focus on premarital issues, family of origin, childhood experiences, and current relationships. The goal of these sessions was twofold: to obtain more information about individual functioning and to discover differences in each partner's behavior and "story" when presented alone.

The couple was brought together again for the fourth session to explore their expectations and perceptions of the marriage. Questions such as the following were asked: How do you see each other as lovers? What were your expectations of marriage? How have those expectations been met and how have they changed? What is your fantasy of a good marriage? The goal of this session was to ascertain the role of the symptom in the marriage, that is, how it was meeting the needs of each partner.

The four sessions produced the following information regarding the couple:

CURRENT SEXUAL FUNCTIONING

Jane and Peter agreed that they had an active and satisfying sex life despite their inability to have intercourse. Peter reported that he was able to have erections during foreplay with Jane but would lose the erection at the time of penetration. He was able to maintain an erection otherwise, including during masturbation. Jane was sexually responsive and orgasmic during manual and oral stimulation, but she experienced difficulty with penetration. They both agreed that they had a loving relationship and wanted the marriage to ultimately be successful. Their words were confirmed by their actions, as they related to each other warmly and affectionately during the therapy sessions.

JANE'S HISTORY

Jane was the older of two sisters in a traditional Irish Catholic family. Her father was an engineer who traveled a good deal. Jane felt closer to her mother, a full-time housewife who devoted herself to taking care of her children and her home. She recalled her parents' marriage as solid and without any major problems, and she remembered her growing up years as happy. She recalled always being the "good" child who tried to be very helpful to her mother, while her sister, 3 years younger, was more rebellious. She described herself as shy but well-liked by boys and girls. She dated in high school and college but was not sexually active before she met her husband. She was educated in parochial schools and went to a Catholic college for both undergraduate and graduate studies. She left home for college and never returned home to live. Because of geographical distance, she sees her parents only two or three times a year, although she talks with them regularly on the phone.

PETER'S HISTORY

Peter was the second child in an Irish Catholic family of three boys and two girls. He was born and reared in the South and was educated in Catholic schools. Mother was extremely religious, attended mass daily, and fully expected that one of her children would become a priest. Peter remembered his mother being very involved with the church and that there were always priests as dinner guests in their home. Peter perceived his mother as very submissive, childish, dependent, and asexual. He was her favorite child. His father was a lawyer whom Peter described as autocratic and preoccupied with his law practice much of the time. Although he had no proof, Peter suspected his father of having affairs with other women. Peter felt that he was put down constantly by his father and that "nothing was good enough" for him. Father's favorite was the oldest brother, who Peter saw as a "crooked lawyer," very selfish and not interested in helping others, just like Father. In contrast, he saw himself as very helpful and interested in others, especially his younger brother and sisters. He was always quite popular with girls, dated a lot, and planned to get married and raise a family. In accordance with his father's plans for him to become a doctor, Peter started school as a pre-med student. He did not think about becoming a priest until college. He entered the priesthood at 21 years of age, a decision motivated not so much by religious conviction as by a desire to please Mother and to antagonize Father, who fiercely opposed it. Father died when Peter was in his late 20s, his mother having died 5 years earlier. Peter never stopped dating, even as a priest. He always had "somebody" and was sexually active, although he denied ever having intercourse. He had masturbated since age 13 or 14 and reported having heterosexual fantasies during masturbation.

COUPLE HISTORY

Jane and Peter met when she was 20 years old and he was 30 years old, and they were both in school. Peter was still a priest during their 2-year courtship, not leaving the priesthood until just before they married. They engaged in a lot of premarital sexual activity, "everything but intercourse." Jane remembers that they both made the decision to refrain from having intercourse before marriage; she does not remember any problems with Peter's erections at that time. Jane felt that Peter was initially more attracted to her than she was to him, but after some time in the marriage she became more attached and dependent on him.

Treatment Plan

After this four-session evaluation procedure, a diagnosis and treatment plan was formulated. There were no apparent problems in the marital relationship, as both partners agreed that it was a close and loving union, and they related warmly during the sessions. Jane's gynecologist had reported difficulty in accomplishing a vaginal examination because of her tenseness, but had finally succeeded and reported no physiological cause for her condition. Initially it appeared that this was a rather straightforward sex therapy case.

The primary diagnosis was vaginismus, a condition often found in Catholic women with a strong religious background similar to Jane's. Peter was seen as having erectile dysfunction related to performance anxiety as a consequence of his inability to penetrate, along with some guilt regarding his abandoned priesthood. The treatment plan consisted of a combination of sex therapy behavioral prescriptions specifically tailored for their dysfunctions, and psychotherapy to focus on their religious backgrounds and resultant guilt. Since I had treated many couples with unconsummated marriages and had never failed to help them resolve the dysfunction, I anticipated a successful outcome.

Process of Therapy

Therapy began with sensate-focus exercises for the couple to reduce tension and relieve performance anxiety for both partners. (See Kaplan, 1974, for a detailed discussion of this and other sex therapy techniques.) This was followed by specific exercises for Jane and for the couple. Jane received the standard treatment for vaginismus, a condition where the vaginal entry literally snaps shut so tightly that intercourse is impossible. Vaginismus is a conditioned response, resulting from the association of pain or fear with penetration. Treatment is aimed at altering the conditioned response and consists of progressive deconditioning of the involuntary spasm of the muscles surrounding the vaginal entry. Jane was initially instructed to touch herself and fantasize. When she was comfortable with this, she was told to insert one finger into her vagina, proceeding to two fingers as she felt comfortable. When she was thoroughly relaxed with these individual exercises, she was to have Peter insert first one finger and then two fingers into her vagina, with Jane controlling the progression as she felt comfortable with the procedure. While Jane was focusing on individual exercises, the couple was also given several prescriptions designed to divert Peter's attention from his erection. These included reading erotic literature, fantasizing, and viewing stag movies in the bedroom. During this initial phase, all went well and both partners accepted instruction, communicated freely, and cooperated fully. Jane was relatively relaxed at each step and was becoming more confident and comfortable with her own sexuality. However, as she became more relaxed and therefore more demanding of Peter, he began to experience more difficulty and became increasingly less potent. When treatment progressed to the stage where Peter was to insert his penis in Jane's vagina, he began to lose his erection prior to attempting penetration. At this point Peter began trying to avoid sex altogether. I was puzzled as to what was going on. Jane and Peter were both verbal and had seemed to be cooperating in the treatment.

One element in the lack of success seemed to stem from the marital relationship. It became apparent there had been a significant shift in the balance of power in Jane and Peter's marriage. In the beginning their relationship could be characterized as one of Father and Daughter, with the older and more worldly wise Peter guiding and taking care of the shy, naive Jane. Peter was an extremely attractive man with a confident and slightly seductive manner. In describing his initial attraction to Jane, Peter had said she was "different from the other girls," since she was unselfish, smart, serious, religious, and somehow chaste. There had been a striking similarity in his description of Jane and of his mother, who was seen as sweet, asexual, and almost saintly. When Jane first came to treatment she was not nearly as "mousey" as Peter's description, but was instead a good-looking, open, and rather up-to-date young woman. As the treatment progressed she became even more gorgeous and free, appearing for a session one hot summer day wearing shorts and a halter, which showed off her body to good advantage. Peter's perception of Jane was clearly not matched by the current reality. Perhaps he needed to deny her sexiness because of what it would say about him to admit to having a sexy wife.

An example of Peter's previous parental control over Jane was the manner in which he had influenced her job decision 3 years earlier. Jane had been offered two counseling positions, one in a highly sought after suburban private school where the salary was $7000 higher, the second at a lower-paying and much less prestigious private school in the city. Although Jane strongly preferred the better job, Peter had convinced her to take the lesser one because it was closer to home. Since that time Jane had clearly become more assertive and less willing to be controlled by Peter.

Although throughout the therapy family of origin issues and guilt arising from their strong religious upbringing had been dealt with, at this point I shifted the focus of therapy to Peter's loyalty conflicts. In exploring Peter's relationship with his family of origin, several important issues emerged. He was currently in touch with only one sister, a psychiatric social worker who still lived in the South along with the rest of the family. Peter was using her as a way to maintain contact with the family without actually keeping in touch himself. He still felt both guilty and bitter about his father and the fact that they were never able to work out their relationship, which had always been stormy. Peter felt as though he was not approved of, and nothing he did was good enough for his father. In turn, he felt that his father was a very selfish man, who was only interested in making money no matter how unscrupulously. When his father died of a sudden heart attack when Peter was in his late 20s, the two of them were not speaking. His father left a great deal of money, which was divided equally among the 5 children. Since Peter was in the priesthood at that time and felt he did not really need the money, he loaned his share to his younger brother to go to college and medical school. This was very much in keeping with Peter's image of himself as a caring person, always more concerned with the welfare of others, especially his younger brother and sisters. The brother became a successful doctor, making lots of money and fulfilling Father's original expectations of Peter. However, the brother never returned the money Peter had loaned him, and Peter felt he was ungrateful. Peter was convinced the younger brother had been "brain-washed" into not liking him by their older brother. In fact, Peter had transferred many of his negative feelings toward his father onto this brother, thus recreating that relationship. Peter had not spoken to this older brother for 3 years, and described him as "just like my father," a "crooked lawyer," selfish and untrustworthy. It was clear that Peter had a great deal of unfinished business with his family, which was interfering with his current life.

To resolve some of these conflicts, Peter was sent home to the South for a family reunion. When this was first suggested he thought it a crazy idea, but as more connections were made between his familial relationships and his current problems he became intrigued and agreed to go. In preparation he wrote to both brothers, reestablishing contact. Jane accompanied him on a week's visit home, where they stayed with the closer sister and saw all of the siblings. For the first time they all talked about their parents and how each of them saw their father and mother. Much to his surprise, Peter discovered that his older brother had always been jealous of Peter's close relationship with their mother and had never felt accepted by her. The older brother did not see himself as Father's favorite, but had only turned to Father because he could not be close to Mother. All of the brothers and sisters saw Peter as a caring, warm, giving person who was the most sensitive among them. The younger brother was greatly surprised when Peter brought up the issue of the money. After their parents died he saw Peter as the "mother" who took care of him, and in that context it had never occurred to him that Peter would want to be repaid. Also, as he told Peter, "You never asked!" When Peter had given the money to his brother, he was a priest with little interest in money, and all of the siblings still thought of Peter in that way. The brother agreed to repay the money. Peter felt that this experience had been most helpful, had cleared up many of his distortions, and had enabled him to reclaim the family he had lost.

When they returned from the visit, Peter felt more content and began to talk about the abbey, where he had lived for many years during his priesthood. As he talked about his life in the abbey, it became apparent that Peter had recreated his family of origin through his relationships there. In his family he had been caught between his saintly mother who wanted him to be a priest and his worldly father who wanted him to be a doctor. He eventually had resolved this by becoming a priest but using his inheritance to make his brother the doctor. In the abbey he was again caught in the middle between Mother Church, whom he loved, and the Father Superior, a strong, dominant man against whom Peter rebelled. Peter was very much a man of the

'60s, participating in antiwar and other liberal activities as a priest, while the Father Superior and others in the abbey were all quite conservative and disapproved of his political activism. He had also rebelled by being sexually active while a priest, but he never took the final step by having coitus. Within the church a priest is not considered to have broken his vow of celibacy unless there is genital intercourse. Thus, Peter fought against the Father Superior and disobeyed, but could never "go all the way" or fully relinquish the relationship. Even though Peter had left the abbey 7 years earlier, it was not acknowledged by the community that he had left at all. Each Christmas the Father Superior sent him a card addressed to "Father P," totally ignoring Peter's marriage and secular identity.

Further exploration revealed that Peter had emotionally never left the priesthood. All of his friends were part of an informal network of ex-priests, who clung together for mutual support and identity. The unconsummated marriage began to have meaning. Peter had never broken his vow of celibacy, and was therefore at some level still a "good priest." Just as he had been unable to let go of his bitterness toward his father, transferring it onto his older brother, he could not be released from his priesthood, by taking the final step in rebelling against the Father Superior and breaking his vows. Peter was encouraged to visit the abbey to resolve these conflicts, but he adamantly refused to make the visit or to explore the issue further. Dealing with his biological family had been easier for Peter than dealing with his spiritual family.

Concurrently, as Jane grew stronger and more free personally she became less willing to tolerate the *status quo*. She began to talk about whether she could go on with their limited sexual relationship, and started to consider separation. Neither this increased pressure from Jane nor any of my therapeutic tactics could budge Peter; he still refused to work on his relationships at the abbey. Indeed, Peter had become steadily more resistant since returning from his visit home and had now stopped working in therapy altogether, only coming because Jane wanted it. Peter was given the option of working either with me or with another therapist in individual psychoanalytically oriented therapy to resolve the conflicts surrounding his dependency needs and priesthood. Because Jane and Peter were about to leave for a month's vacation, we agreed that they would decide what they wanted in the interim and call me with a decision when they returned. Peter agreed to talk to his ex-priest friends to see if they had encountered similar problems and to think about individual therapy.

They never called me; after about 3 months I called Peter. He said he felt the therapy had been useful in many areas, but that there was no change in the sexual problems. In the meantime he had initiated a leaderless support group of ex-priests, and they were discussing some of their common difficulties in adjusting to the secular life, an experience he felt was very helpful. He said he and Jane agreed that it would not be productive to return to sex therapy at this time. Jane called 2 weeks later and asked for a referral for individual therapy for herself.

Analysis of Failure

The failure in this case is directly related to an error in the original assessment of the couple. Because they presented themselves as a close, loving couple and they both seemed relatively healthy psychologically, the diagnosis was of an uncomplicated sexual dysfunction, vaginismus, with erectile dysfunction in Peter due to his inability to penetrate. Based on this assessment, sex therapy began immediately, within the context of marital therapy. In retrospect, this was a serious error. It is still unclear whether vaginismus was ever truly present or whether Jane was willing to accept the role of "symptom bearer" because of the dynamics of the relationship. It is important to consider their relationship within their sociocultural framework. When they first met, Peter was a priest and 10 years older than Jane. Jane had been reared in a religious Irish Catholic home and educated in Catholic schools, and had obviously internalized those values. Within that context a priest is considered to be wiser, stronger, and in every way superior. Clearly, if someone were to be sexually inadequate, it would have to be Jane and not Peter. This complementarity in their marriage is illustrated by the father–daughter relationship they had experienced in the early years.

Peter was originally seen as having the profile of a man with secondary impotence, implying that he was capable of having normal sexual relations. His intact virginity when he entered the priesthood was not considered too unusual since many young men of his age have not yet experienced intercourse. In retrospect, it is apparent that Peter should have been diagnosed as having primary impotence, since the fact that he had never successfully completed intercourse with any women was not a function of his age and priesthood but was related to intrapsychic conflicts. In understanding this one must look to both family and sociocultural factors. Peter's mother was an extremely religious woman and always expected that one of her sons would become a priest. Since Peter was her favorite, he must have known from childhood that he was destined to fulfill her wishes. It is not at all unusual in religious Irish Catholic families for one child to be selected at a very early age to be the family's contribution to the Church. Since Peter's parents were in disagreement over this expectation, with Father wanting Peter to become a doctor, conditions were ideal for Peter to internalize their conflict. Thus he was forever half priest and half not, rebelling against his natural father and his spiritual father, but never "going all the way." This conflict must certainly have been an important factor in Peter's selection of Jane as a wife, since at the time he saw her as pure, serious, and saintly like his mother—the perfect mate to help him rebel but not completely. Through the sex therapy Jane became more sexually comfortable and more demanding of Peter, which had the effect of increasing the pressure on Peter beyond what he was capable of handling. Because of his intrapsychic conflicts surrounding split loyalties between Mother and Father and between priesthood and marriage, he was unable to accomplish penetration. There was no way Peter could consummate the marriage before he had begun to resolve these conflicts.

All good family therapists ask the question, "Why now?"; what has changed in the family to make the dysfunction intolerable now when it was previously accepted? More attention to this question might have pointed the way to success. The stated reason for seeking help at this time was their mutual desire to have a child. It is important to note that the impetus for entering therapy had come from Jane, who had gone to her gynecologist and secured the referral. She was approaching 30 years of age and feeling the pressure of her biological clock measuring the years of her fertility. When Jane and Peter met, she had been a sheltered, sexually inexperienced, 20-year-old "good" Catholic girl, and the lack of intercourse had not been too distressing. However, as she approached 30, one got the sense that she was ready to "grow up" sexually, and was therefore starting to put demands on Peter. She had been willing to accept the problem as "hers" initially, but as she became increasingly competent and comfortable sexually she expected Peter to also change. In contrast, Peter was actually content with their relationship as it was and could probably have gone on like that forever. It allowed him to have both worlds—to be married and sexually active while maintaining his vows as a priest. Thus the function of the symptom both in the relationship and for Peter was not adequately understood.

The view of sexual difficulties as related to the dynamics of the marital relationship and not necessarily expressions of one partner's intrapsychic conflict is indeed a significant advance in the behavioral sciences. However, this case illustrates the importance of also investigating historical causes in addition to the "here and now" interactions of the couple. Certainly Peter had serious unresolved conflicts that prevented him from successfully having intercourse and were quite apart from his relationship with Jane.

One of the attractions of sex therapy for the beginning clinician is that there are definite behavioral prescriptions that are proven to be quite effective in the treatment of specific dysfunctions. The techniques created by Masters and Johnson (1966, 1970) and others, such as Kaplan (1974), are quite useful tools in helping people to resolve their difficulties and improve their sexual functioning. However, this case illustrates the pitfalls of using these techniques without first doing a thorough evaluation of the couple and developing a complete understanding of all the dynamics involved. A couple presenting with a sexual dysfunction cannot automatically be treated with sex therapy. As seen here, even a highly experienced and skilled clinician with a strong systems orientation can misassess a couple and fail.

Hypothetical Reconstruction toward Success

The failure in this case stemmed primarily from a misassessment that resulted in focusing treatment on the sexual problem when this was not the treatment of choice. If Jane and Peter walked into my office today they would receive different treatment. We would start therapy with the same four-session evaluation to obtain the same information. However, more attention would be paid to their motivation for therapy and the degree of distress each partner was feeling. More consideration would be given to the fact that it was Jane who was initiating therapy and to the ramifications that change would have for their relationship. Every effort would be made to clarify the diagnosis, since it turned out that Peter had primary impotence rather than erectile dysfunction related to performance anxiety as a consequence of his inability to penetrate, and it is still unclear whether vaginismus was present at all. The treatment of choice for primary impotence is not sex therapy but either individual or marital therapy with a focus on the intrapsychic conflict leading to the impotence. In this case treatment would start with marital therapy focusing on the dynamics of Jane and Peter's relationship and the ways in which it was changing. It is anticipated that this exploration would have clarified the function of the unconsummated marriage and exposed Peter's split loyalties and ambivalence. Without the pressure created by Jane's increasing demands coming from the sex therapy, Peter might have been more willing to explore the unresolved conflicts. Assuming this was the case, at this point treatment would have included more individual therapy with Peter to resolve these conflicts. Only after this work was completed would sex therapy have been attempted.

This was an unusually difficult case to diagnose and treat correctly. The primary impotence was well-masked, and the original diagnoses of vaginismus and erectile dysfunction related to performance anxiety due to inability to penetrate fit the symptoms as described by the couple. Although one always hopes to learn from one's errors, given identical circumstances one wonders if the therapist might make the same mistake again.

REFERENCES

Ficher, I. V. Treatment of psychosexual disorders in the context of marital threapy. In A. S. Gurman (Ed.), *Questions and answers in the practice of family therapy* (Vol. II). New York: Brunner/Mazel, 1982.

Ficher, I. V., & Eisenstein, T. Obscure causes of sexual dysfunction. *Pennsylvania Medicine*, December 1981.

Ficher, I. V., & Eisenstein, T. Treatment and management of psychosexual disorders: Current approaches. In M. Ficher, R. Fishkin, & J. Jacobs (Eds.), *Sexual arousal: New concepts in basic science, diagnosis and treatment*. Springfield, Ill.: C. C. Thomas, 1984.

Kaplan, H. S. *The new sex therapy*. New York: Brunner/Mazel, 1974.

Masters, W. H., & Johnson, V. E. *Human sexual response*. Boston: Little, Brown, 1966.

Masters, W. H., & Johnson, V. E. *Human sexual inadequacy*. Boston: Little, Brown, 1970.

Sager, C. J. Sexual dysfunctions and marital discord. In H. S. Kaplan (Ed.), *The new sex therapy*. New York: Brunner/Mazel, 1974.

9

A Failure to Keep the Father in Family Therapy

LUCIANO L'ABATE AND MARGARET S. BAGGETT

Introduction

This chapter describes a failure to keep a father in the process of family therapy. Although a variety of direct and indirect techniques were used, none of them succeeded. We are mindful that (1) therapeutic defeats keep us humble; (2) therapeutic defeats can be used as challenges to sharpen our creativity, or they can be ignored or accepted uncritically or with resignation; and (3) therapeutic defeats can be used to improve our practices. This one, we hope, did.

Theoretical Frame of Reference

Our theoretical framework is systematically eclectic and mainly pragmatic. Most of the theoretical background can be summarized through models (L'Abate, in press) derived from a theory of personality development in the family (L'Abate, 1976; elaborated in greater detail in L'Abate, 1983a). These models allow theory to be linked to practice and evaluation to intervention. They are visual or verbal condensations of more complex patterns. In our theorizing, we have found the following four models useful: (1) the E-R-A-Aw-C model of interpersonal competence, (2) the A-R-C model of intimate relationships, (3) a concentric model of priorities, and (4) a model of resources that are exchanged in living.

The E-R-A-Aw-C Model of Interpersonal Competence

The E-R-A-Aw-C model suggests that at least five different components need to function interpersonally (see Figure 9-1). Essentially, information processing flows from Emotionality (E) as input, to cognitive and Rational (R) issues as throughput, to issues of roles and Activities (A) as output. In addition to

Luciano L'Abate. Department of Psychology, Georgia State University, Atlanta, Georgia.

Margaret S. Baggett. Private practice, Atlanta, Georgia.

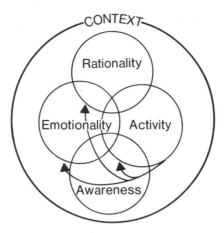

FIG. 9-1. E-R-A-Aw-C model.

Emotionality, Rationality, and Activity, this model includes Awareness (Aw), with some feedback functions, and Context (C) (L'Abate, in press; L'Abate, Frey, & Wagner, 1982). This model fulfills a great many functions, offering (1) a classification of therapeutic schools and methods, (2) a diagnostic scheme, (3) a framework for negotiation, and (4) a definition of love in marriage and the family.

THERAPEUTIC SCHOOLS AND METHODS

"Emotionality" includes the humanistic approaches (existential, phenomenological, and experimental). "Rationality" includes most psychodynamic and cognitive approaches: object-relations, Bowenian, Berne's transactional analysis, Ellis's rational–emotive, and Glasser's reality therapies. "Activity" includes most of the behavioral approaches (social learning, exchange, and equity theories), which are usually based on dyadic and noncontextual viewpoints. "Awareness" includes Eastern philosophies and the social perspectivism of Alan Watts, Fritz Perls, and R. E. Selman. "Context" includes systemic, strategic, and structural approaches, including the paradoxical (Weeks & L'Abate, 1982).

DIAGNOSTIC SCHEME

Diagnostically, the model allows evaluation of where and how the family and the individual members interact or fail to interact. Does the family emphasize R at the expense of E, or A at the expense of R? If a family is explosively emotional, does E move into A or into R? Given the general family characteristic, how do individual family members conform or fail to conform to it?

With an A-E-R configuration, for instance, what pattern will the father follow? What pattern will the mother follow? How will the children imitate their parents?

FRAMEWORK FOR NEGOTIATION

The model also serves as a paradigm for negotiation, following the general dictum that feelings (E) about an issue need to be expressed nonjudgmentally. Various possibilities, including pros and cons, then need to be considered rationally (R), and a plan of action (A) needs to be chosen and implemented. The action is followed by the family's awareness (Aw) of the efficacy of the plan, which they then change and correct as necessary.

DEFINITION OF LOVE IN MARRIAGE AND FAMILY

The model allows us to define love in marriage as seeing the good in one's mate and children (R) and caring, which means physical presence, material goods, and practical activities (A) as well as the sharing of hurts (E), which involves intimacy. Awareness allows correction and change within the context of the marriage and the family.

The A-R-C Model of Styles in Intimate Relationships

The A-R-C model (L'Abate, 1983b) comprises three different styles: (1) apathetic-abusive-atrophied, (2) reactive-repetitive, and (3) conductive-creative-committed to change. Later we will illustrate how this model as well as the other three apply to the family described here.

The Concentric Model of Priorities

The concentric model acknowledges that priorities may shift at different times in the family life cycle. As a whole, however, healthy family functioning is based on clear priorities: self first, followed by marriage, children, in-laws, work, friends, and leisure activities (L'Abate, in press). Self-needs balance and reconcile all of the priorities. For instance, when work becomes identified as part of the self to make up for deficits in identification and self-differentiation, the self ranks lower in the scheme. If children come before the marriage, another dysfunctional shift occurs.

The Model of Resource Exchange

The resource-exchange model encompasses three major classes of resources in life—Being, Doing, and Having (L'Abate, 1983a). We need all three resources: Being, for status and self-regard; Doing, to obtain or give information and services; and Having, which consists of money and possessions.

Most of our clients have deficits in Being, even though they may have jobs (Doing) and possessions (Having).

Therapeutically, these models suggest that a therapist should be interpersonally competent, using all of the components in appropriate patterns and avoiding focus on one component (e.g., focusing on Rationality at the expense of Emotionality or Activity). When the therapist goes into action (A), he or she should have an awareness (Aw) of contextual corrections and changes. Stylistically, the therapist needs to behave conductively with families (who are typically stuck at the apathetic-abusive and reactive-repetitive levels). Priorities should be balanced so that practicing family therapy does not become paramount, offsetting other priorities (i.e., self, marriage, or children). Being a partner and a parent is much more difficult than being a therapist. In resources, the therapist needs to be able to Be—to value self and others, see the good in them, be available to them physically by sharing hurts and confronting intimacy; that is, to Be is to love so that Being balances equally with Doing and Having.

The goals of therapy, then, are to help families develop ways of negotiating constructively and learn how to behave conductively, to balance priorities functionally (for them), and to appreciate Being, loving others as one loves oneself.

Professional Considerations

The following case is on the borderline between two disciplines: clinical child psychology, with its own sets of assumptions and rituals, and family therapy, with its own peculiar sets of assumptions and rituals. Might this failure represent the clash of two different paradigms? Clinical child psychology is usually individually oriented, accepting the child as the identified patient. The child's role as patient is reinforced when the therapist agrees to evaluate and treat the child as an individual. Family therapy rejects the individual as patient, making the family the primary focus for evaluation and treatment.

L'Abate is a former clinical child psychologist who entered the family field in the middle of his career (L'Abate, 1983a). Baggett, who recently obtained her PhD, has a background in both special education and child psychopathology. Both therapists are licensed psychologists. L'Abate is a former teacher and supervisor of Baggett, who is leaning toward a systems approach to child dysfunctionality. The S family was the first that this cotherapy team treated after the transformation from a vertical, hierarchical (supervisor–supervisee) relationship to a horizontal (cotherapists), equally empowered team arrangement. There is no doubt that this shift, from vertical to horizontal, may have had a great deal to do with how the case was managed. When this case began the therapists' interaction was still complementary (i.e., L'Abate assumed a much more assertive, confrontive, directive role; Baggett assumed a more supportive, reflective, nurturant role). L'Abate was stylistically and philosophically oriented toward the more pragmatic issues of therapy (i.e., need to be effective and to accomplish goals). Baggett was oriented toward the softer, more intuitive aspects of therapy.

Background

The S family (Mr. and Mrs. S and their son, R) had been evaluated and treated by another psychologist when R was 5 years old. At that time, R had been experiencing difficulties in a prekindergarten setting, where he was unable to interact appropriately with his classmates or to follow teacher instructions. Because of R's hyperactivity, Ritalin was prescribed; however, his behavior improved only minimally. After a few therapy sessions, Mr. S refused to continue in treatment. Even though Mrs. S attended one or two more sessions, she eventually discontinued treatment as well because she felt defeated by her husband's lack of cooperation and support.

Diagnosis and Treatment Plan

Evaluation

When R was in the 2nd grade, his behavior became of such concern to the school personnel that the former therapist referred him and his family to us. During our first telephone conversation, Mrs. S freely ventilated feelings about her husband's shortcomings and his unwillingness to become involved in therapy. We were very clear from the outset, however, that we would not see either the mother or the son unless the father was involved. Because of the seriousness of their son's difficulties at school, Mr. and Mrs. S agreed to work with us.

R was engaging in such antics as wearing his pajama shirt to school under his clothes, exposing himself in the bathroom, telling bizarre tales, attending to a doll whose clothes he took home and washed, and wrapping himself in coats and remaining under a table for long periods of time while threatening destruction to the doll. When Baggett observed R at school, he seemed to daydream frequently. His written assignments reflected very poor handwriting, and he was unable to complete most tasks. When he attempted to join two other children at play, they immediately rejected him and protested loudly to the teacher that R was interrupting them. R withdrew from the children, slid to the floor, and assumed the fetal position. On the playground R refused to join his classmates for organized group play. Instead, he played alone or with younger children. In general, R presented the picture of a very isolated, unhappy child who was drifting into a world of fantasy.

Baggett conducted a psychological evaluation on R when he was 8 years old. Baggett's behavioral description of R during this assessment period follows:

R is an engaging child, with blond hair, brown eyes, freckles, and a constant smile. He is small for his age. R wears glasses, which slide down his nose, making him wrinkle it in an attempt to reposition the glasses. As he works, he holds his head close to his paper. During this evaluation, R was highly distractible, even in a one-to-one situation. He stood during most of the testing and was in constant motion, chattering about extraneous topics. His fine-motor control was notably poor, and as he worked, he made autocritical remarks, such as "I don't have very good handwriting" and "I'm not very good." His eye contact was fleeting. Reflecting a high level of fantasy thinking, R stated that he had imaginary playmates, two ghosts who visited him at home and at school. These ghosts performed various acts of mischief, such as pushing his pencil to the floor. One of the ghosts was red, covered in blood from having killed his parents.

Intellectually, R was functioning in the superior range, as indicated by the Wechsler Intelligence Scale for Children—Revised Form (WISC-R). Reading achievement was above grade level, but fine-motor skills, auditory reception, math, and phonics were weak. Emotionally, R appeared to be in tenuous contact with reality. His self-concept was exceptionally low. Socially, he was immature and isolated.

At the time of Baggett's evaluation of R, he and his parents had been attending three initial diagnostic sessions with Baggett and L'Abate. From these interviews, the following picture of the marital interaction unfolded. Mr. and Mrs. S came from rather strict fundamentalist backgrounds. They had been married some 20 years; both were well into their mid-30s when R was born. Both had dated very little in late adolescence and had had meager, if any, sexual experiences. They met before Mr. S's induction into military service and married as soon as he was discharged. Mrs. S worked while her husband attended college; however, Mr. S never completed his degree, much to Mrs. S's continued disapproval. In spite of their relatively limited education (Mrs. S completed high school and attended business college for 1 year), both were employed as middle-level managers in large companies. Her salary, however, surpassed his.

The marital interactions of Mr. and Mrs. S can be described, at best, as hostile-distant, with sporadic truces, but as a whole, the interaction was competitively stereotyped in the sense that both had crystallized their roles along fairly traditional lines. Mrs. S was to care for the house, and Mr. S was to bring home the bacon. His responsibilities at home were limited to the absolutely necessary (i.e., mowing the lawn after she nagged him about it or grudgingly grocery shopping when he needed to eat). No matter what, this couple clearly was and still is polarized in a variety of dimensions:

Naughty–Nice. Mr. S attempted to play the nice guy; Mrs. S accepted her role as the naughty one in the marriage and with their child (setting limits and punishing him when necessary).

Perfectionistic–Sloppy. Mrs. S was an extremely efficient, competent manager at home as well as at work. Although we do not know, Mr. S must have been somewhat a perfectionist at work because his job required a great deal of precision. At home, however, he seemed to delight in relinquishing all major and minor responsibilities to Mrs. S, who was quick to take them. For instance, Mr. S would stack daily newspapers in piles beside his recliner until they were so high that they toppled over. Finally, when Mrs. S grew tired of the papers, she would remove them with great resentment.

At home, Mr. S typically watched television while Mrs. S performed her daily housewife chores (cooking, laundry, etc.). When Mr. S did perform a chore, he was either nagged into doing it or he was criticized when he finished for not having done it to his wife's standards or by her criteria.

Emotional–Rational. Mrs. S tended to express her feelings freely and unreflectively, even though she used judgmental blaming styles, considering Mr. S the culprit who was responsible for the way she felt ("miserable"). Mr. S, having read many self-help books, tended to be logical and rational and attempted to appear controlled, forcing Mrs. S to appear uncontrolled or uncontrollable (i.e., "irrational").

Responsible–Irresponsible. As can be deduced from the preceding descriptions, Mrs. S was the responsible one. She paid the bills, performed the chores, answered phone calls, took their child to the doctor and to school, and so on. Mr. S was free of responsibilities and devoted his time to watching television and playing with his personal computer.

Social–Antisocial. Mrs. S craved and sought social contact and wished to have friends and keep in touch with relatives. Mr. S was (and had been most of his life) a loner who avoided all prolonged contacts, had no friends, and made no effort to seek social relationships. He had to be dragged to any social engagement to which they had been invited.

Their sexual interaction was limited and strained. Although they slept in the same bed, Mr. S was extremely nonaffectionate; Mrs. S craved affection and attention. When they had sex (apparently once or twice a year), they did so perfunctorily, without passion or enthusiasm. Apparently, she performed because it was her duty; he performed because he was desperate. Both admitted masturbating solitarily and being as dissatisfied in their sexual lives as they were in everything else.

In brief, this couple had all of the earmarks of the "terrible twosome" frequently described in the literature (Lederer & Jackson, 1969). Miserable with each other but unable to separate or be free of each other, they would probably be just as miserable without each other. Their homeostasis was maintained by continual distance and was occasionally interrupted by an explosive confrontation, mostly about their child. It was clear that the child kept them together and that both did care and were involved (in their own peculiar ways) with him.

The following is a metaphoric example of R's role in the family. One Sunday, Mrs. S surprised Mr. S with apples that she brought home (R and Mrs. S attended church, but Mr. S did not). Mr. S complained bitterly because the apples were not the kind he preferred and accused Mrs. S of having deliberately chosen the wrong variety. Mrs. S was highly indignant because she had thought that she was bringing home a treat for her husband. In the middle of the parents' battle, R spoke up and said to his mother, "I'll eat the apples." He took a bite, then looked at his father and said, "Yuk, ugh! They do taste terrible."

How do these marital polarizations manifest themselves parentally? The bets answer is *inconsistently and contradictorily* (Smith, Smith, & L'Abate, 1985). Mrs. S was certainly more involved with their child than was Mr. S. In her involvement, however, she enacted many of the frustrations that had resulted from the marital interaction (L'Abate, 1975). She lost her temper rather quickly, shouting and punishing R without distinguishing the severity of his "misbehavior." Mr. S tended to counterbalance her "bitchiness" by playing the distant-but-nice father, who uses reasonableness as a way of appearing nice. He frequently criticized Mrs. S's parenting, blaming all of R's problems on her. Yet, his own role was a distant one. Both of them used blackmail and bribery in their interactions with their son—buying trinkets and toys on the slightest pretext but expecting a conditional "good behavior" as a result of the bribe.

The S family illustrates well how the theoretical models can be applied interpersonally. Mrs. S used *E* and *A* at the expense of *R*, reacting to her husband and her child in a repetitive style. Mr. S seemed stuck between apathy and reactivity, a model followed by the son. The parents' priorities, as expressed by them, were child, work, marriage, in-laws, self, leisure, and friends. The validity of this ranking is demonstrated by the isomorphic relationship between their behavior and the expressed priorities. In this regard, the parents were very consistent.

Mr. and Mrs. S represent the overemphasis on Having and Doing at the expense of Being. Their love consisted of working hard (Doing) and accumulating possessions—house, car, computer, and toys (Having). They were unable to Be, alone or with each other. In answer to the question "What do you do when you have nothing to do?" Mrs. S was clear that she either worked or went to sleep. She felt worthwhile only when she kept busy. Mr. S watched television, a pastime that his wife detested. Neither could receive or express unconditional love (Being) to each other or to their child. Their love for each other was limited by habit ("We have been married 20 years"), convenience ("We are used to the same routine"), and convention ("Divorce is not part of our religious background").

The couple was defective, then, in interpersonal competence, intimate styles, priorities, and resources. The models suggest how they need to change to become more functional personally, dyadically, and parentally: They need to learn to negotiate flexibly, become more conductive as partners and as parents, reestablish priorities of self, marriage, child, and the like, and enjoy Being and loving as much as they enjoy Doing and Having.

Mrs. S had assumed the role of the involved but punitive (critical, judgmental) mother. Mr. S had assumed the role of laissez-faire, permissive father. These parents, like most parents of hyperactive children (Smith et al., 1985), were extremely skilled at presenting a facade of competence and functionality. Their relative occupational successes verified their view of themselves as adequate and articulate. In the sanctity and privacy of their home, however, they were able to shed their facade and were free to show the extent of their dysfunctionality. The only one who was permitted to exhibit such dysfunctionality outside the home was the child. Even in this area, the parents were polarized. Mr. S minimized all problems and saw Mrs. S's concern as exaggeration, "making mountains out of mole hills."

Treatment Plans

Considering the interaction of the parents, we can only marvel that their child was not even more disturbed than he was. Initially, our goals were (1) to involve the whole family in treatment, (2) to learn more about how the family functioned as a system, (3) to prevent further deterioration of the child's behavior, and (4) to understand how the child was the recipient and the activator of the system's dysfunctionality. The initial general goals were met. As we learned more about the family functioning, we developed specific goals, such as minimizing the destructive aspects of the complementarity (i.e., polarization) in the relationship. The child's behavior was of course the primary locus of treatment, but it was difficult to separate the child's behavior from his parents' inconsistent parenting practices and the malignant marital interaction. Their boundaries were unclear and permeable (e.g., Mrs. S's use of "we" when referring to R's behavior).

As a general strategy, which developed as we started working with the family, Baggett served as liaison with the school. Mrs. S used Baggett as a consultant, calling her whenever school emergencies arose. Baggett then communicated with L'Abate, always reminding Mrs. S that we were working together as a team and that no "secret" or even less-than-secret coalition between us would be acceptable.

In the course of treatment, many phone calls and school visits were conducted by Baggett; L'Abate made his presence felt in the therapy sessions. Because of her background in special education, Baggett was able to intervene between the school and R's parents, ensuring that therapeutic goals were extended to the school environment as well as to the home (i.e., that R was not able to generate conflict between the teacher and his parents as he was able to do with his parents).

Process of Therapy

Because this case spanned about 3 years from the first session to the less frequent treatment sessions at the end of the 3rd year, a great deal of information (therapeutic sessions, school visits, phone calls, and school and camp reports) will need to be considered. Information from these sources will be discussed as part of the therapeutic process.

During the first few sessions, it became clear that R wielded the power in the family. This child even admitted that he was "the boss" in the family (Johnson, Weeks, & L'Abate, 1979). Concerns centered on parenting for R, with Mr. S refusing to support his wife's disciplinary measures because he viewed her as overreacting and shouting. Other issues also arose, as discussed earlier under areas of couple polarization. When asked why they had entered therapy, Mr. and Mrs. S were able to agree that they wanted to help R and that to do so, they needed to be able to conduct parental discussions about their son. This they had been unable to do. After the first session, the family was sent home with a paradoxical assignment—to read R a note on Tuesday and Thursday after dinner, thanking him for acting out in an attempt to hold their marriage together. R was then to remind Mr. S to start a fight on Tuesday night and Mrs. S to start a fight on Thursday night. The homework was partly done: Mr. S refused to start a fight. R, however, memorized the letter from hearing it and kissed his parents after they read the letter.

During ensuing sessions, both parents were able to cry as they worked through issues of hurt and pain, such as childhood experiences (Mr. S) and earlier happenings in their marriage (Mrs. S). The parents repeatedly asserted that they failed to comprehend how these sessions were of help to R. R's enuresis was one concern, and several interventions had been attempted to ameliorate this difficulty. Mr. S was able to admit that he, too, had been enuretic and thus identified with his son (information that Mrs. S learned only recently).

During one early session, when R was again asked who was the boss in the family, "bronco busting" was used (Johnson et al., 1979). During this procedure the child is safely restrained by the parent (Mr. S, in this case) until he is able to say seriously, without laughter, that his parents are the bosses.

After this procedure Mr. S was observed in the waiting room telling his son several times to put on his jacket so that they could leave; R continued to ignore his father because there was no consequence. The bronco-busting procedure thus appeared unsuccessful, suggesting the notion that defeat is an important aspect of hyperactive child behavior (Smith *et al.*, 1985).

As therapy progressed, we tried to get the parents to initiate negotiation sessions at home (they were to negotiate a time to have a 15-minute argument). Meanwhile, R's parents and his teachers observed that he was making progress at school, although homework assignments were carried out half-heartedly and only partly completed. We decided to declare our ineffectiveness and incompetence, that we were defeated by this defeating family. Mrs. S reacted with anger, asking how we could give up on helping them raise a little boy. The result was that things went well in the household for one whole week. Mrs. S reported that it was the best week they had had in their marriage in a long time.

At this juncture, however, Mr. S protested that the weekly or bimonthly sessions were too frequent for him and that we were discussing the same topics every session and focusing on the marriage rather than on the child. He confessed, furthermore, that he felt tired and emotionally drained after the sessions (expressions of feelings were difficult for him). We changed the sessions to monthly meetings to comply with what seemed to be Mr. S's need to slow the changes. We felt frustrated, defeated, and neutralized. It was clear that we had failed to join with the father and even though we had broken through his intellectual defenses, we became aware that in winning this battle, we had perhaps lost the war. Because the earlier linear approaches seemed to have failed, we tried a more cryptic, circular approach (i.e., paradoxical letters). Another assignment for negotiation was given. In the interim between sessions, the following letter was sent to Mr. and Mrs. S:

> Dear J and H:
>
> After learning to work with you and appreciating where you are, we have reached the conclusion that your relationship is marked by prolonged and frequent defeats. You each have a strong investment in defeating the other in whatever way you can do it. We feel that the defeats are important because as long as you defeat each other, you will be distant from each other; consequently, there is no danger of becoming intimate with each other.
>
> We believe that you both are frightened by the possibility of becoming intimate with each other, and we are aware that intimacy can be seen as a loss of control, loss of self, loss of status, loss of hubris, and in some instances, loss of life. Therefore, we consider the *status quo* the best position for you to maintain. We suggest a few ways to keep things the same:
>
> 1. Bring up the past.
> 2. Use "you," "always," and "never" in conversations.
> 3. Mind-read each other when possible.

4. Correct each other as often as possible.
5. Maintain division of labor—details versus overview.
6. Maintain the complementarity of emotion versus reason.
7. Include R in all issues.

Respectfully,

This letter apparently failed to produce any therapeutic change in the family. At the next session, Mr. S looked pale and said that he did not feel well. The negotiation assignment was completed, but Mr. S had criticized Mrs. S's procedures to the point that she had cried. R was doing better at school and beginning to make friends. In an effort to understand how present conflicts concerning R might be related to his parents' families of origin, we centered much of the discussion on past issues and family history. L'Abate focused on Mr. S during this session, using, as metaphoric language, terminology that Mr. S employed at work. While R was out of the room, sexual relations were also discussed, and more efforts were made at homework aimed toward building negotiation skills.

During the summer R attended a structured program that offered academic remediation in the mornings and camps during the afternoons to aid in building social skills. He received excellent reports. In midsummer Mr. and Mrs. S attended the last therapy session in which Mr. S participated. During one of their arguments, they had been shaken by R's statement, "I don't like living any more because it's no fun in this house."

Because intimacy seemed to be avoided by both Mr. and Mrs. S, L'Abate had attempted to join Mr. S physically (by sitting next to him) and emotionally. During this session, L'Abate was able to get to Mr. S's hurt, and Mr. S broke down in tears about his isolated childhood, the emotional deprivation and distance from his parents, and his inability to get close to anybody. When he broke down, Mrs. S, although she became tearful, was unable to express physically or verbally her recognition of or concern for his hurt.

We consider this episode critical to Mr. S's not continuing in therapy. Very likely, breaking down in front of everybody, including his wife, seemed to him an admission of weakness. He may have felt "embarrassed" or "ashamed" at expressing his hurt through tears, despite the therapists' reassurances that "only strong men cry" and that "weak men do not admit weakness."

We became aware at this juncture that the drama triangle—Persecutor, Victim, and Rescuer—was being played out by the three members of the family. For instance, both Mr. and Mrs. S saw each other as Persecutors and themselves as Victims. Their child was the Rescuer. Without him they probably could not have maintained the marriage as long as they had. R played out the Victim role in his interactions at home and also at school, where he attracted the punishment of his teachers and the rejection of his classmates.

We decided that we should make the family aware of the drama triangle and at the same time express our feelings of helplessness and inadequacy. We thus wrote another letter to Mr. and Mrs. S suggesting essentially that they should continue as they were, with no changes.

Dear Mr. and Mrs. S:

As follow-up to our previous letter, we are now better able to understand the background of the self-defeating behavior exhibited by R at school and at home.

R's behavior derives from love for you and loyalty to you. He personifies aspects of the drama triangle that you both play so well, which is very likely a continuation of the same triangle played in your families of origin.

We wish to make it clear that the triangle is a pernicious and chronic condition that is virtually unbreakable. In our experience, only one or two of ten families can break out of that triangle, which is usually responsible for producing a great percentage of the psychopathology in this country.

We want to close this letter by expressing our pessimism that this triangle will ever be broken in your family. R, like it or not, know it or not, is destined to play out three roles for the rest of his life. We would like to be proved wrong, but at this stage there is no evidence to indicate that our pessimism is unwarranted.

Respectfully,

After sending this letter, we became concerned and, indeed, anxious that Mr. and Mrs. S might construe the letter as too negative and too pessimistic. After a phone call from Mrs. S informing us that her husband had decided to terminate, we agreed to split our functions, allowing Baggett to play out her more nurturant and supportive role, and L'Abate to take the instrumental role. Baggett wrote the following letters (with L'Abate's full knowledge and approval, of course) as a corrective to the preceding letter.

Dear H:

As a follow-up to our last telephone conversation, I want to share some thoughts with you that may not really be very important to you. I know that what I'm saying and how I'm saying it will appear sarcastic and disrespectful to you, but I want to say it because you are important in what you stand for, and I sincerely and seriously believe what I'm saying, even though I could be completely wrong.

I, personally, woman-to-woman, want to express to you my admiration for everything you're doing to protect J. I especially admire the energy you exert in focusing on and bringing up the past, never forgetting or forgiving past hurts. In this way, you are able to keep J distant, protecting him from becoming close to you or having to change in any way. Consequently, I hope you will continue to be inconsistent, never giving up the memory of your past hurts or mistakes made by J, Dr. L'Abate, or me. You are a woman of high standards and, as such, I tend to identify with you. I see in you much of what I also see in myself.

We are strong women. I hope that you will continue to uphold these high standards, no matter what the cost to you, J, or R.

Because there will be such a long time before our next meeting, I thought I must write to you, with Dr. L'Abate's knowledge, to share these thoughts. I hope your summer will be productive, and I look forward to seeing you next fall.

Lovingly and respectfully,

Dear J:

Although I didn't say much during our last session, I have some after-thoughts that, with Dr. L'Abate's knowledge, I want to share with you. These thoughts may or may not be important to you, but I know that I won't be seeing you for 2 months, and I felt that I must let you know before then what is on my mind.

I want you to know how much I admire the efforts you are extending to protect H from getting too close to you. Your emphasis on the avoidance of any display of affection, such as being touched in public, being kissed good-night, or even acknowledging that loving physical contact is pleasant to you, protects H from having to change in any way. As long as you continue this pattern, your marriage (and your fathering) will be predictable, stable, and solid, as it has been for 20 years. I know that your efforts are not easy, but I encourage you to remain consistent in what you're doing, lest there be a dangerous change in your relationship with H. Of course, I may be completely wrong, but I want you to know that I heard, understand, and appreciate what you are doing.

I look forward to seeing you in the fall, and I hope the remainder of the summer is productive.

Respectfully yours,

The rationale for these letters was at least twofold. We believed that straightforward messages, especially verbal ones, could be deflected or forgotten. Furthermore, it was obvious that we were unable to deal with the power struggle (hubris?) between Mr. and Mrs. S.

The course of treatment from then on was based on our seeing the mother and the child or dealing with the mother alone. Both of us telephoned Mr. S and talked with him, but he steadfastly refused to come to the office.

The letters had been our last-ditch effort to keep the father in therapy. We were of course threatened by this loss. We wondered whether we should work together. We questioned the use of letters. L'Abate felt that he had been overly pushy and confrontive, and Baggett agreed with him. Naturally, we also wondered whether we could have done better by staying with a more linear approach and avoiding any paradoxical move. This clearly was the low point of our therapy together.

While this defeat was going on, however, we had considerable success with two other families we were treating together. Furthermore, this defeat, along with similar situations in families with whom L'Abate was working solo, allowed him to become aware of how important defeat is to the whole context of hyperactivity in children and how this behavior, which defeats therapists and researchers of various persuasions and disciplines, is a beautiful metaphor for the marriage. The hyperactive child defeats most professionals who try to get close. The child, after all, learned the techniques from two masters—the parents (Smith *et al.*, 1985).

Outcome

Although R's behavior at school had improved in that he was completing tasks more consistently and behaving more appropriately (the bizarre behaviors had dropped out), he continued to need a structured classroom, to experience academic difficulties, and to withdraw from appropriate peer interactions. Therapy began in January, and R was assessed by Baggett the following summer, before R entered a summer school that combined intensive learning disabilities instruction in the morning with camp activities in the afternoon. We considered the academic and the social experiences important for him.

The following school year, still on Ritalin, still enuretic, R entered a structured school program conducted in a regular school setting. The program was designed to help bright learning-disabled children who would eventually return to a regular classroom and prepare for college. A trained special education teacher taught the class of about eight children. R attended this class during 3rd grade and made substantial progress. His progress is continuing during 5th grade. Enuresis diminished last summer although it resumed during R's 2-week camp experience. R's enuretic behavior stopped completely 3 months later, and Ritalin dosages were reduced, with trials of total withdrawal of medication. Completing schoolwork continues to be a problem; yet, it has improved (unsteadily), and his ability to concentrate has increased. R's teacher reported that his handwriting is now one of the two best examples of penmanship in the class. R has made friends, joined Cub Scouts, takes violin lessons, and has sold school magazines door-to-door, receiving an award for his success. His social skills have improved substantially during the past 2 years; R began making friends with children his own age (before, he had only sought out younger children). Eye contact is now good, and R can engage in a meaningful, coherent conversation with adults; 2 years ago, he hid his face, avoided eye contact, and was generally distractible and tengential when he interacted with adults. His earlier borderline contact with reality has been replaced with more realistic and age-appropriate thought processes.

Of course treatment was characterized by a great many ups and downs, emergencies at the school, and Baggett's many visits and phone conversations with the mother and the teachers. A step forward was usually followed by a half-step backward: A progression was usually accompanied by a regression. In spite of these uproars and turmoils, overall progress was accomplished during the last period of therapy. Improvement might have been more dramatic, however, had Mr. S remained involved in the sessions.

Even with these improvements, R has more progress to make: He is still attending a special class, and he does still manage to produce occasional uproars at home and at school. In spite of his continuing manipulative behavior, his hyperactivity has decreased noticeably.

In a recent telephone conversation (Baggett was telephoning Mrs. S, and Mr. S answered the phone), the father expressed satisfaction with R's improvement. The mother is also very satisfied but wants to continue treatment so that she can improve her parenting skills and receive support from the therapists when she needs it. (Mr. S did, however, tell Mrs. S to share with us this or that issue.)

Analysis of Failure

This failure is noteworthy because of L'Abate's perspective on the role of the father in family therapy (L'Abate, 1983a). One cannot fail to react without looking at oneself and considering possible aspects of countertransference, incompetence, or insensitivity to the father's needs. The basic issue here is that we failed to form a therapeutic alliance with the father. It does not help to characterize him by psychiatric name calling (e.g., "rigid"), to attribute the failure to his investment in the *status quo*, or to hypothesize that he was so satisfied with his life that he was not interested in change. Mr. S is satisfied in his work. His responsibility at home is minimal because his perfectionistic wife clearly protects and shields him from it. Thus, he has power (i.e., maximum authority and minimum responsibility). He may need to resist any change that might threaten the *status quo*, decrease his authority, and increase his responsibility. For whatever reason, he was not about to give in. No role interpretation that we could have given him would have increased his interest in changing.

As most fathers do (L'Abate, 1975, 1983a), Mr. S belittled the intensity of the symptom and viewed it as a manifestation of how he was as a child— lonely and isolated. Yet, he had come out unscathed in his view, at least in his occupational role. Why would his child also not come out intact, as he had done (i.e., without help)?

The father, then, was seen for the first 12 sessions, during a 7- to 8-month period; the remainder of the sessions (spaced approximately 1 month apart over the next 2 years) took place with the mother and the son. We attempted to rationalize the multiple reasons for the father's dropping out.

1. The oppositional quality of the marital relationship may have contributed. As long as Mrs. S was interested and involved in treatment, Mr. S, according to his self-definition (in opposition to her; L'Abate, 1976), would not be. This oppositional and, consequently, negative self-definition is very important because Mr. S seems to assert himself only in reaction to his wife or his child (L'Abate, 1983b).

2. Breaking down in front of others and showing his vulnerability may have been (we can only speculate on this point) a source of embarrassment and shame. If he cannot break down with his wife, how can he do so in front of relative strangers (i.e., therapists?).

3. We may have inadvertently confused and pressured him with our messages—spoken, unspoken, and written (such as phone conversations with Mrs. S)—that we were perhaps siding with his wife and that he was again left out in the cold, a loner, as he has always been.

4. Although Mr. S stated again and again that he was in therapy to improve the functioning of his child, not to look at himself or his marriage, we continued to focus on the dysfunctional marital relationship. Had we dealt with the presenting problem (Haley, 1976; Madanes, 1981), we might eventually have been able to contract with Mr. and Mrs. S to move from the child issue to the marriage.

5. The family seemed to resent the paradoxical approach, labeling it sarcasm. Perhaps a more linear method would have been better accepted.

6. In spite of our development of a joint strategy from the beginning of treatment, some unspoken factors may have influenced our failure. Although we worked as equals, hidden (and not so hidden) issues of dominance-submission may have prevented the development of a coherent therapeutic style, as judged, for instance by how we addressed Mr. and Mrs. S. In the first letter, we addressed them by their first names; in the second letter, L'Abate addressed them as Mr. and Mrs. S. Although we had worked together on a few short cases before, this was the first prolonged case demanding a great deal of us as a team.

From the theoretical models, it is clear that we have helped Mrs. S assume a more competent and conductive role in relationship to her husband, her son, and the school. She has also realigned her priorities to some extent (i.e., realizing the importance of the self, although she continues to place the child before the marriage). Her awareness has increased, particularly her awareness of her own boundaries and those of her husband and her child. R continues, however, to evoke conflict between his parents about homework and school.

Since this experience R's symptomatic improvement and Mrs. S's devoted commitment to both of us have helped us to feel better about ourselves. Furthermore, our relationship as therapists has changed with Baggett's venture into private practice. When we worked with this family, Baggett was still the beginner, the "dependent" one. After 2 years' experience, she has come more into her own; she is more sure of herself and asserts herself more confrontively through her own style. As a result of these shifts in practice and style, L'Abate is no longer the possibly feared, know-it-all consultant and is comfortable allowing Baggett to take the initiative and the responsibility for treatment. We confer and are comfortable in our roles as equals. As a result of this experience, we are trying to be less confrontive with families, being much more careful and selective when we write letters and being aware of the timing that is necessary when we deliver any message—linear or circular.

Hypothetical Reconstruction toward Success

After a failure, a therapist(s) may fall into recriminations (What if I had done this? Why didn't I do this? How could I have done it differently and better?). While we were involved with this case, L'Abate was also working (solo) with other parents of hyperactive children. Perhaps one therapist would have been better than two. Would, then, a male or a female therapist have had a better chance at success? The previous therapist, a solo female, had also failed to keep the father in therapy.

We could have stressed more clearly the nature of the defeats and then constructed for Mr. and Mrs. S a written list of how each defeated the other. This homework assignment, linear as it is, is very useful with families who are characterized by frequent defeats. Once this list had been made, exchanged, and discussed, the positive nature of their defeats (L'Abate, 1985) could have been made known. To counteract their reactive opposition to each other, we could have used a series of exercises designed to make partners aware of their reactivity; they might then have learned to control such reactivity (L'Abate, 1983c).

We should have avoided written letters. They may have confused the father to the point that he was unable to cope. We should have been (1) more straightforward, (2) more gradual, and (3) more consistent in our dealings with them.

Perhaps we should have been more involved in reaching a clear therapeutic alliance with Mr. S by using such interventions as having him come alone or with the child but without his wife.

Probably one of the biggest mistakes we made was in focusing too quickly on the marriage rather than remaining with parenting issues. Even though Mr. and Mrs. S both agreed in the first session that they were unable to have discussions, they must have seen that failure as a parenting issue rather than as part of their marriage contract. Perhaps by working through the parenting, the marriage might have improved, or, at least, we could have reached a point at which we could have specifically negotiated with Mr. and Mrs. S to begin to work on the marriage (Haley, 1976; Madanes, 1981).

Conclusion

This case presentation illustrates our failure as therapists to join the father in being more responsible for and responsive to his son's behavior. We should have concentrated on the symptomatic behavior rather than on the marriage or the earlier personality developments of the parents. We could have used more straightforward, less paradoxical techniques; we could have spent more time reflecting on *what* we were doing, *why* we were doing it, and *how* we were doing it. We have proved again the truism that we learn more from our failures than from our successes.

REFERENCES

Haley, J. *Problem-solving therapy.* San Francisco: Jossey-Bass, 1976.
Johnson, J., Weeks, G. R., & L'Abate, L. Forced holding: A technique for treating parentified children. *Family Therapy,* 1979, *6,* 124–132. (Also reprinted in L. L'Abate, *Family psychology: Theory, therapy, and training.* Washington, D.C.: University Press of America, 1983.)
L'Abate, L. Pathogenic role rigidity in fathers: Some observations. *Journal of Marriage and Family Counseling,* 1975, *1,* 69–79.
L'Abate, L. *Understanding and helping the individual in the family.* New York: Grune & Stratton, 1976.
L'Abate, L. *Family psychology: Theory, therapy, and training.* Washington, D.C.: University Press of America, 1983a.
L'Abate, L. Styles in intimate relationships: The A-R-C model. *The Personnel and Guidance Journal,* 1983b, *61,* 277–283.
L'Abate, L. *Toward a systematic approach to family therapy.* Unpublished manuscript, Georgia State University, 1983c.
L'Abate, L. Distance, defeats, and dependence. In L. L'Abate (Ed.), *Handbook of family psychology and therapy.* Homewood, Ill.: Dow Jones–Irwin, 1985.
L'Abate, L. *Systematic family therapy.* New York: Brunner/Mazel, in press.
L'Abate, L., Frey, J. III, & Wagner, V. Further elaborations of the E-R-A-Aw-C model. *Family Therapy,* 1982, *9,* 251–262. (Also reprinted in L. L'Abate, *Family psychology: Theory, therapy, and training.* Washington, D.C.: University Press of America, 1983.)
Lederer, W. J., & Jackson, D. D. *The mirages of marriage.* New York: Norton, 1969.
Madanes, C. *Strategic family therapy.* San Francisco: Jossey-Bass, 1981.
Smith, M. T., Smith, M. P., & L'Abate, L. Families of hyperactive children: A systemic perspective. In L. L'Abate (Ed.), *Handbook of family psychology and therapy.* Homewood, Ill.: Dow Jones–Irwin, 1985.
Weeks, G., & L'Abate, L. *Paradoxical psychotherapy.* New York: Brunner/Mazel, 1982.

10

Family Therapy versus Schizophrenia and the Psychiatric–Legal Establishment

ISRAELA MEYERSTEIN AND PAUL F. DELL

Introduction

In looking back on the history of the case we are about to present, we discovered that what transpired was not so much a function of our theoretical orientation as it was a matter of context. In particular, there are four major aspects of the context within which our therapy with the Smith family occurred: (1) historical context, (2) work context, (3) ideological context, and (4) the conceptual–theoretical orientation of the cotherapy team. Certainly, a similar set of contexts bears on the treatment of any case, but it will rapidly become apparent that these contextual factors affected the character and outcome of the Smiths' therapy to an unusual degree.

Theoretical Frame of Reference

The Smith family was treated during the 1970s, a period of expansionism for family therapy. It was a time, at least for us, of high enthusiasm, evangelism, and missionary zeal. Minuchin's work on structural family therapy (1974) was being enormously successful in lending credibility to family therapy. Structural family therapy proved to be logical, concrete, and provided an easily grasped diagnostic framework that generates specific treatment goals. We were structural family therapists. We also were significantly influenced by the strategic work of the Mental Research Institute (MRI). As a result, our approach to therapy was active, directive, and made extensive use of planned, structural, and strategic interventions.

Israela Meyerstein. Strategic Family Training Program of the Lehigh Valley, Allentown, Pennsylvania.

Paul F. Dell. Eastern Virginia Family Therapy Institute, Department of Psychiatry and Behavioral Sciences, Eastern Virginia Medical School, Virginia Beach, Virginia.

The 1970s was not only a period of expansionism for family therapy, it was also a period of expansionism for the community mental health movement. Spurred on by the legally mandated deinstitutionalization of chronic (state hospital) mental patients, community mental health programs grew like topsy—and sometimes provided a fertile ground for family therapy. A variety of developments in family therapy during the 1960s lent themselves to the emergence of a natural, harmonious alliance between family therapy and community psychiatry (Zwerling, 1980). The ecological family systems concepts of Auerswald and others, for example (Auerswald, 1968, 1972; Hoffman & Long, 1969; Minuchin, 1969), had already begun to move family therapy out of the therapist's office and into the community. In addition, multiple impact therapy (MacGregor, Ritchie, Serrano, Schuster, McDonald, & Goolishian, 1964) and family crisis treatment (Langsley & Kaplan, 1968) had demonstrated the effectiveness of family therapy as an alternative to hospitalization. Together with Minuchin's successful treatment of high-risk, multiproblem families (Minuchin, Montalvo, Guerney, Rosman, & Schumer, 1967), these innovations in family therapy seemed to be well-suited to community psychiatry. Family therapy simultaneously held out the hope of short-circuiting institutionalization, providing effective treatment to high-risk patients, and maintaining the integrity of the community's natural social units—families.

These are the historical and ideological contexts within which we treated the Smith family. Our work setting was, itself, deeply embedded in these same contexts. We functioned at the interface between a community mental health center and a big city teaching hospital whose residency training program emphasized hospitalization as the treatment of choice. The psychiatrists at the hospital had long ago pronounced our community mental health center clients to be "incurable schizophrenics" who were in need of medication and hospitalization—preferably long-term and probably at the state hospital. In contrast, the community mental health center had been mandated to act as a community "safety net" that would "catch" high risk clients, help them avoid institutionalization (Meyerstein, 1977), and treat them in the least-restrictive possible living arrangements.

At least part of the time, the community mental health center succumbed to the challenge of "curing the incurables." Typically, this challenge reduced itself to a single goal: ending the revolving-door cycle of hospitalization as the means for handling patient crises. Each chronic patient tended to inspire antiinstitutional zeal to succeed in the community where treatment had failed in the institution. Such a conflict of psychiatric ideologies is, of course, a set-up for failure. Not unpredictably, this ideological contest led to a significant level of confusion, power struggles, apparent sabotage of treatment, and, not least of all, schizophrenia.

Background

Referral Information

Joe and Herbert Smith, two brothers in their late 20s, had been attending a medication group at their local community mental health center. This medication group is part of the center's program for clients who had previously been hospitalized and who were considered to be at high risk for additional hospitalizations. At that time Joe and Herbert had both been diagnosed schizophrenic.

Subsequent to an episode the night before (when Herbert had been cursing, storming about, and smashing things at home), his father sought help from the leader of the medication group. Mr. Smith wanted Herbert to be hospitalized—the family's usual response to such crises. With some effort, the therapist convinced Mr. Smith to bring the family for an immediate therapy session. During this session, the therapist calmed the family, prevented them from hospitalizing Herbert, and enlisted the family in ongoing family therapy. Following this initial session, the second author joined the family therapy as a cotherapist. After a period of mostly strategic therapy, the original therapist took another job. Following a hiatus in treatment of 2 months, during which the family took a vacation, the first author was introduced into the therapy as a new cotherapist.

The Family

The Smith family consisted of Father, Mother, and three sons. Bill was the oldest, followed at 1-year intervals by Joe and Herbert, respectively. Father was a hardworking, blue-collar worker on the night shift at a steel mill. He was native to the Pennsylvania community and had worked in the mill and lived in the surrounding countryside for many years. He was devoted to his family and was a steady provider. A self-deprecating man, Mr. Smith frequently avoided eye contact, especially with his wife whom he could rarely be induced to face. He did much to preserve the family myth that he did little at work but sit around. It was always Mr. Smith who initiated contact with some part of the community mental health network when there was trouble with Joe or Herbert.

Mrs. Smith was employed as a sales clerk in a local outlet store. Always neatly dressed and groomed, Mrs. Smith spoke very quietly with a subdued affect. She rarely showed strong emotion. When talking to her, one often had the feeling of not having gained her full attention. She was religious and was responsible for the family's regular Sunday attendance at a local fundamentalist church. Mrs. Smith had been hospitalized for psychotic depression on one occasion.

Bill was his father's namesake. He was the only member of the family who did not live at home. He had an office job involving computers in California and was, therefore, unavailable to participate in the therapy. Described by the family as "very well-organized," Bill was the leader of the three sons.

Herbert was first to have a psychotic break. Since his early 20s he had had multiple hospitalizations. Even though Joe had also had multiple hospitalizations, Herbert was labeled as "the sick one" by the family. Herbert supported this label by typically being slightly confused and several steps behind in family interactions. When talking to him, one never had the feeling of having gained his full attention. He lived at home and had never been able to hold a job.

Joe's behavior during psychotic episodes had been far more lurid and violent than that of Herbert. Nevertheless, Joe was considered to be the competent well sibling of the two living at home. He maintained that he was not crazy, but only had a "nervous stomach." Like his brother, Herbert, he had not been able to hold a job (but did serve an enlistment in the Army). Whereas Herbert tended to engage in childlike fumbling, Joe was forceful, if not aggressive, in his verbal interactions. Of the two, he was unmistakably the dominant one.

Diagnosis and Treatment Plan

Developmental History of the Family

At the time of her marriage, Mrs. Smith was closely tied to her family. For the 1st year or so, Mr. and Mrs. Smith lived with her parents. During this period of time, they seemed to have been quite happy, frequently dining out, going on picnics, to baseball games, and to occasional movies. After about a year, Mr. Smith wrested his wife away from her family, and they bought their own home an hour or so away. Mrs. Smith frequently implied in family therapy (albeit, very indirectly) that even after so many years of marriage, she was still angry that Mr. Smith had taken her away from her family.

Several years into their marriage, Bill was born. A year later, Joe was born and Mother promptly succumbed to a postpartum depression. At about this same time, her mother died. Mr. and Mrs. Smith were very vague about this period in their lives, but imply that Mrs. Smith became rather psychotic and incompetent for an undetermined length of time. Eleven months later, Herbert was born. Mr. Smith completely assumed the role of mother to the children. Throughout this period, Mr. Smith administered all medications to the babies and made all decisions—for fear that his wife would make a mistake. He let her boil the babies' bottles, but would not allow her to prepare their formula. He did this himself. Cast in the role of incompetent, Mrs. Smith was deprived of a major source of gratification and an important aspect of her functioning. In something of a *quid pro quo* for Mr. Smith's having assumed the right to make all decisions regarding the children, Mrs. Smith claimed the right to an extremely intense emotional bond with the children.

As the children were growing up, Mr. Smith extended his control over the mothering functions in the family. His namesake, Bill, cooperated with him by becoming the family cook. Father and Bill did most of the housekeeping. As the children grew, Mother remained closely involved with them, especially the two youngest. Bill emerged as the leader of the boys and blocked his brothers' developing competence just as Father and he had done to Mother. Mother dealt with this by becoming even further involved with Joe and Herbert.

These early developments in the family history had serious and lasting consequences for the marital dyad. Father's usurping of his wife's mothering functions created an imbalance in the relational ledger, which left him unable to lay valid claim to her attentions as a wife. Over the years a great split developed between Husband and Wife. In particular, Mrs. Smith seems to have acquired the right to make a variety of subtle (and not so subtle) verbal attacks on her husband. For example, when asked to plan a family trip for Husband and Wife only, Mr. Smith began to respond with hesitant, anxious pleasure, only to be interrupted by his wife's declaration, "I couldn't imagine going anywhere without at least one of the boys." In response to such rejecting and hurtful statements, Mr. Smith would invariably sit numbly and say nothing.

It was during high school that the coalition of Bill and Father was most powerful and had its greatest impact on family life. Mother and the two youngest were thrown together in their mutual incompetence. In contrast, Bill was competent, popular with girls, and obviously on his way out of the family. Joe, the strongest and most athletic of the three, made a bid for competence and was hoping to follow Bill into the Army. Herbert, however, was unable to keep pace with his brothers; he faltered and fell another grade behind. Mother redoubled her investment in Herbert, thereby allowing Joe to pull free of his mother.

Bill and Joe graduated from high school 1 year apart and each enlisted in the Army. Herbert, gradually losing steam and falling further behind in social development, left high school when he was 17 years old and attempted to follow his brothers into the service. He flunked the physical. Several weeks later he became psychotic. During this same time, Mother had been becoming steadily more depressed about her two sons being away. As a result, she exerted great pressure on Herbert to remain at home. If Herbert left home, she would lose her only remaining source of emotional gratification and self-realization. Thus, Herbert's schizophrenic break was life-saving for Mother. His decompensation not only insured that he would not leave home, but also provided Mrs. Smith with the opportunity to mother one of her children— something which had previously been denied to her.

Joe eventually completed his enlistment and returned home (Bill had completed his enlistment and had moved to California a year previously). Joe promptly precipitated a crisis. His reentry into the family as a competent son immediately subverted the Mother–Herbert, mothering–incompetent dyad that had stabilized mother after Bill and Joe left home. Almost as soon as Joe returned, Herbert began making efforts to leave home to live in an apartment with Joe. Mother promptly became psychotic and was hospitalized for depression. Her illness brought maximum pressure to bear upon her sons. How could they leave when Mother so clearly needed help? As a result, Joe again became ensnared in the family web. Within months, he, too, became psychotic.

The events preceding Joe's psychotic break are revealing. While Joe was in the Army, Father's loss of his coalition partner, Bill, was balanced by Mother's loss of Joe. Father still retained the upper hand in the face of the mother–Herbert pairing. Joe's return, however, threatened to completely supplant Father. Indeed, the family began to settle into a new pattern. Joe provided emotional support for Mother by being a competent, male companion. Father was displaced. He eventually responded to this situation by demanding that Joe get a job or leave home. Joe left to live in a motel, became psychotic, and returned to the house where he threw a brick through the picture window in the living room.

Joe blamed Father for his psychotic break; so did Mother. With this, the mother–Joe–Herbert coalition was reasserted and Father capitulated. Mother gained the right to become the sole determinant of family matters when they involved Joe and Herbert—and she invariably saw to it that all family matters *did* involve Joe and Herbert.

Diagnostic Formulation

The Smith family was a highly enmeshed family with a rigid coalitional structure. Family members fostered a mutual togetherness at the expense of one another's autonomy and differentiation. They were highly reactive to even the slightest changes in each other's behavior. They gave each other total attention and paid little attention to the extrafamilial world. The parents, for example, had no social friends except for a few relatives. Similarly, Joe and Herbert had but one "friend" whom they had seen once in the previous year.

The family had an overfunctioning parental subsystem and a virtually nonexistent spouse subsystem. Mr. and Mrs. Smith were overinvolved with their sons. As parents, they were continuing to function in roles more appropriate to an earlier (normative) developmental stage of family life. As spouses, there was tremendous distance and lack of involvement between Mr. and Mrs. Smith. With very rare exceptions, all interaction between Mr. and Mrs. Smith included Joe and Herbert. This ongoing inclusion of their sons effectively precluded Mr. and Mrs. Smith from dealing with one another as spouses. In addition, their working schedules minimized their time for any kind of interaction. Mrs. Smith typically departed for work before Mr. Smith got up in the morning. He, in turn, left for work in the afternoon before she returned. Finally, Mrs. Smith went to bed before Mr. Smith returned from work at night. Their only opportunities to get together were Monday morning and early afternoon, Saturday evening, and Sunday. Father, however, often worked Saturday evening. Moreover, the family attended church twice on Sunday. Thus, Mr. and Mrs. Smith allowed themselves little time to be together as Husband and Wife.

Joe functioned as Mother's husband. He was the first one up in the morning and prepared the coffee. Mother then woke up and she and Joe retired to the living room where they had their morning coffee and engaged in lively conversation. Meanwhile, Father and Herbert were sleeping. About the time that Father woke up, Mother left for work. Joe and Herbert not infrequently joined Mother on her lunch hour. Mr. Smith, in contrast, had very seldom done this with his wife. It was also not unusual for Joe to drive his mother to and from work. In the evening, Mother and Joe usually spent an hour or two by the fireplace drinking coffee and sharing the day's events with one another. Mr. Smith claimed ignorance of how much time Mother and Joe spent together. Not surprisingly, Joe was quite ambivalent about his almost unbearably close relationship with his mother. Periodically, he gained distance by exploding in anger. In one psychotic episode, for example, Joe attempted to gain some distance from his mother by taking panties from her drawer and slashing them with a knife.

Although the most powerful coalition was that of Mother and Joe, there was also a weaker coalition between Father and Herbert. This coalition was called into play infrequently and was easily overridden by Mother and Joe. It was more often the case that Father or Herbert would seek to gain power in the family at the expense of the other. That is, if Joe and Mother were picking on Herbert, Father might join them in the attack. Similarly, if Father was the brunt of ridicule, then Herbert would pair with Mother and Joe against Father.

From an outsider's perspective Mother appeared to be overprotective and intrusive in such a way as to block her sons from developing autonomy. Similarly, Father gave the appearance that he might have preferred to have Joe and Herbert grow up. Upon closer examination, however, one saw that when Mother was not worrying about her sons' problems, Father was. Thus, there was an infinite dance of shifting coalitions through which the family system continued to function at the same developmental impasse. Namely, the alternating decompensation of Joe and Herbert continued to organize family functioning in terms of parenting. Because they provided the only tie in their parents' marriage, Joe and Herbert could not leave home without precipitating marital disaster or a psychiatric crisis for their mother.

Treatment Plan

In keeping with our formulation we established three treatment goals that we tackled simultaneously. First, we sought to repair the split between Mr. and Mrs. Smith by fostering their participation in mutually satisfying interactions. Second, we sought to decrease the boys' overinvolvement with their mother by encouraging peer relationships and by trying to increase their interactions with their father. Third, we attempted to foster autonomy, competence, and gradual independence from the family for Joe and Herbert. To do this, we asked the parents to insist that their sons attend the community mental health center's independent living-skills program. Our overarching strategy for accomplishing these goals was to align and coordinate all elements of the family, community, and mental health system so that they would work together cooperatively.

Given the long-standing nature of the family's problems, we concluded that the identified patient, Herbert, was the most accessible point of intervention. Accordingly, we devised a series of planned interventions that sought to deal with Herbert explicitly and with Mr. and Mrs. Smith indirectly. In order to free Herbert from his symptomatic role, we worked with Mr. and Mrs. Smith to help them to encourage Herbert's autonomy and, simultaneously, we tried to foster more direct communication between husband and wife.

The therapy was active, problem-focused, and directive in nature. During the early phase of therapy, we used direct, behavioral prescriptions and regularly assigned tasks. Accordingly, a substantial portion of the therapy hour was often devoted to the discussion of task outcome and assigning future tasks. Careful preplanning and on-the-spot planning during sessions (i.e., taking breaks during which we left the room to formulate strategy) were viewed as an antidote to the family's amorphous communication style. The family proved to have great facility at undoing our direct requests; they would ingeniously subvert our prescriptions in a way that prevented us from confronting them with their failure to carry out their assigned tasks. As a result, we relied heavily on paradoxical instructions (Haley, 1973; Watzla-wick, Weakland, & Fisch, 1974).

Their unique ability to retain the upper hand in therapy via confusion and indirection posed a constant challenge to us. Various strategies that we employed to increase our leverage with the Smith family included the follow-ing: more frequent sessions, phone calls between sessions to remind them of assigned tasks, longer sessions, shorter sessions, and sessions with different subgroups of the family. Finally, we considered cotherapy to be the *sine qua non* for successful treatment of this or any other schizophrenic family.

Process of Therapy

The course of therapy with the Smith family was long and arduous. During the 2 years of our contact with them, we plodded through periods of active therapy, vacations, emergency local hospitalization, times of apparent suc-cess, jailings, state hospitalizations, and a courtroom jury trial. Our stamina in this case was probably due to the camaraderie and close working relation-ship of the cotherapists and between them and the team within the commu-nity mental health center. Without this, we would likely have succumbed to early burnout. Certainly, there were many points during treatment where the larger team's infusion of new ideas was all that rescued us from the fate of so many other community mental health workers—chronic undifferentiated treatment.

Moving the Furniture without Changing the Floor Plan

Compared to later stages of therapy, the first 6 months was relatively benign and nonintrusive. During this time the second author and the medications group leader used a nonconfronting, problem-focused, strategic approach (Watzlawick *et al.*, 1974). Most interventions were carefully framed in such a manner as to enlist the parents' cooperation. The "boys" were nudged toward increased autonomy, but not toward independence or genuine competence. This stage of therapy cautiously pursued first-order change (i.e., "moving the furniture without changing the floor plan"). While failing to address the major triadic entanglements, this approach did succeed in establishing rap-port with the family.

Herbert, the identified patient, was considered to be the most accessible (and perhaps the only) point of entry into the family system. Accordingly, the therapists devised a series of strategic interventions that ostensibly were designed to help Herbert; indirectly, they were also designed to alter Mr. and Mrs. Smith's stance as parents. These interventions had three goals: (1) to normalize Herbert's hallucinations (i.e., his voices), (2) to make him more competent and less dependent, and (3) to decrease the parents' "helping" behaviors that were sustaining Herbert's dependence and incompetency. These therapeutic maneuvers produced some early successes. For example, one successful intervention involved the health cards that Herbert and Joe were required to present for mental health services. Father carried the cards because "the boys would be sure to lose them." Father was simply told that "the boys need to carry their own cards." He acceded to this declaration and surrendered the cards to Joe and Herbert who have responsibly carried them from that time forth.

In early therapy sessions the Smiths were quite concerned about Herbert's voices. These voices were usually those of a critical female who said terrible things to and about Herbert. The therapists, however, refused to be impressed by what, to the family, were such obvious manifestations of pathology. The therapists doggedly sought to normalize the voices by relabeling them. In this, they were largely successful. They steamrolled the family with a no-wonder-Herbert-lacks-self-confidence approach to the matter. Henceforth, Herbert's voices were discussed as being a sign of his lack of self-confidence. This redefinition provided the therapists with many more degrees of freedom in planning interventions than "voices" or "hallucinations" could ever have afforded. Herbert's lack of self-confidence was readily apparent to the family; the therapists promptly enlisted their aid in increasing Herbert's self-confidence. Mother, Father, and Joe accepted the assignment to compliment Herbert whenever he did anything correctly. This task, which the family faithfully executed, decreased the parents' infantilization of Herbert and undermined Joe's constant criticism of his brother.

A concomitant assignment dealt with the taking of medicine. All family members, especially Joe, professed great concern that Herbert would forget to take his medication on time and would become violent. To cope with this "problem," the family woke Herbert at 7:00 A.M. every morning and reminded him to take his medicine. In fact, they reminded him at each of his four daily medication times. Failing to persuade the family that this constant reminding of Herbert was destructive to his self-confidence, the therapists assumed their mantle of authority and ordered the family not to wake Herbert at 7:00 A.M. and ordered them not to remind him to take his medicine; Herbert was to handle this by himself. The family agreed. At the next session, the family reported that they had not reminded Herbert to take his medicine in the mornings. Closer investigation, however, revealed that the family had awakened Herbert at 7:00 A.M. every morning. Nevertheless, they insisted that they were not reminding him to take his medicine. When the therapists voiced some incredulity at this rationalization, the family responded with equal incredulity (and impatience) that the therapists could be so dense. After all, they insisted, unless Herbert was up, he would forget to take his medicine and might become violent.

This was the first of many subsequent encounters with such imperviousness. The family was absolutely convinced of the distinction between reminding Herbert to take his medicine, and waking him so that he could take his medicine. Their ability to defeat the therapists in ways that could not be effectively confronted was a hallmark of therapy with the Smiths. Despite the best efforts of the therapists, this sort of maneuver repeatedly subverted therapeutic interventions.

Nevertheless, the therapists continued to eke out a meager schedule of successes. In the 1st week of the family's assignment to compliment Herbert for anything he did correctly, Herbert (reported having) heard no voices. The therapists expressed great concern that Herbert was changing too fast; they instructed Herbert to start hearing the voices again, but to "make them come" while he was walking in the woods. During the 2nd week, Herbert heard no voices. He was again ordered to "make the voices come." Still, he heard no voices. These paradoxical instructions to "hear the voices" took place during the same sessions as the unsuccessful attempt to stop the family from reminding Herbert to take his medicine. Also, the family was still complimenting Herbert for what he did at home. At this point, the therapists cleverly stopped the family from waking Herbert by insisting that Herbert get his own alarm clock—and thereby exceeded the family's tolerance for change. Herbert started to get himself up, but the family suddenly became "too busy" to continue to build up his self-confidence. Herbert began to hear voices again. It is significant in this regard that Herbert hears voices (almost) only when Mother is home. Even when others are home (as well), Herbert invariably receives special attention from Mother because she is the one who is best at calming him down. In order to block this sort of secondary gain, the therapists told Herbert to go for a walk. That is, if he heard the voices while he was home, he was to go for a walk in the woods until the voices stopped. Concomitantly, the family was instructed to tell Herbert to go for a walk if he reported hearing voices.

Early attempts to bring the parents closer together were fraught with frustration. They claimed to be happy and insisted that they did not miss the things that they used to do together. Therapists' suggestions about picnics were discarded by the parents because it was too hot, too cold, too wet, and so on. Any suggestion that they do something together that excluded the boys was likely to elicit one of Mrs. Smith's "it wouldn't be any fun without the boys." On one occasion the therapists reframed this statement by saying that Mr. and Mrs. Smith were excellent, hard-working, devoted parents who deserved a vacation from caring for the boys. The family replied with a one-two combination that floored the therapists. Joe immediately objected, "Even if we weren't mentally ill, they'd still want us to always be with them." Then, almost as one, Mother and Joe put the therapists on the spot by asking, "Isn't it all right for children to live with their parents when they are grown up?" Eventually, the therapists learned to duck such loaded questions, and ceased trying to convince the family that the parents *ought* to spend more time together.

Instead, a few sessions later, the therapists mustered their power and simply decreed that Father was to take his wife out to eat without the boys. This order was framed in terms of his not having paid sufficient attention to his wife. Because this rationale scapegoated Father, it won Mother's support and was successful. Mr. Smith took his wife out to eat at the local Dairy Queen. This homework was successfully reassigned a week later, just before the family went on vacation.

The vacation lasted until the pre-Christmas shopping days and Mother became unavailable for therapy due to her Christmas-season working hours at the store. There was a 2-month cessation of treatment. Perhaps we should have taken Mother's unavailability as feedback regarding our efforts to change the family. Whatever the case, during this period the original therapist took another job and the family's communications with the clinic were vague and confusing. They could easily have been lost to therapy. Persistent contact, however, renewed the therapy.

Major Renovations and Their Cost

Although the therapy had increasingly begun to restructure the family, these efforts vastly increased with the addition of a new cotherapist (the first author) who was a structural family therapist. During this phase of "major renovations," we tried to strengthen the bond between Mr. and Mrs. Smith so that they could, at least, communicate directly with one another, rather than through their sons. We simultaneously encouraged Joe and Herbert to initiate peer contacts outside the family. In short, we wanted to strengthen the diffuse generational boundaries in the family. We did not, however, address the triadic interlocking of family members, which soon thrust its existence into the foreground of our attention.

We told Father and Mother to take each other on a date to a local restaurant once a week. After doing this twice, they began to genuinely enjoy the experience. This was a sizable change that threatened the previous relational structure of the family. Thus, we were not greatly surprised when the parents appeared for therapy one Monday morning without "the boys." "The boys" had refused to come and Mr. and Mrs. Smith did not know why. On the night before, when Mr. and Mrs. Smith had returned home from their date, they had found Joe rather "depressed." Additional questioning revealed that "depressed" actually meant *angry*. We offered the parents our sympathy and support for having to raise such difficult children. The enjoyable experience of the parents' date was discussed and the session was terminated.

A week later the entire family came to therapy in a state of agitation. The parents had gone out again on the previous night and had returned to find Joe depressed, crying, and agitated. Mother had to calm him down. As a result, Father was arguing strongly for hospitalization. The whole family seemed to agree with him. Because we considered Joe's illness to be a blatant attempt to regain Mother from Father, we elected to increase the pressure by not acceding to the family's wish to hospitalize. Instead, we asked Mr. Smith to wake his wife when he came home from work and to ask her how Joe was doing. If there were any problems, both he and his wife were to wake Joe and discuss the matter. Finally, if the family was still uncomfortable with the situation, they were to call us in the morning for an emergency session. This prescription was designed to serve two purposes: (1) to keep Joe out of the hospital, and (2) to prevent him from using his symptoms to steal Mother back from Father. Best laid plans. . . . The family hospitalized Joe later that day. Unlike previous hospitalizations, Joe *voluntarily* admitted himself to the hospital. The ward psychiatrist welcomed our ongoing interest in Joe and supported what we were trying to do. Ten days later Joe was discharged. Because the tension had declined at home, we continued to encourage the spouse relationship.

With Joe (the "well" sibling) reassuming the role of identified patient, our attention turned to him. It was only at this point that we became aware of the extent to which Joe was functioning as Mother's husband. Like Herbert, he was unemployed, had few friends or activities outside the family, and was receiving Social Security Income (SSI) disability payments. Joe hung around the house and kept Mother company when she was home. Joe and Herbert had no household responsibilities because their parents were reluctant to make demands. To compensate for Mother's increased involvement with Father, we encouraged Joe to develop some peer relationships. We hoped that a relationship might develop in Joe's (and Herbert's) weekly medication group. Although both boys voiced discomfort with their parents' growing interest in each other, Joe seemed to have the greatest difficulty. Toward the end of February, after his parents had gone on one of their dates, Joe became violent with the furniture at home. His parents called the police who took him to the hospital. Both parents described Joe as violent and unmanageable; they said they could not handle him.

Rules of the House

This time, Joe's symptomatic behavior succeeded in redirecting our focus. We abandoned our work with the spouse subsystem in favor of devising a plan for Joe. His unmanageability had (at least) two possible interpretations: (1) He needed to be hospitalized because he was violent and crazy (his parents' view), or (2) he did not like the new conditions at home and, therefore, needed to either, (a) learn to accept the nature of his parents' household, or (b) make plans to leave home and live by his own rules. Our family orientation and our philosophy of normalization led us to reject the parents' interpretation and to pursue our nonpsychiatric alternative.

Family therapy continued during Joe's 2-week hospitalization. During this time, we agreed with Father's reluctance to have Joe home again (under the same terms), but we disagreed with his solution to send Joe to the state hospital. We sought to help the parents ensure better cooperation, greater responsibility, and more respect for household rules on the part of their sons. We launched a discussion about what must be different in order for Joe to live at home. As a start, the parents were asked to set clear expectations for Herbert (and for Joe when he came home). With difficulty and hesitation, helped by our support, Mr. and Mrs. Smith worked together and articulated their expectations as the chief executives of the family. This was hard slogging in therapy because the family had so little experience with negotiation, expression of differences, appropriate expression of anger, and the use of clear directives. Still, they made progress. In a homework assignment, Mr. and Mrs. Smith enforced their rules with Herbert and managed him well. As a result, Herbert was becoming more appropriate in his functioning at the same time that Joe was decompensating in the hospital. For example, Joe stormed out of one therapy session after being labeled as "the sick one" by his family.

As Joe prepared to come home from the hospital, we assured the parents of our support and told them that the police department stood ready to help if Joe became violent. During this time period the parents continued to go out and became more committed to each other as a marital unit. Then Joe came home. In response to being "kicked out" of his exclusive closeness with Mother, Joe became sullen. On the positive side, however, Joe and Herbert began to support each other and bonded together as siblings. Unfortunately, this period of progress was short-lived. On the following weekend Joe knocked over some furniture at home, and his parents summoned the police.

This time, they took Joe to jail. There, the forensic psychiatrist examined Joe and transferred him to the mental hospital. The parents contributed the final component to this repetitive cycle by throwing up their hands in helplessness. In the commitment hearing, the judge decided that Joe should receive a 90-day commitment to the community mental health center: first, in its inpatient unit and, then, through its outpatient resources in the community. The judge's commitment decision averted state hospitalization and *specified that treatment should help Joe to live independently* (away from his family). Furthermore, to the parents' great relief (and, perhaps, at their request), the judge *prohibited Joe from visiting his parents' home.* As we watched this repetitive cycle repeat once again, we began to realize the extensive involvement of community helpers in the family's attempted solutions to their problems. Not only did each repetition of the cycle reinforce the likelihood of the same old pathway (violent episode–police–jail–mental hospital–home) but also each successive repetition tended to derail a therapy that was beginning to gather momentum.

All under One Roof—but It Leaks

With Joe's commitment to the community mental health center and the mandated involvement of outside agents of social control, treatment took on a subtle, but significantly different dimension. We launched a valiant effort to centralize the various helping resources and to coordinate a consistent approach to Joe and his family. Our goal, in fact, was to create a kind of airtight, milieu treatment in the community. This arrangement would include structuring and supervising Joe's time; clear expectations and rules from the judge, his parents, and the mental health team; and specified consequences for misbehavior so that Joe would develop self-control and a sense of responsibility.

The team outlined a tentative set of plans for Joe to move into an independent living arrangement where he would share an apartment with a high-functioning mentally retarded client. Joe would have daily, supervised training in independent living skills and vocational preparation. Meanwhile, family therapy continued with the entire family. The goal of family therapy during Joe's month-long hospitalization was to enlist the parents' cooperation in the planned, independent living program for Joe. The parents, although grateful for the support and resources offered through the community mental health center, remained somewhat skeptical and anxious about managing Joe in the community. Thus, a subtle but critical cleavage (to which we were largely blind) began to develop: the therapists aligned themselves with the community mental health center's program to successfully rehabilitate Joe, but the parents (and other previously defeated helpers) remained pessimistic due to the chronicity of the problem. In addition, instead of the parents pushing Joe out, the community mental health center became the executor of the judge's mandate to *pull* Joe out of the home. As family therapists, we found ourselves bridging, and soon participating in, an almost adversarial position. On one side was the community mental health center's program, which sought to "free" Joe from his family; on the other side were the "bad" parents (and others) who did not support the program.

During family therapy sessions the parents received continued encouragement and support (and pressure) to set rules for Herbert. Herbert and Joe were encouraged to plan some activities together to be done upon Joe's release from the hospital. Conjoint sessions with the parents confirmed that they were continuing to go out together and that they were becoming more demonstrable of this closeness in front of the boys. Even Herbert's occasional voices (which he would report to Mother) did not interfere with the parents' plans together. A family therapy session discussed in great detail the issues related to leaving home. The parents expressed their concerns about their boys' welfare and verbalized their difficulties in letting the boys go, especially in such a close and loving family.

Before the community mental health center's plan was fully operational, however, Joe was precipitously discharged from the hospital due to a shortage of beds. Communication between the team and the ward psychiatrist was inadequate in this instance (i.e., we were not informed of Joe's discharge), which highlighted and prefigured our lack of control over significant treatment decisions. Despite the judge's prohibition of home visits, Joe called home and Mother took him in. His visit degenerated into a heated argument, the police were summoned, and Joe was returned to the hospital. As a result of this psychiatric version of the Keystone Cops, we spent the next few weeks planning how to handle all possible pitfalls and, particularly, how to respond "when the roof leaks."

It became apparent to us that a tremendous network of people were activated, helter skelter, each time Joe misbehaved. When Joe made a move, the whole treatment network reacted. In fact, as was comically illustrated by the lawyer on our team in Figure 10-1 (yes, the team even had a lawyer), the team was often in more of a crisis than was Joe. We realized that successful treatment was not possible if different helpers were moving in different directions. Our attempt to prevent "leaks" and gain control over the cycle of home–police–jail–hospital home met with some success and some failure. The challenge of maintaining open communication and close coordination between family therapists, community mental health center staff, ward psychiatrist, police, jail, judge, and forensic psychiatrist was an enormous undertaking (if not Mission Impossible).

Study of the cycle showed that the police were repeatedly called by Mother after Joe had returned home, she had let him in, and things eventually had deteriorated into a family disturbance. Although the parents would claim they did not want Joe to stay, they did not directly ask Joe to leave until a blow-up had occurred and the police were called. Because Joe and Herbert were "mental patients," the mental health officers would come to the house and remove Joe to jail or to the mental hospital. In jail the forensic psychiatrist would routinely evaluate Joe (whom he had known for years) and decide that he was not simply "unruly and misbehaving," but "mentally ill." He would then transfer Joe to the locked ward of the hospital until his release several days or weeks hence. This cycle perpetuated the family's enmeshment, the parents' helplessness, Joe's out-of-control behavior, and the exchange of mixed messages between parents and son about their expectations regarding his behavior. Furthermore, it perpetuated the entanglement of the web of

FIGURE 10-1. Joe Smith in mid-crisis.

conflicting helpers who were out of sync with one another. We decided to break the cycle by altering the role of the agents of social control.

The community mental health center had a contract to train police officers to be "mental health officers"—trained in the skills of family-crisis intervention. We supervised two of these mental health officers and enlisted them to help with the Smiths. The officers had a dual role. As family therapists in training, they were to encourage (and, eventually, require) the parents to give Joe a direct, unified message when he came home and the parents wished him to leave, "We want you to go now and be independent through the community mental health center." As police officers, they enforced parents' authority (if all else failed) by returning Joe to his apartment or to the community mental health center. It was hoped that the police would not only intervene with Joe and his parents, but would also prevent activation of the jail–mental hospital sequence that had proved so detrimental to therapeutic progress.

Moving Day

We set the date for Joe's discharge from the hospital and thought that we had enough control to interrupt the pernicious cycle. In family therapy the parents were involved in our process of reviewing with Joe the details concerning the apartment. They even made an inspection visit. Joe was to share the apartment with a roommate and would have close, supportive, supervisory contact from the group home next door. He took the plans seriously and showed interest. Herbert piped up and suggested that he, too, move in—an idea that was immediately squelched by Mother. The parents approved the plans, but voiced their fears that Joe could not make it on his own and would run home again.

We realized that we could not successfully prohibit home visits because Joe defied the prohibition and his parents colluded with his doing so. We decided not to prohibit what was an inevitability. Instead, we placed the parents in charge of prohibiting or ending Joe's visits, thereby forcing them to take a stand. In family therapy, our goals remained the same: (1) to support the spouse subsystem, (2) to strengthen the executive functioning of the parents, (3) to improve direct, clear communication from the parents to the boys, and (4) to help Joe and Herbert develop more age-appropriate functioning (such as peer contacts outside home). To these goals, we added a new one—helping the spouses to adjust to their upcoming "empty nest" by relearning to be alone together.

Joe and his parents consulted with his caseworker at the community mental health center who planned an intensive, highly individualized program of training and resocialization. A daily schedule of activities (to which Herbert was invited) would closely structure Joe's time in a productive way.

We sought to obtain the cooperation and coordination of all involved before setting the plan into motion. Accordingly, the team convened a large meeting before discharging Joe from the hospital. A ritual signing of a contract took place. Rules, procedures, and consequences were clearly and painstakingly outlined in this several page document which was communicated to at least 15 people in the helping network (many of whom attended the meeting): caseworkers, program directors, chief of the medication clinic, family therapists, mental health officers, judge, police chief, regional director of community mental health services, and the staff attorney. We felt like the conductors of an unwieldy but potentially harmonious orchestra.

In the contract, Joe (who was still under commitment) pledged to participate in the new treatment program, which was designed to help him achieve independence and self-sufficiency. The parents and Herbert signed as well; they agreed to actively support the new program. In keeping with the judge's now-modified ruling that Joe could visit home *only* with explicit parental permission, we assumed that if Joe went home *he had received their permission.* In other words, if he was home, then he had permission to be there *unless they stated otherwise.* If his parents did not want Joe to stay, then they were obligated to tell him to leave, and to call *us* if they needed help; *we* would dispatch the mental health officers. Upon arrival the mental health officers would have the parents clearly state their wishes to Joe to leave and return to his apartment or treatment activities. The mental health officers would then take coercive action *only* if Joe refused to heed his parents' direct request.

The detail and tremendous complexity of Joe's multipage contract will be spared the reader. This document was a central part of the enormous effort we made to develop an "air-tight" plan that would control the community ecosystem. To insure the success of Joe's treatment program, we held weekly meetings with 6–10 team members, family therapists, and staff attorney. In these meetings we exchanged information among the different parts of the program, supported one another, and evaluated our ongoing efforts. We modeled these meetings on Auerswald's (1972) description of the importance of "intersystems linkage" in an ecological approach. We occasionally invited Joe to help plan his schedule, and (we now shudder to think about it) we took turns volunteering our evening and weekend time to keep Joe and Herbert constructively occupied outside their homes.

After "The Great Signing" and Joe's discharge, family therapy sessions were marked by an air of cautious optimism. Mr. and Mrs. Smith weathered the first few days successfully with near disbelief as Joe followed his program and appeared to be motivated. We encouraged the parents' tentative plan to take a vacation alone. Several weeks passed without incident. Mr. and Mrs. Smith became more relaxed about Joe's program and more serious in their intent to take their first vacation without Joe or Herbert—*ever.*

The parents left for a 1-week vacation. Meanwhile, Joe was doing beautifully. While on vacation, Mr. and Mrs. Smith did not call to check on either boy. They returned after a week, seemed to have enjoyed each other, and saw that even Herbert had functioned adequately during their absence.

As part of Joe's separation from his family, we held individual sessions with Joe in order to support his progress in his treatment program. At about this time, both Joe and Herbert became eager for Herbert to move in with Joe (Joe's roommate would soon move out). Joe spent a weekend at home that went well. Matters continued to progress nicely during the following month. By this time Joe had been successfully living in the apartment for almost 2 months.

Toward the end of the 2nd month, Herbert moved in. Initially, this living arrangement seemed to work, but Joe and Herbert soon became embroiled in sibling arguments over space, privacy, possessions, life style, and so on. Herbert, unable to handle his more aggressive brother, would become frightened and call his parents or the community mental health center. Although Herbert provoked many of these altercations (e.g., by taking Joe's belongings), Herbert would blame Joe for the argument, whereupon Joe would blow up and destroy property in the apartment.

The team decided that Herbert's presence in the apartment was creating unnecessary complications; Herbert was sent home. Joe was reprimanded for his unacceptable destruction of property and was told to verbalize his angry feelings, not to destroy things. He was also threatened with loss of access to his car for breaking the rules of the apartment. Herbert was similarly reprimanded and, for 1 week, was banned from visiting Joe and from the day-treatment program as well. We increased the frequency of our sessions with parents in order to deal with Joe's and Herbert's violation of rules. The arguments and destruction of property had reinstated Joe in the role of the "bad boy" in the family.

The Roof Caves In: The Family Calls Other Contractors

A major crisis occurred during a weekend when both therapists were out of town. The effect of the crisis was to derail the parents plans to go away for the weekend. More importantly, it led to a chain of events that spiralled out of our control. Joe drove home with an overnight bag, intending to stay. When Mother returned home from work she found Joe and Herbert arguing in the kitchen. Joe was holding a soda bottle, cocked to throw at Herbert. Joe confronted Mother and demanded to know why Herbert could be crazy and be allowed to stay at home but he (Joe) could not. Mother evaded the question and told Joe to leave. Seeing Joe become still angrier, Mother and Herbert hastily departed the house in order to call the police. Joe proceeded to vent his anger by throwing the soda bottle at the china cabinet, smashing most of mother's heirloom crystal and china, and then through the picture window. When the police arrived they directed Mother to state her wishes to Joe. Joe refused to comply and threatened to kill all of them. The police officers took him away in handcuffs. Mr. and Mrs. Smith decided to file charges: two misdemeanors and a felony.

Father seemed to be panicked by the loss of the male cotherapist's support (he was still out of town). The female cotherapist and Joe's case worker convened a special session to lend support to the parents, especially Father. During this session Mother was half-crazed with anger. The similarity between Mother and Joe was quite striking; both used hyperbole and violent threats to express their anger. On principle the team recommended that the parents press charges so Joe would be held accountable for his behavior. We supported Father's idea of a session with the judge in which the parents would tell Joe how much he owed them (for paying his misdemeanor fines). In order to avert a jail sentence (which would prevent further treatment), we suggested that the parents drop the felony charge. Mother refused. She insisted that Joe be "put away for a long time." On the other hand, however, she was not willing to confront Joe for his responsibility to pay for the damage which he had caused. Father sat silently while she insisted that she had already handled the matter by taking $700 from bonds (held *jointly* with Joe), which she had planned to give to him in the future.

During this special session, much effort was expended to redefine Joe's violence to property as being a "bad temper." It was pointed out that Joe always blew up when he was alone with Mother—never when Father was around. Joe's anger due to feeling rejected by the family and others was discussed. The parents were asked to invite Joe to spend the weekend with them. It was hoped that some supportive contact with his family would help Joe to make it on his own. We wondered how Father kept Joe "so calm." We strongly reinforced Father's positive role and suggested that he might be "the key to solving the problem." Mother, who described Joe as always pestering and upsetting her, was asked to observe what Father did to help her feel safer and less bothered by Joe. Father was labelled "modest" because he could not tell what he did to keep Joe calm. Father clearly perked up from this dose of support. Later that week, we told the caseworker that the parents would drop the felony charge.

In the meantime Joe remained in jail, awaiting trial. The team mood was one of depression, self-critical soul-searching, and relief (because we did not have to worry about Joe's whereabouts while he was in jail). We reevaluated his program and our thinking in family therapy. Joe's treatment program was revised so as to include more specific behavioral goals (e.g., self-control of anger and more adult responsibility for planning his daily activities). In family therapy we gave more attention to the basic triadic pattern of interactions: Joe's fights with Mother served to maintain a safe distance between them by reinvolving the disengaged Mr. Smith with his wife. Mr. Smith is always more attentive to his wife after these episodes and more indignant to Joe (as a way of showing his wife that he supports her). In this way, the mother–Joe overinvolvement helps to bring the parents together. In turn the parents manage to avoid too much closeness by disagreeing about how to handle Joe.

As therapists, we succumbed to obsessional doubting. We questioned the merits of our limit-setting approach and wondered if prescribing the behavioral sequence (i.e., Joe's testing his parents) would work better. Or perhaps we needed to get Father to change work shifts. Or further explore the Smith family's network (we had just discovered that Mother's clergyman was urging her to commit Joe because he was insane). Or could some neighbors help the family?

Meanwhile, the clock of the larger system was ticking away. While Joe was in jail, the forensic psychiatrist examined him and determined that he was dangerous, unable to distinguish right from wrong, and was incompetent to stand trial. He recommended that Joe be committed to a long-term, extended-care facility that provided a structured program with vocational training, recreation, and psychological support (i.e., the state hospital for the criminally insane). He volunteered to testify to that effect in court. We decided that his covert message was, "I'm sick of dealing with this guy in the community; the community mental health center is foolish to think that it can rehabilitate Joe if I never could."

Ever creative, we responded to this devastating plan by capitalizing on Joe's misdemeanor charges. We defined him as an ex-offender rather than a mental patient and succeeded in admitting Joe to the Real Life program for ex-offenders. Real Life provided vocational training, placement, and was guaranteed to treat Joe toughly as an adult. Our treatment team would continue to furnish recreation and psychological support. Although Real Life accepted Joe, its residential facility was full. His old apartment was no longer open to him either. With our resources at an end, we arranged for Joe to stay in a motel while attending Real Life during the day. This stop-gap measure worked temporarily, but Joe went home again several weeks later. His parents filed charges and Joe went back to jail. Father then visited the judge and asked that Joe be given an indefinite commitment to the state hospital. The judge, quite weary of Joe and his family, acceded. Joe was committed to the state hospital for 90 days. While there he maintained contact with his family through letters, phone calls, and a visit home without leave. Joe ran away from the hospital barber shop, hitch-hiked to the vicinity of his home, and called the house. Father and Herbert came and picked him up, claiming that they were "just humoring him." When he arrived home Mother told Joe that he should go back to the hospital. Herbert told Mother that she should go back to bed. Joe stayed, helping himself to breakfast and a cigar. Later that morning, the family secretly summoned detectives to take Joe to jail. He was soon returned to the state hospital.

By this time, Joe's letters home were grandiose, floridly paranoid, and bizarre. We helped his parents write back, "Joe, you are writing crazy things that show you are not ready to come home from the hospital. We will not pick you up if you run away again." We continued to see the parents and Herbert weekly. Herbert was attending a vocational training program.

By December, Joe's 90-day commitment was coming up for review. Joe hired a lawyer who filed a writ of *habeas corpus*, claiming improper trial proceedings and a violation of his rights. This writ was upheld and Joe was released from the state hospital. He went home and, despite his father's misgivings, they let him in. The following day, there was a blow-up between Joe and Herbert. The parents called the police, claiming that Joe had threatened to kill his mother. His parents subsequently dropped the criminal charges and initiated commitment proceedings.

Joe remained in the hospital. His parents insisted that he was the thorn in their side that prevented them from achieving peace. In contrast, they felt good about Herbert. In their view Herbert was making progress and resembled his oldest brother, Bill. Bill, home for the holidays, attended a family therapy session. He appeared to be doing well for himself and was clearly the only brother to achieve a measure of differentiation or, at least, successful separation from the family. We praised the parents for helping and supporting Herbert. We decreased the frequency of therapy sessions to monthly check-ups.

When notified that commitment proceedings were being instituted, Joe invoked his right to a trial by jury. As the trial date approached, Joe remained in the local hospital, consulting with his lawyer. We visited Joe shortly before the trial and were amazed to find him appearing so "appropriate." Gone were the hulking, patient-like mannerisms; gone were the dullness and immaturity. He acted like a normal adult who was managing his affairs with humor and intelligence. We could only surmise that the genuinely paranoid environment that now enveloped him (with family, judge, and forensic psychiatrist seeking to send him away) allowed him to function normally. His context was now overtly paranoid, whereas before his persecution had been denied.

The 5-day jury trial was presided over by the weary and impatient "mental health judge." It pitted two psychiatrists (the forensic psychiatrist and ward psychiatrist who had treated Joe) against the family therapists and the community mental health center's treatment team. A host of other characters in the drama (e.g., the police, Joe, and his parents) were also called to testify. The prosecuting district attorney drew out the lurid details of Joe's past behavior and pointed to Joe's failure to live peacefully in the community. He greatly emphasized the parents' right to protection. In contrast, Joe's attorney described Joe's crazy behavior in terms of his family, emphasizing the interactive nature of the problem. The defense attorney argued that only family and community treatment would adequately address what was happening. In this light, the attorney further argued that it would be countertherapeutic to send Joe to the faraway state hospital. After hours of deliberation the jury decided to commit Joe indefinitely to the state hospital. The parents were angry at us because we testified for the defense and because we had advocated keeping Joe in the community. Nevertheless, another two family therapy sessions were held with Herbert and his parents; they continued to support (mildly) Herbert's efforts outside the home. After a couple of months, Herbert's parents told him that his plans were unrealistic. He promptly dropped out of the day-treatment program. We held one last therapy session with the family. We terminated, leaving Herbert firmly ensconced at home, Joe serving an indefinite commitment to the state hospital, and us feeling demoralized and defeated.

Analysis of Failure

Conceptual-Ethical Errors

Any analysis of "failure" must be founded upon a particular criterion: one's definition of "success." We would argue that this point is not trivial; it immediately brings to light a set of related qustions. What is success in therapy? Who decides what constitutes success? How is success defined if therapist and family (and different family members) have different definitions of success? How much of therapy is conducted in the absence of such considerations?

What we are seeking to bring to light by this series of questions is not the well-taken points (1) that without goals, therapy may drift ineffectively, and (2) that without a clearly defined goal one cannot assess therapeutic effectiveness (i.e., whether or not the goal has been attained). Instead, we are seeking to bring to light that which is *prior* to all such considerations of effective therapy or effective measurement of therapeutic outcomes: values. What *should* the goal of therapy be? What happens if different parties have different desires (i.e., values) about what the therapy should accomplish?

It is always values that determine what will be pursued in therapy. This is true whether what is being treated is cancer, schizophrenia, suicidal behavior, or high blood pressure. It is our values that (may) determine that cancer, schizophrenia, suicidal behavior, or high blood pressure "are" pathological; that is, they are ways of functioning to which we attach a very negative value. In fact, we consider all such functioning to be *mal*functioning (Dell, 1982). Such diagnosable "pathologies," however, are malfunctioning only with regard to what we consider to be valuable: to remain alive, not to suffer pain, to function as a competent person in our society. These are very human goals; they are not, however, intrinsic truths or objective values of the universe.

They are *our* goals, our values. When a woman has cancer, the universe is not malfunctioning; her tumor is not violating the laws of the universe; the atoms in her body are not malfunctioning or behaving strangely. It is for these reasons that medicine has never been able to devise a clear, unambiguous definition of health and pathology (e.g., see DSM-III; American Psychiatric Association, 1980, pp. 5–6). The boundaries of mental and physical "disorders" have no objective existence and cannot be found "out there" in the phenomena of the world; the boundaries of such disorders are defined by the values of human observers. Thus, the diagnostic categories in DSM-III are descriptions of ways of functioning which the majority of us (or, at least, the majority of psychiatrists) *dislike.*

With these considerations in mind, it can now be seen that our knowledge of "pathology" *cannot* tell us what the goal of therapy should be. If it does, we are mystifying ourselves and our clients. A therapist who understands pathology-as-values, must conduct his or her therapy in terms of *values* (rather than a supposedly objective pathology). So, when a client or family desires to pursue different goals than the therapist, the therapist is not able to "know" that their wish to pursue those goals is a further indication of their pathology.

In our therapy with the Smith family, we believed that we knew what pathology was. Our belief in pathology (we want to say that our belief waxed and waned) allowed us to pursue "normal" functioning (i.e., what we and the community valued) in the face of the family's different views (i.e., their values). Too often, we considered their different values (i.e., views) to be just more pathology. Thus, as a result of our "knowledge" of healthy functioning we took it upon ourselves to pursue a variety of ends that the family did not want: A "more functional" spouse subsystem; "normal development" where the boys would "grow up" and leave home. Not surprisingly, that conflict of values bred a myriad of failures in our therapy with the Smiths. The therapy was plagued by an unending series of little sabotages, "forgettings," and "misunderstandings" as the Smiths used their amorphous style of communication to subvert our value-based "therapeutic" initiatives.

Conceptual-Presuppositional Errors

During our work with the Smiths, we espoused an ecological family systems approach. Reflecting on that work, we now see that we were nonecological in many ways. Our comprehension of the ecological approach was probably representative of what Auerswald (1972) describes as the middle stage of shifting cognitive–perceptual awareness *en route* to developing an ecological perspective.

Although we became increasingly aware of the ecological niche in which the Smith family existed, we repeatedly were naive in our thinking about it and were, consequently, the recipient of many rude surprises. Particularly during our initial assessment of the family, we failed to take into account its rich connections to the rest of the ecosystem. We "knew" that the Smith family was a very enmeshed one with an almost impermeable boundary around the family and, therefore, (we thought) very few significant interactions with anyone outside the family. Today, it is common clinical knowledge that chronic patients and their families are strongly connected to the local network of helpers. We had to discover this clinical fact the hard way. For us, the powerful role of psychiatrists in the local hospital and in the medical-legal system became apparent only after they had already impeded our treatment efforts. Similarly, we had not reckoned with the significance of Mother's clergyman, one of the few extrafamilial interactions in which she regularly engaged (i.e., attending church). This minister increasingly served as Mrs. Smith's confidant and as an advocate of sending Joe to the state hospital.

When we finally realized the problems that this larger system of helpers presented to effective treatment, we fell prey to the illusion that we could take control of that system. We attempted to pin down all loose ends and tried to create an air-tight community milieu. We intuitively understood Haley's (1980) claim that successful treatment of schizophrenics necessitated that the family therapist effectively be in charge of all significant treatment decisions (i.e., admission, discharge, medicine, etc.), but failed to achieve this status. We were definitely *not* in charge, despite our best efforts to the contrary. We were never able to exert much leverage on the forensic psychiatrist who remained firmly embedded in his own ideological context; we were never able to convince him to view Joe as "misbehaving and out of control" instead of "mentally ill and dangerous." As a result, we could not stop him from repeatedly transferring Joe from jail to the mental hospital (where Joe would once again not be held responsible for his behavior).

Our work with the Smiths has taught us that Bateson (1972) knew whereof he spoke when he said that belief in the possibility of control is an epistemological error and that the exercise of power in the pursuit of control is a particularly dangerous form of "epistemological lunacy." The therapy of the Smiths often took place in a context of ideology, power, and attempts to control. We were closely aligned with the community mental health center whose mandated task (approximately) was to cure the incurable—those high-risk patients deemed hopeless and chronic by the psychiatric establishment. Our ideological commitment to normalization and to family therapy drove us to prevent hospitalization at almost any cost. As a consequence, we rapidly became embroiled in the encounter between two conflicting models of treatment: community-oriented family therapy and hospital psychiatry. Much like our interaction with the Smith family, these two models proved to be overtly collaborative, but covertly adversarial. They repeatedly struggled about the fate of patients and about how various resources should be allocated (Meyerstein, 1977). Finally, in retrospect, it seems to us that the attempts to exercise power reached toxic levels following the judge's order that Joe could no longer live with his family and that the community mental health center must make him independent. This helped to generate an increasing exercise of power against Joe (i.e., family, mental health officers, court commitments) and increasing reaction on Joe's part (i.e., returning home, destruction of property, threats to kill, and psychotic episodes).

We believe that we were remiss in failing to take sufficient account of the role that we as therapists played in many events. For example, Joe's symptomatic behavior when his parents went out on a "date" cannot be separated from our attempts to foster intimacy between Mr. and Mrs. Smith (which necessarily affected Joe's strong tie to his mother). Perhaps most important, however, is the problem with "pathology." In believing that the atypical behavior of the Smith family was "pathological," we licensed ourselves to pursue therapeutic goals to which the Smiths did not subscribe.

We often failed to be sufficiently systemic in our thinking. Despite being intellectually convinced of the holism of systems, we seemed to frequently become amnesic about holism. Accordingly, we often elected to work with parts of the system (i.e., spouse subsystem, sibling subsystem) without taking into consideration their strong interconnectedness (which would have been quite apparent if we had done a careful analysis of the symptomatic cycle; Hoffman, 1976). In this regard, one of our crucial, irreversible errors was our misunderstanding of the link between the Smith's marital relationship and the symptomatic behavior of Herbert and Joe. We believed that the parents' "faulty" marriage kept the children home to protect the parents from a devastating empty nest syndrome. In believing this, we succumbed to linear causal thinking and the "myth of the contagious bad marriage" (Meyerstein, 1981). Instead of viewing the family in terms of acausal regularities in cross-generational patterns (Haley, 1967), we behaved as if the spouses "problematic" relationship *caused* the boys' problems.

As a result of this conceptualization, our goal was to strengthen the spouse relationship to the point where they would be more comfortable with one another and, then, be able to survive together without need of an identified patient. In short, we sought to free the boys from functioning as the glue in their parents' relationship. We were not so naive as to believe that the boys' symptoms would disappear if we "fixed" their parents' relationship, but it is likely that our focus on the spouse's relationship in therapy gave Mr. and Mrs. Smith the message that they were at fault and must change. This message inevitably begat covert resistance to therapy.

Our intense focusing on the spouse relationship not only did not end Joe's objectionable behavior, but we believe it actually exacerbated the family situation, thereby creating major, new dilemmas. Among these was the explosive issue of who would be Mother's real, emotional husband; it was impossible for two such men to live under the same roof. This situation was made all the more volatile because the family continued to comply with their agreement to participate in family therapy—instead of dropping out of treatment and eliminating our "therapeutic" pressures for change.

When we were not focusing on the spouse relationship, we were focusing on the parental subsystem and thereby succumbed to believing in power and control. We knew that the parents should be in charge in order to clean up the confused generational boundaries in the family. We therefore attempted to strengthen Father's power as the chief executive so that the parents could exercise more might in relation to their sons. In so doing, however, we indulged in the "myth of the fortified split executives" (Meyerstein, 1981). We created a paper tiger; the more forceful and insistent Father became, the more Mother undermined his stands by giving in to Joe. Joe, of course, was physically more powerful than his parents. Despite the combined resources of an entire treatment network (augmented by the police), we achieved only fleeting strength with the parents in relation to their sons. The problem with our approach to the Smiths is that we failed to recognize that effective parenting is not based on strength, but on the alliance between the spouses— their ability to negotiate directly, reach common terms, and to be differentiated in their functioning from that of their children (Meyerstein, 1981).

Errors of Practice

After considerable stewing about various ways to conceptualize how we failed, we have settled on two categories of practical errors in our therapy with the Smiths: (1) Insufficient analysis and assessment of the family's patterns of interactions; and (2) use of power instead of joining or "going with the resistance." As will be seen, both of these errors involve our positioning as therapists in relation to the family.

On our initial diagnostic assessment of the Smith family, we failed to adequately include both ourselves and the ecological network of other helpers. As already discussed, these shortcomings in our analysis of what was happening resulted in many problems during treatment. We also failed to do a careful analysis of the symptomatic crises. For example, we knew that Herbert's voices only occurred when Mother was home, but we did not make a precise inquiry into the family's attempted solution to these incidents (Watzlawick et al., 1974). Similarly, we managed to remain ignorant of the details regarding Joe's eruptions. Our data about this repetitive sequence of behaviors consisted of the following vague account: Joe came home; he and Herbert (or he and Mother) got into an argument; Joe became intimidating and sometimes "violent" (i.e., he destroyed property); Mother called the police. In failing to delineate the exact behaviors constituting these sequences, we undercut our ability to design precise interventions that might interdict these problem cycles.

We also failed to analyze these cycles triadically in terms of patient, Mother, *and* Father. Granted, Father was typically absent when these incidents occurred, but his role both before and after was poorly explored by us. In failing to put the symptomatic cycle in the context of the whole system (Papp, 1980), we were then led to make interventions addressing only a part of the system. We believe that this vitiated many of our efforts.

It now seems clear to us that we repeatedly failed to think systemically or holistically; instead, we were mesmerized by parts of the system that, as a consequence, became the target of a preponderance of our interventions. As already described, we consistently focused our attention on the spouse subsystem. By and large, we refused to be deflected from this course. For example, when Mr. and Mrs. Smith began to "date," Joe became increasingly angry and symptomatic. Faced with the option of shifting the focus of treatment at this point, we elected to continue to concentrate on the spouse relationship. We thought that Joe's misbehavior was an attempt to regain Mother's attention, but decided to pay little attention to his eruptions. By ignoring his reaction, we hoped that it would eventually diminish as he came to accept the new reality of his parents' growing attachment. In fact, however, Joe's upset with these changes did not diminish. Today, we think that we should have been less one-sided in our approach.

Probably our single greatest mistake was our tendency to be too directive and too pushy about treatment goals to which the family did not subscribe. We failed to join with the family around these issues. Said differently, the only customer for these treatment goals was *us*. Armed with our expert "knowledge" of "health" and "pathology," we "knew" that the marital relationship was dysfunctional and "knew" that Joe and Herbert should become independent and move out of the family home. Similarly, we pursued goals and means of treatment that the psychiatric–legal establishment did not share or believe in. We did try to coordinate with the larger network of helpers, but, when faced with glassy stares, we often did not continue dialogue with them. It was much easier to retreat into our determination to "show them" what family therapy could do. In doing that, we set ourselves up for an adversarial interaction, which we lost.

We also had an unfortunate tendency to push for too much change too soon. Looking back, it seems to us that we displayed a remarkable lack of respect for the delicacy required to induce change. We often failed to anticipate the systemic reactions and "resistances" to our forceful interventions. When these things occurred, we were caught by surprise and were often unable to make strategic adjustments. Instead of questioning our premises or strategically disengaging (Stanton, 1981), we succumbed to battling the "resistant" family; we continued to advocate our definition of the problem and continued to press for our goals. Today, it is clear to us who was *really* "resistant."

In our work with the Smiths, we behaved as if success would follow if only we were active enough, directive enough, heroic enough. We became too preoccupied with issuing directives and blinded ourselves to the meaning of the family's responses to our assignments. We very often demanded and received overt compliance, but foundered on their covert defiance to tasks and goals with which the family did not agree. In thinking about it today, we wonder if our tendency to push for too much too soon was not, in fact, creating truly impossible situations. Our insistence that parents "be in charge," the judge's order that Joe be made independent, and the mental health officers' forcing the parents to tell Joe, "I want you to become independent," may have been "be spontaneous" injunctions, which are, by their very nature, impossible to achieve.

Hypothetical Reconstruction toward Success

The Smiths were originally inducted into therapy by a community mental health worker who held different goals (i.e., values, ideology) than did the family. Mr. Smith came to the center seeking assistance in order to hospitalize Herbert. Faced with a therapist whose treatment ideology (i.e., community psychiatry) was opposed to hospitalization, Mr. Smith allowed himself to be convinced to bring in the family for a therapy session. The therapist successfully avoided hospitalization (that time), brought in a cotherapist, enlisted the family in ongoing therapy, and proceeded to try (1) to correct the family structure, (2) to restore the vitality of the marital relationship, and (3) to make Joe and Herbert competent so that they could leave home and start their own independent, adult lives. At no time during the course of treatment did Mr. and Mrs. Smith say that they desired any of these goals. The treatment failed; today we would do it differently.

To begin with, we would not try to convince the family to pursue goals they did not want. Similarly, we would not covertly pursue unannounced or unnegotiated goals of our own. We would, in fact, conduct our encounter with the family from a stance of being willing for the family to remain exactly as it is. We would ask the family what they wanted and, then, help them to achieve it. If they wanted to hospitalize Herbert, we would ask them what they wanted from us. If they wanted him to stop causing trouble and to continue to live at home with them (which we think is probably the most accurate portrayal of Mr. and Mrs. Smith's goals), we would help them to achieve that. If different family members had conflicting goals, we would serially assist each to pursue his or her goal. In the unlikely event that the family wanted to pursue a goal that was unacceptable to us (murder, suicide, child abuse, etc.), we would refuse to help them pursue that goal—but not directly try to *persuade* them to have a different goal. If necessary, however, we would report them to the police.

The goals of treatment therefore, and the criteria of success, are defined by the client. In keeping with this view, we are quite willing for our clients to change their goals during the course of therapy. This, in fact, is a common occurrence when we take the client's goals seriously. By helping clients ferret out what is preventing them from achieving what they want and by pointing out what needs to be done (without arguing that they do it), we often bring clients to the point where they decide to alter their goals. They may decide that they are not willing to do what must be done to achieve their original goal. They may come to see that they really want something different. Or, they may decide to do what it takes to get what they want.

If the Smiths told us that they did not want Joe and Herbert to be belligerent and destructive of property, we would ask them why they put up with it. If they claimed that they did not know what to do or that they were physically unable to control Joe and Herbert, we would ask them what they would do if a stranger came to the house and was belligerent and destructive to their property. If they claimed that they could not call the police on their own sons, then we would tell them that they would have to put up with what Joe and Herbert were doing. If they claimed that Joe and Herbert were sick and did not know what they were doing, we would suggest that they hospitalize them. If they complained that the doctors never did much good and that Joe and Herbert always became belligerent and destructive after they came home, we would ask why they let Joe and Herbert live with them since they were often belligerent and destructive. If they said that they could not throw their sons out, we would ask, "Why not?" If they finally insisted that they would not tell their sons to leave, then we would ask if they were willing to learn to accept belligerence and destruction of property. And so on.

By our willingness to accept the client's evolving position, we would never be faced with a so-called "resistant" client. There can only be "resistance" when the therapist thinks that the client somehow ought to be behaving differently than he or she is currently behaving. Our willingness to accept the client's position profoundly alters the therapeutic landscape. Instead of a field of sick patients, we find clients with interesting problems. These problems are typically maintained by the client's use of inadequate solutions (Watzlawick et al., 1974) which, in turn, are based upon unquestioned (and counterproductive) presuppositions (Shaw, 1982). Thus, in working with clients, we are quite willing to accept their goals, but routinely call into question the presuppositions that "cause" the client to continue to use ineffective solutions or that prevent him or her from employing other solutions that would be effective.

In many respects this is a difficult approach to carry out because we so easily slip back into "knowing" that the family's behavior is "pathological." Whenever we make this slip, we moved toward goals that are ours rather than the family's. In this moment the therapeutic endeavor goes awry. This is a recurring point of choice in therapy. Will we draw upon our armamentarium of techniques, strategies, and so-called paradoxes in order to move the family toward *our* goal (i.e., that which we consider to be "healthy")? Or, will we detach ourselves from our conception of "the healthy" and recommit ourselves to an unequivocal effort to help the client pursue his or her stated goal? We believe that effective therapy follows from consistently choosing the latter.

Although we place our commitment to the client's values at the center of the therapy, we are not espousing an antitechnique philosophy. Many techniques can be used in the service of helping the client to achieve his or her stated goal. We would not, however, use techniques that are designed to "cause" the client to pursue our goals or that are designed to "cause" the patient to see that his or her approach to the problem will not work. Thus, for example, we would not use "symptom prescription" or "going with the resistance" as a means of achieving goals or standards of "health" that *we* have chosen. Instead, if we slipped into pushing the family toward our own goal, we would recommit ourselves to unequivocally supporting the family in the pursuit of their own goal—even when (perhaps, especially when) they are clearly determined to continue a particular course of action that is not working. This may look like "symptom prescription," but our attitude is not one of manipulation or winning a contest. It is our belief that "symptom prescription" is most effective when used by therapists who have a deep respect for the family, the family's values, and the family members' need to behave as they are doing.

Today, we have rather different thoughts about the Smith family than when we "treated" them. Had we approached the Smith family in terms of our current thinking, there is an excellent chance that they would never have entered family therapy in the first place. Father, after all, was only seeking to hospitalize Herbert. If the family did enlist in family therapy, the next most likely outcome is that we would have helped restore the precrisis equilibrium and terminated—in accordance with the family's wishes. Had the family expressed interest in additional work beyond reequilibration, then—and only then—would we have had the opportunity to help the family work more effectively with their "boys." Finally, no matter which of these avenues the family chose to pursue, we doubt that the therapy would have culminated as it did—in the scapegoating and extrusion of Joe from his family and from the community.

REFERENCES

American Psychiatric Association. *Diagnostic and statistical manual of mental disorders* (3rd ed.). Washington, D.C.: Author, 1980.

Auerswald, E. H. Interdisciplinary versus ecological approach. *Family Process*, 1968, *77*, 202–215.

Auerswald, E. H. Families, change, and the ecological perspective. In A. Ferber, M. Mendelsohn, & A. Napier (Eds.), *The book of family therapy.* New York: Jason Aronson, 1972.

Bateson, G. *Steps to an ecology of mind.* New York: Ballantine, 1972.

Dell, P. F. *Pathology: The original sin.* Paper presented at the First International Conference on Epistemology, Psychotherapy, and Psychopathology, Houston, Texas, September 1982.

Haley, J. Towards a theory of pathological systems. In G. Zuk & I. Boszormenyi-Nagy (Eds.), *Family therapy and disturbed families.* Palo Alto: Science & Behavior Books, 1967.

Haley, J. *Uncommon therapy.* New York: Norton, 1973.

Haley, J. *Leaving home: The therapy of disturbed young people.* New York: McGraw-Hill, 1980.

Hoffman, L. Breaking the homeostatic cycle. In P. J. Guerin (Ed.), *Family therapy: Theory and practice.* New York: Gardner, 1976.

Hoffman, L., & Long, L. A systems dilemma. *Family Process,* 1969, *8,* 211–234.

Langsley, D. G., & Kaplan, J. D. *The treatment of families in crisis.* New York: Grune & Stratton, 1968.

MacGregor, R., Ritchie, A. M., Serrano, A., Schuster, F. P., Jr., McDonald, E. C., & Goolishian, H. A. *Multiple impact therapy with families.* New York: McGraw-Hill, 1964.

Meyerstein, I. Family therapy training for paraprofessionals in a community mental health center. *Family Process,* 1977, *16,* 477–493.

Meyerstein, I. Unlearning myths about family therapy. *International Journal of Family Psychiatry,* 1981, *2,* 203–219.

Minuchin, S., Family therapy: Theory or technique? In J. Masserman (Ed.), *Science and psychoanalysis* (Vol. 14). New York: Grune & Stratton, 1969.

Minuchin, S. *Families and family therapy.* Cambridge, Mass.: Harvard University Press, 1974.

Minuchin, S., Montalvo, B., Guerney, B. G., Jr., Rosman, B. L., & Schumer, F. *Families of the slums: An exploration of their structure and treatment.* New York: Basic Books, 1967.

Papp, P. The Greek chorus and other techniques of family therapy. *Family Process,* 1980, *19,* 45–47.

Shaw, R. *Principles of contextual therapy.* Workshop conducted in Boston, Massachusetts, October 1982.

Stanton, M. D. An integrated structural/strategic approach to family therapy. *Journal of Marital and Family Therapy,* 1981, *7,* 427–439.

Watzlawick, P., Weakland, J., & Fisch, R. *Change: Principles of problem formation and problem resolution.* New York: Norton, 1974.

Zwerling, I. Family therapy and community psychiatry. In M. Andolfi & I. Zwerling (Eds.), *Dimensions of family therapy.* New York: Guilford, 1980.

11

We Were Somebody's Failure

ANONYMOUS

With SANDRA B. COLEMAN

Our Background

I remember the day I was to find out if what I suspected was, in fact, a reality. It was rainy, bleak, and miserable. My nervousness mounted with each passing hour, and I was even a bit amazed as I became aware of my extreme anxiety when I anticipated confirmation that very day that I was pregnant for the third time.

I tried to convince Steve (my husband of nearly 11 years) to drive me to my gynecologist, but he was in no mood to be bothered with doctors. He had just returned from running a series of errands accompanied by our two rather rambunctious daughters (aged 7 and 9 years), and he considered that enough of an imposition. Although he dearly loved the girls, he didn't particularly embrace the art of parenting, particularly when they were as cantankerous as they were that day. Steve was a firm believer in the adage that children should be seen and not heard, and he was displeased that I had somehow been unable to imbue the kids with as much of that as he would like. Because of my unusual amount of tension, I countered his refusal to drive me with one of my rare but massive bursts of rage. Our argument ended when Steve conceded to at least pick me up at the conclusion of my appointment.

When I learned that I was most assuredly pregnant, I registered no surprise. In the months that followed, I tried to put aside the fears and uncomfortable feelings that kept flashing through my mind. I had two healthy, beautiful daughters; why shouldn't I be lucky enough to have another? Perhaps this time Steve would even get his son. I could not fathom my almost constant worry. Surely there was no reason for the panic I felt.

Actually, the pregnancy turned out to be an easy one. Despite my emotional distress, my physical health was good and I gradually became pleased with the idea that we would have another baby in the house. As I approached the end of my 9th month I became a bit more relaxed, but the birth process quickly reversed my momentary feeling of ease. I began labor at 6 A.M. and arrived at the hospital at 8 A.M. expecting a quick and uncomplicated delivery. (My other deliveries were uneventful, and I really didn't know why I'd have trouble now.) My labor was prolonged, however, and my obstetrician was moody and unpleasant. He seemed unusually curt and insensitive to my struggle. At one point after checking my progress, he obnoxiously said to the labor room nurse, "just throw a sheet over her if she yells," and he rapidly left. Later he broke my water and returned to his office. He was not there when the baby started to arrive, and I readily accepted the relief of gas offered by the nurse, although I heard her say, "I never saw anyone drink that down like that!" This statement echoed back to me many times in the months to follow, bringing with it guilt and remorse.

Tina was a lovely baby girl; she was quiet and appeared to be perfectly fine at birth and during her first 2 months. My previous anguish rapidly disappeared, and I suspected no problems until I noticed that she continually held her right hand in a tight fist. From 3 months of age on, Tina and I spent countless hours among a bevy of pediatricians, neurologists, and superspecialists who ultimately diagnosed Tina as having right hemiparesis. The cause—unknown. My obsessive investigations and soul-searching were fruitless. Of course, a birth injury was suspected but no viable evidence was ever produced.

Physical therapy began during Tina's 1st year, although it was always pretty clear that she would never have the normal use of the one side of her body. At 18 months she had a grand mal seizure, the first of many, many more to follow. By the time Tina was 6 years of age, she was diagnosed as having borderline intelligence, which translated meant that she was retarded but educable.

Although we were not a perfect family before the trauma of adding a special child, this additional stress was profoundly felt by all. I had always wanted and tried to involve Steve in spending more time with the children and me. It appeared that as Tina's problems pyramided during her early years, so did the demands of Steve's work. His usual 12-hour, 6-day-a-week preoccupation with work rapidly became a 7-day phenomenon. When he had a few rare hours off, he wanted time to himself. Because I was a full-time mother, he delegated all the responsibility of the three children to me, especially when it came to Tina. He refused to acknowledge her problems and because he was rarely around her, his denial seemed to work. His schedule appeared to collaborate with his need to avoid facing his handicapped child, and it was I who spent most of the torturous time rushing Tina by ambulance to the local hospital during her many status epilepticus seizures, which are grand mal convulsions, usually persisting without periods of consciousness for 5-6 hours. They came suddenly without warning, and I coped with each one with fear and aloneness. Although I desperately needed Steve's help during these painful experiences, he just was never around.

After several years I knew that we needed some kind of help beyond that provided by the rehabilitation specialists and physical therapists. Because our middle daughter, Valerie, was causing a great deal of trouble by her almost constant arguing, screaming, and noncompliant behavior, I suggested to Steve that we consult a child psychiatrist. Steve supported this idea but at the time of our appointment was unable to leave work, and I alone accompanied Valerie. Dr. Thomas recognized the problems Valerie was having as being highly related to larger, more pervasive family problems. He recommended that the next appointment be made at a time when Steve could be present; despite my attempts to accommodate to Steve's schedule, at the last moment he never arrived.

Dr. Thomas saw Valerie for approximately 6 months. I also saw Dr. Thomas and when Valerie's visits seemed less necessary I continued alone. Despite my repeated attempts to comply with Dr. Thomas' many requests to see Steve, he never came.

Tina's yearly evaluations and physical therapy treatments became a part of our lives, and we gradually adapted to her special medical, physical, and psychological needs. We also adapted to her outbursts, her violent temper tantrums, her impulsivity, and her ever-present coyness and manipulative yet innocent cleverness. We adapted to her demandingness, her egocentrism, and her helplessness. Steve worked ambitiously to support her many expenses, and I stayed home caring for her and always preparing for those overwhelming seizures. I also fought for her educational rights, formed parent interest groups, and forced state legislature to provide for such children in more adequate ways. I even became a classroom assistant in the special education program. Steve was pleased with my obsession with Tina's "cause," and he rarely intervened except when he didn't care for my discipline of the girls. Generally the only time he got directly involved with the family at all was during the times when Tina was having a tantrum and I was "not handling it right."

Dr. Thomas said that the whole family needed therapy. Although Valerie was functioning better, our eldest daughter, Susan, was becoming increasingly more sullen and withdrawn. She was the only one other than me who could handle Tina, and she was so skilled at understanding and coping with Tina's many moods that I hadn't realized what effect this had on her own development. She was now almost a teenager and I hadn't even noticed that she "hung around the house" more than any of the other kids her age. Beyond all the problems with the kids, Steve and I had managed to put up with our marriage, each of us feeling misunderstood by the other and each of us angry yet committed to maintaining the best possible kind of life under the circumstances.

During the months and years to come, we considered family therapy several times, but each attempt was somehow aborted. Although it was easy for me to blame Steve for resisting help, I knew that I couldn't place all the responsibility on him. I think we were all afraid of what we might find if we sat down together in the presence of a trained therapist.

Our Therapy Experience

Introduction

Each year Tina had a complete physical examination and evaluation. This was one annual event that usually got Steve's attention. It seemed that during the intervening years after Tina's problems were initially diagnosed, the rehabilitation center had become more and more family-oriented. At first the staff focused almost exclusively on Tina, requesting only specific answers from us about medical issues. Occasionally, behavioral management was discussed with the social worker, but the only interactions we ever had with the staff psychologist were after his evaluations, which were done every 2–5 years.

As Tina approached preadolescence, however, our visits changed. The psychologist and social worker often talked with us together and the concerns were obviously more family-focused. Questions regarding Tina's effect on each one of us became routine. Gradually I gained hope that this might provide the opportunity I had been waiting for—a perfect excuse to get everyone in therapy together; maybe someone would see that there were stresses beyond those associated with Tina. Because I was enormously afraid of Steve's anger, it was difficult for me to come out and openly declare that there were problems. Unfortunately I never learned to speak up to my husband, as I desperately feared his temper. When he hollered and stormed out of the house screaming at either the kids or at me, I retreated, completely unable to handle the situation. I was a very private person, and coupled with this fear of him I knew I could never push for help without someone else's urging.

At Tina's 12th-year assessment, the opportunity came. The chief pediatrician, who had been one of the first rehab doctors to ever examine Tina told us directly what we were facing with our multihandicapped daughter who was now almost a teenager. Dr. Avondale was sensitive but firm. She did not elaborate or pontificate but confronted Steve and me with the "team's observations and recommendations." She told us, "You and your entire family have been through years of hell trying to cope with the many severe problems associated with raising an epileptic, cerebral-palsied, retarded child. You've done an admirable job, but you can't do it all alone. The next several years are going to be extraordinarily rough and you must have professional assistance. The team feels that it is imperative that you have a consultation with our affiliates at the Mainstream Family Therapy Center." Dr. Avondale briefly elaborated on the many fine contributions of the Center emphasizing their expertise in working with families. "They are so widely known," Dr. Avondale stated, "that professionals from all over the world are honored to be accepted in their family therapy training programs." Steve and I agreed to gather the girls together and to begin family therapy at the appointed time the following week.

Our Therapy Session

It was questionable as to which one of us was the most nervous when we arrived at the Center. We entered a freshly painted room with a circle of matching chairs carefully centered in front of a draped wall and a border of ogling cameras. As if by magic, when we arrived the drapes mysteriously leaped aside revealing a large bright mirror. A brief introduction made by a "Dr. Somebody or Other" was rapidly followed by a request for "permission to tape your session." My heart immediately sank. I knew myself and I knew how hard it was for me to speak up. To have to do this before these cameras was a real downer. It seems like we all rather timidly said, "Oh, sure, that's fine," but none of us meant it.

When we talk now about our reaction to these first moments at Mainstream, even some 8 years later, Steve comments that as he said, "Okay," to the request for filming, "I pulled up my armour, locked it, and tossed away the key." Valerie too remembers that, "I said, 'sure just let me find the first corner to hide in so no one can see me.'" Susan recalls little about this except that she was "awfully nervous, and I thought that whatever happened there was going to be big trouble."

Dr. Somebody encouraged us to "have a seat, wherever you feel comfortable." Immediately I realized that they wanted to see where we would sit, but before I could think through how I thought we should place ourselves, Tina sat down and Steve sat slightly behind her. I joined them by sitting on Tina's other side and Susan and Valerie took seats next to me. The doctor sat across from us, separated by a coffee table with an ashtray and a telephone. I remember thinking that I was glad that they had a phone in the room because if Tina had a seizure we could summon help. It's interesting now to speculate on why I would find that reassuring or necessary in view of the fact that we had a doctor right there in the room with us.

Dr. Somebody began the session by asking our names, where we lived, what we did, and if we got lost on the way to the Mainstream Center. I thought he was nervous and was just chatting away. Of course we didn't get lost; if we had we wouldn't have been 30 minutes early!

After 10 or 15 minutes of what seemed like idle conversation, the phone rang. Dr. Somebody picked it up, listened, hung up, and then asked if any member of the family would like to begin. Before anyone could speak Tina leaned back and kissed Steve on his cheek. He responded by moving closer, reaching out and hugging her. Dr. Somebody looked at me and remarked "They really love each other, don't they?" Before I could think of what to say he turned to Steve and said, "You two really have a close relationship. I'm just wondering what you do when Tina does something that is not so lovable. How do you handle disciplining her?" Before Steve could answer, he asked, "Is that different from how you discipline your older daughters?" Steve responded by stating, "Oh, I always sit down and talk to them about whatever the situation may be. We usually just have a nice discussion together."

At this point Susan began to giggle nervously. Dr. Somebody asked, "What is so funny?" Susan said, "Oh, I'm just thinking about something that happened at school." How could she let out what she was really thinking? As her father so calmly went on about level-headed talks with "his girls," Susan saw visions of hamburgers flying through the air as the almost weekly volcanoes erupted at the family dinner table. She saw her father charging like a bull out the front door, her mother sobbing, and her sisters running up to their bedroom retreats. All this flashed in front of her and she anxiously fought every urge to yell, "He's lying . . . make him tell you what he really does, please . . . don't let us get away with this 'Oh, we sit down and talk routine!' Please help our family to get things straight; we need help to learn to work better together." But Dr. Somebody accepted Susan's explanation about her laughter and didn't push her for any further information.

Dr. Somebody then turned to me and asked how I dealt with disciplining the girls and if it was different for each one. At this, I merely said that since Susan was away at college and Valerie was a Senior in High School, this really wasn't much of an issue for me anymore. I did say that I found Tina the most difficult to handle, particularly when I had to set limits. He asked if Steve helped me with this, if he supported my denial of her requests. Before I could answer, the phone rang and he left the room.

When Dr. Somebody returned he asked Tina if she wanted to say anything about anyone in her family. Tina talked for several minutes about how strict we were with her and how she felt her older sisters were too bossy. Steve joined in and said he felt that the older girls were very involved in "mothering" her and that they always seemed to feel the need to help me handle her. This took away from the original question about Steve's ability to support me in disciplining Tina. It seems like the major portion of the time remaining in the session focused on this issue of Susan's and Valerie's roles in taking care of their sister.

Several times Dr. Somebody answered the phone and left the room. Each time he left I kept thinking about the fact that there was obviously someone calling him out to tell him something. Because he looked terribly young, I assumed that whoever was dialing in was also making comments about what was happening. I knew that the phone caller must be watching either on a TV screen or through the mirror. Each time our therapist left, I anticipated that something special would happen when he came back. I expected some terrific maneuver, but it never happened. I even hoped his mysterious supervisor or boss would come in and help. In fact, nothing ever happened. The session continued pretty much as it had begun. Dr. Somebody would make a comment about something. One of us would give a monosyllabic response; Dr. Somebody would generally say, "Yeah," or "Uh-huh"; the phone would ring; he would leave the room only to return and make a comment; and the whole thing would revolve again without anything else ever taking place. I kept waiting for something dramatic but it never came. In fact, the most remarkable thing was that I said so little and Valerie never said anything. Most of the dialogue was really between Steve and Tina who continually displayed a father–daughter love affair, the likes of which I'd never ever seen before nor was I to ever witness again.

After what appeared to be the 10th or 11th phone call, Dr. Somebody left a final time and somewhat abruptly returned. He walked over to Steve held out his hand, and said, "You certainly have a fine family and, well (somewhat hesitantly) you seem to handle things very well. Thank you so much for coming." He did not mention anything about us ever returning and that was the end of our experience at the Mainstream Family Therapy Center.

Our Analysis of the Therapy Experience

I think the whole family was stunned by our experience at Mainstream. I don't believe that any one of us could understand what happened that day. I know that my first feeling was one of disappointment. We were a family struggling in our own way to handle the constant tensions under which we lived. Our oldest daughter, Susan, was always trying to ease these tensions and was constantly in the middle trying to maintain her identity and not get lost in the shuffle of all the attention bestowed on her youngest sister. She kept seeing her parents struggle to be husband and wife at the same time that they needed to be parents and cope with everyone's hurt. One of us kept trying to run away and the other was consumed with over-involvement. We needed balance and we wanted an opening to discuss all the pain. We needed so badly to find alternative ways of working together, rather than fighting with and against each other. We needed a therapist to expose us to ourselves. This is what I hoped and expected would happen at Mainstream. I know that I was too afraid to expose it. So were all the others. But why did the therapist let us get away with the same kind of escape that we used on our own? I truly expected that a professional would realize that we were there for a serious problem and that if people show up in therapy it is *not* because all is well and they can handle things okay. I was so disappointed in the questions that were asked and the easy acceptance of what seemed to be "off-the-wall answers." I hoped that when we began to talk about discipline that we would now find better ways to handle the children as well as the communication among all of us. Certainly we needed help with Tina and I felt that this was an opportunity to find an outlet for our troubles. Family therapy was an avenue of hope for handling and dealing with things more effectively, and we all flubbed it, including the therapist. If only he had questioned more with each person and had tried to dig deeper into the responses instead of so easily accepting their casual, matter-of-fact answers. He really never pushed or led the way to an opening. All the tears, anger, and frustration were right there, right on the very flip side of each answer. Every emotion could have been so easily scratched open but we needed a little bit of help. Perhaps we needed someone to say, "It's okay to hurt. Families with your kind of problem always feel sad and angry and afraid." It felt to me that he expected us to be terrific and fine and he really didn't want to probe for anything other than that.

I kept wondering why he didn't question all the ridiculous giggles or nods or glib "Yeahs" and "Nos." When Steve and Tina got into their "passion," the therapist started to move in a positive direction. Certainly he had to know that there was a connection between Susan's well-timed giggles and their display of affection. He was on target when he questioned the way that Steve disciplined the girls and whether he supported me when I needed help. Why then did he stop so suddenly and turn the whole thing over to the kids? We were the parents and we needed to work with each other. If only he had tried harder.

Susan reflected later that she wanted him to probe:

I wanted him to ask me to say things so I couldn't be blamed. I was feeling like I might explode with all kinds of information if he just tactfully opened Pandora's box. When Daddy was doing all that hugging and kissing with Tina I was angry and thought she'd be in big trouble. Here I was laughing and thinking the therapist would have to know how crazy it was for me to laugh but he just said "Uh-huh." So I knew right then that I couldn't trust him. He was not a good enough leader to pick up on things, which meant that he wouldn't be able to handle what came out. I felt somehow safe that I didn't have to go through what I had expected, but I was tremendously let down knowing now that nothing could change. The experience was like being held hostage and saying everything is fine. It was like being caught in a big fight but not letting anything out so I was still in jail. In some ways this felt like a safe enough environment for these things to come out yet it obviously was not going to happen. I was upset because I had thought that he would know what I was thinking. Such forced laughter—and the guy says "Oh" . . . and walks away. I didn't care if anyone did see it all because I wanted everyone in the family to know how I saw things. I just needed someone to help me feel that there was a safe place to let it out. And I stayed afraid because I needed the therapist to make me say it. I just didn't feel strong enough to do it—not of my own free will!

Valerie said that she went into the session thinking that maybe she would hide for awhile until things really got going. Then, when she learned about the taping she said, "Well, I guess I'll just keep hiding. Nobody's going to look at my face and see me somewhere at some later date. I guess there are students observing us like monkeys. Well, they'll get nothing from me in this session. I'll be as unnoticeable as possible and will make no moves or say anything to draw attention while they're all watching and taping. Not one or a million people will ever see me open up to a whole bunch of strangers."

I'm not sure how Steve felt after that session. Initially I thought that he was probably relieved. Recently I asked him if he could reach back in his memory and share any of his impressions or feelings regarding the session at Mainstream. He knew that I was contributing this chapter to a volume on failure in family therapy, and he had been somewhat interested in what I was going to say. Thus, it was evidently something he had begun to think about again. He showed no objection to my working on this; of course he knew that it would be an anonymous authorship, and yet ordinarily he might still have raised some doubt about the possibility that our family life would be in some way exposed. From his response to my writing this chapter, I almost had the feeling that he supposed it was a good way for me to get rid of some negative connections that I might still have with the "Mainstream incident," as we called it.

After several days of silence, he offered this personal memory. "They asked if I minded if they taped the session and I said, 'No, that's fine!' as I pulled on my armour and pulled down my football helmet. Susan looked at me and said with silent eyes, 'Who's that man sitting over there?' I said, 'It's me, it's your father, this benevolent man who is sitting here . . . it's me."

Steve said that he was confused, and one of his greatest frustrations was that we had received such a buildup about the Center's fine reputation. He expected an excellent therapist, a "man at the top." He knew how much we all hurt and he felt choked by his own anguish. "When Tina reached out to me, I needed her love even more that moment than she ever could have needed mine. I thought someone would ask 'which of you is protecting the other?' But none of this happened and no one ever discovered our internal distress. Yes, I'm sorry it didn't work then . . . so much might have been better."

Tina never commented at all. When I asked her if she remembered going to Mainstream she just shrugged and murmured something about all doctors and hospitals being "a big, rotten pain."

Tina has been a difficult experience to write about. I knew that it wouldn't be easy. I think that Steve was right—I needed to let go of that negative connection. So many times over the years I thought about the terrible failure we had with each other in our very first attempt to enter therapy as a family. I, like Steve expected a supertherapist. Instead we obviously were greeted by a trainee with little experience or knowledge. The telephone conversations between him and his superiors added nothing to the session; it just left us feeling that he was as incompetent at figuring out what to do as we were. When he walked out each time, we felt that we were under constant scrutiny, and no one would even talk to each other. We felt so unsafe. The secure environment that we each were looking for never emerged, and so our problems, like our lives, remained unchanged by the Mainstream encounter.

I often wonder how our lives would have differed had that session taken another course. I also wondered why the therapist never asked us to return. Perhaps a second session would have been different. Why didn't he perhaps consider speaking to us alone or in smaller groups for a few minutes just to break the ice? No one could really be as in control as we sounded. Why didn't he or his supervisor realize that? Why weren't they more patient about finding our pain? I think we all felt such a tremendous let down that things could have happened but didn't. Instead of a door opening, we were again at *status quo* with just regrets and even more self-recriminations. We couldn't help but feel that Mainstream could not understand or cope with us and our inadequacies were exaggerated as a consequence of that single session. Although we probably would have liked to blame the therapist and the Center, we really could not. After all, they were the experts and we were the failure.

Personal Note

It is important to let the reader know that I can share what happened to us at Mainstream because of the current experience we are all having in family therapy. Shortly before I learned about this book, Steve and I agreed that we had to do something about our relationship. This was extremely critical at this time because Tina had graduated from high school and was having a great deal of difficulty finding a place for herself in society. She was still living at home, dependent on us for the major portion of her existence. Steve and I were also still dependent on her role between us. With the exception of Susan and Valerie who left home and are independently doing their thing, these dependencies are much the same as they were back in 1975, when we were seen at Mainstream. We felt very frightened about trying again, but this time we were reassured that the therapist had many years of private practice experience, and was particularly skilled in treating families with special children. This is so. Our present family therapist is sensitive and caring. She understands what we have been living with and what we need to do for ourselves to make the necessary changes. We feel mutually pleased about her relationship with our family and we are all growing, even though the changes cause us to stretch and moan and at times we all really hurt. I think the difference is that we feel connected to her, which helps us to feel connected to each other in a more mature way. Most important we no longer feel like we are a failure of a family or a family therapy failure.

12

Circumlocution and Nonresolution

FLORENCE W. KASLOW

Introduction

The roots and branches of my professional genogram are varied and diverse. In the pursuit of knowledge and truth, I have read and studied with most of the leading theoreticians or their key disciples, trying to understand and extract the essence of each theory. I have gained respect for all—coming to believe each has its own validity, explanatory power, and intervention efficacy with certain kinds of families, problems, and situational constraints. My initial grounding was psychoanalytic theory. From this, I retain my belief that even while utilizing a family systems approach that assesses and attempts to modify dysfunctional communications, conflictual interactions, unclear or inappropriate boundaries, and other structures within the unit, I also am concerned about the intrapsychic dynamics of each member as an individual. Thus my therapy reflects operating at both the intrapsychic and interpersonal levels of functioning, seeking, when deemed necessary, to bring about the return of relevant unconscious repressed material as well as to uncover salient family secrets and to understand family myths, traditions, and expectations.

Theoretical Frame of Reference

I believe that the three timeframes of past, present, and future are all significant, and so I do a brief history in the initial session—particularly in relation to the presenting problems and why therapy is being sought at this moment in time. If I think more in-depth historical material is essential for a sufficient assessment upon which to predicate interventions, I will obtain this by doing an extensive genogram with the family (Guerin & Fogarty, 1972), utilizing their family photographs to prod their memories and enable reminiscences to occur (Kaslow & Friedman, 1977), and perhaps recording the data on a chronological chart (Duhl, 1981). Material on the present circumstances and how the family wishes to change them will be obtained through listening

Florence W. Kaslow. Private practice, West Palm Beach, Florida; Florida Couples and Family Institute, West Palm Beach, Florida; Department of Psychiatry, Duke University Medical School, Durham, North Carolina.

to family communications and observing nonverbal behavior such as sculpting, play, and drawings. Any or all of these data-gathering and intervention strategies are utilized when deemed appropriate in order to enrich the flow of the therapy process. Concern for the future is evidenced in terms of ascertaining how much the family desires to change themselves and the situation and in terms of linking this to goal setting. My approach is encapsulated in my dialectic integrative model, which is described in prior writings (Kaslow, 1980, 1981a, 1981b) and exemplified in graphic form in Figure 12-1 in terms of the major theoretical schools from which it draws.

Background

It was a dreary wintry day in the Northeast when the referral call came. Dr. X was calling from an inpatient unit that treats substance abusers. Mitzi, a 21-year-old woman, had been in residential treatment at the unit for 4 weeks and was to be discharged at the end of 6 weeks. The director of the facility supported a family systems approach to understanding substance abusers and often involved significant family members in treatment as copatients. In this case Mitzi's parents had attended sessions intermittently, but had not yet become inpatients. Dr. X did not want to discharge Mitzi until she and her family had begun outpatient family therapy and he was reasonably certain a beginning therapeutic alliance had been established. He described them as a physically handsome, wealthy family who were used to "calling the shots" and who were not easy to deal with nor very responsive to therapy. All had denied the existence of Mitzi's problem for several years; they still avoided recognizing the severity of her addiction and were unwilling to have her

FIG. 12-1. Major family therapy theories. (*Note*: "Multimodal" is the term utilized by Lazarus, 1981, for his integrative approach.)

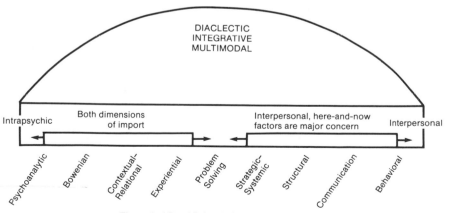

Theoretical Focal Points in Assessment and Treatment

remain in the hospital an additional 2 weeks as recommended by staff. She had been a resistant patient, and the staff were not optimistic that her recently detoxified state would be maintained. The family had reluctantly agreed to have Mitzi return one evening a week to the hospital for a former patients' two hour group meeting. This agreement followed their refusal to permit her to live in a halfway house for several months postdischarge. Her parents believed she should reside with them while finishing her recuperation and continued to indicate they thought too much fuss was being made about a little drinking and drug taking.

Since this unit periodically referred patients to me, they knew I would try to solidify the gains already made and would support Mitzi's attendance at evening group therapy. They also thought my style of family therapy could incorporate enough ego-supportive appreciation of the family's strengths and accomplishments, enough gentle identification with Mitzi and a younger brother (staff suspected him of also being an addict), and enough confrontation and mirroring to eventually demolish the family's superciliousness and heavy defensive armor. And so the challenge was undertaken.

For the first session, five of the six members of the Grande family arrived. They were, indeed, strikingly attractive; they were an on-stage "show biz" family through and through. Dad stopped at the mirror in the waiting room to comb his hair before coming into my office; his greeting of "Hi! I've been *so* eager to meet you!" would have been more appropriate at a business gathering or social event where he was the host. He was determined to establish himself quickly as the incomparable male lead, the indisputable family patriarch, whose ambition had been to sire a "family dynasty" along with his beautiful wife, and whose plans had been temporarily derailed. At 56 years of age, he was erect and dapper.

Mrs. Grande was tall, trim, and elegantly groomed—a striking 52-year-old woman. She had abandoned her promising fashion design career in favor of becoming the ideal wife, lover, and mother. She shared her husband's dream of amassing a fortune through his own tenacious efforts and had willingly and happily undertaken all of the social functions incumbent upon the spouse of an aspiring corporate executive in the fast-paced world of high finance. She had taught the four children all of the social amenities required for gracious living, made sure they had appropriate designer-clothes wardrobes for every occasion, had supervised their education in the best available private schools, nurtured the considerable artistic and theatrical talents of her two beautiful daughters, and turned over much of the formative instruction of their two sons to her husband. After all, the sons were to be socialized to enter the financial empire Mr. Grande was building and therefore were thought to require a strong guiding influence from their father. She was well compensated materialistically for her excellent playing of her role in the unfolding team drama and, ostensibly, Mr. Grande had been an appreciative and adoring husband.

In accordance with the script, the oldest son, Craig, had finished college and joined the large brokerage firm of which his father was then president. Although Craig appeared to be of above-average intelligence, neither in the first nor in subsequent interviews did he seem to possess the high-voltage energy or creative brilliance that it takes to become a branch manager earning $100,000/year at age 28 without special connections. Yet he had zoomed quickly upward—following Dad's instructions and being careful not to overtly rebel or "make waves." Dark complexioned, expensively tailored, and attractive, Craig was still single. He had his own bachelor quarters in a luxury center-city condominium. He appeared appropriately concerned about his two younger siblings, willing to be counted on in contributing to their recovery, and possibly to be playing a go-between and buffer role between the senior and junior adult subsystems in the family.

Next in line in terms of ordinal position was Thea, the absent member during the initial session. Thea was a professional dancer and choreographer who had been residing in New York for the previous 3 years. Although she had had some chorus line roles in Broadway productions, she was not rising as quickly as a dancer must if she is to really "make it big" while she is in prime, fit condition. She could not make the session because she was involved in tryouts for a show then being cast. She was described as lovely to look at with a fine ballerina's figure, talented, somewhat quiet and even a little shy, and quite disappointed at not being selected for better lead roles. It sounded like a replay of *A Chorus Line* and *Dancin'* scenarios.

Mitzi was the identified patient. With her eyes downcast and covered by unruly hair that drooped carelessly, shoulders sagging and clad untidily in jeans and a cotton blouse, it was hard to imagine that she had already been a successful starlet. The family reported that she had begun acting early and had lived in New York or California off and on since she was 15 years old. She had had lead roles in several major television and film dramas. She had travelled "in the fast lane" off and on location; she drank heavily with other cast members—many of whom were considerably older—for pleasure and to relax after a gruelling day of filming. As many of her cohorts also indulged in smoking marijuana and snorting cocaine, she too engaged in these pastimes—sometimes with quite heavy usage. Mitzi was isolated from any protective family support system, imbued with the family's clear message to excel and become rich and famous, young and highly suggestible, and craved acceptance in the sophisticated world of theatre. Over the prior 3 years Mitzi had become a polydrug abuser. Usually she only indulged heavily on the weekends and was able to sober up and act sufficiently well to camouflage her malady by Monday morning. But she finally crashed, and was unable to continue working. The producer, who had seen other actors and actresses decompensate in this way, called the parents and forcefully alerted them to their daughter's condition. He suggested she fly home and they make arrangements for inpatient rehabilitation.

The parents had already refused to acknowledge some indicators from Mitzi that she was having difficulty coping and was drinking quite a bit, which they chalked up to "normal work stress" and the fact that "everyone drinks and occasionally gets smashed." They assumed the producer was exaggerating and decided to wait until Mitzi got home before doing anything. When she arrived they saw how distressed and confused she was and so arranged for residential treatment in a well-reputed drug and alcohol inpatient facility. During her 4 weeks there, she had been sullen, morose, and generally indifferent to the other patients and to staff efforts to engage her in the treatment process. Although younger than many of the patients, she stayed aloof and indicated that she had little in common with them.

All members of the nuclear family had visited, except Thea, and Mom had participated most actively as the copatient, but had not joined her in residence. The family had colluded with Mitzi in denying the addiction by indicating that they considered it a passing phase and that once she had recuperated she would be able to drink and even "do drugs" in moderation. They wanted her discharged at the end of a 6-week stay, despite the staff recommendation that she remain at least another 2 weeks. If they were to admit to deep-seated and severe problems, the family image of being outstanding and invincible would be shattered. That would have been intolerable in terms of the family's myth and mystique.

The youngest child, Richard, was a freshman at a "preppy" upper-class suburban university. A tanned, well-built "Jock" image was projected. Despite his active participation in sports, the family admitted they knew he had been going with a fast crowd and doing drugs. Not only was his college work not up to his usual performance and family expectations, but he was making errors in his part-time work in the cashiering department of Mr. Grande's firm. Like all employees, he had had to take a lie detector test. He had not fared well on questions regarding substance abuse, denying any usage. During the first session, he and Dad had quarreled about this, with Richard asserting his anger that they believed a machine rather than him and avowing he was no longer taking anything.

This then comprised the contemporaneous family portrait that emerged during the first session. I indicated the need for at least two more family sessions and urged that Thea attend the next one so a more complete and accurate picture of the family's dynamics, structure, and functioning could emerge.

Diagnosis and Treatment Plan

The family was seen as high-achieving, high-pressured, and perfectionistic. Mr. Grande was a charmingly authoritarian self-made man who believed that clear-cut goals, talent, and perseverance lead to success and that one could and should overcome all problems and obstacles on his or her own. Narcissistic, self-satisfied, and even smug, he had provided generously for his family while expecting them all to be achievers in their own right. The undisputed head of the family, he was accustomed to people trying to please him and following his instructions, and to getting his own way. Because of his fierce pride and ability to dictate and make shrewd, good decisions, he had not responded well to the treatment center's confrontational approach and diagnosis of his daughter as an "Addictive Personality" evidenced in a "Substance Abuse Disorder."

Mrs. Grande clearly supported her husband's primacy in the family, and their relationship had both complementary and symmetrical aspects (Pollack, Kaslow, & Harvey, 1982). It was complementary in that she occupied a "one-down" position in the realms of power, authority, and decision making. It was symmetrical in that they held the same values, goals, and beliefs and had built their family and other aspects of their life-style together in accordance with a shared dream of a family dynasty and a jointly devised road map for establishing it. Mrs. Grande functioned as partner–supporter for her husband and as planner and implementer for the home, family activities, and pursuits. She was a devoted mother who invested time, money, and energy in her children and expected huge dividends in return in the form of high profile and remunerative accomplishments. For 25 years she had derived pleasure from her wife–mother roles and had willingly subjugated her own career interests to be a professional Mom. Now, with her discouragement that the children were not each fulfilling the life scripts so carefully written for them, and the dawning realization that Mitzi, and probably Richard too, were profoundly disturbed, Mrs. Grande seemed more ready than her husband to reassess her daughter's condition and to consider channeling some of her aspirations into resuming her own career in fashion, abandoned many years earlier. She expressed some willingness to attend Al-Anon meetings and evidenced some receptivity regarding reevaluating her family's expectations and the demands for the pursuit of excellence at all costs.

Similarly, Craig seemed receptive, even intrigued with the prospect of therapy and articulated interest in getting to understand himself and his family better. He expressed his recognition that both Mitzi and Richard were having difficulties and indicated he had been aware of this earlier and tried to press his folks to do something, but they had ignored his pleas. His reality testing and grasp of the situation seemed the best in the family.

Mitzi indeed appeared to be a young woman with many borderline and narcissistic features, who fell into the classification of an "addictive personality." She was depressed and forlorn; some of her underlying anger at her parents for not recognizing her dependency needs and insisting she get help earlier broke through in spurts. Each of her parents had been in individual treatment with a psychiatrist to whom they had also sent Mitzi when she was in town. She held him in disdain, as he had not even recognized when she came in high, or that she sometimes went into the lavatory to smoke a joint during a session. He had never asked to see the family as a unit.

Richard also had many features of the borderline personality—ingratiating, impulsive, manipulative, and deceptive. He seemed, more than Mitzi, to be the scapegoat on whom his father's disappointment and distrust were focused. In turn Richard was the most overt bearer of the family's anger against the autocratic, critical, and righteous father.

It appeared that the family had maintained a dynamic and satisfying equilibrium while the children were growing up. They had many exciting trips together, and all of the children seemed to fit into the master game plan. While the parents felt in control of their good-looking and talented children, they fostered the children's careers and motivated them through approval and the prospect of huge rewards. Once Mitzi moved out, 6 years earlier, the existing homeostasis had changed markedly. By then the two older children were also gradually asserting their independence, though less compellingly than Mitzi. During the ensuing years, Craig had become more sure of himself in business; he sometimes questioned Dad's policies and had moved out of the family household. Thea also was living out of town and although she was described as being in great shape, that seemed unlikely. That left only Richard living very close to home and being home from college on many weekends, holidays, and vacations.

Some preliminary hypotheses were:

1. As Mr. and Mrs. Grande faced living together without children present on a daily basis, they sensed something amiss in their seemingly wonderful relationship. Each seemed to project blame onto the other for the nonfulfillment of the dream of a family dynasty made up of Mr. Grande and the four children as five stars with Mrs. Grande as director–coordinator. Either Mitzi or Richard could have been acting out to unite their parents and hold the marriage together.

2. Mr. Grande may well have had one or more extramarital affairs to keep his great ego needs gratified, to substantiate his belief in his ability to make any conquest he desired, and to replace the diminished affection he had received from his lovely daughters after they departed.

3. The referral source had hinted that they suspected father–daughter incest but had been unable to broach the subject. It seemed strange that in this upper-class, success-oriented family, concerned about reputation and esteem, the two sons had remained close to home, while the two daughters had moved far away when still very young. It was somewhat conceivable that the daughters were fleeing from an incestuous relationship. Further, if Mitzi's alcoholism was associated with incest, it would be consistent with recent findings regarding female drinking patterns (Crigler, 1984). Therefore, the incest theme loomed as plausible.

4. Mitzi had been precocious and had developed a pseudosophistication, having left home to live relatively autonomously at age 15. Her dependency needs had surfaced when she was under intense pressure in the adult world, and she had resorted to escaping into the hazy world of the substance abuser, thereby gratifying her oral-dependent cravings and, perhaps unconsciously, exhibiting behavior that would lead her back home, where she could take refuge. At the same time, if the assumption of incest were correct, at home she might be able to determine why her mother had not protected her and try to rework her relationship with both parents to see if they could love and accept her for herself and not for what she represented—a child prodigy about whom they could brag and who everyone saw on display as a tribute to the Grande family.

5. Richard was also testing the limits and seeking greater acceptance and protection from his own impulses. Acting out sufficiently to embarrass his parents seemed the only way to break through the family's veneer of cool perfection and arouse some genuine—even if negative—feelings.

6. The parents preferred to exclude Thea from the therapy, keeping up the deception that she was not part of the family's current dilemmas, and in fact was healthy and living a satisfying and productive life.

7. The family system pathology was deep rooted with many triangles abounding (Bowen, 1978), several major secrets, a strong mystique and mythology of family invincibility and perfection, much surface pseudomutuality (Wynne, Ryckoff, Day, & Hirsch, 1958), and an inadequate and inaccurate communication network.

Given all of the preceding hypotheses, it was recommended that they enter family therapy and that, given the distance they had to travel and the fact that all were loquacious, sometimes double sessions would be scheduled to run 1 hour and 40 minutes. It was agreed that they would make every effort to have Thea come home, which they did the following week, and two double sessions were held while she was in town. Both Mitzi and Richard said they had some matters to discuss privately. Given that they were young adults engaged in individuating while also attempting to become connected to their family in a new and more wholesome manner, it was agreed that they could each have individual sessions in addition to the family sessions.

The spoken treatment goal was to have both Mitzi and Richard stay off alcohol and drugs. Yet both were denying the extent of their chemical dependence and abuse. Therefore, I planned to encourage them to join either Alcoholics Anonymous (AA) or Narcotics Anonymous (NA) and to sincerely "do a program" in addition to working in therapy. I intended to reinforce Mrs. Grande's willingness to attend Al-Anon meetings and hoped Mr. Grande might also decide to participate, though this looked dubious. While the system was in such a state of flux, and its equilibrium unfrozen, I hoped (1) to enable the parents to appreciate their children more for who they were,

(2) to diminish their pressure on the children for exceptional performance and continual achievement, and (3) to encourage the children to fashion their own identity. Further, I intended to try to help Dad become a little more relaxed and less of a martinet, more able to enjoy "being," and not always measuring his and other people's worth by how much they earned and their list of titles or credits. It was felt that Mom's vicarious overidentification with her daughters and her covert encouragement of extreme seductiveness was detrimental to them and that therefore she should be helped to actualize her own recently reawakened desire to return to work. The sexualized nature of various alliances needed therapeutic attention and some strengthening of the real rather than pretend marital bond seemed indicated. In keeping with my diaclectic approach (Kaslow, 1981a, 1981b), I decided on a combination of therapeutic techniques of analytic guiding to uncover the secrets and deal with the affect and interpret interactions and transactions; utilizing the transferences the young adults seemed to have begun developing; contextual emphasis on the loyalty bonds and joining with each member at different times through multidimensional partiality (Boszormenyi-Nagy & Spark, 1973); structural interventions in regard to generational and personal boundaries (Minuchin, 1974) and trying to enhance the sexual and cognitive bonding of the spouse dyad; strategic–systemic techniques of paradox and reframing; and Bowenian detriangulation (Bowen, 1978). Each approach was to be interwoven in the tapestry of the therapy process when it seemed most appropriate.

Process of Therapy

Subsequent to the initial interview, the course of therapy entailed two 2-hour sessions with the entire family plus two 1-hour sessions with Richard. The following paragraphs are summary notes from the two family sessions, which illustrate the focal themes and therapy process as chronicled when it was fresh in the therapist–author's mind:

Mr. and Mrs. Grande and their four children came together. Thea had flown in from New York just for the therapy session, and we scheduled a second session for the same week because of her being in town. Also, Mr. and Mrs. Grande spent 3 days at the substance abuse treatment facility in Parents and Co-alcoholic groups. By our Friday afternoon session (the second) they were quite exhausted.

Some of the themes that emerged during these 4 hours together follow:

1. Mr. Grande enjoys relaxing in the evening with several drinks. Mrs. Grande finds him more lovable and humorous when he is a little bit high. We looked at the addiction theme in the family, and it turns out that his main addictions are being a workaholic and his almost desperate desire to create a dynasty.

2. Richard is very distressed and what spilled over is his guilt about his part in "causing" Mitzi's break. Earlier this year when she was home, she had given him somewhere between $2000 and $2500/month to supply her with cocaine. They often enjoyed drugs together as this made them feel closer. Mr. Grande has accused his son of causing her break, and we looked at their closeness and the contributory factors. Richard feels quite distressed and confused by all of this.

3. In addition, Richard is terrified of staying in a business requiring taking a polygraph test and yet very much wants to be part of it. My own impression is that he has become quite frightened of the drug scene and might be able to pull himself out of it given enough space and the family's willingness to trust him with another chance. Consequently, since his parents will be out of town next week and Richard seems to have moved toward a therapeutic alliance with me, I offered him a separate appointment, which he accepted with alacrity.

4. There is conflict between Mr. Grande and Craig—who until the second session seemed like the "cooperative son." Craig has played a buffer role between Father and Richard and is only now pulling himself out of the middle and telling them they must communicate directly. Despite Craig's earnings of about $100,000 a year as a branch manager plus another $25,000 a year in "perks," he feels that he should be paid quite a bit more because his friends are. His friends are in comparable positions in their fathers' businesses; also his life-style is quite expensive. He has what sounds like an elegant apartment in the country and another in the city. He drives a Mazaratti and "lives it up." Dad and he have many disagreements about this and also have their differing concepts about what is a fair distribution of the family's wealth. There are trust funds in each of the children's names, and Mr. Grande is so intent on treating everyone equally that he does not yet seem to differentiate that Craig is making a time and energy investment in the business while the others are not. Mr. Grande said that perhaps the two of them needed to see a referee and asked whether I knew enough about business to enter this. I handled it purely factually by saying that I had some business consultation experience particularly with family corporations, and felt that I could.

5. Richard is somewhat jealous of the salary that Craig receives. I indicated that at 18 years of age, Craig certainly had not been getting that salary and that they had to look at the age difference. The boys seem to have gotten along well until Richard got deep into drugs, and Craig resents covering for him and being the intermediary.

6. Thea emerged as the "good child" during the first interview she attended. She is exquisite-looking and apparently quite talented. Here again, it is hard to assess in this setting. Dad is willing to buy a dance company or back a Broadway production or do anything else to further her career. In the second session Thea indicated some reluctance to return to New York, and it seemed that we were on the tip of unearthing some family secrets. One secret that came out is that she is cohabitating with a nonJewish divorced man with two children. Her Dad objects vehemently and has not visited her in New York. After his somewhat "mind boggling" few days at the substance abuse treatment facility as well as his few sessions with me, he is more willing to say that Thea is entitled to choose who she wants yet to hold firm that he has a right to voice his opinion that this is not what he would want for her. The man Thea is involved with apparently is a successful theatrical entrepreneur.

7. What emerged is that Thea had been married briefly. One wonders at her divorce, her confirmed inability to make a deep commitment, and the kind of man to whom she has gravitated when on the surface she has absolutely everything to offer.

She is quite likeable and appealing and seems genuinely concerned about Mitzi. She has been close to Mitzi in the past and offered to be available to her as needed now, but without being intrusive.

8. It was again hard to see Mitzi's face because of the bangs and the disheveled hair. She seemed to rapidly become attached to me and by the end of the session asked if I would become her therapist when she left the substance abuse treatment facility. Since I feel a good ability to work with her, I have agreed. She thinks the hardest part of going back to work will be not getting high, and we all talked about experiences other than chemical abuse that can lead one to great heights and peak experiences. To not indulge will mean that she will often be alone on weekends.

9. At one point, we were talking about privacy versus connectedness, and the need for boundaries regarding one's own bedroom behavior. Dad blurted out something about an affair some years back that Mom had learned about. This was what initially catapulted her to seek psychotherapy with Dr. T, and later Mr. Grande also saw Dr. T. Mitzi had apparently resented the affair and thrown this up to them. All the children seemed vaguely aware of it. There was some not too good natured kidding that Dad is jealous of Craig's girlfriends. Any overtures I made to obtain psychosexual developmental history data on the children were blocked either by Mr. Grande saying it was drugs and booze, not sex that was causing the problem, or by Mrs. Grande adeptly changing the subject. Any lead to exploring possible incest would have seemed capricious; it did not flow from any verbal or nonverbal clues and so was delayed for a future session—when more trust had been established. Queries about what else was transpiring when he had the affair also went unanswered; both said that this had been adequately dealt with during therapy with Dr. T, had been painful enough then, and the door was closed on that phase. Now everything between them was just "fine."

10. Only once did Mother emerge as a real person—when she let the children know that she and her husband are "at peace" and that she really resents that all of the things they tried to do for the children have been so misinterpreted. This included taking them out of school each winter for 2 months so they left the cold Northeast for warm Florida. Craig was left in private school in their home city and the other three had to continually adjust. The parents seem to have been unaware of the toll that this took on the children, who never felt that they belonged anywhere for long and who all seem rootless.

My roles in these two sessions were multiple: information gatherer; conductor—leading through queries; attentive and empathic listener; information provider regarding addiction and the half-life of some drugs and alcohol, indicating that I did hear the substance usage as serious; gentle confronter regarding how much pain was emanating from Thea as well as Mitzi and Richard and about the numerous dyadic and triadic conflictual relationships; interpreter of the importance of maintaining intergenerational boundaries, respect for individual privacy and right to make one's own choices, and the need to be allowed to be responsible for one's own decisions, errors, and accomplishments while still feeling a sense of real belonging and attachment to the family unit.

At the end of the second of these two sessions, the family affect seemed less morose, a little less conflicted, and a trifle more optimistic. It was agreed that various individuals and subsystems would be seen and that Thea would come to town monthly so that we could hold full-family sessions. The four young people all indicated that they thought this kind of family conference was long overdue and very helpful. Thea particularly said she welcomed the opportunity to talk about her problems in relation to her parents' very specific and rigid expectations regarding her career and love interests. Richard made an appointment for the following week when his parents were to be away. Mitzi was to call before her release from the substance abuse treatment facility for an appointment, and Craig had stated he wanted to come in with Dad upon the latter's return.

Richard was seen twice alone in the next 2 weeks. Case notes indicated the following:

Richard was on time, and these seemed like productive sessions. He claims that he has not touched any drugs or liquor in 3 weeks and that he is feeling much better during the day. His eyes looked less glassy and bloodshot. He enjoyed his parents being away and his girlfriend seemed to have come and stayed with him for a few days. They had a rather casual and quiet good time. The biggest complaint is that he is having great difficulty sleeping, and this seems to be the main withdrawal symptom. We looked at former night fears and how much sleep he really needs. I suggested he might try hot herbal tea and a hot bath before bedtime and also to consider reading. Reading is something he has not done in a long time and will start again. We also explored his numerous interests from the past and channels that he might now pick up again, like skiing and water sports, as ways of both burning up energy and providing highs without the use of drugs. We also dealt with the importance of his seeking out friends who are not part of the drug culture.

He is to remind his mother to call me to set an appointment for the family. No word yet from Mitzi.

Mom did indeed call the next week. Richard had gone on a binge. They were furious that he violated their trust again, and there was an implication that my belief in the sincerity of his desire to "go straight" was partly at fault. They wanted to know if I thought he too should go into an inpatient rehabilitation program, and I supported their moves in this direction.

An appointment was made for Mitzi for the next week and then cancelled by Mom because it was too far for Mitzi to drive alone in her still shaky condition and everyone else had other commitments. After a lapse of several weeks, I sent them completed medical insurance forms, which they had asked us to fill out, and a brief summary of our five sessions pointing out the major issues that appeared suspended in midair and waiting to be resolved.

Two weeks later I received a handwritten note from Mrs. Grande. The important portions are excerpted below:

I tried to call you—I just returned from New York where my husband and I took care of some business. Since I"ll be leaving again Tuesday for the Islands, I wanted to touch base with you. I received your letter—thanks.

I do want to tell you that we all came away better, in our own individual ways, from having spent our sessions with you. Please understand that the combination of time, distance, and the usual complications were the real reasons for our not continuing, for now. Richard was not happy about the fact that he had been caught betraying our trust (and for that time, he was angry and didn't want to see you or anyone. He has improved a great deal, much of which I attribute to your counseling, in spite of his "slip"). Mitzi has been seeing Dr. P here, to great advantage. She feels comfortable and trusts her, so that, for now, is okay. Thea would like to see you on one of her visits. My husband and Craig are seeing Dr. T and seem to feel good about that. You opened up some necessary areas. So, I just wanted to "clear the air" and let you know what's been going on. I think the world of you and what you've done for us. I do hope your door will be open to us in the future—the question is when.

Nothing further was heard from the Grandes and any overtures on my part seemed unwarranted.

Analysis of Failure and Hypothetical Reconstruction toward Success

In light of the data acquired in the first session about the great emphasis this family placed on power and the father's desire to control every one in his immediate world, it was important for the therapist to win the "battle for structure" early (Napier & Whitaker, 1978). Given the severity of the problems, the family's denial of this, their skill at manipulation, the realities of their residing hours from my office, their numerous work and travel commitments, and Thea's living in a different city, it was urgent to contract for weekly or at the least, bimonthly family sessions, affirming that this would definitely constitute the treatment of choice. This I failed to do, believing I would alienate them by generating too much resistance. Instead, I opted to be cooperative with their wishes (demands?) and see individuals and subsystems, thereby hoping to "hook them" into treatment.

In replaying the tapes of these sessions, I was struck by Mr. Grande's extreme male chauvinism—his attitude that all of the important work and decision making is done by men and that women are meant to be ornaments, handmaiden–partners, or dilettantes. Ordinarily I am quite effective in engaging men of this genre in therapy, where they have an experience with a competent woman who appreciates and supports their masculinity rather than competing against it; my male patients usually grow toward greater respect for a woman's intelligence and ability, which reverberates into their out-of-therapy relationships with women. Therefore, I had naively assumed I could do the same with Mr. Grande, and I missed the extent and intensity of his attitude.

In retrospect, he might have been more willing to continue if a skilled, assertive male therapist had joined me to comprise a therapy team. (As it was, he later returned to his former male therapist, Dr. T.) Inclusion of a male cotherapist might have enabled Mr. Grande to form a therapeutic alliance and might have served to deflect his attention away from dealing with me as he did other women, either trying to direct my actions or to make another conquest. Further, as cotherapists we could have modelled open and sincere communication, techniques for confronting and resolving issues between us instead of denying them, respect for each other's individuality and integrity, and less stereotypical sex-role functioning and interaction (Kadis & Markowitz, 1972; Kaslow & Lieberman, 1981). While one therapist empathized, supported, and soothed, the other could have zeroed in to focus on the addiction theme in the family to which all had fallen prey and pursued the deeper family secret—which was probably father–daughter and brother–sister incest. It was the attempt to begin to explore this at the third family session that may have hastened their retreat from family therapy and the return to individual treatment where they could deceive themselves by dealing with their individual intrapsychic dilemmas and keep the troubled transactional and interactional processes and relationships hidden. This repressed material, which I believe was there, seemed to be literally driving three of the children to very masochistic, destructive behavior. Conceivably, Mom was consciously uninvolved and unaware, and Dad was not about to have this mysterious causative enmeshment unveiled. A cotherapy team might well have handled it through generating a systemic hypothesis, strategically intervening to unmask the secret, and helping them rework the relationships.

In addition, I was somewhat gullible regarding Richard's desire and ability to go "cold turkey." He seemed so well-meaning and sincere, and I wanted to believe he was a substance user, not an abuser, so I allowed myself to be taken in. Given what we know about substance abusers and their families (Stanton, Todd, & Associates, 1982; Kaufman & Kaufman, 1979), and how difficult it is to stop "doing drugs" and recover—particularly when denial is a major defense mechanism and the family dynamics are not undergoing change (parents were to be away) while the symptomatic individual is waging his battle—I should have predicted several relapses if he tried to do this alone and thrown my weight on the side of combined inpatient treatment for Richard and frequent concurrent family sessions for all. Likewise, it would have been judicious to press for Mitzi to go to a halfway house rather than home. That would have allowed the detoxification and rehabilitation process to continue unabated in a protected environment until her ego strength and abstinence were sufficiently integrated that she could withstand the pressures of home and ultimately of her career back "on the set." Meanwhile the rest of the family should have simultaneously undergone conjoint family therapy—in light of Richard's and Mitzi's symptomatic behavior,

Thea's inability to sustain object constancy in relationships, and Craig's mounting disgruntlement with all of the sham and pretense regarding the family's image and their ability to set everything right by "buying their way."

In closing, I want to add that this chapter has been purposely written in very basic concepts and vocabulary so that abstract premises and sophisticated phraseology would not obscure the problems in the case and the lack of much progress. I cannot help but ponder what we mean by "failure." Undoubtedly in the Grande case, the premature termination and visible outcome fell far short of the articulated goals. It would be fascinating to know how another therapist would have proceeded. Would therapy have been more effective if I had followed the course charted in the section above? Answers can only be speculative. Perhaps in the cases we deem to be failures, we must also consider what Mrs. Grande alluded to in her letter—the uncomfortable issues that are highlighted, and though not dealt with immediately, can no longer remain dormant. These issues may bubble in consciousness to be dealt with by the individual and family outside of the specific therapeutic context— perhaps on their own, with relatives or friends, or with another therapist. Is this then failure, or the beginning journey and quest of which the final destination and results may remain unknown to the therapist? This is part of the ambiguity and mystique of the life of the therapist.

REFERENCES

American Psychiatric Association. *Diagnostic and statistical manual of mental disorders* (3rd ed.). Washington, D.C.: Author, 1980.

Boszormenyi-Nagy, I., & Spark, G. *Invisible loyalties.* New York: Harper & Row, 1973.

Bowen, M. *Family therapy in clinical practice.* New York: Jason Aronson, 1978.

Crigler, P. W. Incest in the military family. In F. W. Kaslow & R. I. Ridenour (Eds.), *The military family: Dynamics and treatment.* New York: Guilford, 1984.

Duhl, F. The use of the chronological chart in general systems family therapy. *Journal of Marital and Family Therapy*, 1981, *7*, (3), 345–352.

Guerin, P., & Fogarty, T. Study your own family. In A. Ferber, M. Mendelsohn, & A. Napier (Eds.), *The book of family therapy.* New York: Science House, 1972.

Kadis, A., & Markowitz, M. Short term analytic treatment of married couples in a group by a therapist couple. In C. Sager & H. S. Kaplan (Eds.), *Progress in group and family therapy.* New York: Brunner/Mazel, 1972.

Kaslow, F. W. Stages in the divorce process: A psychological perspective. *Villanova Law Review*, 1980, *25* (4/5), 718–751.

Kaslow, F. W. A diaclectic approach to family therapy and practice: Selectivity and synthesis. *Journal of Marital and Family Therapy*, 1981a, *7*, (3), 345–351.

Kaslow, F. W. Divorce and divorce therapy. In A. Gurman & D. Kniskern (Eds.), *Handbook of family therapy.* New York: Brunner/Mazel, 1981b.

Kaslow, F. W. Profile of the healthy family. *Interaction*, 1981c, *4*, 1–15.

Kaslow, F. W., & Friedman, J. Utilization of family photos and movies in family therapy. *Journal of Marital and Family Therapy*, 1977, *3* (1), 19–25.

Kaslow, F. W., & Lieberman, E. J. Couples group therapy: Rationale, dynamics and process. In G. P. Sholevar (Ed.), *The handbook of marriage and marital therapy.* New York: Spectrum, 1981.

Kaufman, E., & Kaufman, P. (Eds.). *Family therapy of drug and alcohol abuse.* New York: Gardner, 1979.

Lazarus, A. *The practice of multi-modal therapy.* New York: McGraw-Hill, 1981.

Minuchin, S. *Families and family therapy.* Cambridge, Mass.: Harvard University Press, 1974.

Napier, A. Y., & Whitaker, C. A. *The family crucible.* New York: Harper & Row, 1978.

Pollack, S. L., Kaslow, N. J., & Harvey, D. M. Symmetry, complementarity, and depression: The evolution of an hypothesis. In F. W. Kaslow (Ed.), *The international book of family therapy.* New York: Brunner/Mazel, 1982.

Stanton, M. D., Todd, T. C., and Associates. *The family therapy of drug abuse and addiction.* New York: Guilford, 1982.

Walsh, F. (Ed.). *Normal family processes.* New York: Guilford, 1982.

Wynne, L., Ryckoff, I., Day, J., & Hirsch, S. Pseudo-mutuality in schizophrenia. *Psychiatry,* 1958, *21,* 205–220.

13

Struggling with the Threat of Suicide

KARL TOMM

Introduction

In retrospect my experience with the L family had an extraordinary impact on my development as a professional. It prepared me for a major shift in my thinking about mental process and in my method of conducting therapy. I had worked extremely hard in trying to help the L family break out of a pattern of repeated suicide attempts but failed. The experience left me disillusioned with my knowledge and skills. I became much more receptive to seriously consider some radically new developments in the field. As a result, my whole orientation changed. Thus, the type of work I now do differs significantly from what I did then. This is not to say that what I do now necessarily would have been successful then, but I suspect it could have been much more facilitative in helping the family discover alternative solutions.

Theoretical Frame of Reference

Prior to this experience I had elaborated my own integration of existing theory and technique in family therapy and published it as a model moving "towards a cybernetic–systems approach" to family therapy (Tomm, 1980). The integration was based on my understanding of von Bertalanffy's (1968) notion of hierarchical systems and Wiener's (1948) notion of cybernetic feedback. Problems were differentiated according to system level (individual, dyadic, triadic, whole family, family–community etc.) and efforts were made to identify self-perpetuating patterns of interaction at each level (Tomm & Sanders, 1983). The integration allowed for the inclusion of concepts and techniques from psychoanalysis, behaviorism, ethology, and communications theory. One idiosyncratic feature of the assessment aspect of the model was to draw a circular pattern diagram of dyadic interaction that reflected the core maladaptive process in an important relationship. This circular or homeostatic pattern then would become a target for therapeutic intervention. A large number of specific skills were defined (Tomm & Wright, 1979), which were used to break up the maladaptive pattern. Many of these skills were

Karl Tomm. Department of Psychiatry, University of Calgary Medical Clinic, Calgary, Alberta, Canada.

oriented toward providing feedback to the family about their problematic patterns and stimulating new adaptive patterns of interaction between family members during the session itself. The approach was quite directive with deliberate attempts to restructure interpersonal relationships and to enhance the family's cognitive awareness and understanding of their interaction process. The model allowed for intervention at different levels simultaneously including the use of biological methods (medication) and social methods (hospitalization), in addition to family therapy.

During the year following my experience with the L family, however, I came across the work of the Milan team in Italy. Initially, I found their book (Selvini-Palazzoli, Boscolo, Cecchin, & Prata, 1978) difficult to understand. I nevertheless explored their innovative methods and became intrigued, eventually elaborating my own understanding of the Milan systemic model (Tomm, 1984a, 1984b). It was true that with my earlier work I was moving "towards" a cybernetic–systems approach, but the next step turned out to be a different move than I had expected. It was a leap, not a step—a discontinuous rather than a continuous move. The Milan approach is based on a very different view of systems, namely that of Gregory Bateson (1972, 1979). It is based on a more complex version of cybernetics, namely the cybernetics of cybernetics or second-order cybernetics (Keeney, 1982). Whereas von Bertalanffy's ideas of systems appear to be based on the interaction of units of mass and energy, Bateson's ideas of systems are based on the interaction of bits of information, differences, and patterns. The primary focus of analysis and the resultant methods of intervention in the Milan systemic approach differ from the systems approaches based on general systems theory. It is hoped that some of these differences will become evident to the reader by the end of this chapter, where the alternative interventions that could have been used with this family are described.

Background

The L family was originally a very typical nuclear family. It consisted of a 44-year-old pharmacist, a 39-year-old homemaker, a 13-year-old girl, and a younger boy. The couple had been married 17 years. There had been a planned pregnancy that miscarried prior to the birth of the girl. The couple attributed the spontaneous abortion to the inordinate physical demands of the mother's job. She thereafter assumed the role of a full-time homemaker. Serious family problems began 6 years prior to the referral, when the second child, the boy, was diagnosed as having a malignant tumor. The mother felt guilty about the tumor, because she had had some X-rays early in the pregnancy prior to knowing that she was carrying the child. The father, who had wanted a large family, went to extraordinary efforts to obtain the best possible medical care. However, his efforts were taken to an extreme. For instance, he insisted that the child undergo further painful treatments even after it was obvious the child was dying. Conflict between the parents emerged regarding the boy's medical management when the mother (with the physician's support) tried to spare the boy further pain. This escalated to the point where eventually the mother took an overdose in an apparent suicide attempt. Shortly thereafter the boy died at the age of 5. One hour prior to the boy's death, the father had administered some medication and he wondered if he had given the boy too much.

Within a few days of the death, the husband decided unilaterally to move the family closer to his family of origin. The couple found it extremely difficult to talk about the wife's suicide attempt, the loss of the son, and the move. (Prior to the marriage the husband had had a girlfriend who he was trying to break off with. She had made several suicide attempts presumably in an attempt to save the relationship, but eventually killed herself.) Once the L's were resettled, the father invested himself heavily in his career, which was very successful. He even did some extra volunteer work for young children who were dying. However, tension in the home gradually mounted. Two years later the wife's father, who had been an alcoholic, died. The wife felt increasingly abandoned and depressed. Another 6 months later when she could no longer tolerate the stress, she made a second suicide attempt. At this point she entered a course of intensive individual psychotherapy with Dr. N, a friend of the family.

Frightened by the second suicide attempt, the father tried harder to help his wife and to spend more time with his daughter. However, he secretly began taking stimulants to maintain his activity level. The mother found her husband's attempts to help rather patronizing and manipulative. She began to suspect his drug abuse and withdrew even more. Over the next 2 years, she made four more suicide attempts, all by taking overdoses after an argument with her husband. She was hospitalized three times while she continued under the care of Dr. N. Eventually she was seen by Dr. M, a biologically oriented consultant. He diagnosed her as manic–depressive and initiated treatment with lithium carbonate. During this time the husband also began seeing Dr. N individually. Dr. N conducted a few conjoint marital sessions, but apparently these did not go well. About 9 months prior to the referral for family therapy, Dr. N recommended separation because of the wife's continuing suicide attempts. He suggested that the husband seek therapy in a specialized drug abuse treatment center, which was located about 1000 miles away. The husband refused to leave the city. He did agree to move out of the house to live with his sister. However, he began to abuse both drugs and alcohol more frequently and his work deteriorated rapidly. Two months later, when his wife made another suicide attempt (on the anniversary of the boy's death), he stopped working altogether because of "depression."

After further encouragement to seek therapy elsewhere, the father moved to the city where the son had died and initiated psychoanalytic therapy. Three months later he broke off this treatment (against the analyst's advice) and returned to stay with his parents. A week later he was found semiconscious in his bedroom and was hospitalized overnight. He admitted that he was medicating himself but denied that he was suicidal. Pressure mounted (from Dr. N, his wife, and his family of origin) for him to go to the drug abuse treatment center. He set out to do so but kept phoning his sister after he was a few miles out of the city. She became suspicious and eventually found his car at a motel with him deeply unconscious in one of the rooms. After extensive resuscitation efforts in another hospital, he fully recovered. For a while he was obsessed with the thought that he may have caused himself some brain damage. He wanted to be treated with electroconvulsive therapy (ECT), but Dr. S, the psychiatrist in charge at this hospital, was hesitant to administer it. Two weeks later Mr. L eloped from the hospital, checked into a hotel, drank a couple of bottles of liquor, and slashed his wrists with a broken glass. Dr. S was away at the time. He had signed out to Dr. R, who immediately initiated ECT. A total of seven ECT treatments were given. These were discontinued after a friend of the patient informed the hospital staff that Mr. L was still abusing medication even while receiving this treatment in the hospital. When confronted with this information, Mr. L withdrew dramatically from all social contact and virtually hid under his bed covers for several days. Dr. S spoke with Mrs. L, who informed him that her husband had been phoning her repeatedly (since being asked to leave several months earlier), asking to return home. Although she wanted him back, she refused to have him home for fear that his addictive behavior was not yet under control.

Engagement

It was at this point that I was asked by Dr. S to initiate family therapy. I first saw Mr. L in the hospital individually and found him alert and coherent but extremely despondent about his life situation. He wept when he spoke of his son's death and expressed resentment towards his wife for not being as supportive to him as he had been to her. He felt somewhat suspicious of Dr. N and jealous of the relationship Dr. N had with Mrs. L. He felt that if he could not get back with his wife and daughter there would be nothing for which he should stay alive. He wholeheartedly agreed to a proposal to be involved in family therapy. I called Dr. N to discuss the possibility of doing therapy with the family. Dr. N pointed out that he had known the family for a long time and that the husband had a tendency to try to "possess his wife" even to the point of "strangling her emotionally." Dr. N emphasized that the wife had been doing much better recently (while on her own with the daughter) but that she had not yet decided on a formal separation or divorce. Dr. N was now seeing her primarily in a group (twice a week) rather than individually. Dr. N was aware of Mr. L's jealousy but attributed it to paranoid ideation associated with repressed homosexual attachment that came to the surface when Mr. L was abusing Ritalin. Dr. N advised against family work and indicated that it would be more useful for the husband to go to the specialized drug abuse treatment center that he had proposed earlier and then perhaps get involved in conjoint therapy after he had made some progress individually. Mr. L had emphasized to me that there was a greater probability that he would commit suicide if he went away. He wanted to be treated locally where at least he had his family of origin to depend on. I then called Mrs. L and found that she was very interested in marital therapy. However, she did not trust her husband's sincerity and insisted that Mr. L control his drug taking before she would participate. At this time Mr. L was still hospitalized and under constant observation, because he was considered an acute suicide risk. Mrs. L was afraid to visit him and usually only did so when accompanied by his sister. The daughter was terrified and tried to avoid the whole situation by keeping herself focussed on her work in school where she was doing quite well.

I reviewed the situation with Dr. S. It was clear that Mr. L did not want to be sent away. He had tried once before to obtain therapy at a distant center but suddenly interrupted the treatment. The suicide attempt leading to this admission to hospital had occurred *en route* to the recommended center. We thus agreed that he should be treated locally and that family therapy was worth a trial. I devised a plan that was designed to engage the wife and daughter. It was proposed to Mr. L that he write a letter to his wife and daughter outlining the plan and his commitment to it. If Mrs. L and the daughter agreed, Dr. S would give Mr. L an opportunity to demonstrate his willingness to cooperate by allowing him full privileges to leave the hospital on pass whenever he wanted on the condition that he return daily at certain specified times in order to have his blood and urine checked for drugs. If and when Mr. L had managed to remain totally free of drugs for 7 consecutive days, a family interview would be arranged and everyone would be expected to attend. Mrs. L agreed and the plan was implemented successfully.

The first family assessment session was 2 hours long and seemed to go quite well. A number of important conflictual issues were defined, and everyone agreed to further assessment with a view towards the possibility of an extended course of family therapy. However, I was in for a major shock. The very next day Mr. L checked himself into another hotel, ordered a large number of drinks to his room, wrote a suicide note and took a lethal overdose of Elavil (an antidepressant). Because of his bizarre behavior in the hotel, he was identified as a patient from the hospital and was discovered in time to be lavaged, intubated, and placed on renal dialysis. After 2 days of intensive medical treatment, he recovered consciousness and was transferred back to the psychiatric unit under constant observation.

Fortunately, the first interview had been videotaped, so it was possible to review what had transpired. Mr. L was anxious in the session but was quite pleased that he had achieved a drug-free period. He was obviously hoping for more recognition for his efforts, but was met with a rather cool response from both his wife and daughter. Mrs. L indicated she was interested in the possibility of eventually getting together but was "never going to be under anyone's thumb again." She defined his drug taking as manipulative and extremely guilt-inducing. He pointed out how he began taking drugs when she began pulling away from him when she started therapy. Later he admitted that he first started taking Ritalin after the son died. She pointed out that she was particularly vulnerable to his drug taking because her father had been an alcoholic and she always felt responsible for her father's "sickness." Mr. L indicated that he was angry about Dr. N's involvement in their family, but she quickly reacted by saying how much better she had been doing lately. She resented his efforts to curtail her outside relationships. I clarified the circular pattern of him trying to control her and her withdrawing from him, which in turn activated his efforts to control, and so on, and pointed out how both of them would have to change. She then made it very clear that she was not yet ready to have him back home. In the hopes of engaging her in the therapeutic process, I then temporarily joined her and focussed more on his contributions to the pattern. I confronted him on the intensity of his demands on her and suggested that "your chances of getting together again are better if you let her go." Mr. L became angry "What freedom does she want? . . . Then go! . . . I won't tolerate an affair!" The wife indicated that she had never been interested in other men. I apologized, saying that I did not realize how sensitive he was to loss. There was a brief discussion about the loss of the son and both agreed they had been profoundly affected by his death. The husband openly admitted that he had overreacted in the session. He realized that he had "put all [his] eggs in her basket" and needed to develop a broader network of supportive relationships for himself. It was agreed that an interview should be arranged with his family of origin to explore the possibility of him living with them while conjoint therapy took place. In the meantime he would remain in the hospital under Dr. S with full privileges and continue to have intermittent "drug screens." The daughter declined repeated invitations to offer her opinions and to make comments. It was clear that she wanted to stay out of the struggle between her parents. On the other hand both parents were very protective of her and emphasized her need to avoid missing school. Her nonverbal behaviors suggested that she was aligned with her mother. It was agreed that she would come to some but not all the sessions. The problem of multiple professional involvements was brought up. I indicated that if I was to work with them, I wanted to be in charge of all aspects of therapy including hospital management. Mrs. L insisted that she had to continue her group therapy with Dr. N for emotional support, and I reluctantly agreed, thinking that she would probably give it up once family therapy was under way.

Thus everyone seemed quite content with what had been achieved in the first interview. The wife and daughter volunteered to accompany the husband back to the hospital. On the way back he apparently invited them to spend the weekend together but the wife rejected the idea. The next morning the nursing staff noted that he seemed in good spirits when he left the hospital. After he left he called his wife and spoke to her on the telephone. The wife subsequently reported that the only thing that was unusual about the call was that when it ended he told her that she "need not bother to come to any more sessions" and hung up. Thus everyone, including the wife, was surprised and shocked when he was found unconscious a couple of hours later. The suicide note contained an apology for his actions and a request that he be buried beside his son.

The situation was obviously extremely labile. After this latest suicide attempt, Mr. L was appropriately remorseful. He readily accepted the removal of pass privileges and voluntarily gave up his clothes, which he had resisted in the past. He insisted that he definitely wanted to continue the plan of family therapy and proceeded to arrange for the family of origin interview. Mr. L, his mother, two married sisters, and a brother-in-law attended the second assessment session. They all encouraged him to give up his current marriage and start again. They attributed most of the problem to Mrs. L, who they said obviously was not responding to his needs. He defended his wife against their accusations and emphasized that she was the only woman that he loved and that he could not live without her. None of the relatives were willing to accept him in discharge for fear of his suicidal behavior.

Mr. and Mrs. L, their daughter, and Mrs. L's mother attended the third assessment session. Just prior to the interview, Mr. L passed me a note saying that he felt we should not convey to Mrs. L the negative feelings expressed about her by his family of origin in the second session because she probably "could not take it." On the suggestion of the therapist, Mr. L took full responsibility for his latest suicide attempt. His wife responded by saying that she felt partly responsible because she could not be open and honest with him about her fear of him committing suicide. The daughter also apologized for being so cool towards her father in the previous interview. Mrs. L's mother asked her daughter and son-in-law why they wanted to stay together when their interaction was so catastrophic. Both hedged in their responses, but indicated that they wanted to pursue family therapy whether or not they stayed together. I concurred and made a definitive commitment to the family to take over their treatment. A formal transfer of care from Dr. S subsequently was arranged in the hospital.

Diagnosis and Treatment Plan

In keeping with the assessment model I was using at the time, problems were differentiated according to system level, that is, individual problems, family problems, and family–community problems.

Individual Problems

The husband-father appeared to have the most severe problems. He was depressed, had little self-esteem, and was seriously suicidal. Although there were some indications that his depression included an endogenous component (loss of 10–15 lbs and difficulty sleeping), he had not responded to traditional methods of treatment, namely antidepressant medication and ECT. My impression was that his depression was predominantly reactive. He had lost a son that he desperately tried to save and probably was carrying a great deal of unresolved grief. He now was struggling with the loss of his wife, his daughter, his home, and his capacity to work. There were narcissistic features in his personality makeup in that he tended to assume that he had the correct view and that he had the right to impose this in any situation. Hence he experienced more frustration than others when he did not achieve his goals and felt justified in using whatever means were necessary to reach them including the use of deception and the abuse of drugs and alcohol.

The wife–mother was more frightened and angry than depressed at the time of the family assessment. In the prior therapy with Dr. N, she had made substantial progress in working through the loss of her son. However, she now was extremely ambivalent about the marital relationship. On the one hand, she had been dependent on her husband financially and emotionally for many years and valued continuity of family life. On the other hand, she resented being confined and trapped emotionally. She had recently become profoundly disillusioned with the "strength" of her husband because of his addictive behavior that reminded her of her "weak" father. She was frightened and repulsed by his suicidal actions yet felt a strong need to help him.

The daughter was an early pubescent girl who seemed bewildered and confused about what was happening around her. She reacted by avoiding the marital problems as much as possible and focussed her energies on her schoolwork. While this tendency to avoid problems was seen as potentially problematic, it appeared to be an adaptive response to the current crises.

Family Problems

The major interpersonal problem was the escalating conflict in the interaction between the couple. The hypothesized underlying dynamic of the repetitive sequences of maladaptive interaction is illustrated as a circular pattern diagram in Figure 13-1. The diagram includes inferences about their intrapsy-chic processes, both cognitive and affective, and the resultant communicative behaviors that connected their interaction to create a cybernetic loop of positive feedback or escalation. Both husband and wife were frightened but for different reasons. He was terrified of losing the relationship he had with his wife, and she was afraid of losing her autonomy and being engulfed. Their predominant mode of responding to fear also differed. His was one of attempting to manipulate and control, hers was one of withdrawing from him and rejecting controls. These individual patterns when connected together created a positive feedback loop in the marital relationship. Each spouse's "corrective" actions may have had a negative feedback *intent* for self but had the *effect* of defeating the intended goals of the other. That is, negative cybernetic feedback at the individual level inadvertently resulted in positive cybernetic feedback at the interpersonal level.

Since the pattern was circular, the description of a typical sequence could begin at any point. The wife seemed to be grappling with a sense of entrapment in the marriage. Her struggle against this entrapment by with-drawing from her husband and rejecting him eventually led to the separation. His pleading and repeated demands to return home activated her fear of losing her emerging autonomy. As a result she became more determined to keep him out even though she wanted to continue the marriage. On the other hand her rejection of his initiatives and her associated tendency to reach out

FIG. 13-1. Maladaptive circular pattern of interaction.

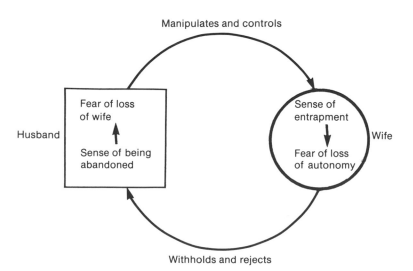

to others for emotional support increased his fear of losing her. Thus he redoubled his efforts to manipulate her into accepting him, even if it meant becoming devious and dishonest or using guilt induction (to which he knew she was vulnerable). Each became increasingly frustrated and angry with the other's behaviors, became less and less able to empathize with the other's needs, and became increasingly hostile and destructive in their own behaviors. Hence the escalating viciousness of the marital pattern illustrated in Figure 13-1.

At the triadic level there appeared to be an alignment between the mother and daughter with the father split off from the rest of the family. While this pattern did not have the malignant qualities of "a coalition against" the father, it was an additional strain for him. He probably experienced having "lost" his daughter emotionally after he began making suicide attempts. Prior to this, when the mother had been the identified patient, he had spent extra time with his daughter, going out for drives, taking her out for pizza, and so on. During that period he probably had the major alignment with the daughter. Thus at the time of the assessment when it appeared as if the girl had aligned herself with the mother, the father may have been experiencing some betrayal regarding the realignment.

Other family problems included financial difficulty and inconsistent support by families of origin. The husband had some disability insurance, but there was considerable conflict about how he had handled a number of bills. The wife's mother and sisters lived far away and were not readily accessible for support. The husband's parents and sisters were available but generally were not supportive of the marriage. While they provided encouragement, most of them (with the notable exception of one sister and one cousin) were too frightened or busy to become very involved.

Family-Community Problems

The family was involved with multiple professionals whose views on the nature of the problems and the most appropriate solutions differed. Dr. S and Dr. R both felt there was a major biological component to Mr. L's depression and strongly supported organic treatment methods. I felt that the marital relationship was the major problem and was worried about the continuation of antidepressant medication because of the potential for abuse and its labeling effect. Dr. M felt that Mrs. L had a manic-depressive illness. Dr. N and I both felt that each spouse had significant intrapsychic problems. However, we differed on how these should be dealt with. He felt strongly that the solution was separation, physical, emotional, and eventually legal. I felt that his proposed solution and his involvement with the wife was a problem. It aggravated the husband's perception of them in a coalition against him as evidenced by his paranoid jealousy. These different points of view must have increased the confusion in the family. Thus there needed to be some coordination of therapeutic efforts.

Plan of Therapy

My goal was to integrate the therapeutic management by taking over full responsibility for treatment of the whole family. Because the father was still in the hospital, his care was to be transferred to me, and I was to conduct the family therapy as well. The main thrust of treatment was to proceed on two fronts: individual therapy of the father in the hospital and marital and family therapy in an outpatient clinic on another site. The individual treatment would only continue as long as the father remained in the hospital.

The individual treatment plan was (1) to control Mr. L's suicidal behavior by curtailing his privileges as required, (2) to explore the psychodynamics of his depression, mobilize a catharsis of anger and sadness, and enhance his insight into his own problematic patterns, (3) to build his self-esteem by guiding him into constructive activities and more gratifying interaction with his family and friends, and (4) to expand his social relationships and his capacity to be self-disclosing.

The plan of therapy based on the marital assessment was (1) to raise the corrective negative feedback loop from the individual to the interpersonal level and (2) to replace the existing maladaptive positive feedback loop with a more adaptive one. The first part was to be achieved by the therapist providing feedback in the therapist–family system and by the therapist stimulating appropriate feedback between the spouses themselves. Both these maneuvers were to be oriented towards helping each spouse recognize the consequences of his or her own behaviors in triggering unwanted behaviors in the other. In addition, I wanted them to understand the connections in the interpersonal pattern, and hence was to stimulate interpersonal perception so that they could identify and respect each other's vulnerabilities. The second part of this plan of therapy for the marital problem was to orient them to identify and reinforce constructive changes in each other. This would be carried out by pointing out and clarifying the adaptive interaction process as it occurred during the immediacy of conjoint marital interviews as well as in their interaction between sessions. For instance, efforts were to be made to help him recognize her initiatives for more contact with him as a consequence of his initiatives in allowing her more autonomy and *vice versa*. This adaptive interaction pattern is illustrated in Figure 13-2. Once established, this pattern would become self-perpetuating and lead the couple out of the malignant pattern in Figure 13-1.

Because it was assumed that both parents had unresolved feelings concerning the loss of the boy, attempts were to be made to uncover these feelings and to stimulate mutual support. It was also felt that they both

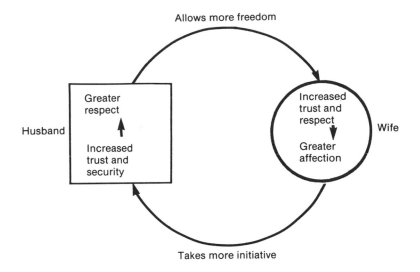

FIG. 13-2. Adaptive pattern of interaction.

carried a great deal of underlying bitterness and resentment toward one another for what had happened around the time of the death and since then. An effort was to be made to uncover and discharge these feelings in the context of support.

A decision was made that the daughter not participate in the marital sessions but that she be brought in intermittently to share in planning for family activities. The extended family would also be invited in as required for discharge planning.

Process of Therapy

Over the ensuing 3 months, there appeared to be slow but steady progress. The treatment plan described in the preceding section was implemented, and during this period there were no further suicide attempts. Mr. L remained in the hospital where he was treated intensively as an individual. At the same time there were 15 conjoint sessions most of which were marital interviews. A couple of sessions included the daughter and a few others included members of the extended family on each side (the wife's mother visited briefly while on vacation).

The following modifications were made in the treatment plan as therapy progressed. Mr. L's anger proved extremely difficult to mobilize in the individual psychotherapy interviews. Eventually the Gestalt two-chair technique was utilized and a surprising amount of intense rage emerged. He felt very guilty, however, about expressing aggressive fantasies regarding his wife and insisted the therapist keep these secret. Once his anger was mobilized, he was encouraged to continue to express his hostile feelings openly in the hospital and he did so. For instance, because he was found to be extraordinarily dependent on his wife, major efforts were made to enable him to initiate other social contacts. This was done by deliberately placing him in a four-bed room and starting him in a psychotherapy group. He was openly angry about both these moves, and in both situations a compromise was negotiated. His tendency to rely on drugs and alcohol also was explored in depth with an attempt to encourage him to use interpersonal support as a substitute for chemical agents. In addition to the individual sessions with me, he was provided with extensive support by the nursing staff. While in the hospital he gradually spoke more openly about his suicidal impulses and on occasion even spontaneously asked to have his clothes removed so that by wearing only his pajamas his impulse to elope would be curtailed.

In addition to the directive method of interactive marital therapy previously described, both husband and wife were shown videotapes of prior sessions in order to help them attain a more objective view of their own behaviors and the related interaction patterns. During the videotape feedback sessions, both spouses were surprised at the intensity of their own anger. On a few occasions either the husband or the wife had left the room in a rage but usually they returned to continue the session. Indeed, there was increased openness in the expression of a wide range of affect in the marital interviews. Efforts were made to reduce each spouse's expectations of the other and to loosen their controls over each other. An example of the latter was an attempt to negotiate personal "private time" but this was rejected by the husband. Each spouse was asked to prepare lists of reasonable expectations of the other should they live together in the future or should they obtain a divorce. These lists were discussed. Notably the husband had great difficulty visualizing himself having any contact with his wife if they were to divorce.

As therapy progressed, Mr. L began to think more realistically about the possibilities of a permanent separation. There were transient moments when he actually felt that he would feel freer if divorced. The couple spontaneously began to spend some time together on their own. They would often have meals together before or after sessions. While he was out on pass on weekends, he would stay with his family of origin, usually his younger sister, but he visited his home briefly. The husband began thinking about work again and started making inquiries. Everything seemed to be going well.

During the 4th month there was a turn for the worse. It was time for my vacation, and arrangements were made for Mr. L to be discharged and stay at the home of his cousin. The cousin was a recovering alcoholic and felt he understood Mr. L's problems regarding the drug abuse and could provide some useful support. Mrs. L made arrangements to take her vacation while I was away in order to avoid getting into problematic patterns with her husband when I was not around to sort things out. She and the daughter thus would be out of town as well during this period. Dr. R, who had previously been transiently involved in managing the case, was asked to provide ongoing psychotherapeutic support for Mr. L during the 5-week interval.

Two weeks after I left on vacation, Mr. L was found at his cousin's home in a stuporous state. He had taken some "extra" medication because he "wanted to blot it all out." He denied that the episode was another suicide attempt. Apparently, prior to this event he had visited his home (which he had previously agreed not to do) and gone through some of his wife's belongings. He became increasingly jealous of her possible involvements with other men. He was readmitted under Dr. R. Back in the hospital Mr. L expressed annoyance that his wife and I were away on holidays at the same time, and he wanted Dr. R to inform his wife immediately about what had happened. When this was not done, he insisted that he wanted to be discharged to go to the drug abuse treatment center. Dr. S was consulted at this point and felt suspicious that Mr. L might just want to go out in pursuit of his wife. Mr. L was persuaded to remain in the hospital. Two weeks later while out on a pass, he checked himself into a hotel and took another massive overdose of antidepressants and sleeping pills. At this point Dr. R was also convinced that Mr. L should be sent to the drug abuse treatment center, but by this time Mr. L had changed his mind.

When I returned from vacation the next week, I was profoundly disappointed. However, I immediately resumed individual sessions with Mr. L, and as soon as his wife and daughter returned, family interviews were resumed as well. He was again advised to take responsibility for his self-destructive behaviors in the conjoint sessions, and his wife responded positively to him when he did this. As things began to improve, the cousin suggested that Mr. L invite his wife to spend a night at their place. Mr. L phoned her but when she was hesitant he became very angry and suicidal. I confronted him on this impulsive reaction as guilt-inducing and controlling, which he accepted. As therapy progressed, Mrs. L began to take initiative to have her husband home more often while on pass. There was some exploration of sexual issues. He admitted to feeling somewhat impotent as a male when he was not able to control his wife's responsiveness to him. Both spouses maintained that they had had a mutually satisfying sexual relationship in the past, but there had not been any intimacy for some time. Neither felt ready to resume sexual relations at that time. There was more video feedback and this time things improved more rapidly than before.

Within 4 weeks he was discharged to the care of his cousin and began spending weekends with his family. The first weekend went well but during the second weekend there was an argument between the couple over the husband's reluctance to follow through on an appointment he had made regarding work. The husband left the house in anger. In his typical pattern he checked into a hotel and took another overdose. Again he was found by his sister who suspected that something was amiss.

By this time I realized that the whole treatment plan needed to be reassessed. I questioned my objectivity. The family had become very dependent on me, and I was deeply involved with them. Treatment was not progressing as I had expected. I arranged a review meeting with Dr. S, who suggested that because of the repeated forging of prescriptions, Mr. L should be asked to voluntarily relinquish his pharmaceutical dispensing privileges. I felt that this might be a further blow to his already precarious self-esteem, but Dr. S felt that the move would impress upon him the gravity of his self-prescribing behavior. Since things were not going well according to my plan, I complied. At the same meeting, we agreed that I explore the possibility that Dr. J, another family therapist, join me as a cotherapist in the conjoint sessions.

The conclusions of our review were presented to the couple. Although they agreed, their response was rather cool. In retrospect they probably sensed that I was losing confidence in my work with them. The very next day Mr. L secretly wrote himself another prescription. When this was inadvertently discovered by his wife, she became infuriated with him and walked out. He immediately barricaded himself in his room, took the medication, and attempted to cut his throat. Once again he was returned to the hospital.

He subsequently did write an official letter to revoke his dispensing privileges. The proposed cotherapist, Dr. J, first met with the couple independently and correctly noted that a disproportionate amount of the focus in therapy had been placed on the husband. Dr. J indicated that there needed to be a shift to redress this imbalance and pay more attention to the problematic contributions of the wife. Understandably, Mrs. L then refused to accept Dr. J as a cotherapist. To say the least, their responses to our new proposals were not very reassuring.

By now, I very seriously questioned my capacity to manage the situation. I began to wonder if I had erred in not involving Dr. N (who I discovered was still seeing Mrs. L). Thus I decided at this point to call a case conference including all the professionals involved with the family, namely Dr. S, Dr. N, Dr. J, and myself. After being informed of this plan, both the husband and wife declared very strongly their wish to have me continue in my work with them. I was quite candid in pointing out my limitations and my lack of success with them. I indicated that a decision about me continuing or not would be made at the conference.

Shortly thereafter, during the course of a conjoint session, the wife angrily announced her decision to divorce her husband. She also expressed a great deal of anger toward me and "all [my] plans." After the interview, however, she returned to the hospital ward to tell her husband that she was "just angry" and did not intend to obtain a divorce. But the next week she announced her intention to obtain a legal separation. This time she seemed more serious, and the husband angrily took off her wedding ring but returned it when the therapist intervened. The wife stated that she did not want any more family interviews. When seen individually after the conjoint session, the wife was offered support in having made a difficult decision. During this individual interview she expressed some confusion about whether she was divorcing her husband or whether she was really "divorcing the therapist and family therapy." Two days later the wife phoned her husband to say that she wanted to work on the marriage again.

However, when she appeared for the next marital interview a few days later, she was extremely anxious and depressed. She requested that she be admitted because of increasing suicidal ideation. It was close to the anniversary date of the death of the son. Because of her prior history of suicide attempts and her obvious agitation, she was admitted. The husband, who appeared to be coping fairly well at that point, was allowed to go home to take care of the daughter. The following week, however, when the case conference was actually convened, he surprised us all by presenting himself in a sluggish state of mind, as if he had been drugged. He denied taking any medication, but the hospital staff checked his car and found two bottles of pills. It was obvious to me that I had "lost control" of the situation and my judgment in anticipating his behavior was grossly inadequate.

The case conference was quite tense. Mr. L was at times rather incoherent. He expressed a great deal of anger about the proceedings. Dr. S became openly angry with him and threatened to have him committed involuntarily if he did not agree to be readmitted. He refused. His wife intervened and pleaded with him to accept rehospitalization. He eventually agreed on the rationale that it might be possible to make some progress with both spouses in the hospital at the same time. Although Dr. N did not say so, he appeared to feel (quite correctly) that the case had been terribly mismanaged. In our discussion after the couple was dismissed, he indicated that some time ago he had diagnosed Mr. L as "an inevitable suicide." I asked him what he meant by this and he explained that in his practice over the years he had seen a number of cases that appeared to enter a self-destructive pattern that inevitably led to suicide. He felt that Mr. L had the same characteristics as these cases. I had never heard of this label before and recall feeling shocked when it was applied to Mr. L. In the ensuing discussion Dr. N emphasized that the best solution would be for Mr. L to be sent to the drug abuse center. I felt too defeated to object. Whether or not Mr. L accepted this recommendation, it was decided that I should terminate my therapy with the family over a period of 4 weeks and arrange for a transfer to some other therapist who was not as deeply involved. The group also decided that a separation of 6 months with individual therapy for each spouse separately would be recommended.

Predictably, Mr. L refused to move away from the city where all his family and friends were located. He was very upset about the decision for me to terminate family therapy. Mrs. L was more accepting but also disappointed. I indicated that I would consider resuming therapy with them after 6 months if they both wished to do so. The wife settled down very quickly in the hospital over the next couple of days and was discharged. The husband also pulled himself together quickly. He promptly found another psychiatrist (a condition for discharge) and then dismissed me, indicating there was no need for me to continue for the 4 weeks. The last conjoint session was held about 1 week later and I remember a chill running through me when Mr. L refused to shake my hand when I said goodbye and wished him well.

I had no further professional contact with the family. About 1 month later I received a large box of fresh pears as a gift with a thank you card from all three members of the family. Another 5 months later, however, I received a phone call from a friend of the family saying that Mr. L had been found dead in his room. I called Mrs. L to express my condolences, and she offered the following information. After therapy terminated with me Mr. L moved in with his sister's family and continued with his new therapist, Dr. O, whom he saw two or three times a week. He was placed on another antidepressant, but because he repeatedly abused this it was eventually discontinued. He and his wife began seeing each other from time to time while he continued to live at his sister's home. He started doing some volunteer work on a part-time basis and seemed to be coping well. Mrs. L reported that she then started to see him regularly and they often had meals together and took long walks. One month prior to his death he unexpectedly moved out of his sister's house and found a room for himself. His sister became alarmed and made inquiries, but was reassured by both Mr. L and Dr. O that everything was okay. Shortly thereafter, the sister left on a holiday for a couple of weeks and the contact with the wife increased. Two weeks prior to his death, Mrs. L noted that he began to have paranoid ideas of a jealous type. He accused her of sleeping with another man and insisted that he knew where she was going and the names of the men with whom she was involved. She denied this because it was untrue, but Mr. L did not believe her. She had the impression that he was abusing medication once again. He became increasingly bizarre. Finally, the evening before his death, he suddenly appeared at his former residence making accusations about his wife. This time he initiated some violence and the couple got into a scuffle. The daughter also became involved in an attempt to break them up. Finally, Mr. L left and returned to his own apartment. His wife phoned him the next morning to be sure that he was okay. Both agreed over the telephone that perhaps Mrs. L should join him at the scheduled appointment with Dr. O later that day. However, when Mrs. L called Dr. O, he disagreed with the idea. She then called her husband back stating that she would not be at the session but that the therapist was expecting him. However, he never did show up at Dr. O's office and was found dead the following week when his sister became concerned when there was no answer to her phone calls. Mrs. L indicated that before her husband died, they had considered contacting me again for further marital and family therapy. Ironically, it was almost exactly 6 months from the date of our final conference that he was found dead.

It was not entirely clear how he died. In contrast to the previous occasions when he made suicide attempts, the room was in order this time and there were no pill bottles or evidence of alcohol abuse. There was however, a short note on his dresser stating "we always hurt those closest to us." On autopsy the pathologist was unable to find a cause of death. The concentration of medication and other drugs (that were screened) was not abnormally high in his blood, liver, or stomach contents. Thus, although his death was probably due to suicide this could not be established with certainty.

Subsequent to his death the wife and daughter moved to be closer to her family of origin. The last contact I had with them was a card another 6 months later indicating that they were well settled in their new home.

Although I felt very strongly that I failed with this family at the time of termination, I felt it even more acutely when I heard the news of Mr. L's death. I had had ample opportunity to help them discover an alternative solution to their problems but had failed. The description of their interaction in the final days was isomorphic to their pattern when I first met them. Nothing had changed.

Analysis of Failure

This whole report is, of course, my own idiosyncratic construal of a series of events and their meaning. I am certain that any of the other professionals involved (let alone various family members) would construe much of what happened very differently. Therefore, my report must be regarded as biased and incomplete.

To state with certainty whether or not there could have been a different outcome entails a philosophical problem regarding determinism. If the outcome could not have been any different, then it would be inappropriate to consider the therapy a failure. However, I choose to regard my management of this case as a therapeutic failure for several reasons. First, I experienced it as a personal failure. Second, I prefer to believe that more creative solutions to family problems are always possible. Third, it is useful for my development as a professional to recognize and understand my errors so that I can try to avoid them in the future. Fourth, other professionals reading this may learn from my mistakes and assist me in learning more as well. Some readers will undoubtedly be able to identify therapeutic errors that I have not recognized. I would be grateful if some of these readers would take the time to drop me a note to share their views. I expect to learn still more from this tragic experience.

What follows is a summary of the major factors that I have identified (thus far) as contributing to the treatment failure. These factors have been divided into two categories: (1) tactical errors and (2) epistemological errors. "Tactical errors" refer to errors in the management of the case given the theoretical framework and treatment model that I was operating with at the time. By "epistemological error" I refer to the more comprehensive issue of how a therapist "knows" the problems with which he or she is working and how this knowledge leads him or her to make errors that are only evident when viewed from another perspective.

Tactical Errors

The first mistake probably occurred at the beginning of therapy, when I allowed myself to become engaged primarily with the husband rather than with the whole family (or couple) as a unity. Having seen the husband alone in consultation in the hospital, I should have insisted on seeing the wife alone for long enough to establish an equally strong engagement with her in order to attain a position of neutrality vis-à-vis the couple prior to initiating the family interviews. If this had happened I would not have felt the need to focus so heavily on the husband's contributions to the problems in the marriage during the first session, and perhaps the first setback could have been averted. In order to maintain this neutrality while I was working with the husband in the hospital, it would have been necessary for me to see the wife individually as well. As it turned out I did see the wife alone occasionally but never enough to redress this balance and hence her continuing reliance on Dr. N.

Given my orientation at the time, I should have insisted that the wife break off the therapy with Dr. N as a condition for assuming overall responsibility for the case. This would have been problematic at the outset, because she had more confidence in him than in me. Perhaps this could have been negotiated through Dr. S, who initially asked me to take on the family. At the very least I could have requested a joint conference with Dr. N and Dr. S to discuss the potential problems that I saw in the triangle between Mr. L, Mrs. L, and Dr. N. The brief telephone discussion that I did have with Dr. N was not enough, particularly since he appeared to be influencing Mrs. L in the opposite direction that I was. His bias was toward separation; my bias was toward reconciliation. His continuing involvement with her probably undermined the work that I was doing with the couple, and the work I was doing with the couple probably undermined the work Dr. N was doing with the wife. Unfortunately, this never became an overt issue and hence was never seriously considered after the beginning of therapy until just before termination. In all probability it was, however, a strong covert issue. Dr. N was obviously aligned with the wife, and I was predominantly aligned with the husband. The discrepancy in orientation and the opposite alignments in effect constituted a form of covert conflict between Dr. N and myself, which was channelled into the marriage and undoubtedly served to aggravate rather than ameliorate the couple's problems. Thus if I could have engaged the wife and the husband equally and convinced Dr. N to relinquish his professional involvement, the potential of my therapeutic efforts may have been enhanced.

The full significance of Dr. N's involvement never became apparent to me until after the terminal conference. His belief that Mr. L was an "inevitable suicide," although probably never openly expressed to the wife, may have had an unintended covert malignant effect on the family. For instance, such a belief would justify his suggestion that the couple should separate, that the husband should leave the city, and that the wife should keep her distance from her husband (presumably in order to help insulate her from the intensity of another major loss). All of these moves aggravated the husband's turmoil. Thus the belief in itself could have been operating as a self-fulfilling prophecy. Furthermore, the wife's continuing dependence on Dr. N for emotional support created a triangle in which the husband was the jealous outsider. My lack of attention to the potential role that Dr. N was playing in the dynamics of the larger family–community system was an error of major proportion.

The fact that my therapeutic gains over the first 3 months collapsed shortly after I went away on vacation suggests that the break in therapy was inadequately planned. I did not realize how heavily Mr. L had come to depend on me; the transference was very strong at that point. With his wife and daughter gone at the same time, he must have felt totally abandoned. Although I had arranged for Dr. R to see him during the interval, there was not an adequate transition period for Mr. L to experience his support. Furthermore it was an extremely inopportune time to arrange for a discharge. He also lost the support of the nursing staff.

With respect to the internal dynamics of the family itself, I underestimated the significance of the role of the daughter. Her presence and more active participation in more of the sessions could have been of enormous benefit for everyone. I seemed to have been stuck in adhering to a covert family rule: "Let's not put any pressure on the one remaining precious child." Her observations of what was happening would have been of great value to me as therapist. Furthermore she probably was not entirely "an innocent bystander." I recall the mother once saying that she stopped making suicide attempts after she solemnly promised her daughter that she would never make another attempt. It was probably at about this point that the daughter switched her alignment from the father to the mother, possibly in gratitude for the promise. Subsequently, the girl probably felt trapped in this realignment and unable to help her father. If she rejoined her father, the mother may have felt betrayed and could have broken her promise. During the time I was working with the family, the daughter rarely took any initiative with her father.

Although it may be a misperception, I think that I was on track with respect to the core marital problem. Given the model I was using at the time, I probably was doing a reasonably good job. Perhaps I allowed too much intensity to emerge in the conjoint interviews as evidenced by the episodes when one or other spouse suddenly left the room in anger. In retrospect, the degree of focus on negative affect and destructive behaviors as opposed to positive exchanges must have been disproportionately high. This negativity (which will be discussed below) made it extremely difficult to create the context of mutual trust and support that I was trying to establish. More attention should have been paid to the issue of sexual jealousy that sometimes surfaced when the husband was impaired with drugs. While jealousy was discussed, it was not explored in sufficient depth. If it had been, perhaps the covert issue with Dr. N could have emerged more clearly. Mr. L found it very difficult to openly criticize Dr. N, because Dr. N had indeed helped his wife; she felt more secure in herself and was no longer making suicide attempts.

Another oversight was my failure to adequately assess Mr. L's position in his family of origin. He obviously had a significant amount of continuing contact, particularly with one sister, which I accepted as constructive. However, it is possible that there were additional family dynamics at work that may have contributed to the unpredictability of his behavior. For instance, the continuing closeness between Mr. L and his younger sister must have interferred with the wife's role of being a source of support to her husband. Thus, there should have been more sessions that included the wife and members of his family of origin in order to understand these dynamics more fully.

Epistemological Errors

As mentioned earlier, my experience with the L family prepared the way for a major change in my orientation to mental health problems and to therapy. The experience of failure shook me to my roots, my "epistemological roots." Undoubtedly it was because I invested so much of myself in trying to help the L family and that my efforts failed, that it was possible to be shaken so deeply. It was only after some time (i.e., after I had assumed a new epistemological stance) that I was able to redefine certain therapeutic moves within my previous orientation as errors. What seemed perfectly "correct" then, now appears "wrong." Consistent with my present position, however, I recognize that my present designation of these interventions as "errors" is relative. Perhaps a brief theoretical discussion may help to explain.

I am using the term "epistemology" here in the sense that Bateson does (1972) to refer to how we "know" our world, which determines how we think, act, decide, and organize our existence. My epistemological error was my "knowledge" of the "reality" of mental problems. I "knew" that these problems existed independent of my thinking about them and independent of family members' and other professionals' thoughts about them. My error was rooted in my naive belief in the objectivity of my own observations and in the objectivity of the events that our language describes. I did not realize the degree to which I and other observers (family members and professionals alike) were, in fact, specifying certain phenomena as problems through our own cognitive actions. I now believe that through our actions of drawing certain perceptual and cognitive distinctions (e.g., happy vs. sad, control vs. freedom), of specifying certain linguistic entities (e.g., depression, autonomy) and of employing them in our interaction (e.g., conversation) we are continually cocreating and maintaining our "reality." Rather than regarding perceptions, words, ideas, and beliefs as objective and "true," I now tend to consider them as reflections of distinctions that we have drawn. Thus (when I am able to do so) I prefer to regard a family member (or anyone) who is describing his perceptions or expressing his ideas as selecting certain distinctions in order to "make a move" in a "game" of social creation, exploration, and regulation. In adopting this view I have moved from a position of objectivity towards one of relativity; from empiricism towards constructivism. I say "towards" advisedly. I have not gone all the way. I have not adopted a position of complete relativity; somewhere there is probably a "bottom line." Furthermore, some distinctions are more highly interrelated than others and thus appear to be more "stable." Hence, some perceptions may be regarded as more "real" than others and some ideas as more "true" than others. This makes it possible to state that one word, idea, belief, or perspective is more useful than another. They "fit" better with our past histories of action and experience. Nevertheless, I now find it very useful in therapy to consider whatever "fits" and appears to be "objective" and "true" as *relative*, as a concrete specification that is *more* or *less* useful. On many occasions it is, of course, extremely useful to "act as if" various events and phenomena are objective and real. Thus my present epistemological frame of reference includes my previous orientation as a subset.

How did my previous epistemological orientation lead to error? The propensity to objectify by drawing attention to discrete "objects" tends to obscure the more fundamental relations entailed in phenomena. For instance, when I regard the wife as afraid of the husband's actions, I tend to objectify her fear and make it a descriptive quality of the wife. It becomes "located" inside her rather than in the relationship with her husband. This leads me to orient my therapeutic efforts predominantly towards her as an individual rather than towards the relationship. Her fear thus becomes the context for defining the relationship as distancing rather than the distancing relationship being the context for defining the phenomenon of fear. This difference may be subtle but its effects in the thinking and behavior of the therapist is significant, regardless if he or she is seeing the couple as individuals or conjointly. It promotes a drift toward an individualistic as opposed to an interpersonal orientation in therapy.

Another effect of objectification is that it creates the illusion of certainty. The therapist comes to "know" what is wrong and what needs to be corrected. This "knowledge" then inevitably leads the therapist into a moralistic stance *vis-à-vis* the family and even other professionals. Because we do not like to consider ourselves as moralistic, this position is usually disguised. However, it does have its effects just the same.

How did my epistemological "errors" manifest themselves in my work with the L family? First, I was much more individually oriented than I could admit. Although I espoused an interpersonal systems perspective, I focused predominantly on individuals. Second, I tended to handle "depression, control, fear, withdrawal, separation, repressed anger," and so on as if they were real objective phenomena. My "knowledge" led me to organize my therapeutic activity to try to manipulate these "objects" in a way that would be helpful to the family. For instance, I would orient my interventions to *block* the husband's controlling behavior by pointing out to him how it led to his wife's withdrawal. Thus his fear of loss was "moved in" to block his control by directing him to perceive the consequences of his own behavior. In this way I was trying to build in a negative feedback loop, which at the time I thought was a good way to conduct therapy. The relationships between these phenomena of fear and control are extremely important and their "movement" in relation to one another is potentially very useful. However, the manner in which I did this was problematic. Thus, the third and most significant effect of my epistemological errors was to inadvertently contribute to increasing the negativity in the system. Insofar as I "knew" that Mr. L was depressed and was afraid of losing his wife and that Mrs. L was resentful and was afraid of being controlled and that these characteristics interacted with each other, I "knew" what to do. I "knew" what was "right" and what was "wrong" and my job was to "correct" what was "wrong." This epistemological orientation inevitably led me into a moralistic stance *vis-à-vis* the family and the family members. I was "led" to point out to the family what mistakes they were making. I did this both directly and indirectly; directly by giving them "corrective feedback" by pointing out the "mistakes" they were making with each other and indirectly by stimulating them to give "corrective feedback" to each other directly. Little did I realize at the time that in so doing I was adding fuel to the fire. Corrective feedback of this type essentially entails telling another person to stop doing something because it has an undesired consequence or effect. It is constraining, inhibiting, and negative. Telling others the "right" things to do is hardly any less moralistic. The negative judgments are merely implicit rather than explicit.

In conducting therapy the way I did then, I was adding further constraints to a system that was already too constrained. Family members were already blaming each other for acting in ways that were "wrong." Mrs. L was blaming Mr. L for abusing drugs, controlling her, and so on. He was blaming her for not being supportive enough, rejecting him, and so on. The system was already stuck in a tangled knot of mutual blame, disqualification, inhibition, and constraint. Unfortunately, my orientation placed me in a position where I was, in fact, continually adding my "blame" as well. At the time I did not, of course, see it this way. I had rationalized my "blaming" as corrective feedback. It was more precise and correct than theirs, and hence I assumed that it could "really" set things straight. My feedback may have been offered in a more gentle and supportive manner, but it was predominantly negative just the same. By pointing out their mistakes with one another (directly or indirectly, explicitly or implicitly), I was blaming them, when one of their major problems was that they were already in a desperate struggle of blaming each other.

Another contributing factor to my epistemological error was my "knowledge" about psychiatry. At the time, I believed in the value of insight and conscious understanding of interpersonal process. This belief helped justify my action of being explicit about the corrective feedback. Not only was I open and direct with them, I actively encouraged them to be that way with each other as well. I failed to recognize the escalating negative effects of expressing negative thoughts and feelings. I also believed in the theory of repression, which resulted in unnecessarily activating further fear, pain, bitterness, rage, and depression.

Finally, my narcissistic belief in the correctness of my beliefs and in my competence as a therapist maintained my (initial) blindness to the ineffectiveness of my work with the family. In part, this narcissism was driven by my competitiveness—my desire to show my colleagues that I could succeed where they had failed. Perhaps this is why I "forgot" about Dr. N's involvement. It took more than one catastrophic suicide attempt to impress upon me that my "solutions" were mistaken and that possibly my whole approach was incorrect. Unfortunately, the recognition of my errors came too slowly to be of any help to the family. Ironically, the family helped me far more than I helped them. The failure experience turned out to be an antidote to the incipient escalation in my professional narcissism. It helped me become a little more humble and opened me to reconsider my understanding of psychiatry and of human relations in general.

Hypothetical Reconstruction toward Success

The possibility of trying something entirely different with the L family actually occurred to me toward the end of my involvement with them. I began to
consider doing something paradoxical. At the time, I thought of paradoxical
interventions as prescribing escalation of the symptom. However, I was too
frightened of the possibility of suicide to give that a try. It was just as well. I
did not have sufficient understanding of therapeutic paradoxes then. Subsequently, when I came across the Milan approach, I was captivated by their
use of paradoxical strategies (Selvini-Palazzoli *et al.*, 1978). After studying
their work, the nature and relevance of paradoxical interventions became
much more understandable to me. The key is to positively connote and
prescribe the *pattern* including the symptom, not the symptom itself, and to
prescribe *no change*, not escalation. However, this is not exactly easy to carry
out.

     In order to use Milan-type paradoxes well, one needs to understand the
basis of the approach. As implied already the approach is relativistic and
constructivist. The therapist tries to enable the family to entertain alternative
realities by (1) "releasing" new perspectives in the course of asking carefully
chosen questions and (2) constructing alternative "truths" and offering them
in the form of interventions. Specific behaviors, ideas, and beliefs of the
family are of interest by virtue of their *effect* in the ongoing process, not
because they are "right" or "wrong." The symptom is taken as a "message" in
the context of the interactional process. As such, the symptom is regarded as
having certain effects in the system because it is different than what is
expected or desired. These effects, in turn, have other effects, and so on,
which are eventually recursive. For instance, following the Mental Research
Institute (MRI) understanding of problem formation (Watzlawick, Weakland, & Fisch, 1974), the problem may trigger various attempts to solve it,
and the attempted solutions may eventually result in the recurrence of the
problem. The recursiveness or circularity in these patterns of interaction
creates the illusion of stability, "resistance," or "homeostasis" of the problem.
However, in contrast to the MRI approach of correcting the inappropriate
"solution" behavior, the Milan systemic approach utilizes a position of neutrality and questions the whole notion of correctiveness. Rather than regard
the attempted solution as the problem, the problem may be regarded as an
interim "solution" to some other difficulty. The task of the systemic therapist
is to keep asking questions to facilitate the kinds of new cognitive connections and behavioral effects that are required for the family to discover their
own alternative solutions that are not symptomatic. Where this process
appears to get stuck because the family "knows" too clearly what is wrong,
the therapist introduces confusion through the use of paradox. Where there is

too much confusion, the therapist introduces clarity through prescription of behavioral ritual.

In trying to understand the family, the therapist assumes that "things have to be the way they are" because of how the family "knows" and organizes their existence. The therapist tries to understand how the family's organization of reality, requires the presence of the symptom. Thus, the therapist is oriented to be intensely curious. The therapist keeps asking questions (usually referred to as circular questions) that might clarify relevant issues and trigger family members to revise their own views. The therapist does not decide what is wrong and provide corrective feedback on the basis of his or her "objective" understanding. The pattern of questioning triggers the release of new information (inherent in the system) without blaming. This enables the family to mobilize their own self-healing capacity rather than constraining it further.

When the therapist does offer an opinion, it is selected because it is different than the prevailing beliefs in the family, and the difference is anticipated to have a useful effect. In such an opinion the behaviors of various family members usually are connected and positively connoted in such a way that the meaning of the symptom is redefined in a paradoxical manner. The absurdities inherent in the paradox tend to "loosen the grip" of prior assumptions that may have contributed to the patterns that included the symptom. Alternatively, a ritual may be prescribed. A ritual is a carefully prepared behavioral directive. However, it is not offered in the sense that "this is the way the family should behave." It is prescribed in the sense of a useful experiment, a rite or an exploratory task.

If I were going to treat the I, family today, I would approach the situation very differently. My work would be exploratory throughout. In other words I would not conduct a definitive assessment at the beginning of therapy and then devise an overall treatment plan. The therapeutic direction would be tentative with continual reassessment on the basis of the family's responses to my actions. I would not make a diagnosis, but devise tentative hypotheses to be tested and revised again and again. I would not assume that I "knew" the nature of the problem. Instead, I would continually evaluate the consequences (in my own behavior) of what I thought the problems were. The latter would determine the kinds of questions that were asked and consequently what kind of "reality" was being cospecified during the course of the interview.

Thus, each session would begin with a reassessment of the most relevant systemic unity and its dynamics at that time. The unity could be a belief system entailing the dynamic interaction of certain ideas, expectations, and fears. Or it could be certain interpersonal relationships entailing particular behavior patterns. Whatever unity is specified as the most relevant during a particular session, the intervention would be based on the hypothesis that fit best to explain the dynamics. The therapeutic actions contained in the intervention would be selected according to their anticipated effect in liberating the system to change on its own. The actual effects of the intervention would be carefully noted and used to guide the creation of future interventions. Thus, therapy would evolve in the emerging dynamics of the therapist–family system. Given this orientation of continually responding to the responses of the family, it is impossible to specify exactly how therapy may have proceeded with this case. All that I can do is try to provide the flavor of the approach by describing a few things that I may have tried.

The initial focus would have been to ask a variety of questions (difference questions, triadic questions, behavioral effect questions, reflexive questions, and future-oriented questions) with a view toward developing a more and more systemic understanding. For instance, I would try to "discover" why the drug taking and suicidal behavior of the father and related behaviors of the mother and daughter were "necessary" and "good" for the family (as an interim solution to some other hypothetical problem). Among the questions might be: "Which parent was closer to the daughter 2 years ago? Do the father's suicide attempts bring the mother and daughter closer together or push them further apart? Are the mother and daughter closer now than they were a year ago?" A hypothesis generated around their responses could then be offered to the family in the form of a reframing intervention. An example of the latter might be that the suicidal behavior was a way that the father discovered to help his wife and daughter rebuild their relationship. He realized that a gulf had developed between them over the last few years. By behaving in a manner that he knew would worry them both very deeply he had been helping them to come back together again. With a positive connotation of this type, confusion and uncertainty about motivation and intention is introduced. With less certainty about presumed malevolent intentions and effects, family members are freer to behave in different ways than before. The paradox could even be strengthened by prescribing no change, "And until your wife and daughter can convince you that they are a strong enough couple, you should continue in this work that you have decided to carry out for them." Note that the suicidal behavior is not positively connoted, but the interpersonal *pattern* in which it is embedded. A directive to do what one is already doing is hardly constraining; it is confirming. What is even more therapeutic, however, is the new meaning that is attributed to the behavior. If this new meaning has some degree of validity, its clarification enables family members to entertain nonsymptomatic ways of fulfilling the same underlying function so that the symptom may be relinquished spontaneously.

The potentially problematic issue of Dr. N's involvement could be handled in a similar manner. A paradoxical opinion might be generated to explain why the wife needed to continue to see him in order to help her husband. The therapist might say, "It is clear that you have lost confidence in your husband's love for you. It is hard for you to see his love when he is abusing drugs. But you have found a way to help him show his affection more strongly. By sharing your inner thoughts and feelings with Dr. N instead of your husband, you are helping your husband discover how much he loves you and wants you for himself. By helping him think you are having 'an intellectual affair' with Dr. N, you help him become jealous. And it is good that he shows you his jealousy, because in this way he is showing you how strong his love is for you. It is also useful that his love is somewhat possessive at the moment rather than purely affectionate, because this makes you wonder if it is really love. In this way he is helping you slow down in trusting his love, so you can build your confidence in him more slowly." In anticipation of an immediate disqualification of the reframe one might add, "And of course, it is better for you to believe that you are only seeing Dr. N for support because you would never want to make your husband feel jealous. But because jealousy is so necessary for your relationship at the moment, you should continue to see Dr. N for the time being in order to help your husband with his affection for you." Alternatively, Dr. N could be invited to a session and he could be congratulated for helping the wife help the husband in this way. The goal in delivering such an intervention would not be to interrupt the wife's therapy with Dr. N. It would be to give the complex interaction between the three parties a different meaning which could liberate any one or all of them to a number a possible changes in their pattern of interaction. The wife might change her attitude toward Dr. N and convey this to her husband. The husband might change his view of their relationship and his ways of showing affection to his wife. Dr. N might spontaneously decide not to continue his work with the wife, or continue in a different manner.

If the suicidal behavior continued, the issue of death and dying would be explored in greater depth. This would be done with the assumption that (for some unknown reason) the family needed to continue "playing" with death. For instance, there could be a need for the famly to express their continuing loyalty and connectedness to their dead son. There could be a need to expiate real or imagined guilt for current or past events. Once again the focus would be to reconnect thought and action of various family members in new and novel ways emphasizing the positive aspects of whatever patterns were discovered. Alternatively, a ritual could be devised to further clarify and "challenge" the relevant dynamics. The family could be instructed in preparing for a more "creative" death and a funeral "celebration." For instance, the father could be assisted in planning an "alternative suicide." Rather than trying to constrain his freedom even more by restraining him from entertaining suicide, it might be better to "go with the need to kill" and agree with him, "Yes, something definitely needs to die, but I wonder if it needs to be your physical self. Perhaps some of your ideas, attitudes, beliefs, or behavior patterns need to die. Those things that are forcing you down this path to suicide need to be destroyed." A method of "killing" these ideas and the like rather than his body could become the primary focus of a ritualistic enactment (if the father chose to opt for an alternative suicide). For example, the father might be instructed to write on pieces of paper those beliefs that needed to die and then burn and bury them in a carefully prescribed manner. The wife and daughter might be asked to participate by preparing suitable gifts for the father's "sacrifice." Just exactly what type of ritual might be devised would depend on the precise details of the beliefs and behavior patterns that were salient for the family at the time.

Having employed a particular intervention, the therapist need not (indeed, should not) remain committed to it. He or she should carefully note its effect on the family (or other relevant systems) and move on to generate new hypotheses and interventions. If, for instance, the family failed to carry out a ritual, the therapist would accept responsibility for prescribing it too soon, rather than blaming the family for not following through. The goal is not to correct the family but to enhance their effective freedom to entertain and explore alternative (nonsymptomatic) solutions on their own.

Included in this orientation is the realization that the therapist cannot and should not attempt to control the behavior of others. He or she should continually work towards the enhancement of responsible autonomy. At moments of extreme suicidal or homicidal risk, however, the therapist deliberately may choose to temporarily relinquish the role of therapist and assume that of a social control agent. In the latter role he or she may call the police or mobilize whatever other resources are required to restrain someone from violent action. When he or she subsequently resumes therapy, he or she needs to examine (from a neutral position) the messages in the therapist–family system that led to his or her action. With respect to my work with the L family, being in the dual role of a facilitative therapist for the whole family and a social control agent for Mr. L's suicidal actions probably resulted in considerable confusion both for myself and the family. It is possible to carry out these incompatible responsibilities by separating them in time. However, it should be made clear to all parties concerned when one is in each role. Splitting these roles between two colleagues who are able to collaborate with each other would make the therapeutic work easier to carry out.

Thus, in the Milan systemic approach, the therapist does not assume any direct responsibility for family members' behavior. He or she takes responsibility for his or her own actions in the therapist–family system, where he or she specifies and respecifies "realities" that he or she anticipates may have a useful effect on the famly's problem-solving capabilities. If the family remains stuck in their pattern, then the therapist must keep changing his or her own thinking and behavior and not also remain stuck by hanging on to prior hypotheses and intervention strategies. The therapies must always be prepared to consider how his or her own actions are possibly contributing to the maintenance of family patterns and consequently the problem itself. The most important focus in systemic therapy is the dynamic and changing relationship between the family and the therapist.

I have no way of knowing if this approach would have led to a successful outcome. Implicitly, by defining some of my interventions as mistakes, I am assuming that the outcome could have been better. In summary then, my first failure with the L family was my inability to reconstrue their situation so that they could discover alternative behavior patterns to those that led to Mr. L's recurrent suicidal behaviors. My second failure was my inability to change my own pattern of working with them to help liberate both of us from a therapeutic impasse.

REFERENCES

Bateson, G. *Steps to an ecology of mind.* San Francisco: Chandler, 1972.

Bateson, G. *Mind and nature: A necessary unity.* New York: Dutton, 1979.

Keeney, B. What is an epistemology of family therapy? *Family Process,* 1982, *21*(2), 153–168.

Selvini-Palazzoli, M., Boscolo, L., Cecchin, G., & Prata, G. *Paradox and counterparadox.* New York: Jason Aronson, 1978.

Tomm, K. Towards a cybernetic–systems approach to family therapy at the University of Calgary. In D. S. Freeman (Ed.), *Perspectives on family therapy.* Vancouver: Butterworths (Western Canada), 1980.

Tomm, K. One perspective on the Milan systemic approach: Part I. Overview of development theory and practice. *Journal of Marriage and Family Therapy,* 1984a, *10,* 113–125.

Tomm, K. One perspective on the Milan systemic approach: Part II. Description of session format, interviewing style and interventions. *Journal of Marriage and Family Therapy,* 1984b, *10,* 253 271.

Tomm, K., & Sanders, G. L. Family assessment in a problem oriented record. In B. Keeney (Ed.), *Diagnosis and assessment in family therapy* (*The family therapy collections,* Vol. 4.) Rockville, Md.: Aspen Systems, 1983.

Tomm, K., & Wright, L. Training in family therapy: Perceptual, conceptual and executive skills. *Family Process,* 1979, *28,* 227–250.

von Bertalanffy, L. *General systems theory: Foundation, development, application.* New York: George Braziller, 1968.

Watzlawick, P., Weakland, J., & Fisch, R. *Change: Principles of problem formation and problem resolution.* New York: Norton, 1974.

Wiener, N. *Cybernetics or control and communication in the animal and the machine.* Cambridge, Mass.: Technology Press, 1948.

PART THREE

EMERGING PRINCIPLES OF FAILING

14

An Analysis of Family Therapy Failures

SANDRA B. COLEMAN

In Collaboration with ALAN S. GURMAN

> In Silent Mid-night
>   Our Old Scarecrow
>   Topples Down . . .
> Wierd Hollow Echo
> —Boncho (*Japanese Haiku*)

The echo of the failures described in the previous chapters resounds, leaving behind a hollowness of disappointment for the families and their therapists as well. Beyond the intricate dissections and explications of the authors for what went wrong, many basic and general issues are raised by the preceding cases. Although the families presented here all posed extraordinary problems and complications, their therapeutic chronicles strike a cautious note in a field that unabashedly flaunts its many achievements and creative methods. It is always quite tempting to "Monday morning quarterback" the failures of others, yet it must be recognized that there do exist certain kinds of problems and problem contents that transcend the clinical competence and creativity of individual clinicians and that, in fact reflect the current impatience of our field to respond to effectively.

Some of the questions raised by the very issue of failure follow:

• Are there specific, identifiable warning signs that failure is imminent, and do they vary according to one's "school" of therapy?

• Is there any consistency in the timing of these failure cues—for example, early in the course of therapy—or is there considerable variation across cases?

• Are there general hypotheses that can be formulated about failures?

Sandra B. Coleman. Family Guidance Center of Bucks County, Yardley, Pennsylvania; Department of Mental Health Sciences, Hahnemann University, Philadelphia, Pennsylvania.

Alan S. Gurman, Department of Psychiatry, University of Wisconsin Medical School Madison, Wisconin.

- Are there qualitative differences in failures linked to specific types of family problems; for example, do families with a schizophrenic member produce failures that differ from families presenting a school-phobic child?
- Similarly, are certain types of presenting problems more apt to result in failure?
- How does the family life cycle intersect with therapeutic failure; that is, is there an interaction between normal family life cycles and therapy failure patterns?
- How do current theories of change account for the course of events in both the cases presented here and in other potential therapy failures?

Beyond all these questions is the overriding issue of the meaningfulness of exploring a concept as complicated as failure. One might well wonder if the attempt to probe the innards of efforts that do not succeed has any more than philosophical value. Pragmatically, one might ask if there is any functional benefit to be derived from such a study. Further, if a precise model of failure can be developed, how would it affect current theories and practices of family therapy? What would such a paradigm contribute?

Emmelkamp and Foa begin their recent book on behavior therapy failures (1983) with a chapter entitled, "Failures are a Challenge." At the time that I (Coleman) originally conceived of *Failures in Family Therapy*, I was unaware of the Emmelkamnp and Foa work; thus, the present book was developed and written without ever having read their material.

This chapter focuses on three major areas that unify many of the aspects of failure that are discussed in the preceding chapters. The first section explores the cases described in the preceding chapters in an attempt to draw inferences and develop possible tenets of failure associated with family work. The second section attempts to develop a general position on family therapy failures by taking a critical look at both treatment attitudes, values, and real-life facts. Finally, a practical application of what has been learned about failures is suggested with the hope that an epistemology of failures in family therapy will in some way offer a potential means of reducing the incidence of failing. Perhaps these ideas will raise the consciousness of those in whom our families in treatment place their trust, often when they are in extreme desperation.

Factors Related to Case Failures

An overview of the 12 cases in this volume indicates that they were all remarkably difficult. Clearly, these failures do not represent the usual garden variety of presenting problems or of family conflicts, dynamics, and histories. This does not imply that one only fails with the most complicated families, but it may reflect that, when asked to present a failure, each of us is most apt to remember our most extraordinary and perplexing experiences. Thus, it is important to keep in mind that the analyses of the therapies exemplified here may not apply to family therapy failures in general. Still, because there are many common factors that do prevail across these cases, the findings should generalize to the more troubled families seeking professional help.

An attempt to derive common factors linked to failing suggests a central definition of failure. Although this is a reasonable expectation, this premise was not adopted. A very specific model within which each author described his or her case was used, but the term "failure" was left to be idiosyncratically determined. It seemed that such a powerful concept could only be defined as a result of serious thinking and exploring multiple failure situations. A definition involving less than that seemed haphazard and presumptuous. Because the contributors are all outstanding therapists and thinkers, the task of delineating just what a failure is was felt to be best served by allowing their clinical experiences to lead the way toward explication. Therefore, one of the products of this volume will be a definition. The concerned reader is encouraged to examine the following ideas and to consider the amalgam of circumstances that he or she would associate with family therapy failures.

Pretreatment Factors

FAMILY

History. The family's history prior to referral is important in predicting a likely therapy failure. Although not every case description provided this information, most of the families had a long history of problems prior to entering treatment; some problems were specifically related to the presenting problem, and some were tangentially associated with the current situation. Of particular importance is the length of time that the presenting symptom had been present. As can be seen in Table 14-1, all the cases were symptomatic for a significant amount of time with a range of 3–35 years.

Also highly important was the family's previous therapy history. Among the families described here, only three (Ficher & Kaplan, Chapter 8; Jacobson, Berley, Melman, Elwood, & Phelps, Chapter 4; Wynne & Green, Chapter 5) had not had some form of previous therapy. Although our sample is relatively small and is not a product of systematic research, it is nonetheless striking and clinically significant that 75% of these cases had former treatment.

In addition to the family's psychological history, their physical health or medical history should be considered. As Beavers (Chapter 7) implies, a family's biological factors are an issue. Thus, genetic limitations or advantages need to be determined in compiling a comprehensive historical perspective. Similarly, the family's socioeconomic status and cultural background need consideration in view of their potential contribution to success or

TABLE 14-1. Length of Time Family Symptom Existed

Therapist(s)	Years
Beavers (Chapter 7)	12
Coleman (Chapter 2)	35
Ficher and Kaplan (Chapter 8)	7
L'Abate and Baggett (Chapter 9)	3
Kaslow (Chapter 12)	3–5
Jacobson *et al.* (Chapter 4)	[a]
Liddle (Chapter 6)	16
Meyerstein and Dell (Chapter 10)	[b]
Segal and Watzlawick (Chapter 3)	11
Wynne and Green (Chapter 5)	[b]
Anonymous (Chapter 11)	8
Tomm (Chapter 13)	6

[a]Uncertain but said to be a continuation of patterns that began in family of origin.
[b]Unspecified but it is assumed that it approximated at least 5 years.

failure. The latter did not seem to play an important role in most of our cases, but it would be remiss not to at least mention the influence that demographic and ecologic factors may have on case outcome. The one situation that was affected by a religious–cultural issue was that of the former priest and his wife (Ficher & Kaplan, Chapter 8). In reconstructing the case the authors demonstrate their awareness of the misassessment of the problem relative to the sociocultural factors. It is understandable that part of the problem was most likely due to the threat imposed by encouraging the couple to use such explicit sexual methods as masturbation, erotic literature, and stag movies. In view of their strict Catholic background, this couple may have needed a rather different and perhaps more subtle approach, even if their sexual problems might eventually require direct confrontation.

A final piece of information that is essential to understanding the family is the type of former therapy that they had received. For example, in the case of the Anonymous family (Chapter 11), the mother had a history of several years of individually oriented therapy. Because her therapy had been largely psychodynamic in nature, it precluded any in-depth understanding of how the system was affected by the handicapped daughter and how the mother's therapy intruded upon the system. How that variable interacted with their disastrous initial family session is unknown but it certainly had an influence. Since the mother was the therapy motivater for the family, the knowledge that she had been in individual treatment could have been used to more effectively join her first as a means of connecting with everyone else. Thus, just as the family's own history is important prior to initiating treatment, their experiences in earlier psychotherapy encounters need serious consideration.

This may be especially salient, as suggested above, not so much because of the amount of previous therapy logged by the family or by individual members, but in terms of the focus of those prior experiences, that is, the level of the system toward which professional attention has been directed in the past. Because it is well known that patients in psychotherapy, especially effective therapy, tend to take on the sets and even the language systems of their therapists, extensive previous individual (especially psychodynamic or psychoanalytic) therapy experience, or extensive experience even in systemically oriented therapy of a style very different from the current therapy, may have trained into family members certain expectations about the way the current therapy should operate. Such sets may unfortunately block the establishment of a strong working alliance with the present therapist. For example, the kind of psychological mindedness usually seen as desirable in a candidate for intensive individual therapy, especially if reinforced by previous treatment experiences, may pose problems for working with many family therapists, especially those whose clinical focus is more interactional. If, as we believe, a natural inclination to view oneself and one's problems in living with a more circular, relational, and interactional set is a good prognostic characteristic for the eventual outcome of family therapy, then family therapists may need to pay special attention to inducing such a set with families, or individual members of families, whose natural orientation is more intrapersonal, especially if such a proclivity has been reinforced in earlier therapeutic encounters. This is a particular issue when a family or couple presents with a clearly identified patient, especially one with obvious and undeniable severe individual psychopathology, as was true of many of the cases described in the preceding chapters.

Current Status. One of the first questions asked usually pertains to the presenting problem and the person who is identified as the "patient." Even though some family therapists prefer to minimize the emphasis on patient status, they still acknowledge that the family has one. We are especially interested in this when the initial referral is made. It is interesting to note that in 7 of our 12 families, the identified patient was an adult. Two of the cases were couples and the remaining three presented problems involving a child. Table 14-2 contains information about the diagnostic categories[1] associated with the family problems. Although some family therapists try to avoid using labels, they are of importance in the context of this discussion. As can be noted, 75% of our families contained members who were either schizophrenic or borderline. In addition, five of the families (42%) also had a drug or alcohol problem that was either identified as part of the presenting problem or emerged at a later point in treatment.

Because of our awareness that life-cycle issues play an important role in

---

1. Diagnoses of cases were made in some instances by authors; in others I (Coleman) assigned diagnoses, to the best of my judgment, consistent with DSM-III classifications.

TABLE 14-2. Diagnostic Category Associated with Families Treated by Particular Therapists

Schizophrenic	Borderline	Neurotic	Character disorder
Beavers[a] (Chapter 7)	Coleman[a] (Chapter 2)	Anonymous (Chapter 11)	Wynne and Green[a] (Chapter 5)
Meyerstein and Dell (Chapter 10)	Ficher and Kaplan (Chapter 8)	Jacobson et al. (Chapter 4)	
Segal and Watzlawick (Chapter 3)	Kaslow[a] (Chapter 12)		
	Liddle (Chapter 6)		
	L'Abate and Baggett (Chapter 9)		
	Tomm[a] (Chapter 13)		

[a]Also had known drug or alcohol problem.

family adjustment, this is another pretreatment factor that deserves attention. In all cases, with the exception of Jacobson's couple, the prevailing stage-relevant issue was "growing up and leaving home." Although this is the stage that is often associated with family problems, it still seems astounding that slightly more than 90% of our contributing therapists experienced a failure where the "empty nest" or "preempty nest" was the dominant developmental problem. Even more fascinating is the fact that in almost half of these cases the separation dilemma was rooted in the older adult, that is, Harry Haverman (Coleman, Chapter 2), the ex-priest (Ficher & Kaplan, Chapter 8), Herbert and Joe (Meyerstein & Dell, Chapter 10), Mary Lou (Liddle, Chapter 6) and Mr. L (Tomm, Chapter 13). Because these families all experienced their life-cycle crises in pathological rather than in normative ways, it is predictable that, given the nature of their associated diagnoses, these cases could be expected to be particularly resistant to primary, deep-rooted change.

A final pretreatment factor is related to the referral circumstances. A major question is whether the referral was family-motivated, initiated by another institution or source of influence, or legally adjudicated. The only two examples of self-motivated families in our set of cases were Mary Lou (Liddle, Chapter 6) and Jane and Jack (Jacobson et al., Chapter 4). All the others were referred by another doctor, institution, or involved third party. None were legally sent to treatment although the T family (Wynne & Green, Chapter 5) would have been so ordered if they had not immediately arranged for an appointment for Floyd.

When one combines the major historical pretreatment factors with each family's current status, a pretreatment cluster of failure variables emerges. In summary, this cluster of pretreatment variables includes a rather lengthy history of problems including extreme tenaciousness of the major symptom; previous history of therapy, generally focused on one individual rather than the family system; a relatively severe diagnosis associated with the identified patient, who is most apt to be an adult with a life-cycle conflict centering around separation from the family; and an entry into treatment vis-à-vis a source external to the family.

THERAPIST

In addition to the pretreatment variables associated with the families in their own right, there are factors surrounding therapists that can potentially affect case outcome. Both professional and personal elements are influential.

Professional. Professional factors have an undisputed claim toward affecting treatment outcome. Experience level alone is considerably important and treatment retention is consistently shown to have a positive correlation with therapists' level of experience. In a broad sense, to insure some degree of potential success, a therapist assigned to working with families should have considerable training and experience as a family therapist. There is no necessary, or in our view likely, equivalence between the possession of family therapy skills and those necessary for individual therapy. Because of the vast differences between the theory and practices of individual versus family therapy, there is no reliable transfer from individual to family treatment, despite such obvious commonalities as the necessity of the therapist's capacity for empathy, caring, and the like.

Beyond the general training in family work, lies another more specific issue, that of the therapist's experience and knowledge relevant to the presenting problem. One might wonder about the likely effectiveness of a therapist treating a schizophrenic family if that therapist, although very experienced, had never worked with schizophrenics. Although perhaps not constituting quite as much of a mismatch of requisite skills and knowledge as sending an individual therapist into a family situation, the family therapist should have a working knowledge of the vicissitudes of the problem that he or she is about to treat. Without this knowledge, the likelihood of successful outcome is severely compromised.

Another related issue is that of doing cotherapy. Many family therapists have not had a great deal of experience in working with another therapist on a true peer level. More frequent is the student–professor cotherapy relationship. This was demonstrated here in several cases, all of which seemed to involve unfortunate complications for the treatment of the families. As a pretreatment variable, the cotherapy team must explore the same factors as a solo therapist and, in addition, must determine whether or not he or she is willing to cope with the additional problems likely to arise from the cotherapy situation. These include the cotherapy relationship with one another, the impact of that relationship on the family being treated, and the inherent competitive striving for power, status, control, and so on. Furthermore, a poor cotherapy alliance will gravely affect the process of therapy and is probably a reliable predictor of failure (e.g., Rice, Fey, & Kepecs, 1972). On the other hand, if the team has worked together previously and has resolved some of its relationship conflicts, cotherapy is likely to enhance the treatment process, particularly when the problems are as serious as those discussed here. Unfortunately, the cotherapy teams illustrated in this volume were more problematic, and the cotherapy relationships and interactions seemed to have been clinically associated with the negative effects of treatment. This may have been largely due to the fact that they involved either trainee–supervisor teams or teams that had just emerged from such a hierarchically ordered situation. More about the effects of cotherapy will be discussed in the following section.

In addition to the therapist experience factor, the therapist's enthusiasm and interest in the case is a determinant of the eventual outcome. As evidenced in the contextual atmosphere of the referral in Chapter 2 (Coleman), the therapist's positive attitude toward working with addiction and the challenge of the case history were major aspects of accepting this family into treatment. Perhaps two of the most vital questions a family therapist should ask prior to accepting a case are (1) "Do I really like working with this presenting problem?" and (2) "What specific information from the referral data interests me?"

Clearly, practical considerations limit some of the idealism discussed here, but given families as complicated as those that have been presented, special consideration with regard to the therapist's own circumstances is a necessary means of attempting to avoid failure.

Personal. The person of the therapist has been a central point of concern in almost all schools of psychotherapy (Gurman & Razin, 1977). It is a *sine qua non* that a therapist needs to possess excellent relationship skills (Gurman, 1977). A recent article by O'Malley, Suh, and Strupp (1983) underscores the fact that patient involvement is the most consistent predictor of therapy outcome. Perhaps nowhere is the therapist's capacity to relate more essential than in treating families. One's ability to form an alliance and to join family members is the bottom line of treatment (Gurman & Kniskern, 1978). How clearly this inadequacy is demonstrated in the session with the Anonymous family (Chapter 11); the most obvious factor in the sessions' gradual deterioration was the therapist's lack of empathic connection to the family.

In marked contrast to the relationship deficiency in the latter situation, the quality of real understanding and caring pervades many of the cases presented here. Liddle's feeling for Mary Lou and her mother is highlighted by his description of them "as, in the main, lovable, rather cranky eccentrics" (Chapter 6). The tenderness felt toward Harry Haverman pervades the Coleman case (Chapter 2) and the overwhelming commitment that Meyerstein and Dell had toward Herbert, Joe, and their parents (Chapter 10) further exemplify the emotional "pull" toward a family that lets them know that their therapist cares. Even though, as Liddle notes, this can occasionally have a negative effect, unless a person is able to have genuine concern for another, a profession other than therapy should be considered.

The therapists' own family history and current state of being are also important. Although the authors did not allude to their own personal lives, it would not be surprising if a few of them might have been struggling with some of the same issues as their treatment families. One would hope that the therapists' resources and coping mechanisms were superior to their patients, but it is hard to imagine that among the contributors none was experiencing any personal dilemmas, marital conflicts, separations, or empty nest crises, and so on. Hopefully, the major difference between the professionals' family struggles and their treatment families is the degree to which the conflicts persist. It is not expected that any of the therapists had been experiencing the emotional distress over the very same problem for a decade or more, like several of the families that have been described.

If a therapist is going through a personal bout with a problem similar to that of a referred family, he or she might wisely consider sending that case to someone else. Unfortunately, the demands of one's practice and the lack of time generally spent on studying pretreatment variables usually precludes doing this. Moreover, if this option were adopted as a rule, many couples and families, such as those going through the process of divorce might find it difficult to receive treatment (cf. Gurman, 1983). Yet, one would wonder how much the time spent in self-assessment *vis-à-vis* a new referral would help to prevent an ineffective treatment liaison.

Although each family treated by our therapists presented most of the characteristics associated with pretreatment failure criteria, their therapists did not. Each of the therapists who presented a case is an expert in family therapy; indeed, the essential factor in selecting contributors for this volume was that each be an undisputed leader in the field. Thus, in terms of the qualifications for working with families, the authors represent a selective group. The effectiveness of their relationship skills and ability to treat the types of families they described have been demonstrated over and over. These therapists include experts with impressive accumulations of experience in the treatment of a very wide range of clinical problems, including the most recalcitrant and difficult disorders brought to clinicians. Moreover and not surprisingly, most of the clinical problems described in these case studies were the very types in which these therapists have, to varying degrees, specialized during their years of clinical practice. Why, then, did they achieve such disappointing results? The next section will intensively explore some tentative answers to this fundamental question. Before glancing ahead, however, the checklists in Table 14-3 are offered as a means of reviewing important pretreatment factors associated with potential case outcome. It is our clinical impression that, singly or in some (as yet empirically undocumented) combi-

TABLE 14-3. Pretreatment Checklist

Family

1. What is the family's history relative to the current presenting problem? What additional symptoms or problems have they previously exhibited? Is there an apparent functional connection between previously treated (or untreated) problems and the current problem(s)?
2. How long has the present symptom persisted? What efforts have been made (outside a professional treatment context) to deal with these symptoms or problems? What is the pattern and flavor of the family's previously attempted solutions to the symptoms or problems?
3. Are there factors in the family's medical and genetic history that may be relevant to the current problem? Are there predisposing characteristics that could affect treatment?
4. In what ways may the family's socioeconomic status, religion, and ethnic cultural background influence treatment process and outcome, for example, expectations regarding the therapist's role, length and intensity of treatment, and so on?
5. What has been the family's previous experience with therapy? What schools or models of treatment have been used with what level of success?
6. Who is the identified patient and how do his or her symptoms or problems ripple through the system; that is, what is the function of the presenting problem and what is the feedback loop within which it is enacted?
7. In traditional psychiatric nomenclature, that is, according to *DSM-III* (American Psychiatric Association, 1980), what is the identified patient's diagnosis? Are there known effective "nonsystemic" treatments of the central problem or disorder, such as antidepressant medication for certain affective disorders? If so, and if such treatments are to be used, what will be the impact on the family, especially in terms of nonsymptomatic family members' interactions with the identified patient?
8. What life-cycle issues or developmental transitions are the family experiencing at present? Are these related to the central complaint?
9. What are the referral circumstances; for example, what is the source of therapeutic motivation, and so forth?
10. What is the family's attitude toward family therapy in general and/or toward particular methods or styles of family therapy?

Therapist

1. Does the assigned therapist have training and experience in working with the type(s) of problem(s) presented by this family?
2. Will the therapist be working with a cotherapist? What previous experiences have they had in doing cotherapy in general and with each other?
3. If cotherapists will be involved, what roles will they take, that is, colleagial, student–teacher, and so on? How do they feel about working together?
4. What interest and degree of enthusiasm does the therapist (and/or cotherapist) have for this particular case?
5. What factors surrounding this family are of special interest to the therapist?
6. What personal characteristics of the therapist will facilitate his or her work with this family?
7. How may the therapist's own family history possibly help or impede his or her work with this case?

TABLE 14-3. (*Continued*)

---

8. Is the therapist currently experiencing any personal problems or crises similar to those presented by this family? If so, how will their potential intrusion into the treatment of this case be minimized?
9. What problems does the therapist anticipate having with this family?
10. What would be the therapist's loss (e.g., financial, case census quota, etc.) if he or she did not treat this family?

---

nations, adequate attention to each of these matters may help to guide the family therapist's work in ways that will help to reduce the chances of treatment failures.

Early Treatment Factors

REFERRAL AND ASSESSMENT

Significant pretreatment issues surrounding family therapy referrals have already been discussed. In some of our own cases, referral circumstances were particularly complicated, helping to contribute ultimately to the unsuccessful outcome. Coleman (Chapter 2) elaborates on several of the issues surrounding the Haverman referral including an assortment of "good and bad" reasons for her involvement. Certainly she was fascinated by the case and found it a challenge. However, she was pressured by the clinic and its administration to assume major responsibility for a family that had all the signs of needing an enormous amount of time and care, which she was unable to sustain because of a conflict of interests and responsibilities. Similarly, although Tomm (Chapter 13) does not say why he accepted the L famly, there were overwhelming issues associated with their referral. In the midst of a complicated situation—Dr. N, a personal friend of the family, was recommending that Mr. L go to an inpatient substance abuse treatment center rather than family therapy, Dr. M was consulting as a biological–organic expert, and Dr. S was urging the L's to participate in family therapy—Tomm moves into the case. Perhaps not quite as complicated but also important were the conditions encountered by Wynne and Green (Chapter 5) and Kaslow (Chapter 12). In each instance, the referrals were from other sources that were applying rather strong pressure to the families to seek therapy post haste. Thus, it is apparent why they sought treatment; what is not clear in the latter two situations is why the therapists accepted the referrals.

Although not mentioned, the practice of psychotherapy is remunerative and provides support for ourselves and our families. In public agencies, and particularly in private therapy settings, it is possible that referrals are accepted for financial reasons. This is, of course, a valid, pragmatic reason to treat a family, yet not one contributor to this volume discussed the influence of economics on their acceptance of the family referrals. It would be interesting to know how often economics do enter into the decision to treat a particular family. Many of the cases seen by our experts were clients being treated at nonprofit institutions and might have been accepted by the therapists because of caseload or teaching requirements. One might speculate, however, that in the private sector the primary criterion for case acceptance is the family's ability to pay.

Closely aligned with referral factors are those associated with assessment, and many of us consider the two as a single process. Regardless of whether referral and assessment factors are discussed separately or combined, the circumstances surrounding referral are an essential part of the entire case assessment.

Nine of the twelve families presented here were considered by their therapists to have been inadequately or inaccurately assessed. The Anonymous family (Chapter 11) describes how it felt so misunderstood, that is, misassessed, from the very beginning; L'Abate and Baggett (Chapter 9) failed to determine that, "a more linear, step-by-step" approach would have probably been much more effective with the S family, particularly with Mr. S. Their experience demonstrates the flexibility that the therapist must have in order to make the treatment fit the family rather than the reverse. In Liddle's case (Chapter 6) the easy joining and the family's unusual psychological awareness interfered with the assessment of the case and, in conjunction with the other factors of failure, served as a false-positive aspect of the unusually complex mother–daughter relationship. Ficher and Kaplan (Chapter 8) originally diagnosed the case as one of "complicated sexual dysfunction." This they viewed as their most serious error. The entire treatment approach followed from this misassessment, preventing other more important issues from emerging and being resolved. Meyerstein and Dell (Chapter 10) felt that one of their two practical errors was "insufficient analysis and assessment of the family's patterns of interactions"; they also discuss how they "failed to adequately include themselves and the ecological network of other helpers." These factors were associated with some of the difficulties that arose doing treatment. Like Liddle (Chapter 6), Meyerstein and Dell were too intrigued by the family, ". . . we were mesmerized by parts of the system. . . ." Jacobson et al. (Chapter 4) describe the couple as having bipolar states of being, "in crisis or 'recovered.'" Jacobson et al. view their appearance during the pretreatment assessment in a "recovery" phase as leading to later difficulty during treatment. Evidently this relationship "mood swing" was elusive during early assessment. Kaslow (Chapter 12) mentions an important assessment issue when she states that she failed "to give recognition to their value system. . . ." She further notes that she had not "sufficiently conveyed [her] cognizance of the family's strengths and accomplishments." Coleman (Chapter 2) discusses several of her own omissions related to life-cycle factors, loss, and family of origin. In marked contrast to L'Abate and Baggett's assessment error that led them to overlook the need to use a more linear approach, Coleman is self-critical about being too linear. She questions, "In this family the cybernetic paradigm hits one in the face; how then could I have missed it?"

From the examples given it is possible to formulate some basic guidelines for checking the thoroughness of one's assessment to also take into account the important referral issues. The checklists in Table 14-4, although hardly exhaustive, should cover the major components.

A common problem encountered in all therapies is that of the values and attitudes of the participants. One must be aware of one's own value system relative to each new family seen in treatment. Also, a therapist should try to understand the family's value system, particularly as it affects therapy goals, strategies and techniques, and so on, and should be aware of value differences among family members. This was a problem in a few of the cases and is most obvious in the treatment of the ex-priest and his wife (Ficher & Kaplan, Chapter 8). A frequent intervening variable is the therapist's own goal for the family's relational health. Although not offering an iron-clad guarantee, the use of a formal assessment process will assist in making treatment goals clear. Furthermore, even in the case of experienced professionals, a written assessment forces one to more closely examine the realities and fantasies surrounding our patient families.

The need for accurate and comprehensive assessment cannot be overstressed. The difficulty of nearly all of our therapists (83%) derived, in part, from this phase of treatment. Clearly, in relationship to failure, there is strong evidence that errors made in the referral and assessment period have profound and perhaps irreversible effects on eventual outcome. The field of family therapy is fortunate to have a large body of enthusiastic professionals eager to learn and practice the most *avant garde* methods in vogue today. Perhaps we need to temper our pace, however, before we zoom in to try promising, but highly experimental interventions. A more cautious and thorough effort to understand families at the beginning may help to lead to a more successful treatment outcome.

Treatment Factors

The attempt to analyze the failure path of our 12 cases imposes an arbitrary division between stages of therapy. It also forces one to separate concepts and constructs, thus making family therapy appear to be a function of disparate units, somewhat like a model made from a set of Tinker Toys®. What makes family work so complex is that all its components are not discrete. Unlike a Tinker Toy®, if you remove one section of a family the new construction may

TABLE 14-4. Treatment Checklist: Comparing Referral Issues to Therapist's Assessment

---

Referral

---

1. Why was the case referred to *this* institution, practice, or therapist?
2. Why was the case referred at *this point in time*?
3. Was the case referred for positive reasons—such as this institution, practice, or therapist is apt to be most effective with the family—or was the case "dumped" by other agents who were defeated, perplexed, or angry?
4. If the referral has been made by another professional person (physician, psychotherapist, clergyman, etc.), and the initial contact was made by a family member, has the current therapist discussed the referral with the referring person?
5. If the referral was made by a friend, relative, or nonprofessional personal acquaintance of the family, what was said about the present therapist that made the referral to *this* therapist seem attractive?
6. *Who* in the family made the *initial contact* and why was he or she selected to do so? What are the overt and covert messages relative to this person's position in the family and role in the presenting problem.
7. What characteristics, associations, and attitudes surround the initial contact? Is there chemistry? Is it negative or positive?
8. *How much resistance* is noted during the referral contact, such as difficulty arranging appointment time, bringing other members, and so on?
9. How difficult is it to *engage* the caller?
10. *Does the therapist have the experience* to treat the presenting problem?
11. Does the case seem like a challenge?
12. Does the therapist look forward to the prospective session or would he or she prefer someone else to see the family?

Assessment

---

1. What type of assessment is being used? Is it written and does it conform to a uniform outline? Is it merely done in one's head?
2. What theoretical framework guides this assessment?
3. Are hypotheses formulated and do they include the presenting problem?
4. Are life-cycle issues integrated into the assessment?
5. Are intergenerational issues included in the assessment?
6. Is the history of the family of procreation included in the assessment? The history might reveal the loss of a child, significant separation(s), previous medical and psychological problems, treatments, and the like.
7. Are all systems levels assessed: family as a system, marital subsystem, and each individual as a psychological subsystem, and as a biological subsystem?
8. Are therapy goals established? By whom (therapist or family)?
9. Are planned interventions consistent with the stated goals?
10. If the therapist's goals are different from those of the family, are they made explicit or kept quiet?
11. What likely outcome(s) are anticipated as a result of this assessment process?

---

not be substantial enough to stand on its own. The material being discussed here is really continuous, and it is important for the reader to keep in mind that the issues are isolated for purposes of explication; the template itself must always be kept in sight.

As one moves into the midst of the cases, several major factors relative to failure emerge. Some failure factors are offshoots of the initial assessment problems; others, however, are more specifically related to treatment techniques and interactional difficulties between family members, family and therapist, or therapists. For the sake of clarification these issues are divided into (1) theoretical issues and (2) process issues.

THEORETICAL ISSUES AND FAILURE

Academic training generally reinforces the idea that all therapy must be done within the context of theory. A student is taught to do what he or she does with patients as a result of having a theoretical framework as a constant guide. As we move away from the university setting, theory-based practice still prevails but often becomes more loosely constructed. Also, as therapists mature they become less theory bound. Lest one accuse family therapists of being heretics, the history of psychoanalysis lends credence to this normative process.

Theoretical problems relative to failing emerged for several of our therapists. Coleman (Chapter 2) points out that she even abandoned her own theory of addiction, which was developed from working with families like the Havermans. In the final section of her chapter, she discusses the many loss issues associated with the Havermans' lives, noting with apparent regret that those issues were never brought into therapy. Loss and separation issues were similarly embedded in nine (75%) of the cases, some more subtly than others (see Table 14-5). In Tomm's case (Chapter 13), death was a constant issue, from the loss of a 5-year-old son from cancer and the death of Mrs. L's alcoholic father to the ever-present suicidal gestures of both parents. It was perhaps predictable that, with so much apparent counterphobic behavior, one of the L's would eventually succeed in bringing about another death. Perhaps less apparent, but certainly significant, was the fear of the potential loss of John to residential treatment if the D's did not attend family therapy (Segal & Watzlawick, Chapter 3). Mrs. Smith's (Meyerstein & Dell, Chapter 10) mother died at the same time that her middle son was born, causing one to wonder about the effect of her death on his birth and the subsequent burden accompanying these two closely aligned events. It is not possible to directly attribute the lack of success in these cases to these unresolved losses, but it is important to be aware that almost all of the families experienced rather significant losses or separations, and in most of the cases the focus on them in treatment was minimal.

TABLE 14-5. Loss Issues in Family Life

Therapist(s)	Family issues	
	Death	Separation
Beavers (Chapter 7)		X
Coleman (Chapter 2)	X	X
Ficher and Kaplan (Chapter 8)	X	X
Jacobson *et al.* (Chapter 4)	X	
Kaslow (Chapter 12)		X
Liddle (Chapter 6)		X
Meyerstein and Dell (Chapter 10)	X	X
Segal and Watzlawick (Chapter 3)		X
Tomm (Chapter 13)	X	X

Note. "Loss" includes death, direct and indirect suicide, and separation.

One of the most pervasive theoretical issues affecting a number of cases is that of power. Power frequently resides in a subsystem composed of persons who are in a seemingly less potent role who appear to control persons who normally would be expected to wield greater influence by virtue of age, position in the family, or experience. Sometimes power seems to lie in a parent–child coalition. Such hierarchical inversions or cross-generational liaisons were apparent in eight of our cases (66.6%) as follows:

- Anonymous (Chapter 11)
- Coleman (Chapter 2)
- Kaslow (Chapter 12)
- L'Abate and Baggett (Chapter 9)
- Liddle (Chapter 6)
- Meyerstein and Dell (Chapter 10)
- Segal and Watzlawick (Chapter 3)
- Wynne and Green (Chapter 5)

The siblings in the Haverman family (Coleman, Chapter 2), are excellent examples of how a junior subsystem gains power, infiltrates the larger family system by disrupting it, and helps to bring the entire family to eventual destruction. An astounding example of power was that held by the son (Segal & Watzlawick, Chapter 3) who was able to "send" his parents to family therapy while he stayed home to reinforce the symptom. Mary Lou (Liddle, Chapter 6) similarly was able to maintain control by saving paper bags and by shoplifting, rendering her too immature and ineffectual to leave her aging mother. Dual cross-generational subsystems existed in the Smith family (Meyerstein & Dell, Chapter 10) in which initially Mr. Smith and Bill were in control of the functional or instrumental aspects of the family, while

Mrs. Smith, Joe, and Herbert were responsible for the expressive part. Between the two complementary subsystems there was some maintenance of harmony until Bill grew up, leaving behind a cacophony of psychotic behavior. The subsequent coalitions between Mrs. Smith and Joe and between Mr. Smith and Herbert were less effectual, often breaking apart, and pitting one lone family member against a more formidable threesome.

Similar examples are found in the other families. Certainly, one can see how each component permits the power to reside in the subsystem, thus forming a very adequate feedback loop that keeps the symptomatic behavior in fine tune. It is fascinating to note how many of the cases (67%) presented here had either a hierarchical inversion or a cross-generational coalitionary unit orchestrating the family theme.

The influence of intergenerational patterns on present behavior is viewed differentially as a consequence of one's theoretical vantage point. Depending on the degree of significance placed on these factors, intergenerational issues are either used merely for intake or background data, or may become central foci for therapy (see Table 14-6). Thus, intergenerational factors are theoretically relevant and frequently involve important process issues. Table 14-6 indicates the role of previous generations in the cases described here. It is somewhat amazing to see that the only case where intergenerational issues were taken seriously and dealt with explicitly in the process of treatment was the Ficher and Kaplan couple (Chapter 8). Six of the therapists did not use

TABLE 14-6. Intergenerational Considerations among Treatment Families

Therapist(s)	Type of use in treatment			
	Not used	Minimal use	Used for back-ground information only	Used directly in therapy
Anonymous (Chapter 11)	X			
Beavers (Chapter 7)	X			
Coleman (Chapter 2)		X		
Ficher and Kaplan (Chapter 8)				X
Jacobson et al. (Chapter 4)			X	
Kaslow (Chapter 12)	X			
L'Abate and Baggett (Chapter 9)	X			
Liddle (Chapter 6)				X
Meyerstein and Dell (Chapter 10)		X		
Segal and Watzlawick (Chapter 3)	X			
Tomm (Chapter 13)		X		
Wynne and Green (Chapter 5)	X			

intergenerational material at all, three of them used it rather minimally, and two apparently acquired such information largely for record-keeping purposes. It is difficult to know what this reflects. It may well be a function of the "here-and-now" orientation of the models used by this group of therapists. It may also be a significant aspect of failing. It is not possible to make any assumptions without having a comparison group of more dynamically oriented cases; however, what is striking is that even those therapists who were more psychodynamically oriented (Kaslow, Chapter 12; L'Abate & Baggett, Chapter 9) were no more apt to integrate transgenerational data with the current problems than were the structural–strategic therapists. One might speculate that in these very complex cases, intergenerational factors are too important to be overlooked. This may be a highly important area to pursue further, but on the basis of what we have here, one can only wonder what would have happened if more ancestry had been allowed to enter the therapy room.

Process and Content Issues

The subgrouping and labeling of family therapy constructs, as previously noted, is arbitrary. An example is the issue of intergenerational factors. Although theoretically derived, the likelihood of intergenerational factors becoming pragmatic issues in treatment depends on how a therapist functions. Among our cases antecedent family patterns received minimal attention as either process or content variables.

THE ROLE OF THE PRESENTING PROBLEM

In contrast, although the therapists may have paid little heed to the role of "inheritance," the presenting problems clearly received more concentrated attention. The presenting problem or symptom was dealt with in all cases but the Anonymous family (Chapter 11) where the problem never got a chance to be presented. Perhaps one of the difficulties with initiating the session was related to the way the problem was amorphously distributed across the entire family, making it difficult to focus.

What is perhaps more interesting than whether or not the presenting problem was dealt with explicitly during the course of therapy is the status of the presenting problem at the conclusion of therapy. The varying circumstances surrounding the presenting problem when treatment ceased are worthy of review. In one of the most hopeful cases (Beavers, Chapter 7), the identified patient, Donna, was less psychotic at the conclusion of the second round of therapy. One does not know, however, if this was the result of the renewed therapeutic effort, the cumulative beneficial effects of multitreatment approaches, or remission in the usual bimodal states of psychotic and nonpsychotic functioning of schizophrenic families. Jane and Jack (Jacobson *et al.*, Chapter 4) were also moderately improved at the termination of therapy. It was suggested by the therapists, however, that the accomplished gains might also have been a function of the couple's recurring cycle of crisis and recovery. If therapy ended during a recovery phase, the end result would look significantly different from that attained if treatment had stopped during a crisis.

In the S family (L'Abate & Baggett, Chapter 9), some definite improvement was noted in son R, with shifts seen in several of the behaviors associated with his presenting symptoms. It is doubtful, however, whether permanent changes took place within the family system, and the readministration of R's Ritalin after only a 2-week hiatus suggests that the improvements were likely to be temporary. Similarly, limited change occurred in Mary Lou (Liddle, Chapter 6) as a result of threatened eviction. Here, too, although there was some individual change, the interpersonal transactions between mother and daughter did not differ markedly from those seen initially.

In six cases the presenting problem was still present at termination, and in two instances (Coleman, Chapter 2; Tomm, Chapter 13) the identified patient died. In the Coleman case the presenting problem of drug abuse became the legacy of the next generation, and one could speculate that the threat of suicide would hover over future generations of the family that Tomm treated. Thus, for the families discussed in this book and probably in most cases of unsuccessful family therapy, the status of the presenting problem is a central and imposing dimension of failure.

Motivation and Consumerism

The issue of whether or not family members are real "customers" for therapy was raised by Segal and Watzlawick (Chapter 3). Before therapists assume excessive blame for family therapy failures, we should determine if the families we are seeing are serious "buyers." Assessing the status of the presenting problem at the conclusion of treatment necessarily involves consideration of the motivational factors that influence the entire process of therapy.

In the previous section one of the pretreatment issues we considered were the circumstances of referrals. The prevailing conditions that lead a family into treatment are not always connected to their (self-generated) desire to be in therapy. In considering the role of motivation it is important to periodically review the conditions surrounding the initiation of treatment, searching for cues pertaining to a family's intrinsic drive for treatment. Initial motivation may be an important predictor of outcome. Thus, the clinician's review of motivation at critical stages of therapy or when treatment energy appears to be waning is a possible means of preventing failure.

One of the ways to assess motivation during the treatment process is simply by noting who comes to the sessions and the consistency of their attendance. Early in the development of family therapy, much meaning was ascribed to the absent member. This was considered so important that therapists at times would send families home without treating them unless all members were present. Perhaps the most basic premise behind the "missing-person theory" was that whoever was not included was a significant member without whom treatment success was unlikely (Whitaker & Keith, 1981). The missing member was viewed as the preserver of the family's homeostatic functioning. Further theories about the role of the absent member were proposed but as the field grew and models changed, becoming more present-oriented and interactional, many therapists began to work with whoever appeared at the scheduled session. Some strategic approaches advocate asking family members to bring who they think is important, thus giving sanction to leave some members home. Today, there is growing acceptance that whom one chooses to bring and omit from therapy is of major significance, often contributing to treatment success (Gurman & Kniskern, 1978).

Among the cases presented in this book, the configuration of members who attended regularly varied remarkably. The identified patient was never seen by Segal and Watzlawick (Chapter 3); the father dropped out in L'Abate and Baggett's family (Chapter 9), and there was repetitive truancy among the family members seen by Wynne and Green (Chapter 5), which the authors felt was a major aspect of their failure. The mother in the family seen by Beavers (Chapter 7) dropped out at a critical time; the absence of the Haverman children was a central issue in the Coleman case (Chapter 2). The configuration of attending members in the sessions conducted by Kaslow (Chapter 12) was topsy-turvy, fragmenting the family before it was clear what was really going on. This, in addition to having another therapist in the background, probably contributed heavily to the family's being noncustomers for family therapy. Even among those families whose members attended sessions regularly, other types of absences may have been overlooked and not brought into the sessions. For example, Mary Lou (Liddle, Chapter 6) had an older sister who had left the nest much earlier. One might wonder if the hoarded bags had anything at all to do with her; whatever her role, there did not seem to be an attempt to bring this potentially important sibling "into" the therapeutic process.

It is not possible to know whether a change in the configuration of those attending sessions would have any effect on making families become *bona fide* customers. Nor do we know if changing these configurations would have changed the participants' motivation and influenced eventual outcome. One might wish to examine such issues, however, when therapy is not progressing in a positive direction. Detecting these potential impediments to success during the process of treatment might offer an opportunity to detour an oncoming failure.

The issue of motivation is complex and needs to be understood in relationship to each family member, therapist, and network of involved institutions, particularly the referring agent. Motivation can be explored in terms of the *type* and *amount*, but most significant is the determination of who in the therapeutic constellation of players has the most drive toward therapy.

Among our cases therapist's motivation often seemed to be heightened in the therapists who often were willing to go beyond the realm of the therapy sessions to make things better. Meyerstein and Dell (Chapter 10) were compulsively involved in keeping Joe and Herbert out of the hospital and worked overtime and on weekends for their cause, which retrospectively they acknowledged as inconsistent with the family's goals. Coleman (Chapter 2) went after the family in order to hold their final session. This too, was probably more a reflection of her motivation than that of the Havermans.

With regard to motivation, Tomm's family (Chapter 13) experienced enormous emotional suffering, sometimes reflected by their painful and persistent way of seeking help from several doctors at once. One might think this was indeed indicative of their motivational drive for relief; yet another interpretation might view such behavior as an attempt to prevent anything at all from changing.

Kaslow's family (Chapter 12) also seemed to dart from treatment to treatment. Again, is this a reflection of the family's motivation to be rid of their problems or is it a symptom-maintaining effort?

In some instances motivation appeared to reside more exclusively in one person, not necessarily the identified patient. The mother in the Anonymous family (Chapter 11) was ostensibly the motivator, but when one considers that she did nothing to offset a session that she had to know was going to impede her purpose, some doubt is raised about how much she too was just a part of a system that really did not want to change. After all, she was the experienced therapy patient who had to know when things were not going right. Why then did she not balk at what was happening? She also could have encouraged the other members to be more honest. As leader, had she taken a risk, the others might have followed. Mary Lou (Liddle, Chapter 6) had several therapy experiences, representing her "marriage" with her mother, although her partner previously remained absent. Was she more eager to change than her mother? Realistically, one might think so in that she had more to gain by growing up and leaving home than her mother, who would inevitably be left to live and possibly die alone, a prospect that the mother obviously did not encourage. If one explores the systemic rigidity, however, one may conclude that although Mary Lou may very well have been seeking therapeutic assistance, her motivation may not have had anything to do with her wanting to change the configuration of her homelife. She may have merely wanted someone to talk to, a confidante, perhaps a "father." Liddle was clearly eager to move in to restructure the pair, but even with Mother's presence in treatment this was not about to happen.

These cases all seem to suggest that the assessment of motivation is probably intimately related to the issue of goals. Consistent with our discussion on goal setting (see following section), it is highly important for the therapist to accurately assess *whose* goals are being established in treatment. We view motivation then as a function of one's desire for something, and if that something is not valued by the family but is determined as important by the therapist or some external force (Wynne & Green, Chapter 5), motivation will be less than optimal. Thus, any attempt to look at motivation as keen or dull is useless without reviewing the assessment phase of treatment and insuring that the goals of treatment are consistent with the *family's* needs and expressed desires.

Goal Setting and the Product

Related to the issue of consumerism in psychotherapy is its product, which is associated with the establishment of initial treatment goals. In the preceding section on assessment, goals were discussed in relationship to values and attitudes. As noted, the family and the therapist may differ markedly in what each views as a viable and desirable treatment goal. It is unlikely that a family will seriously work toward a goal that is not intrinsically related to something they value or want. This became a major factor in Meyerstein and Dell's failure (Chapter 10) with the Smiths. As the authors suggest, ". . . our knowledge of 'pathology' cannot tell us what the goal of therapy should be. If it does we are mystifying ourselves and our clients. A therapist who understands pathology-as-values must conduct his or her therapy in terms of values (rather than a supposedly objective pathology). So, when a client or family desires to pursue different goals than the therapist, the therapist is not able to 'know' that their wish to pursue those goals is a further indication of their pathology."

Meyerstein and Dell (Chapter 10) take themselves to task for believing that they "knew what the pathology was." Thus, they established goals for the Smith family according to what they (the professionals) and the community valued, thereby breeding a conflict between established "normal" values and those the family might have deemed more important. As the authors reflect, ". . . the only customer for these treatment goals was *us*."

A conflict in goals was also noted in the Ficher and Kaplan case (Chapter 8). There, the therapists' value was sexual expression without constraint. Perhaps what represented adequate sexual freedom for the former priest and his wife was the very act of marriage. Clearly, the goals they might have set for themselves independently might have differed a great deal from those of two sexually aware, self-actualized therapists who had never been infused with stringent religious doctrine.

In some cases treatment goals remained rather ambiguous (Kaslow, Chapter 12; Segal & Watzlawick, Chapter 3), and in some instances it was difficult to know if there were goals at all (Jacobson *et al.*, Chapter 4). Thus, in exploring the degree to which a family is a real consumer, one must determine if what is being offered is attractive enough to make working for it worthwhile.

Alliance

As discussed in the pretreatment section, the relationship between the therapist and the family being treated involves without question one of the most significant and multidimensional factors in treatment outcome. In all schools and theories of psychotherapy the therapist–patient bond is studied and discussed. There is ample evidence suggesting that the alliance factor plays a central role in treatment outcome; when positive, these relationship dimensions may transcend varying models, schools, and techniques of therapy.

In family therapy the therapist must first have the necessary personal skills to relate to others and to be secure in doing so in a group situation. The attempt to connect with a family is perhaps one of the greatest challenges of all therapies because, unlike a group without continuity or history, the family has years of experience with each other and in dealing with strangers. The family therapist is an unusual stranger who intrudes upon the family at a time when they are vulnerable and who offers assistance, but not without eroding some of the family's congealed patterns and behaviors and exploding and exposing their long-term intrafamily modes of interaction. Unless the therapist can somehow connect with *each* member and offer believable evidence that each member's feelings and ideas will be respected, no treatment can ever take place. Each member of the family must feel safe with the therapist in order to take the risks that will inevitably be required for significant and lasting change.

Among our cases alliance factors were considered to be a problem in many of the failures. This is particularly interesting since, as noted earlier, all of the therapists are experts, with many years of experience with families and many triumphs in succeeding with difficult problems, and are unquestionably superior in their capacity to connect with families in treatment. Nonetheless, many were unable to make the kind of connection that might have fostered success. In his hypothetical reconstruction, Beavers (Chapter 7) notes, "I believe I have learned that equivocation when a family is desperate—in effect, offering a peanut when a steak dinner is needed, even demanded—does not have a good chance of success. I will either make room in my schedule for daily visits or throw in the towel immediately. It is quite likely that if I had given enough attention to the whole family quickly enough the desperation would have been less and would not have proceeded to the point of the extrusion of Donna."

Tomm (Chapter 13) also includes among his "tactical" errors not seeing the wife alone, which might have facilitated his connection with her. Even more to the point is his remark that "The first mistake probably occurred at the beginning of therapy, when I allowed myself to become engaged primarily with the husband rather than with the whole family (or couple) as a unity." Tomm also views his own vacation at a time when Mr. L.'s transference was at a peak as another tactical error causing the patient to feel abandoned. The therapist in the Jacobson *et al.* case (Chapter 4) overly identified with the wife and never formed a good working alliance with the husband. Like Tomm's overinvolvement with one member that left the other therapeutically bereft, the skewed connections compounded the other failure issues. Similarly, Coleman (Chapter 2) had too much affection for Harry and Connie while never establishing a bond with the siblings. These faulty, or at least incomplete, alliances are in contrast with those formed by Meyerstein and Dell (Chapter 10) and Liddle (Chapter 6), all of whom were so fascinated by what was happening that they may have become overly involved to the extent that one might consider their alliances too tight. Without the room to gain perspective, a therapist can develop an overalignment with the family, creating an enmeshed structure. Although this extreme may not have been reached here, it is important to note that too much alliance may lead to (or be) a kind of overidentification, which unfortunately can render therapy impotent.

Cotherapy

Problems in working with another therapist were discussed in the previous section of this chapter, where the focus was on the pretreatment considerations relative to cotherapy. Within the treatment process itself, when family difficulties often become increasingly complicated, cotherapy is apt to have either an ameliorating or disastrous effect. In the families presented here, cotherapy unfortunately may have been linked to the latter result. Not one of the cotherapy teams appeared to benefit the family. Even more critical is the fact that cotherapy may have contributed substantially to the ultimate treatment failures.

In 50% of our cases, a traditional cotherapy team was used. In their case reviews, some of the therapists discuss the impact of cotherapy on the family, while others merely allude to it. Coleman (Chapter 2) emphasized the issue of symmetry, reflecting that "Greg and I were the wrong pair for the family. There was just too much symmetry between us and Harry and Connie. No matter what I did, Greg came off looking inadequate. . . ." Even though both therapists were aware of the effect of their relationship patterns on the Haverman family, their cotherapy behavior was as resistant to change as the family's behavior patterns. Attempts to look at this more deeply vis-à-vis supervision, "never helped our relationship which, at best, remained tenuous."

The imbalance of status between cotherapists was apparent in several cases; the prevailing pattern was that of supervisor–trainee. As L'Abate and Baggett (Chapter 9) suggest, "In spite of our development of a joint strategy from the beginning of treatment, some unspoken factors may have influenced our failure. Although we worked as equals, hidden (and not so hidden) issues of dominance–submission may have prevented the development of a coherent therapeutic style. . . ."

Liddle (Chapter 6) states that he decided to see Mary Lou and her mother with a student because of the "complexity and difficulty of the case." When reviewing this decision he remarks, "In retrospect, it is clear that this experience was an instrumental and formative one in my ultimate decision to abandon this technique as a viable teaching format." Clearly, this statement is not an endorsement of the traditional cotherapy model.

In their hypothetical reconstruction, Wynne and Green (Chapter 5) still advocate the use of two therapists but suggest a change in role definition, making each role specific and structured while also working more as a team of colleagues, reversing roles with a series of families patterned on the Milan model. These authors point to the "hazards of a loosely structured cotherapy relationship . . ." which makes it "all too easy for the therapist to evade dealing with differences and responsibility about what should be done. Each therapist can unwittingly assume that the other will take the responsibility, resulting in a lack of effective leadership by either. In effect, the avoidance of the divergence constitutes a pseudomutual cotherapy relationship." A similar issue of structure and role definition appeared in the L'Abate and Baggett case (Chapter 9) and to some degree in the Meyerstein and Dell case (Chapter 10).

The traditional cotherapy model may invite a pseudomutual relationship. It also has a tendency to elicit power and hierarchical conflicts between therapists. Unless they are truly peers, having had similar experiences in life and in their professional work, one will most likely emerge as more dominant. Perhaps what the experiences cited here suggest is that (1) structure and role definition in cotherapy are essential and that (2) the newer team models that place one therapist in the room with the family while a team of one or more additional therapists observes the session, as demonstrated by the Milan model, may provide optimal benefit to both therapists and families in treatment. Again, one can have no sense of certainty that the multiproblem families presented in this book would have experienced more favorable outcomes had they been treated by a Milan-type team, but one should at least entertain the thought that this may be an effective way of coping with the treatment difficulties such families pose.

Professional Transitions

Like families, therapists also experience developmental changes in their professional growth. Most family therapists were originally trained in an individual framework that was often psychodynamic in orientation. A major shift has to occur in the family in order to treat a family successfully. A central problem for a therapist making that change lies not only in learning the techniques of treating family members together, but in learning how to think in terms of systems, a long difficult process. Years of work often are involved before thinking in terms of systems becomes an internalized, automatic sensing device—the major core of a family systems therapist. Within a systems model one finds several major schools that further dictate how a therapist thinks and how he or she conducts therapeutic interventions (Gurman & Kniskern, 1981). A family therapist thus develops along many different lines, frequently beginning to do family therapy one way and eventually shifting to schools or models that impose very different treatment methods yet still fall under the rubric of general systems theory.

As already suggested in the previous section on cotherapy, several therapists treating the families presented in this book were experiencing transitional states in their own professional development. Liddle (Chapter 6) discusses the problems inherent in his treatment of the M family as a function of an inadequate integration of models. Specifically, he suggests that there were "problems in construction (as well as the problem of implementation)." His overemphasis on technique was perhaps related to his own transitional processes as a family therapist. As a 2nd-year postdoctoral trainee in structural and strategic family therapy, Liddle was obviously making major conceptual shifts away from his previous eclecticism. As he states, "The case was thus begun on the cusp of a change within a change."

Tomm (Chapter 13) discusses the impact of his experience with the L family on his professional development. He suggests that his failure "shook me to my roots, my 'epistemological roots,'" making "what seemed perfectly 'correct' then, now appear 'wrong.'" One would suspect that Tomm was somehow ready for personal change and that the L family became the viable catalyst. As Tomm reviews his epistemological errors, it becomes increasingly apparent that his previous integration of concepts and techniques must have been open to modification. How often a therapist is on the edge of making a developmental transition is not known, but given the advances that are constantly being made in family therapy, professional growth must be an integral component of being in this rapidly advancing field of behavioral science. Thus, as we explore dimensions of pretreatment circumstances relevant to treatment failure, the therapist's own stance on the professional continuum and his or her stage of epistemological development must be kept in mind as important variables.

Ecological Collisions

The role of other systems colliding with family therapists and families in treatment is often significant and it has proved to have effects on almost all the cases described here. These "alter" systems included ghosts of therapists seen in the past, as well as nonfamily therapists who were involved with one or more family members at the same time that they were being treated in family therapy; schools (L'Abate & Baggett, Chapter 9; Wynne & Green, Chapter 5); the police (Meyerstein & Dell, Chapter 10); child welfare agencies (Wynne & Green); nonpsychiatric physicians of various specialties (Anonymous, Chapter 11; Ficher & Kaplan, Chapter 8; Wynne & Green; Coleman, Chapter 2; Beavers, Chapter 7); and additional psychiatrists or mental health specialists (Anonymous; Beavers; Coleman; Kaslow, Chapter 12; L'Abate & Baggett; Liddle, Chapter 6; Meyerstein & Dell; Segal & Watzlawick, Chapter 3; Tomm, Chapter 13). It is rather alarming to note that except for the husband and wife in Jacobson et al. (Chapter 4), all of the other families had antecedent or on-going collisions with other professional systems.

Some of these systems were more directly involved with the families, yet others were more subtle in their influence. In the case of the Anonymous family (Chapter 11), Tina's mother had a continuous line to her own therapist to deal with her own intermittent anxieties. Although her therapist was supportive of the family's being seen by someone else, the enormous power of his relationship with the mother certainly interferred with her willingness to open up to another therapist. Thus, direct "hands-on" behavior with a family may not be necessary in order for other systems to intrude upon the basic therapist–family group.

Wynne and Green (Chapter 5) felt remiss in not including the school official in the treatment process. They note, "It is striking that it was only shortly before termination that we learned that the real legal responsibility lay with the Child Protective Unit and not with the school." With hindsight they realized that ". . . we should have clarified explicitly the formal relationships between each of the community agencies, between each of them and the family, and our potential role with each of them. . . ."

In addition to the interface between other institutions and family therapy, there are the therapist's own competing roles and or responsibilities. Few of us are able to limit ourselves to working exclusively with only special types of family problems. Most of us, like the therapists presenting cases in this book, treat an assortment of dysfunctions. Similarly, most of us have multidimensional types of professional responsibilities. It is hoped that our many-faceted career interests are well integrated and complementary. At certain times, however, our interests may not be synchronized, at which point they can become competitive and conflictual. When this happens our various career interests may negatively affect our work with families, becoming as disruptive as competing institutions or professionals.

Coleman (Chapter 2) previously mentioned how her research imposed time constraints on her attention to the Haverman family, particularly when the case became more drawn out than she anticipated. Her own values were tested as she wrestled with wanting to be creative and therapeutically responsive to the family's needs, while feeling compelled to accomplish research goals that had specific time and funding limitations.

Liddle (Chapter 6) also discusses his joint roles as case supervisor, cotherapist and clinic director. In each of these three situations he had to be administratively responsible while at the same time giving attention to the constant demands of Mary Lou and her mother. Although his activities were all clinical in nature, thus more interrelated than Coleman's diverse responsibilities, the burden of each aspect of his work must have been intensified when the mother and daughter became, "the stars of the clinic." A great deal of attention to one particular family always increases one's anxiety about success, sometimes imposing an additional demand that adds just one more burden to the therapist's already over-worked internal system.

Time and Energy

Beavers (Chapter 7) suggests that one of his problems was not having the time or energy in a busy private practice to attend to all the demands placed on him by Donna and her family. The issue of time and energy is a salient one; it is rarely mentioned in professional literature or in training programs although it is probably more subtly subsumed under discussions on therapist "burnout."

Among our cases there is a definite sense of weariness that often emerges, suggesting that like Coleman (Chapter 2) and Liddle (Chapter 6), the case "got" to many of the therapists after awhile. One can easily understand why burnout could happen due to the families' complexity, demands, and uncanny ability to defeat everyone who ever came into contact with them. This is succinctly underscored by Jacobson et al. (Chapter 4), who describe the therapist as "exhausted at the end." It is interesting that with only two exceptions (Anonymous, Chapter 11; Wynne & Green, Chapter 5) the therapists persisted in treating these families for rather long periods of time ranging from 18 sessions (Jacobson et al.) to many sessions over a period of several years (L'Abate & Baggett, Chapter 9). Thus failure in and of itself cannot be attributed to insuffient time or concentrated effort. If the construct of time has any relevance at all, it does not appear to be in relationship to the number of sessions or total period of case involvement.

The timing of events has major consequences in several aspects of therapy, particularly when planning interventions. Segal and Watzlawick (Chapter 3) note that, "One might say that our error was one of timing and pacing. Therefore, in reconstructing the case, the therapist, having correctly assessed Mrs. D's lack of motivation would refrain from making any interventions aimed at interrupting the problem-solution loop. Instead, his or her initial goal would be to convert Mrs. D into a 'customer' for treatment." These authors further imply that along with first attempting to increase Mrs. D's motivation for treatment, slowing things down would have helped them to develop better rapport.

The value of slowing things down is addressed by L'Abate and Baggett (Chapter 9), who felt that they focused too quickly on the marriage instead of first joining the parents to alleviate the symptom. Wynne and Green (Chapter 5) suggest that one of their alternatives might have been "to acccpt initially the community," thus allowing thc community to be "in a position to help the family with an acknowledged family dilemma." Similarly, Meyerstein and Dell (Chapter 10) felt that they "pushed too soon for change."

Timing was also a significant factor in overall case management and decision making. Tomm (Chapter 13) felt that his case discharge was "untimcly" as did Coleman (Chapter 2). It is interesting that both therapists retrospectively viewed thc families as needing more support, more therapy— more of everything. One wonders if the enormous demands of the ever-needy, suicidal, drug-abusing families bccame too overwhelming, thus making their premature discharge more a function of the therapists' exhaustion. Untimcly discharges were also experienced in the cases seen by Jacobson *et al.* (Chapter 4) and Beavers (Chapter 7), both of whom were fortunate enough to be able to "recall" the family and accomplish a modicum of success the second time around.

There are no easy solutions to warding off the pernicious effects that a therapist's weariness or work overload can have on case outcome. Perhaps the most hope can be found in recognizing one's own inner state of being. Certainly, without awareness there is little optimism for change. Once a therapist can acknowlege that the problem of burnout exists, there is an opportunity for resolution. An effective method of altering a failure course due to therapist burnout is for the clinician to seek a consultant or team of colleagues to share in the case. This can be accomplished through either indirect (presenting the case at a staff meeting) or direct (live consultation with the family) methods. In either situation the therapist is availing himself or herself of support and innovative approaches, which can lighten the burden and create a sense of shared responsibility. After exploring all the long-term troubles that these families have had, ongoing consultation—even for the highly experienced family therapist—seems to be a major prerequisite for working with cases similar to those presented here. If there are any doubts, one might ask if a medical specialist is likely to treat an intractable carcinoma without a team of competent medical consultants.

Summary of Treatment Factors

Although we have elaborated on the major factors that we feel are related to failure in family therapy and that are particularly applicable to multiproblem families such as those presented here, the issues raised are not exhaustive. Additional parameters of failure may be significant, perhaps even more than those we have delineated; we thus encourage and invite the reader to propose his or her own. We feel that we have exposed a bit more than just the tip of the iceberg, and in review of our findings we suggest that any cluster of several of the failure constructs explored here are apt to render a family therapy case in jeopardy unless the therapist is able to offset the downward trend by developing diversionary treatment methods that overcome the problems we have encountered here.

In summary, the following are treatment factors that appear to be most frequently associated with failure:

- Inadequate understanding and analysis of the circumstances surrounding the referral, particularly with regard to the assessment of the problem.
- Overlooking the systemic nature of the problem, that is, not understanding the feedback loop.
- Insufficient goal setting, particularly with regard to who sets the goals.
- Inconsistency or contradictions between theoretical framework and applied interventions.
- Theoretical oversights or omissions, that is, not dealing with major family traumas, power issues, or intergenerational patterns that pervade the present.
- Overlooking the role of the presenting problem.
- Failing to notice the pervasiveness of motivation and consumerism.
- Conflictual goals that affect therapy outcome (product).
- Insufficient therapist–family alliance.
- Incompatible cotherapists and treatment-defeating cotherapy models.
- Treatment disruption due to the therapist's professional transitions.

    • Ecological collisions such as inadequate involvement with other institutions, therapist's multiple role conflicts, and so on.
    • And the erosion of treatment due to constraints of time and waning professional energy.

In an effort to assist others who may wish to review the failure potential of a particular case, the treatment checklists are offered in Table 14-7.

General Conceptual Issues of Failure

> MACBETH: If we should fail—
> LADY MACBETH: We fail!
> But screw your courage to the sticking-place,
> And we'll not fail.
>   —Shakespeare (*Macbeth*, I, vii)

The multifaceted components of failure have been extracted from our case studies and examined in detail. Without systematic sampling methods and a reliable research design, it is obviously not possible to provide statistically significant probabilities regarding the proportion of variance accounted for by each factor in our failure paradigm. Ample evidence does exist, however, for the development of a clinical model of predictors of family therapy failure. When taken individually any single factor may have only a weak association with treatment outcome, whereas the synergistic power of the failure variables are likely to have a major impact on therapy.

    The microanalysis of failure, as suggested by our findings from the case presentations, is incomplete without looking at the issue of failure more globally. This section explores some of the more general situations related to failure and suggests an epistemology of failure relative to treating families.

    In struggling with the concepts of failure and success, Keith and Whitaker (Chapter 1) found guidance in their dictionaries, which revealed that the root word for failure, "fallire," implies purposive behavior, deceit, or escape, while success derives from the word "cede," the act of giving over. Both definitions impart a sense of intentionality or implicit motive. A more benign definition, and surely one more consistent with what both Lady Macbeth and our contributing authors might embrace, is found in the *Random House Dictionary* stating that the verb "to fail" is "to fall short of success or achievement in something expected, attempted, desired, or approved."

    If one searches for a unitary concept of failure for the entire range of our family therapy cases, the view of failure as an unfortunate end result of one's sincere goals or expectations is more applicable. Failure here is thus imbued with initial hope, or honorable intention. Using the same dictionary as a

TABLE 14-7. Treatment Checklist

Theoretical issues

1. What is the theoretical basis for the treatment approach to this family? Are the techniques and interventions consistent with this theory?
2. How are theoretical constructs that are applicable to all theories (loss issues, power, and so on) being incorporated into the treatment with this family?
3. How are intergenerational patterns and/or major issues being incorporated into therapy?

Process issues

1. How is the presenting problem being approached? Are the interventions designed to incorporate the essential elements of the presenting problem?
2. Has there been a change in the family's interactional sequence of behaviors as it enacts the presenting problem?
3. Are the noted changes in the family's behavioral sequences indicative of first-order change; that is, someone or something within the feedback loop changes, but the systemic linkages are the same? Or is there evidence of real second-order change; that is, is there a change in the system itself (Watzlawick, Weakland, & Fisch, 1974)?

Motivation and consumerism

1. To what extent do the members of this family appear to be real therapy "customers"?
2. With what degree of regularity does the family attend sessions?
3. Are there members who consistently fail to appear for sessions?
4. How does family member absence support the hypotheses about the family's presenting problem? What role do the absences play in the system's operation?
5. How would the system be affected if the configuration of members attending sessions changed? What is the anticipated outcome?

Goal setting and product

1. As therapy progresses, is there a shift in goals, or are the goals toward which the family is working the same as those originally established?
2. Is there any emergence of a conflict in values or goals, either between family and therapist or among family members?
3. Do the original goals still seem viable, or should there be a reassessment of the product being sought?

Alliance

1. What is the nature of the therapist's alliance with the family, initially and as treatment progresses?
2. Are there any members with whom the therapist is not making a successful connection? What factors are preventing this from occurring?
3. Is the therapist pitting one member against another in a manner that is not constructive to the therapeutic process?

TABLE 14-7. (*Continued*)

4. Is there a way to correct a faulty alliance or is there an unyielding impasse that appears to be unresolvable? What could be done in the event that this impasse cannot be resolved?

Cotherapy

1. How well are the cotherapists able to work together with this family?
2. Is the team a positive or negative contribution to treatment?
3. Does this cotherapy system in any way complement the family? On the other hand, are the team and the family too symmetrical?
4. Does each therapist have a clearly defined role with this family? Would a change in roles produce a more successful shift in treatment progress?
5. If the cotherapists are both in the room with the family, would therapy be more effective if one would remain outside as an observer–consultant?
6. What mechanisms are the cotherapists using to cope with their own relationship? Is there a supervisor or consultant for the team?

Professional transitions

1. Is the therapist currently experiencing any changes in his or her professional model at this time?
2. If in transition, how does the new professional training interact with previous approaches to treatment?
3. Is this case being supervised? Is the supervision a proponent of the "old" or the "new" model? What is the effect of this on the family in treatment?

Ecological collisions

1. In addition to the family and the therapist, what other ecological systems are involved with this family?
2. To what extent are these systems incorporated into treatment?
3. If they are not directly involved with therapy, how are they being considered and is this sufficient?
4. In view of the family's goals, how will the ecostructures cope with the anticipated outcome of family therapy?
5. Does the therapist also have multiple roles in addition to being this family's therapist?
6. How is the therapist handling his or her role conflicts and how do these conflicts affect working with this family?
7. What would have to happen in order for the therapist to be more effective with this case?

Time and energy

1. To what extent is therapist "burnout" limiting the family's progress?
2. What solutions are there for reenergizing either the therapist or the family?
3. What is the anticipated case outcome if the therapist does not address this problem?

reference, the verb "to succeed" means "to happen or terminate according to desire; turn out successfully; have the desired result." Thus, the distinction between failure and success in our view is a function of process and not something that is due to conscious or unconscious wrong-doing motives. All of our family therapists set forth hoping to succeed; only when they became inextricably caught in unforeseen entanglements and insurmountable situations were they struck with the fact that the case might not conclude as expected.

In the preceding section we have attempted to analyze the complex processes in which these cases went askew. Each author's review of therapy provides insightful material from which we can hopefully learn. From these case-specific issues, an effort has been made to develop categories and constructs that may help others to avert failure. Beyond this classification there are some major conceptual issues that need to be addressed.

Validity of Failure

> Truth happens to be an idea. It becomes true, is made true by events. Its verity is in fact an event, a process: the process namely of its verifying itself, its verification. Its validity is the process of its validation.—William James (*Pragmatism—Lecture 1*)

One might endlessly debate the validity of failure, that is, its truth. One important concern in writing a book on family therapy failures was that truth would be distorted and the failures whitewashed. It was not hard to project that brilliant semantics could metamorphize almost any failure into the wings of success. Fortunately, this did not happen; the therapists boldly acknowledged their blunders. This lends support to our central position that failures in treating families do, indeed, happen (even to some of the very best clinicians among us). Despite our ever-increasing information base and growing sophistication in family therapy theory and techniques, we sometimes err, occasionally with tragic results.

The discussion of failure is always juxtaposed with success because the two are intimately and undisputedly related. Keith and Whitaker (Chapter 1) define success in family therapy as "when the family achieves a sense of wholeness or integrity, absurdity, and the capacity to deal with the community in relation to its problems as individuals and as a group. Success is intensifying the family organization and administrative competence." In contrast, they think failure occurs when the therapist fails to care, becomes deceptive, or backs out, "failure to maintain integrity." They further question if the failure to have any effect at all on a family is perhaps even more pernicious.

Some might challenge the Keith and Whitaker (Chapter 1) view of failure, thinking it too general or ambiguous. Before we elaborate on the more specific nature of failure, we need to underscore the fact that although it appears in diverse forms, failure, as applied to treating families, does exist.

Failure Due to the Limitations of Human Nature

Limitations will bring progress. Harsh limitations, however, are not a virtue.—
I Ching (Hexagram 60)

Although we need to examine more fully the range of failure categories, we must consider that the bottom line of all therapy is that those responsible for its administration are human. Despite their heterogeneity, people who choose to work with families are probably more similar to one another than are the treatment models to which they subscribe. One of the most obvious commonalities among therapist is the unfortunate fact that they have limitations. This element of being human receives rare attention in an era where expanded consciousness and the development of one's infinite potential are highly valued and often sought. The possible limitations of family therapists in both professional and personal contexts were discussed in the previous section. The limitations referred to here are those that apply to a more general human condition. For example, despite the vast store of information that a therapist can acquire from a family, the human mind can only integrate, correlate, and retain a finite amount of information at any given time. Unlike a computer, our own retrieval systems are dependent on restricted memory banks, which limits the number of permutations of family facts and events that can be assessed simultaneously.

Each case presented in this volume had enormous quantities of data offering potential treatment cues. It is interesting that none of the therapists mentioned forgetting significant material or being unable to handle the massive information associated with the case. All of us regarded failure as a function of errors in assessment, theoretical oversights, misguided goals, and so on. It is perhaps incredibly revealing that we all view ourselves as failing due to our own shortcomings, that is, intrinsic failings.

Also important and related to the discussion of cognitive limitations is the emotional drain in working intensively with families. There are implicit demands that are imposed by continuous involvement with severe human conflicts. No one has studied the long-term effects of being a family therapist, but one might speculate that, mingled with the wonderous joys felt when families achieve their goals, there are periods of disappointment and frustration. Even when a case is not beset by major problems of suicide, divorce, and despair, therapy sometimes concludes on a depressive note. A current example is illustrative of such an experience:

Mrs. Z was referred for individual therapy by another therapist who had treated her husband for more than a year for agoraphobia. The original therapist suggested that the wife needed treatment in order to better understand her husband's anxiety states. Also, some of her own worries were being somaticized. Since Mr. Z had terminated therapy with his doctor, the second therapist (Coleman), in response to the husband's resistance to being involved in more therapy, suggested that treatment would be enhanced by the husband's participation, since such a caring spouse could help his wife do better by being present.

After several months it became apparent that Mr. Z was not going to attend therapy sessions. He felt he was doing the best he could to prevent his agoraphobic episodes from interfering with his primary function as sole breadwinner for his wife and four young children. He did not express a desire to do more than that. He rarely enjoyed outings with his children or other social situations and he led a very restricted existence. His wife gradually began to function more independently, began to develop some long-term plans to return to graduate school, and realized that her husband (still angry yet insistent that things were going well) was not likely to make major behavioral changes in the near future. She also was aware that what she really wanted from life could not be achieved in this marriage. Because of her desire to acquire more education and more potential financial security before leaving him, she was resigned to stay in the marriage for several more years. Her short-term and long-term goals were compatible; she described therapy as "helpful" and said that her somatic problems had virtually disappeared and that she did not want anything additional at this point in time.

This case exemplifies a therapy situation that probably leaves both the couple and the therapist feeling apathetic. Nothing went particularly wrong but it certainly was not terrifically right. In such a situation, therapy ends on a flat note, yet that is all the Z couple was seeking. Such cases are not failures in the same sense as those presented in this book, yet they represent common experiences that all therapists have in working with the wide range of problems that people present. Although these cases do not take the same kind of energy as the Havermans (Coleman, Chapter 2) or the Smiths (Meyerstein & Dell, Chapter 10), they have a depleting effect on the therapist, contributing to the emotional hazards of working with troubled human beings.

As just discussed, families, too, are human and have their own boundaries and limitations. Could it be that the multiple problems of many of the families seen by our contributing authors would render any therapist ineffectual? What is being suggested here is that there are certain cases that seem "doomed" to fail. This is not to imply that there is something basically malevolent about a family, but rather that there may be a set of circumstances or events that cannot be changed, at least at the time that therapy is undertaken.

When psychological disorders are contrasted with physiological infirmities, an interesting observation is made. Those in the medical professions know that some diseases cannot be cured. They also assume that some illnesses with the potential for cure cannot be cured in some people. The medical profession abounds with vignettes of patients who "should" have died but did not and cases of those who "should not" have died but did. Physicians know that their treatment with some will probably fail, and although they may continue to experiment with nontraditional approaches long after the more usual ones have proven useless, there is a point where it must be conceded that nothing can save the patient. Similarly, one might wonder if there are certain intrinsic factors that render family therapy hopeless. This notion is apt to be received with initial defensiveness and refute, even though we have all had experiences that probably engender such thought. What is being suggested, however, is that just as therapists may be impeded by their own human limitations, so are some of the families that we attempt to treat. Despite what we believe to be the genuine desire among people we call "patients" not to suffer, and despite the selective presentation in the professional literature and in clinical workshops of brilliant and masterful pyrotechnical "cures" by numerous family therapists in cases in which even minimal success at first seemed impossible, failures do occur, at least for mortal family clinicians.

An example of a family with limited potential for successful treatment outcome was recently seen in consultation by one of the authors (Coleman):

Dr. and Mrs. P and their three daughters were referred for a family therapy consultation by the director of Stay At Home, a short-term residential program for runaway girls. The presenting problem had been the eldest daughter's obsession with running far away from home and getting involved with young men who committed petty burglaries, abused drugs, and so on. Although only 14 years old, Felice had already had two abortions and was probably pregnant for the third time when the family arrived for their first consultation. The other two daughters, aged 11 and 7, were beginning to demonstrate early signs of acting out behavior such as declining grades, unexcused absences from school, and so on. Dr. P was a well-known scientist who was also a multimillionaire, having inherited a huge estate as the only surviving son of enormously wealthy parents. His inheritance was used to keep the family comfortable, while he devoted his entire life to his scientific research in an obscure but fascinating field.

His first wife, and the mother of the two older daughters, had been found dead 10 years previously by Felice, then 4 years old. The cause of death was attributed to an aneurism of the brain, but some confusion surrounded the circumstances. At the time of her death, Dr. P was in Australia working on a scientific experiment. He returned, too late for the funeral, and after 3 weeks flew back to Australia, leaving Felice and her younger sister, an infant, with the housekeeper, nurse, and other household help.

Dr. P returned periodically for brief periods of time and at one point introduced the second Mrs. P, by that time pregnant, to his two young daughters who had had no previous knowledge of his marriage let alone their prospective sibling. The new Mrs. P stayed home with all the children while Dr. P continued to lead a lifestyle of being at home for only brief periods of time. Although Mrs. P tried diligently to handle all three daughters, the two eldest refused to accept her, constantly testing her and rejecting her efforts to "love" them.

Felice ran away the first time at age 9. This was followed by a continuous pattern of running away and being returned by authorities. At the age of 12, she had her first abortion and was placed in a residential treatment program. This pattern of running, being caught, and placed in treatment continued with no significant change despite the help of many professionals.

Consultation with the family at each time of placement led to strong recommendations of family therapy. The broad range of mental health specialists all saw the unresolved loss of the first Mrs. P and the simultaneous and continuous loss of Dr. P due to his career as central issues. Although Dr. P agreed on the importance of his relationship with his daughters and his need to be involved in family therapy, he rarely attended sessions due to travel and professional obligations. Mrs. P conscientiously did her best to cooperate with all the professionals, but the conflict was not hers to resolve. Despite the consistency of the recommendations made by all who assessed the family, no one could alter the obsessional pattern of Felice, who was merely replicating that of her father.

An interesting additional aspect of the case surrounded Mrs. P, who had been in individual therapy for more than 12 years with the same therapist. Although he had known her prior to her marriage, even the therapist had evidently accommodated to the family pattern.

This case clearly demonstrates the type of toxic but stable family functioning that is likely to be a family therapy failure. Short of paralyzing the family's physical and economic means of functioning, there is no viable intervention that will create the impetus for constructive change.

Failure Occurs when It Is Unexpected

In marked contrast to the previous case, there are families that present with problems that can reasonably be expected to result in successful outcome but do not. This is especially so when the symptoms are child related and are reported in the literature to have good to excellent treatment outcomes. Symptoms of this type include psychosomatic problems, childhood behavior problems, "soft" delinquency problems, and so on (Gurman & Kniskern, 1981). In this category of failure, the anticipated changes do not occur even though success could have been predicted on the basis that therapists typically do succeed with such families. This type of situation may be one in which a different therapist using a different approach might produce a significantly different result.

The following example is taken from a case recently published to illustrate a particular strategic approach (Coleman, 1983):

The Frolick family was referred by the school for family therapy in conjunction with their 13-year-old son's acting out behavior. The initial session revealed that the family had seen another therapist for 18 months of weekly family therapy sessions. From all that was learned it was apparent that the first family therapist had done an excellent job of assessing the problem as more related to a developmental issue than delinquency. He had used appropriate and well planned behavioral techniques to reinforce more appropriate behavior. The family had seemingly cooperated and yet, 18 months later, the presenting problem was still present. Neither the first therapist nor I could determine what went wrong.

Because I had the advantage of knowing my predecessor's logical but unsuccessful course of action, I designed a strategic method of treatment that I hypothesized might be more successful. My prescription was "no therapy." The family was only to be seen if the acting-out youngster got into trouble. Weekly contacts with the family were by telephone. Follow-up treatment indicated that this strategic approach was effective in eliminating the behavior. (For a complete review of the case, see Coleman, 1983.)

There was no way of knowing beforehand why the first therapist's interventions failed. His level of experience and soundness of treatment were beyond question. This type of failure probably occurs much more frequently than is realized, for in most instances one might never know what went wrong or how to prevent a repetition of the same experience.

Failure Is Expected but It Does Not Occur

There are families seen in treatment with seemingly unsuccessful outcomes for whom follow-up indicates that what initially appeared as a failure ultimately proved to be successful. Generally, these families attend sessions with a moderate amount of involvement, although treatment goals are often loosely defined, such as "We want to communicate better." Insights are gained, but there is no concrete evidence that any real change has taken place. An example of such a case is the Thomas couple:

The Thomases were originally referred (to Coleman) by Mrs. Thomas's psychiatrist, who had been treating her for manic depression and felt that the couple needed adjunctive therapy; a couples group was his recommended treatment choice. After being seen conjointly for approximately six sessions, Mr. and Mrs. Thomas were placed in a small group with three other couples. Their initial anxiety was so intense that it appeared that they might not be able to remain in the group. When their tension subsided they began to participate, but, although they were quite able to give meaningful suggestions to others, Mr. Thomas in particular reacted defensively to almost any insights or suggestions offered to him. Although Mrs. Thomas was more open and able to share her marital concerns, her husband was rarely able to do so. He focused more on his somatic complaints or his discomfort in sitting on pillows on the floor. The group consistently tried to make him emotionally and physically comfortable, each week saving him a space next to a wall, which he could lean against to ease his persistent back pain. Despite their efforts he never seemed to really get into the group. Positive change appeared particularly unlikely after one critical session in which Mrs. Thomas talked about her disappointment in her husband's low sex drive. He withdrew into the wall, his face reddened, and he then angrily made it clear that he would not discuss this in either group or individual therapy. Although to everyone's amazement he returned the following week, the sexual issue never surfaced again. When the group terminated at the end of 4 months, each person evaluated its effectiveness on the marital relationship. It was surprising to see that in all areas, including sex, both Mr. and Mrs. Thomas noted positive change. Telephone follow-up months later indicated that the Thomas couple had sustained the improvements in their relationship. Mr. Thomas stated, "I can't believe how much we each got from the group."

This case is fairly typical of those who show no evidence of more than minimal benefit from treatment yet for whom, at some point in time after therapy is concluded, significant change becomes evident.

Neither Better nor Worse, but Sometimes Worse

Two additional situations deserving attention involve (1) cases that do not improve as a result of family therapy but also do not deteriorate and (2) cases that deteriorate as a consequence of family therapy. The deteriorative or negative effects of marital and family therapy have been documented and discussed by Gurman and Kniskern (1978). Although these authors found that outcome studies including a "worse" category were rare, 10 studies of nonbehavioral marital therapy reported "worsening," a 53% deterioration rate, yet 5 family therapy studies reported a 29% deterioration rate. The deterioration rate in outpatient family therapy was only 2.1% but was based largely on families with presenting problems related to a child or adolescent. The authors suggest that the low rate may be due to the fact that family theory predicts less frequent negative outcome because of the greater number of involved members. Also, when a child is the identified patient, there is a greater probability that some of the difficulty will diminish as the youngster progresses developmentally. Furthermore, problems focused on a child are less apt to have persisted as long as those associated with an adult. As emphasized in the earlier portion of this book, the identified patients in our cases were mostly adult who had experienced the presenting problem for an unusual amount of time.

In reviewing the more specific factors influencing deterioration in family therapy, Gurman and Kniskern (1978) emphasize the role of therapist variables, particularly those associated with "relationship-building skills":

> A particular therapist style also seems to increase the chances of negative therapeutic effects on marital-family therapy. It is perhaps best described as one in which the therapist does relatively little structuring and guiding of early treatment sessions (Shapiro & Budman, 1973); uses frontal confrontations of highly affective material very early in therapy (Guttman, 1973; Hollis, 1968)

rather than reflections of feeling; labels unconscious motivation early in therapy rather than stimulating interaction, gathering data, or giving support (Postner *et al.*, 1971); or does not actively intervene to moderate interpersonal feedback in families in which one member has very low ego-strength (Alkire & Brunse, 1974; Guttman, 1973).

Gurman and Kniskern (1981) further suggest that family therapists need to be much more active than those administering individual treatment and that the therapist's affective response is an important factor in treatment retention. It is interesting that among the cases presented in the preceding section of this book, there is little evidence of case failures due to the specific therapist characteristics mentioned by these authors. What seems significant in a few cases, however, is that failure was, at least in part, attributed to the absence of the father being directly involved in treatment. This was a major issue in the case described by L'Abate and Baggett (Chapter 10) and was suggested by Gurman and Kniskern to be associated with family characteristics associated with deterioration.

Finally, Gurman and Kniskern suggest that family therapy offers an opportunity for "powerful learning encounters in which changes of both positive and negative sorts can occur" (1981). Thus, it is important to consider instances where there is no immediate observable change in family functioning subsequent to treatment. One must also search to discover whether therapy served to exacerbate or prevent further deterioration of the system or of individuals in the system. This is even more difficult to assess since one can only speculate that a system might worsen had there been no therapy. Although deterioration after therapy terminates may be obvious, it is unlikely that one can unequivocally state that the family problems would have intensified had they not been involved in treatment.

> See . . . the heavy leaf
> On the Silent
> Windless day
> Falls of its own will
> —Boncho (*Japanese Haiku*)

An Epistemology of Failure

We have looked at failure in a rather fragmented way, dissecting it into many parts and subsections, always searching for clues to prevent its occurrence. We have somewhat obsessively been able to categorize and outline important family therapy variables that are often associated with cases that do not have successful conclusions. A major purpose in our analysis of failure in family therapy has been to support the validity of this analysis as a construct and to attempt to delineate its components. From an intricate search of an amalgam of 12 very complex cases, it is evident that failures in working with families do take place. It is also possible to predict that when several of the described variables form an aggregate, family therapy failure is more than likely. This aggregate of failures is especially apt to appear in complicated, multiproblem families whose presenting symptoms have persisted for a long period of time.

Despite our ability to label factors as having considerable failure predictability, we also recognize that, as with all living organisms, there are indescribable, unobservable, and unexpected consequences of intervention or non-intervention that impose unexplained and often unanticipated results. This is perhaps a reassuring though puzzling reminder that no matter how skillful we become in treating families in distress, there may still be something outside our consciousness that can make us pause in wonder.

One of the final elements to explore in our search to understand failure is that of mind, asking ourselves how we perceive our work and what we think about our thoughts of a particular family—the metaperceptions of who the family is, what it can or cannot do, what it is, and what it might become.

Problems of Mind

A fool sees not the same tree that a wise man sees.—William Blake (*Proverbs of Hell*)

The first experience of a family takes place with referral. Either through some intervening system, a phone call, or an in-person meeting, a first impression of the family is made. How we perceive the family—how they look, sound, and feel; their pattern or their system; their imagery—becomes a unique mental representation, a family landscape to wander in through time. Although that imagery may later blur and be refocused, that first vision becomes the dominant construction of mind that guides what occurs throughout the treatment period. How we "know" that family to be is our initial source of potential success or failure. Thus, our primary error may be one of perception, of mind.

The ancient Chinese painter Wang Wei noted that "the painter must transcend the limitations of the eye and delve deeply into the spirits and interactions of nature; that paintings should express the ever-changing processes of nature. . . ." In Western society the left hemisphere of the brain, with its emphasis on word sounds, is instrumental in determining what a family is. We search for the appropriate words to describe and define the images the family conveys. Perhaps we would do far better if our right hemisphere dominated our perceptions, creating an ideogram or visual design imbedded with intuitive symbols. Silent, like a family sculpture, the initial imagery might be free of the distortions emerging from our tendency to classify what we see in neat verbal packets of diagnostic nomenclature. Perhaps it is our descriptors that chattel us and limit our vision of families, the use of our models and our means of applying what we academically know instead of what we might experientially come to learn.

LIMITS OF VISION

Unfortunately, we have little control over how we perceive objects. As Bateson (1979) states:

> The processes of perception are inaccessible; only the products are conscious and, of course, it is the products that are necessary. . . . The two general facts—first, that I am unconscious of the process of making the images which I consciously see, and second, that in these unconscious processes, I use a whole range of pre-suppositions which become built into the finished image—are, for me, the beginning of empirical epistemology.
>
> Of course, we all know that the images which we "see" are indeed manufactured by the brain or mind. But to know this in an intellectual sense is very different from realizing that it is truly so. (p. 32)

LIMITS OF LANGUAGE

Bateson points to another limitation imposed by our right-brain dominance—the limitations of language. Expressing an idea that is consistent with the view of general semanticists, Bateson (1979) states:

> It is necessary to be quite clear about the universal truth that whatever "things" may be in their pleromatic and thingish world, they can only enter the world of communication and meaning by their names, their qualities and their attributes (i.e., by reports of their internal and external relations and interactions). (p. 61)

Similarly, Korzybski (1958) states, "The map is not the territory." Weinberg (1959) reflects:

> The non-verbal quality of the sensory world—the world of thingness—is the large fish which escapes the net of language. . . . [Weinberg stresses that] words are not things. They are on the next level of abstraction. . . . The object "is" the mass of sensations (color, smell, taste, etc.) which are produced within us by the reaction of our nervous system to stimuli from the submicroscopic level—the event. We project our auditory and visual sensations "out there." The object is not words. Whatever you say a thing "is," it is not. (pp. 35, 94)

In developing an epistemology of failure, it may be that the very root of our error is in believing that the family (the object) is what we project it to be (through our language), but what it "is," it is really "not." Weinberg (1959) suggests:

> Because of this total reaction of the nervous system at all levels to any kind of stimulus, the patterns of linguistic usage can have a profoundly disturbing effect upon it if they cause us to confuse the different levels of abstraction, as when we act as if inferential knowledge were factual knowledge or as if words were things. (p. 95)

Explaining the Unexplained by Making It Explainable

What is being suggested is not that we enter the war zone of pragmatics versus aesthetics (Allman, 1982a, 1982b). What is being said is that the nature of failing in family therapy (and perhaps in all therapy) is a function of interactive processes, some very explainable and capable of residing in the pragmatic camp, while other more abstruse errors in treatment may fall in the domain of aesthetics. The difficulty in dealing with aesthetics is that its abstract nature paradoxically renders it less potent when translated into written language. An apparent paradox arises from the assumption that failure can be objectively explained while at the same time we realize that it is never objective. Both views are possibly correct and worthy of exploration when our therapeutic efforts do not succeed.

One danger in trying to apply these concepts to clinical treatment lies in becoming too intellectual and too philosophical about our failures. A greater danger, however, lies in not accounting for the effect of our perceptual errors on failure. The understanding of this aspect of therapist behavior is not easily grasped and rests largely on learning to grapple with issues that sometimes appear far too esoteric. Here, Bateson (1979) again serves as a reference point in his discussion of how human beings perceive similarities between abstract relations. He assigns the word "abduction" to describe a process in which we look at one object and "then look around to find other instances of the same abstract relations in other creatures" (p. 142). He noted this in art, religion, and even physical science.

The abduction process may be a large part of the unconscious process that we experience in our first contact with a family. Upon meeting family X could we not rapidly scan through our previous cases and see the family Y? Our associations immediately take hold and become integral parts of the treatment process that follows. Obviously, this can have positive and negative value; however, because no two experiences can ever be the same, our use of the abduction process can, at times, be defeating unless we are more flexible in our application. The difficulty with this suggestion is that it makes it sound as if abduction is a "thing" like a can opener; when a therapist needs it, he or she yanks it from the drawer, places the family under the magnetic lid, and turns the crank. *Voilà!* Here is the difference that makes the difference!

Demand for Coherence

> If I don't know I don't know
> I think I know
> If I don't know I know
> I think I don't know
> —R. D. Laing (*Knots*)

Bateson (1979) believed that not only was abduction essential to the process of thought, but epistemological change was not likely without it. Bateson suggests that in order for change to take place there is a double requirement placed on "the new things," as compared with the original "thing." The new thing must fit the organism's internal demands for coherence and must fit the external requirements of the environment. This whole concept of coherence has to do with balance within a system's internal and external environment. Coherence is similar to but different from homeostasis, seems more ecosystemic, and when applied to famlies means that the family system has to fit its own internal and external environment.

Our failures may have something to do with not knowing or not understanding a family's state of coherence. By not shifting our system of abductions we may too rigidly superimpose family X on family Y, thus preventing the Ys from reaching their own unique state of coherence.

One of the essential issues in how one knows a family and understands its coherence lies in one's cultural point of view. Dell (1981) contrasts the Western concept of "essential qualities" intrinsic to human beings with Eastern thought that ". . . reality does not lie in a set of characteristics inherent in objects, but rather in the set of events from which Westerners abstract property-bearing 'objects.'" These cultural differences affect our perceptions and, as Keeney (1982) suggests (in discussing cybernetic epistemology), determine whether we come to know things because of the primacy of their patterns or their "materiality." Thus, in discussing the "fundamental act of epistemology" Keeney separates figure and ground and declares, "All that we know or can know, rests upon the distinctions we draw" (1982, p. 156). These distinctions, or "punctuations" as Bateson (1979) viewed them, assist us in understanding how families organize their experiences. Keeney notes that, "A complete epistemology of family therapy must therefore look at how both the client and therapist construct a 'therapeutic reality'" (p. 157). This again underscores our need to understand a family's state of coherence. Keeney views family therapists as epistemologists because ". . . they embody patterns of knowing and constructing a therapeutic reality . . . [which requires that] . . . one knows about one's knowing. That necessarily requires that we see ourselves constructing and construct ourselves as seeing." The recursive nature underlying this epistemological view Keeney sees as "a process of knowing, constructing and maintaining a world of experience."

In addition to all the pragmatic issues previously discussed, our failures were also a product of Western vision. Unable at the time to reach for Keeney's "epistemological knife" we attempted to treat and to reconstruct the treatment from a point of objective reality. Each family's state of coherence was relative to something familar, describable, and amenable to being mapped. We sometimes tried to separate ourselves from the interactive process of failing; later we viewed our experiences from what we hoped was a distortion-free lens. Despite all the obvious pragmatic factors, something still seemed to be missing.

Impotence of Control

> No human being can really understand another and no one can arrange another's happiness.—Graham Greene (*The Heart of the Matter*)

Consistent with our cultural belief in *real* objectivity is our adherence to the concepts of power and control. The attitude that therapists either prevent or allow things to happen in therapy implies that we are omniscient, always directing the flow of behavior from a point of superior knowledge. Much of the analyses of our failures suggests that although we did not know what we were doing when things went askew, we certainly were capable of knowing once we assumed a position of hindsight. Just as none of us claimed to have trouble juggling all the information and events surrounding a family, none of us reflected that we did not know what happened. Such an admission is probably not admissible. This would imply that we knew that we did not know and know that we still do not know—an unlikely acknowledgement, especially in view of the limitations of conscious self-perceptions.

Bateson (1979) saw power as "one of the most dangerous" metaphors, the "myth of 'power'" being especially pernicious since it leads to the belief in one's ability to control—a major epistemological error.

When we, as therapists, accept the metaphor of control, we automatically accept the premise that we, as the primary agents of change, can design the correct interventions, assign appropriate tasks, and develop systemic prescriptions, all of which will produce a significant reduction in family psychopathology.

Dell's attitude toward control is dogmatically expressed when he states:

> To believe that one might control what happens is to aspire to the stature of the gods. This is overwhelming pride, the first of the seven cardinal sins. The error inherent in the notion of control is the equation, "A causes B," or "A can make B happen." No one can ever cause something to happen. Therapist's interventions do not cause a patient to change. The organization of the system (i.e., patient) determines what will happen, not the intervention. Put simply, man proposes, but the (organization of the) system disposes.

Dell links control to epistemological error, which he defines as "the misunderstanding of, or the outright refusal to accept, reality. The most destructive way to refuse to accept reality is to believe in the possibility of control. Control licenses the use of power. . . . Control wreaks havoc."

In exploring the epistemology of failure from an aesthetic point of view, we see that even our hindsight assessment of what went wrong and what we would do if we had another chance invokes the myth of power. Implicit in all of our thinking is that if we did not make it work right the first time, we could *make* it better the next time, "A causes B" but "A can make B happen" later.

Epistemological Truth

> Nothing is so firmly believed as what is least known.—Michel Eyquem de Montaigne (*Essays to the Reader*)

Along with Dell, who underscores Bateson's notion of the impossibility of control, we believe that what "really" determines behavioral change is not the therapist's brilliantly conceived and controlled interventions but coherence. The reactions to another's attempts to induce change are more than likely a function of the family's coherence. If therapy is successful it is probably because both therapist and family were able to discover an acceptable means of transforming the sequence of problem behaviors—they were mutually able to uncover the epistemological truth that happened to fit the family's behavioral coherence.

This process, in Maturana's (1978) philosophy, is due to a "triggering" mechanism that leads to system transformation. According to Dell (1982), Maturana views the family therapist as using "behaviors (i.e., interventions) that differ from those already being used within the system." He further believes that ". . . the behavioral coherence of each family member specifies those interventions that will trigger behaviors that may transform the system" (p. 35). Maturana suggests that behavioral coherence "is the lock—and the therapist's interventions are the keys" (1978).

Epistemological truth can only emerge from the therapist's acceptance of the family's state of coherence and from the therapist's understanding that in disturbed families, members have fine-honed ways in which they "repeatedly inflict epistemological errors on each other and on those around them" (Dell, 1982, p. 38). Further, the therapist, in order to facilitate change, needs to adjust a three-way visual lens in order to see epistemological errors from inside the family, inside himself or herself, and the interaction between them. Such a demand appears overwhelmingly difficult to achieve often, and yet many of us do it most of the time. Much of what we accomplish when we succeed in family therapy is a result of "knowing" and integrating all the epistemological truths that will lead the family toward its goals.

What seemed to have happened in the families we presented here, and perhaps what happens in many situations that result in failure, is that we, like the family, repeatedly committed the same errors—one active, the other passive (Dell, 1982). We tried to control others (active error) and we resisted the acceptance of reality, "What is is; what ain't ain't" (passive error). In our symmetrical dance with the family we got out of step and lost our footing too late to gain the advantage of another chance.

In summary, along with the many pragmatic factors that were clearly related to the failures experienced with our treatment families, we have attempted to present the more aesthetic problems of mind that also seem to have had an impact on case outcome. Thus, in looking for an epistemology of failure we must consider that there are always information and behavior that remain outside our consciousness. This contributes to our perceptual short-comings—the limitations of our visual imagery of a family and of our attempts to explain their system or pattern of behaviors in verbal language. There are unexplainable issues that are sometimes forced into explanation by our associative processes (abduction). Sometimes we just do not understand how families organize their experiences (their coherence) and we miss seeing or knowing the therapeutic reality of the situation. It surely is not likely that we can always have a metaview of what our "punctuations" are as therapists and how they fit with those of the family. Perhaps, we are stuck with the limitations of the Western mind, believing that we ultimately have the power and control to change others to be something we think they want or need to be. Finally, our most serious error may go beyond the myth of power; the ultimate factor in failing our families and ourselves may well be the truth that we are, in fact, only human. If this is so, then the limitations we must accept may be not merely those of Western mind, but of universal mind.

A Saddening World:
Flowers Whose Sweet
Blooms Must Fall . . .
As We too, Alas . . .
—Issa (*Japanese Haiku*)

Wherefore Go'est Failure

Our minds thus grow in spots; and like grease spots, the spots spread. But we let them spread as little as possible: we keep unaltered as much of our old knowledge, as many of our old prejudices and beliefs, as we can. We patch and tinker more than we renew. The novelty soaks in; it stains the ancient mass; but it is also tinged by what absorbs it.—William James (*Pragmatism*)

How much we learn from the failures presented here can only be determined at some future point in time. As the philosopher William James suggests, "Our minds . . . grow in spots." Whether or not the issues and concepts derived from an in-depth journey into failures will affect our work in any serious way remains unknown. We analyzed the specific elements involved in cases that had unsuccessful outcomes at the time that therapy terminated. We also considered some of the more global aspects of failure. Finally, we attempted to develop an epistemology of failure. None of what has been presented here is complete; we have only begun to open up an area of family therapy that needs exploration. More searching for a systematic method is necessary to obtain a substantive data base on the vicissitudes of failure. Thus, before bringing this book to conclusion, we will present a few possible directions to guide the continued pursuit of understanding failure.

The Clinical Route

The effort to compile a book on family therapy failures initially came from a clinical source. As mentioned in the Prologue, the failure video tape became a prized possession, not because of the pain unfortunately experienced by the family in that session, but because of the important and serious message conveyed by the system of family members and therapist who mutually fell apart. Thus, if there is any benefit at all to producing an entire volume on failure, the clinical community must derive the largest portion.

The first by-product of such work is the awareness that we do fail in treating families. Because the contributors to this volume are widely known, well published and respected by many, it is important that they have acknowledged their point of being stuck. This demonstrates that failures do not hang only around the meek and less experienced, but are born out of the efforts of the strong and agile as well. It is hoped that our presentations have made us all aware that although failure in family therapy is never sought or embraced it is a realistic piece of the less-desired aspects of treatment.

Awareness is the starting point, but it is only that. After we accept the idea that failure is one of the possible treatment outcomes, we must ask, what happens next? The answer is an idiosyncratic one in that there are no universal ways for therapists to incorporate the information presented here. As with any smorgasbord of ideas, some readers will grasp one offering and others another. One possibility is for family clinicians to spend time exploring previous cases that were not successful. An attempt at follow-up would help to confirm or dispute one's impressions. A very thorough analysis of what went wrong in each situation may very well provide consistent evidence of a repetitive trouble spot. Obviously, this would suggest an area for further supervision. Although a few of us may be adept at monitoring our own deficiencies, most of us, particularly in the heat of working with families, are not. Two of the most useful developments in the field of family therapy supervision are the use of the one-way mirror and video tape. These tools provide a more realistic means of monitoring what takes place within a session, giving a far superior edge to training than that of the pad and pencil method of the earlier days, when one took one's notes to supervision.

Once identification of one's weaknesses takes place and a solution for strengthening is found, new family therapy cases can be handled with prevention strategies. Here, with the assistance of the supervisor and with our own self-monitoring behavior, we can begin to cope with the failure-prone area.

Although not entirely foolproof, this is a viable means toward overcoming an important block as a therapist.

In addition to discovering one's therapeutic inadequacies, we also need to determine how much any specific problems encumber us with likely failures. This obviously taps into our own intrapersonal issues and suggests that we either examine them (in supervision), work them through (in our own therapy), or decide to avoid treating particular kinds of family dysfunctions (refer such cases to someone else). In some situations, referring cases to others when they are not likely to succeed with us is a wise decision, particularly if the presenting problem is not frequently encountered (e.g., dog phobias, etc.). If the clinical problem is a common one (e.g., alcoholism), however, it might be very important for the therapist to overcome the prejudice or conflict surrounding the symptom.

Once a family is accepted for treatment, preventative strategies can be incorporated. The first part of this chapter delineated factors most frequently associated with failure, particularly in complicated, multiproblem families. Reference to these failure variables can provide a system of checks and balances on one's work; the use of the summary checklists can be of further help in self-assessment and avoidance of failure.

More difficult to apply are the concepts presented in the section on the epistemology of failure. Here the retort, and a valid one indeed, is probably, "How can one possibly know one does not know if one does not know what one does not know?" This is true enough, however, the point to be made from this very abstruse material is that we need to acknowledge that there are unknowns in our work. There are also perceptual distortions, visual and language limitations, and culturally determined elements that impede our view. We are capable of recognizing that there is no objectivity and that there is no *real* reality; all reality lies within the experience of the person who is perceiving it. When someone says that her husband is trying to kill her, it does not matter that the therapist knows that it is not so. What matters is that the therapist accept *her* perception, delusional or not, and plan interventions that will fit her perception.

Perhaps the most important concept to wrestle with clinically is that of power. If we can begin to abandon our own attitudinal distortions that the decisive difference in what happens in treatment is our design of that all-powerful intervention, we will have started to chip away at a belief system that dominates the family therapy field. In almost every decade there is a novel method, a new dogma, that promises to supercede all previous dogmas. Like the Pied Piper, someone or some mystical system charismatically leads us away, toward that ultimate moment of family therapy *nirvana*. If we could grasp the myth of power and loosen the mental knots that bind our thinking, we might fail less. If we can stop feeling gulity when we are not using the method in vogue, if we could fit our own internal demands for coherence with what is really comfortable for us in the environment, rather than what we believe the environment demands for us, we might fail ourselves less, and our families in treatment might do better. In feeling the seductive power of the Pied Piper of family therapy, we support the myth of power, for to be controlled implies that we, too, possess the power to control others.

Instead of using so much energy in attempting to control the sequence of events in therapy, family therapists might do better to sharpen their perceptual capacities to make better interpretations of the family's universe. Perhaps every clinician needs to have an out-of-body experience by moving into the form of every member of the family, to feel the sensations of what it is like to be in the body of the family. Before the advent of the video tape era, students used to role play being in the family. One of the limitations of the visual mode of perceiving the family via tape is that important kinesthetic information is missing. When we are stuck in our work today, we are more apt to review a tape or consult with supervisors or colleagues behind the mirror. It is doubtful that we think of understanding the lack of progress or change from within the soma of the family. This is a vital source of data that we eliminate by relying too much on advanced technology and dramatic techniques. We sometimes need to go back to basics to learn what we do not know and what might be significant particles of information.

Family therapists need to blend the ambitious quest for learning the elusive *what* it is that makes people change with a more complete understanding of *who* the families really are—the actual sensations of families' internal phenomena. Thus, in confronting our clinical limitations we most likely need to get in touch with more than just cognitive sources of inspiration. Perhaps we should all pause every now and then to consider, as Nagel (1981) suggests in his essay, "What Is It Like to Be a Bat?," that ". . . no matter how the form may vary, the fact that an organism has conscious experience at all means, basically, that there is something it is like to *be* that organism" (p. 393).

The Training Route

A widely circulated anecdote from the annals of graduate school psychology is told about the behaviorist Ogden Lindsley, whose graduate students were said to get no credit for his practicum until their patients got better. The source of this vignette is unknown and its truth or fiction probably insignificant. What does matter, however, is the implicit message it conveys, for it raises a rarely discussed issue, the degree to which training is focused on treatment outcome. It would be extremely interesting to learn how many family therapy training programs look at outcome as a factor in evaluating graduating students. It is doubtful that many do this on any regular, systematic basis. However, a follow-up of cases to determine the relationship between successful therapy outcome and performance characteristics of student trainees would be highly revealing.

Although there is definite responsibility on the part of the clinical supervisor to see that cases treated by trainees do not terminate poorly, failures may occur more frequently than one would suppose. This may be due to the tenets of the model being taught, the nature of the training program itself, the unspoken, unwritten *folie à deux* between supervisor and supervisee, and the lack of well-developed and clearly articulated performance standards.

Schools of therapy—such as structural, strategic, behavioral, Milan systemic, or Mental Research Institute (MRI) Brief Therapy—that emphasize goal setting are more likely to focus on assessment that is closely linked to families' initial and presenting problems. In contrast, process-oriented models that are psychodynamic and transgenerational (Bowen) are more likely to concentrate on affective material and emphasize resolution of intrapsychic issues and three-generational conflicts in addition to symptomatic changes. Experiential family therapy takes on an atheoretical point of view that incorporates a great deal of the therapist's use of self and attempts to release a creative force within the therapeutic relationship. Focus is always on the symbols and experiences associated with the therapy sessions. Family therapy students will obviously be imprinted by the methods learned during training. When affective communication and content are major values, assessment will be more related to those aspects of treatment. On the other hand, students trained to help families articulate and pinpoint their goals will be more interested in looking at goal attainment at the conclusion of treatment. There is nothing new or surprising about this. What is important to consider, however, is whether some models are more successful than other. Because the failures presented in this book were not systematically selected to represent a cross-section of schools of famly therapy (although this was the initial plan), at present we can do no more than speculate that one's investment in the choice and emphasis of selected domains of outcome criteria is dependent, to an important degree, on the model of training to which one is dedicated.

Also important is the attitude that training programs have toward the supervisor–trainee relationship and the type of commitment that it engenders. We do not know if training institutes actually have clearly formulated principles or guidelines. In one of the author's (Coleman's) experiences as a faculty member in a family therapy graduate school program, there were several instances in which students who were performing poorly in class and in the clinic with families were discussed extensively in faculty meetings. Here, all the faculty members agreed on the inadequacy of the students, yet nevertheless they were still graduated with a degree in family therapy. One of them is currently a doctoral student at another university and received recommendations from some of the very same faculty who attested to his remarkably poor level of performance. Another student was put on probation, despite good grades, because his family and marital therapy skills were consistently ineffective and his ability to relate to people was grossly insufficient for a field where relating is a *sine qua non*. After much soul searching, tape monitoring, and consultations with field supervisors, the student was finally not permitted to graduate. A year later, however, he received his degree and is now working as a professional family therapist. There is no evidence that his therapy skills have improved.

The issue of responsibility is tantamount to this discussion. We must look at both the responsibility of the trainee and that of the supervisors. We wonder how often a trainee is imbued with the idea that his or her major responsibility is to families in treatment. Too often the student is misled because our tests measure what the student has gained; rarely do we attempt to estimate how much the families acquired. What happens when a student's therapy skills are mediocre? There are situations where serious errors are committed, but more troublesome are cases that suffer from sins of omission. Such therapists often seem to have what one of us (Gurman) refers to as "wimpy outcomes." These are the garden variety of family therapists who do not produce glaring failures but who are unable to give families enough of what they might reasonably expect to get from treatment, given the present status of family therapy as both art and science (Gurman & Kniskern, 1978, 1981).

The ultimate responsibility for "wimpy outcomes" belongs to the supervisors, but here several other variables often intervene. Training supervisors question and debate the issue of how much a trainee's inadequacy is related to his or her own unresolved family dilemmas. How dependent one's therapy skills are upon this and how much a supervisor's role is expected to embrace these issues is a point of great debate. Here, too, the answer is more apt to be a function of one's training model. A Bowenian student would have no choice but to go back to his or her own family and confront the conflict, while Haley's student would never have to meet an ancestor in a thousand hours of supervision.

Related to the role of the therapist's own family in supervision is the degree of sensitivity a supervisor has toward dealing with the student's personal life. Even when personal issues are not considered to be the supervisor's domain, therapists are unusually sensitive people. How much we allow our own protectiveness and fear of hurting others to interfere with our training decisions is unknown but it is a very likely concomitant of the training situation. Also, supervisors are competitive in addition to being caring. Too often we invest too much of our own egos in our students and, in typical pseudomutual fashion, we become unable to "see" their shortcomings.

This can easily lead to a kind of meta failure that is an occupational hazard. Perhaps supervisors need to be evaluated according to the outcome of their trainees' patient outcomes.

In addition to the question of how to handle a situation where the student is not doing very well, another perplexing problem arises. What does the supervisor do with regard to the family who is not progressing because of the student's difficulty? Does the supervisor step into the session and take over? Is a cotherapy model more effective? If the supervisor has been using a direct feedback approach (closed-circuit videotape observation, one-way mirror, intermittent consultation directly with the trainee and family, etc.), some of the more obvious problems with the student's feelings of impotence when a supervisor makes a sudden live appearance may be avoided. If these methods have not been used, the problems are increased. One would imagine that the use of the direct supervisory model might eliminate having to make much of the decision, because these methods expose the student's difficulty much more rapidly and are not subject to as much distortion due to time lapse. Many new issues and problems are raised, however, when the supervisor has to respond to a floundering family being treated by a floundering trainee.

It is not the purpose of this book to answer the questions we are raising. One thought-provoking idea will be offered. The leniency of the field's acceptance of less than adequate performance among our students introduces a less than adequate standard in our profession. It also reduces the chances that the senior people in family therapy in the future will be as skilled as their predecessors. Such a feather-ruffling statement obviously reeks with elitism but without pedantry, family therapy is more apt to suffer a greater flood of failures, a situation that could make extinct a still struggling profession yet to establish itself as a distinct discipline.

The Research Route

It is obvious that research on failures in family therapy can only enhance what has been presented here. From both a descriptive case study level (the method we have used) and an empirical level, additional studies will provide the field with a more reliable data base, which it is hoped will lead to better failure-prevention strategies. The way in which our cases have been analyzed provides a clear model for developing future research. With solid sampling methods and randomization of cases, any family therapy program or institute that treats a large number of families could readily set up a research project. The variables can easily be lifted from the first part of this chapter and set into a multivariate design. What is lacking from our work is an accurate way of determining how much of the variance can be accounted for by any one of the many factors discussed here. The next step requires that we discover this.

In addition to exploring the specific variables we have identified, there are other elements of research on failure that are important. One might want to learn whether there are specific aspects of working with families or being in family therapy that are unique to these types of therapy. The question is, are there characteristics and dimensions of the experience of family therapy that do not apply across therapies such as individual, group, and so on? As mentioned previously, the family is the only group that comes to treatment with a history of having been together in a broad spectrum of experiences. As we know, despite what we may clinically describe as pathological, family members have enormous resources and when all is said and done they will go home together, hopefully using newly learned patterns, but assuredly holding on to old behaviors. Thus, comparative analyses across therapies are necessary in order to understand the uniqueness of family therapy and some of the possibly unusual ways in which family therapy both fails and succeeds. One might also want to ask if a particular presenting problem is more apt to result in failure as a function of the type of therapy administered. Family therapists, collectively speaking, need to be involved in two major, but different, types of research on clinical failures. First, comparisons of family therapy with more traditional treatments such as individual therapy are called for, and such comparisons will speak especially to the nonfamily therapists. Second, comparisons between alternate family treatments may help to refine both the practices of family clinicians and the teaching emphasis in training programs.

In addition to research across methods there is still a need to continue to explore aspects within the various major family therapies. Of special relevance to such within-school research will be studies that aim to isolate both technical and personal factors on the part of both the therapist and family that are regularly associated with failure within a given school of family therapy. Obviously, some of the variables studied can be expected to be quite different from school to school.

Finally, on a more applied level, as mentioned in our discussion of implications of failure for the clinician, therapists themselves need to do some retrospective accounting of their case outcomes. Follow-up can easily be done by an assistant or secretary who can use a concise follow-up questionnaire to determine the effectiveness of therapy at least 6 months, but preferably 1 and 2 years, after termination. Without sophisticated computers, descriptive statistics can assess and compare the effects of working with varying approaches and diverse presenting problems. It is valuable to know if, as individual clinicians, we do better work with families with some types of presenting problems than with others. It can be argued that we are ethically responsible for attempting to identify the parameters of our own failures as well as our successes; evaluation of our own practices is a means of doing this.

This book merely provides a beginning, a way of thinking about our work that is not always comforting. If we have aroused some energy, some conflict, if we have tapped some new ideas and stimulated emotion, then the purpose in preparing a book on family therapy failures has, in itself, not failed.

REFERENCES

Alkire, A. A., & Brunse, A. J. Impact and possible casualty from videotape feedback in marital therapy. *Journal of Consulting and Clinical Psychology*, 1974, *42*, 203–210.

Allman, L. R. The aesthetic preference: Overcoming the pragmatic error. *Family Process*, 1982a, *21*, 43–56.

Allman, L. R. The poetic mind: Further thoughts on an "aesthetic preference." *Family Process*, 1982b, *21*, 415–428.

American Psychiatric Association, *Diagnostic and statistical manual of mental disorders* (3rd ed.). Washington, D.C.: Author, 1980.

Bateson, G. *Mind and nature: A necessary unity*. New York: Dalton, 1979.

Coleman, S. B. The non-treatment treatment of a non-problem problem. *Journal of Strategic Therapy*, 1983, *2*, 62–66.

Dell, P. F. Some irreverent thoughts on paradox. *Family Process*, 1981, *20*, 37–42.

Dell, P. F. Beyond homeostasis: Toward a concept of coherence. *Family Process*, 1982, *21*, 21–43.

Emmelkamp, M. G., & Foa, E. B. Failures are a challenge. In E. B. Foa & M. G. Emmelkamp (Eds.), *Failures in behavior therapy*. New York: Wiley, 1983.

Gurman, A. S. The patient's perception of the therapeutic relationship. In A. S. Gurman & A. M. Razin (Eds.), *Effective psychotherapy: A handbook of research*. New York: Pergamon, 1977.

Gurman, A. S. The therapist's personal experience in working with divorcing couples. *American Journal of Family Therapy*, 1983, *11*, 75–79.

Gurman, A. S., & Kniskern, D. P. Deterioration in marital and family therapy. *Family Process*, 1978, *17*, 3–20.

Gurman, A. S., & Kniskern, D. P. Family therapy outcome research: Knowns and unknowns. In A. S. Gurman & D. P. Kniskern (Eds.), *Handbook of family therapy*. New York: Brunner/Mazel, 1981.

Gurman, A. S., & Razin, A. M. (Eds.). *Effective psychotherapy: A handbook of research*. New York: Pergamon, 1977.

Guttman, H. A contraindication for family therapy: The prepsychotic or postpsychotic young adult and his parents. *Archives of General Psychiatry*, 1973, *29*, 352–344.

Hollis, F. Continuance and discontinuance in marital counseling and some observations on joint interviews. *Social Casework*, 1968, *49*, 167–174.

Keeney. B. What is an epistemology of family therapy? *Family Process*, 1982, *21*, 153–168.

Korzybski, A. *Science and sanity: An introduction to non-aristotelian systems and general semantics*. Lakeville, Conn.: Institute of General Semantics, 1958.

Maturana, H. R. Biology of language: The epistemology of reality. In G. A. Miller & E. Lenneberg (Eds.), *Psychology and biology of language and thought*. New York: Academic Press, 1978.

Nagel, T. What is it like to be a bat? In D. R. Hofstadter & D. C. Dennett (Eds.), *The mind's I*. New York: Bantam, 1981.

O'Malley, S. S., Suh, C. S., & Strupp, H. H. The Vanderbilt psychotherapy process scale: A report on the scale development and a process outcome study. *Journal of Consulting and Clinical Psychology*, 1983, *51*, 581–586.

Postner, R., Guttman, H., Sigal, H., Epstein, N., & Rakoff, V. Process and outcome in conjoint family theapy. *Family Process*, 1971, *10*, 451–473.

Rice, D. G., Fey, W. F., & Kepecs, J. G. Therapist experience and "style" as factors in cotherapy. *Family Process*, 1972, *11*, 1–12.

Shapiro, R., & Budman, S. Defection, termination, and continuation of family and individual therapy. *Family Process*, 1973, *12*, 55–67.

Watzlawick, P., Weakland, J. H., & Fisch, R. *Change: Principles of problem formation and problem resolution.* New York: Norton, 1974.

Weinberg, H. L. *Level of knowing and existence.* New York: Harper & Row, 1959.

Whitaker, C. A., & Keith, D. V. Symbolic-experiential family therapy. In A. S. Gurman & D. P. Kniskern (Eds.). *Handbook of family therapy.* New York: Brunner/Mazel, 1981.

Epilogue

SANDRA B. COLEMAN

This book began with a warning about the dangers of linearity that might lurk among some of the material presented here. It ends with a more circular theme. Consistent with *I Ching* philosophy, one must not conclude one's efforts by thinking that a matter is complete. As Wing (1982) notes:

> . . . it would be a mistake to imagine that by achieving your aims you will bring matters to a close, that good judgement and order will prevail. The time Before the End can be compared to a lengthy trek over a high mountain. At some point, before reaching the peak, you can see in detail exactly how much farther you must travel. You will know what is involved in reaching the top because of your experience in the climb so far. However, when you do reach the peak, which has been in your sight for many long days of effort, you will have done only that. You will have acquired little information and no experience whatsoever about descending the other side. To rush up and over the top in an overly confident manner could bring disaster. (p. 149)

> Before the End comes progress. But
> if the young fox, having nearly crossed
> the stream, gets his tail wet,
>   there will be no advantage.
>   *I Ching* (Hexagram 64)

REFERENCE

Wing, R. L. *The illustrated I Ching.* New York: Doubleday, 1982.

Sandra B. Coleman. Family Guidance Center of Bucks County, Yardley, Pennsylvania; Department of Mental Health Sciences, Hahnemann University, Philadelphia, Pennsylvania.

Name Index

Subject Index

Page numbers in italics indicate material from tables or figures.